Java™ Developer's Guide
to Servlets and JSP

Bill Brogden

SYBEX®

San Francisco • Paris • Düsseldorf • Soest • London

Associate Publisher: Richard Mills
Contracts and Licensing Manager: Kristine O'Callaghan
Acquisitions and Developmental Editor: Denise Santoro Lincoln
Technical Editor: Ashok Hanumanth
Book Designer: Robin Kibbey
Editorial: Argosy
Book Production: Argosy
Graphic Illustration: Argosy
Indexer: Matthew Spence
CD Coordinator: Kara Eve Schwartz
CD Technician: Keith McNeil
Cover Designer: Design Site
Cover Illustrator/Photographer: Jack D. Myers

Library of Congress Card Number: 00-106433

ISBN: 0-7821-2809-2

SYBEX and the SYBEX logo are trademarks of SYBEX Inc. in the USA and other countries.

Screen reproductions produced with FullShot 99.
FullShot 99 © 1991-1999 Inbit Incorporated. All rights reserved.
FullShot is a trademark of Inbit Incorporated.

Internet screen shot(s) using Microsoft Internet Explorer reprinted by permission from Microsoft Corporation.

TRADEMARKS: SYBEX has attempted throughout this book to distinguish proprietary trademarks from descriptive terms by following the capitalization style used by the manufacturer.

The author and publisher have made their best efforts to prepare this book, and the content is based upon final release software whenever possible. Portions of the manuscript may be based upon pre-release versions supplied by software manufacturer(s). The author and the publisher make no representation or warranties of any kind with regard to the completeness or accuracy of the contents herein and accept no liability of any kind including but not limited to performance, merchantability, fitness for any particular purpose, or any losses or damages of any kind caused or alleged to be caused directly or indirectly from this book.

Manufactured in the United States of America

10 9 8 7 6 5 4 3 2 1

Java™ Developer's Guide to Servlets and JSP

*To my wife, Rebecca, my unfailing support
through many years.*

ACKNOWLEDGMENTS

I would like to thank the following people for their help:

As always, to my wife, for her support over many, many years.

To my fellow LANWrights, Inc. employees Ed Tittel and Dawn Rader for their guidance and editorial expertise, respectively.

Thanks to Paul Wheaton for his contribution to Chapter 12.

Finally, to all the wonderful people at Sybex for being a great group of people to work with!

CONTENTS AT A GLANCE

CONTENTS

INTRODUCTION

The great potential for Java use in Web applications has been obvious for years. Even the earliest public releases of the language provided extensive support of networked communications. Various software vendors—both non-profit, such as the World Wide Web Consortium (W3C) and the Apache organization, and for-profit vendors—developed Java-based server technology.

Even the first versions of what would become Java servlets enjoyed great success because of Java's proven advantages of multi-thread execution, memory management, object orientation, and a powerful standard library. After release of the Java Servlet API version 2.0 in late 1997 and Sun's Java Servlet Development Kit in 1998, servlet development really took off.

As Sun developed and integrated the various technologies that were to be packaged as the Java 2 Enterprise Edition, various problems with security and integration with large applications led to modification of the API. During development of this book, the current Java Servlet API has been version 2.2, the final release version of December 1999. This API incorporates many changes over the previous version, particularly in the areas of integration into Web applications and standardized configuration using XML.

Standardization of the technology of JavaServer Pages has occurred much more slowly. The API was stuck at version 0.92 for quite a while. In the absence of a clear path from Sun, many software companies developed their own technologies for combining custom tags in HTML with database search and similar capabilities.

As Sun developed what would become the Java 2 Enterprise Edition, it became clear that JSP had a big part to play in the overall Web application picture, so API development proceeded rapidly to version 1.0 and then 1.1. With the publication of the Java 2 Enterprise Edition, it appears that Java Servlets and JSP have become well integrated into the bigger picture of Web application development with Java.

A most significant event occurred in October, 1999. Sun turned over all Servlet 2.2 and JavaServer Pages 1.1 code to the Apache organization for further development of reference implementations of open-source Java servlet and JSP engines. This development is independent of the J2EE specifications and ensures that there will always be a free and up-to-date implementation of the servlet and JSP APIs.

One of the other spectacular trends in Web technology has been the rise of the widespread use of XML for packaging data. This technology is now well established as the method of choice for many functions, including configuring complex applications, and as XHTML. It appears likely that XHTML will be the Web page markup standard of the future. Fortunately, this trend became clear as the JSP API was refined, so the JSP tag grammar is now compatible with XHTML.

Intended Audience

I assume that the reader of this book will have basic familiarity with HTML, Web servers, and the Java language, and that he or she will have access to a computer capable of running a small-scale Web server, the standard Java compiler, and other utilities. You can work through every project in the book without spending a cent—all you need can be downloaded for free.

The small-scale Web server I use most of the time is the free Jakarta-Tomcat development kit (`http://jakarta.apache.org`). Tomcat is a good place to start if you don't already have a Web server. I have also used the JRun server (`http://www.allaire.com`) both freestanding and as an add-on for Microsoft's PWS and IIS Web servers. Another server I have tested these examples with is the Orion server (`http://www.orionserver.com`), which has a nice JSP tag library tutorial.

The examples in this book are intended to provide you with a working starting point for your own applications, both as Java servlets and JavaServer Pages. Because so many technologies can be combined with servlets and JSP, I have tried to cover as wide a range as possible instead of digging deeply in one direction.

What's on the CD

This book contains a great deal of working code. This includes a number of Java servlets and JSP applications. The source code is on the CD-ROM in directories following the chapter organization. If I come up with additions and improvements, they will be posted at

```
http://www.lanw.com/java/jspbook/
```

Conventions Used within the Book

I have tried to keep the layout as simple as possible. The typography convention will be familiar to all readers, with all code in a monospace font as in the following method declaration example:

```
public void _jspService( HttpServletRequest request, HttpServletResponse ➡
response )
```

NOTE   Occasionally I will use this Note format to present an aside from the main text.

WARNING   This is the warning style that is used to call your attention to possible problems, such as a deviation from standards.

Contacting the Author

I would be delighted to hear from any reader. You can reach me at wbrogden@bga.com in cyberspace. My real-space address is William Brogden, 130 Woodland Trail, Leander, TX, 78641.

Reports of errata or other problems should be sent to me so I can post corrections. Errata sent to me will be posted at http://www.lanw.com/books/errata.

CHAPTER 1

The Basic Servlet API

- How a Web Server Handles HTTP Requests
- How an HTTP Request Is Passed to the Servlet Engine
- How to Get Input Data from a Get or Post Operation
- How to Create Web Page Output with Java
- Understanding the Implications of the Servlet Thread Model
- Setting Up a System for Servlet Development

The use of Web servers is a recent addition to the phenomenon known as the Internet. In 1993, messages sent in the Hypertext Transfer Protocol (HTTP) format used by Web servers were only a minute portion of the traffic on the Internet. HTTP's tremendous functionality led to a rapid expansion in both the number and capabilities of Web servers. Essentially, it was HTTP that made the World Wide Web possible.

Originally, a basic Web server simply returned a text page when it got a correctly formatted request message. However, it did not take programmers long to discover that great things were possible if some extra functionality was added, such as forms and graphics capabilities.

The Common Gateway Interface (CGI) standard enables the user of a Web browser to submit data from a Web page to a server for further processing. Programming with Java servlets and JavaServer Pages builds on this universal standard and makes it easier to use. To understand how this works, you must understand how a Web server processes HTTP transactions and how these transactions are related to the servlet Application Programming Interface (API).

How a Web Server Handles HTTP Requests

The current standard for Web servers, HTTP version 1.1, is maintained by the World Wide Web Consortium (W3C) organization (www.w3.org). The widely used HTTP 1.0 standard has many problems that have been uncovered as the use of the Web has expanded; the 1.1 standard, which has been in development for a number of years, is expected to greatly reduce such problems. Fortunately, we don't have to delve into the intricacies of HTTP to understand how to get something done.

A simple HTTP transaction between a Web browser and a Web server takes place in several steps. If you enter http://java.sun.com/jsp/simplepage.html into a browser connected to the Internet, the following actions occur:

1. The browser establishes a TCP/IP (Transmission Control Protocol/Internet Protocol) connection to the server represented by java.sun.com.

2. The browser sends a request message for the page represented by jsp/simplepage.html to the server.

3. The server sends a response message that includes either the text of that page or an error report.

4. The TCP/IP connection is closed.

In this case, the server only has to locate the text file represented by the jsp/simplepage.html part of the request, which it does by using conventions the Webmaster has set up to map from requests to the local file system. The text file contains all the HTML markup needed to create the page display on the browser, so it is passed through unaltered by the Web server.

Request Message Contents

The request message from browser to Web server starts with one or more text lines terminated by carriage return - line feed (crlf) characters. The first line specifies a method, a Uniform Resource Identifier (URI), and an indicator of the HTTP version being used. The standard methods in the HTTP 1.1 protocol are OPTIONS, GET, HEAD, POST, PUT, DELETE, TRACE, and CONNECT. The request for a plain HTML page uses the GET method. With JSP and Java servlets, the most important methods are GET and POST. The following sections describe the process with JSP and Java servlets.

The GET Method

The GET method is used to request a resource, such as an HTML page. When you type a request, such as http://www.someserver.com/index.htm, the request message to the server specifies the GET method, and the URI is index.htm. In this case, the requested resource is an HTML page, but it can also refer to a process that creates data on-the-fly. A GET request can include some additional information appended to the URI string as a query string. You have undoubtedly seen this in action at Web shopping sites.

The server process is passed this query string when it is executed. Due to restrictions on the size of the request header that servers can handle, the total of URI and query string should be less than 240 characters. Listing 1.1 is a simple HTML form that uses the GET request.

Listing 1.1: An HTML page with a form

```
<html><head>
<title>Chapter 1 GET example</title>
</head>
<body><font size="4">
<center>Please enter your name and password then press Start<br>
<form method="GET" action="http://localhost/servlet/GetDemo" >
Name: <input name="uname" value="" type="text" size="20"><br>
Password: <input name="userpw" value="" type="password" size=10>
<input type="submit" value="Start" ><br>
</form></center>
<hr></body></html>
```

The resulting page will be rendered as shown in Figure 1.1, where the fields have been filled in by the user. Note that because the password type is used for the second field, the browser shows "*****" instead of the actual characters.

FIGURE 1.1
Browser rendering of the
GET example HTML page

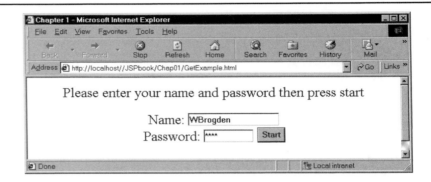

NOTE   A note about HTML tags. Although most browsers can parse both uppercase and lowercase letters, you are probably used to seeing HTML tags and attributes such as <FORM> in uppercase. The reason I use lowercase tags and attributes is that the HTML 4.0 standard uses them, and we all might as well get used to it.

When the Start button is clicked, the browser submits a GET style request line that includes the form data in the URL. The first line is followed by several lines that take the following form:

```
keyword: value
```

These lines define various bits of optional information about the browser and are followed by blank lines. Listing 1.2 is the complete request (note that certain lines are wrapped in this display):

NOTE   Please note that some lines of code in this text are broken for print purposes only. All code for this book is included on the accompanying CD-ROM and is not broken.

Listing 1.2: The request generated by the example form
```
GET /servlet/GetDemo?uname=WBrogden&userpw=java HTTP/1.1
Accept: application/msword, application/vnd.ms-excel,
    image/gif, image/x-xbitmap, image/jpeg, image/pjpeg, */*
Accept-Language: en-us
Accept-Encoding: gzip, deflate
User-Agent: Mozilla/4.0 (compatible; MSIE 5.0; Windows NT; DigExt)
Host: localhost
Connection: Keep-Alive
```

The Web server has been set up to associate the use of servlet in the URL with the servlet engine so this request is passed to the servlet engine for processing. The servlet engine creates a Java object that implements the HttpServletRequest interface and an object that implements the HttpServletResponse interface. It passes references to these objects by means of a mechanism (see "Inner Workings of a Servlet Engine" later in this chapter) to the doGet method of an instance of the GetDemo servlet. Listing 1.3 shows the Java code for the GetDemo servlet.

Listing 1.3: Source code for the GetDemo servlet

```java
// demonstrates handling of a GET request
import java.io.*;
import javax.servlet.*;
import javax.servlet.http.*;

public class GetDemo extends HttpServlet
{
  public void doGet(HttpServletRequest req,
        HttpServletResponse resp)
  throws ServletException, IOException
  {
    resp.setContentType("text/html");
    PrintWriter out = resp.getWriter();
    String username = req.getParameter("uname");
    String password = req.getParameter("userpw");
    out.println("<HTML>");
    out.println("<HEAD><TITLE>GetDemo</TITLE></HEAD>");
    out.println("<BODY>");
    out.println("Hello " + username + "<br>");
    out.println("Your password was: " + password + "<br>");
    out.println("</BODY>");
    out.println("</HTML>");
    out.close();
  }

}
```

Note how the getParameter method is used to get the values of the uname and userpw parameters that were in the URL from the HttpServletRequest object. Having these parameters parsed out of the GET request by the servlet engine vastly simplifies servlet programming.

The following steps describe how the output that goes back to the browser is created using the HttpServletResponse object:

1. The setContentType method sets the MIME type of the response that will be sent to the browser. The response creates all the other header lines using default values.

2. The getWriter method returns a PrintWriter object named out so that we can output plain text.

3. The various calls to out.println send text creating the HTML page to the output stream.

4. Finally, the call to out.close flushes the output stream buffer and terminates the sending of the response.

Response Message Contents

The response message from Web server to browser always starts with a status line composed of the protocol being used, a numeric status code, and a text version of the status code. This is followed by various lines of additional information in the keyword: value format, followed by a single blank line. The HttpServletResponse object takes care of creating these lines, but the servlet has control over the values that are returned. The response continues with the data that were written to the output stream by the servlet. Listing 1.4 shows the complete response text generated by the GetDemo servlet. Note the blank line that is required to terminate the header area.

Listing 1.4: The text of the GetDemo response

```
HTTP/1.0 200 OK
Server: Microsoft-PWS/2.0
Date: Sat, 26 Feb 2000 22:34:04 GMT
Content-Type: text/html

<HTML>
<HEAD><TITLE>GetDemo Output</TITLE></HEAD>
<BODY>
Hello WBrogden<br>
Your password was: java<br>
</BODY>
</HTML>
```

When the browser receives this data, it decides what to do with it on the basis of the response code and content type. In this case, the content is displayed as an HTML page, as shown in Figure 1.2. Note that the userpw parameter value is readable in the browser's address field for the URL request sent to the server, making GET a less secure way to send sensitive information than the POST method.

FIGURE 1.2
The browser display
generated by the
GetDemo servlet

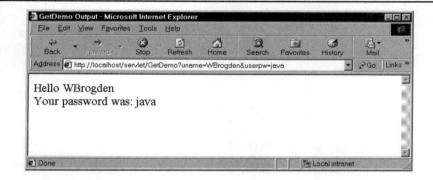

The POST Method

When the method specified in a request is POST, the request can contain any amount of information because it is sent as lines of text, and the URL contains only the name of the servlet to process the request. Listing 1.5 provides an example of an HTML form using the POST method.

Listing 1.5: An HTML page with a form using the POST method

```
<html><head>
<title>Chapter 1</title>
</head>
<body><font size="4">
<center>Please select topics of interest<br>
<form method="post"
    action="http://localhost/servlet/MultiDemo" >
<select name="topic" multiple >
<option value="a">APL
<option value="b">Basic
<option value="c">C++
<option value="e">Eiffel
<option value="f">FORTH
<option value="j">Java
<option value="p">Pascal
</select><br>
<input type="submit" value="Submit Selection" >
<input type="submit" value="Cancel" ><br>
</form></center>
<hr></body></html>
```

If the user selected APL, Eiffel, and FORTH in the list box and then clicked either of the buttons, the transmitted request would include the following text:

```
topic=a&topic=e&topic=f
```

Because there are three name-value pairs with the same name, we can't just use a `getParameter("topic")` method call. Instead, as shown in Listing 1.6, the servlet API provides a `getParameterValues` method that returns a `String` array that preserves the order of the selections as presented on the page. In this case, the array has three `String` objects, with the values "a," "e," and "f."

Listing 1.6: The doPost method handles POST requests

```java
public void doPost(HttpServletRequest req,
    HttpServletResponse resp)
    throws ServletException, IOException
{
  resp.setContentType("text/html");
  PrintWriter out = new
      PrintWriter(resp.getOutputStream());
  String[] topics = req.getParameterValues("topic");
  out.println("<HTML>");
  out.println(
      "<HEAD><TITLE>MultiDemo Output</TITLE></HEAD>");
  out.println("<BODY>");
  out.println("Selected " + topics.length +
      " topics<br>");
  for(int i = 0; i < topics.length; i++){
    out.print( topics[i] + " " );
  }
  out.println("</BODY>");
  out.println("</HTML>");
  out.close();
}
```

Inner Workings of a Servlet Engine

You can think of the servlet engine as acting like a container for the servlet code, just as a Web browser is a container for applet code. The servlet engine performs many tasks that greatly simplify the programmer's job. Here are the stages of the lifecycle of a servlet that uses the standard threading model:

1. *Servlet instance creation.* The servlet engine loads the Java classes to create a servlet instance either when the engine is started or when the first request for a particular servlet arrives. When this happens depends on settings for the particular servlet. Typically, the engine creates only a single copy of the servlet object and reuses the object for every request, even if more than one request is being processed at the same time.

This saves the time that would be required to create a new servlet object for every request, but it requires careful planning by the programmer. However, see the `Single Thread Model` interface for alternatives.

2. *Instance initialization.* The engine calls the servlet's `init()` method. With this method, you would typically set up parameters that are going to be constant for the life of the servlet, such as paths to files or a pool of database connections. After initialization, the servlet instance sits in memory until a request is directed to it.

3. *Request handling.* Each request that an engine gets is handled by a separate Java `Thread`. The engine may create a new `Thread`, or it may assign one from a pool. The `Thread` creates request and response objects as previously discussed and then calls the servlet's `service()` method. The `service` method is responsible for deciding how to handle the request.

4. *Thread management.* Any number of threads may be executing the methods of an object at the same time, each with its own request and response objects. Designing your code so that it is thread-safe is a major part of learning servlet programming.

5. *Other services.* A typical service provided by an engine is session tracking. This provides a method by which your program can keep track of data belonging to a particular user.

6. *Instance destruction.* When the servlet engine needs to shut down completely, or just to recover memory, it calls the servlet's `destroy()` method. At this point, the servlet can close files and otherwise shut down gracefully.

One of the services the servlet engine provides to servlets is management of the standard outputs, `System.out` and `System.err`. Text output to these streams will be directed to log files. The exact location of the files varies between engines. When writing information to one of these streams, remember that other servlets may also be writing data, and be sure your message is labeled so you can tell which servlet it comes from.

The Servlet API Packages

The Java servlet library is elegantly simple, considering how much power it gives the programmer. We will be concerned with the following packages:

`javax.servlet` The basic generalized servlet package.

`javax.servlet.http` Specialized extensions for Web pages.

`javax.servlet.jsp` Classes for creating JavaServer Pages.

`javax.servlet.jsp.tagext` Specialized extensions to jsp classes.

The following sections cover these packages in more detail.

The javax prefix indicates that these classes are what Sun calls *standard extensions*. Although standard extensions are part of the official Java standard, developers of Java Virtual Machines are not required to provide them. Examples of other standard extensions are the "Swing" GUI interface, Enterprise JavaBean, and the accessibility packages.

The javax.servlet Package

The javax.servlet package contains a number of interface definitions that provide the basic structure of the entire API. The interfaces you will be using most often are listed here:

Servlet   This interface defines the methods that all servlets must implement. The GenericServlet class implements the Servlet interface.

ServletRequest   All information about a client request is accessed through an object implementing this interface. Creating a ServletRequest object is the responsibility of the servlet engine.

ServletResponse   An object implementing this interface must be created by the servlet engine and passed to the servlet's service method to be used for output of the MIME body to the client.

In addition to the interfaces just listed, the javax.servlet package has the following utility interfaces:

RequestDispatcher   This powerful interface permits you to forward a request from the current servlet to another servlet or a JSP page for additional processing.

ServletConfig   Objects using this interface are used to hold information used during servlet initialization.

ServletContext   Objects using this interface let a servlet locate information about the servlet engine it is running in and its environment.

SingleThreadModel   This interface contains no methods. It is a marker that forces the servlet engine to ensure that only one Thread executes an instance of the servlet at one time. The servlet engine can do this either by restricting access to a single instance of the servlet or by creating a separate instance for every Thread.

The classes in the javax.servlet package provide basic bare minimum functionality. In general, you will work with classes that extend these for more specific applications.

GenericServlet   This provides bare minimum functionality.

ServletInputStream   A class for reading a stream of binary data from the request.

ServletOutputStream   A class for writing a stream of binary data as part of a response.

Only two exceptions are defined in the javax.servlet package. These classes do not descend from RuntimeException, so if a method declares that it throws ServletException, a calling method must provide for catching it.

ServletException   A general purpose exception used throughout the servlet API.

UnavailableException   This exception is to be thrown when a servlet needs to indicate that it is temporarily or permanently unavailable.

The javax.servlet.http Package

When programming servlets to create Web pages, you will be dealing with classes in the javax.servlet.http package. To give maximum flexibility to servlet engine designers, most of the package functionality is defined in interfaces.

HttpServletRequest   This extension of the ServletRequest interface adds methods specific to HTTP requests such as typical Web applications.

HttpServletResponse   An extension of the ServletResponse interface, which adds methods specific to HTTP transactions.

HttpSession   Objects implementing this interface allow the programmer to store information about a user between individual page visits or transactions. Servlet engines provide methods for keeping track of HttpSession objects using unique IDs. We discuss the use of these objects in Chapter 3.

HttpSessionBindingListener   This interface is analogous to the many listener interfaces in Java GUI design. A programmer would implement this interface in an object that needs to be notified when it has been attached to or detached from an HttpSession object.

HttpSessionContext   This interface is deprecated as of version 2.1 of the API due to security concerns about letting one servlet find out too much information about other servlets on the system.

The following are the classes in the javax.servlet.http package:

HttpServlet   This abstract class is the one you will usually extend to create useful Web servlets. The methods are discussed in detail below.

Cookie   These objects are used to manipulate cookie information that is sent by the server to a browser and returned on subsequent requests. Cookie information in a request is turned into Cookie objects by the HttpServletRequest.

HttpUtils   Static methods in this class are useful occasionally.

HttpSessionBindingEvent   Objects of this type are used to communicate information to HttpSessionBindingListener objects when they are attached to or detached from an HttpSession object.

Implications of the Servlet Thread Model

If you are not used to programming multi-threaded applications in Java, you will probably need to change some of your programming practices. The significant points to emphasize include:

- There is only one instance of your servlet class, and many Thread objects may be executing methods in this instance at any one time.
- This instance remains in the servlet engine memory for long periods of time. Any errors in memory management that might go unnoticed in a short-lived application will eventually show up.
- Because there is only one instance, all instance variables or static variables are open to modification by more than one Thread simultaneously.

Variable Storage Considerations

There are three ways to organize storage of variables in your servlet program: as static variables, instance variables, and local (or automatic) variables. Recall that static variables in Java belong to a class as a whole and exist independently of class instances, so they clearly should not be used for data related to a particular transaction. However, the distinction between instance variables and local variables sometimes trips up first time servlet programmers.

The code fragment in Listing 1.7 is from the GetDemo servlet shown at the start of the chapter. Because the String variable password is declared inside the doGet method, it is a local variable. The storage location that holds a reference to the actual String object is on the stack belonging to the Thread executing the doGet method. If two Thread objects are executing doGet, each will have its own stack and its own password variable.

Listing 1.7: GetDemo with password a local variable

```
public class GetDemo extends HttpServlet
{
  public void doGet(HttpServletRequest req,
       HttpServletResponse resp)
  throws ServletException, IOException
  {
    resp.setContentType("text/html");
    PrintWriter out = new PrintWriter(
       resp.getOutputStream());
    String username = req.getParameter("uname");
    String password = req.getParameter("userpw");
    // method continues .....
```

In contrast, the code fragment in Listing 1.8 shows how we might define password as an instance variable. If there is no chance of more than one Thread executing doGet in the same object, this will not cause a problem. However, in the normal servlet environment, any number of requests may be processed simultaneously, and there is only one copy of the servlet object. Thus when a Thread retrieves the password value, it could be from a different request from the one the Thread is working on.

Listing 1.8: GetDemo with password an instance variable

```
public class GetDemo extends HttpServlet
{
  String username ;
  String password ;
  public void doGet(HttpServletRequest req,
      HttpServletResponse resp)
  throws ServletException, IOException
  {
    resp.setContentType("text/html");
    PrintWriter out = new PrintWriter(
        resp.getOutputStream());
    username = req.getParameter("uname");
    password = req.getParameter("userpw");
  // method continues.....
```

Unfortunately, the conceptual error of using an instance variable in a servlet will probably not show up as a bug in normal testing. Because it takes multiple simultaneous requests to create the error, the problem will show up at irregular intervals and be almost impossible to duplicate—a real programmer's nightmare.

If for some reason a servlet can't be written using local variables, it can implement the SingleThreadModel interface. This interface does not specify any methods but serves as a signal to the servlet engine to ensure that only a single Thread can be using an instance at one time. Because this implies extra delays when handling multiple requests, the normal practice is to take the appropriate precautions for multiple Thread access.

Synchronized Access to Resources

In many servlet applications, you need to control access to resources that are managed outside of the servlet object. Typical examples include access to databases and files. Careful use of Java's synchronization mechanism is needed to ensure that threads managing different requests do not interfere with one another. Listing 1.9 shows a code fragment from a servlet that records comments in a guest book log file. Here, synchronizing the critical part of the code on the gbPath object prevents collisions between threads.

Listing 1.9: Synchronizing on the gbPath object prevents interference between Threads writing to a file

```
public class GuestBook extends HttpServlet
{
  static String gbPath = null ;
    // gbPath must be set in the init method
  static void addToLog( String usr, String cmnt )
      throws IOException{
    if( gbPath == null ) return ;
    synchronized( gbPath ){
        // open file in append mode
      FileOutputStream fos = new FileOutputStream(
          gbPath, true );
      PrintWriter pw = new PrintWriter( fos, true );
      pw.println("User: " + usr + " Says " + cmnt );
      pw.println(); // blank line
      pw.close();
    } // end block synchronized on gbPath
  }
  // class continues ....
```

One technique for resource management that you are sure to run into is object pooling. This is particularly useful with objects that are time consuming to create and/or that use scarce resources. Database connections are frequently managed in object pools.

- On servlet startup a specified minimum number of connection objects is created.

- When a servlet needs a database connection, it requests one from the pool manager. If none is available and the number in the pool is less than the maximum, a new one is created. If the pool is at maximum size and none is available, the servlet thread is blocked until a connection object becomes available.

Parts of a Basic Servlet

The life cycle of a servlet has three main phases: initialization, response to requests, and destruction. We will now take a closer look at each of these phases.

The init Method

Because servlet methods are defined in an interface and interfaces cannot define constructors, all initialization of a servlet is carried out in the init method. The servlet engine is guaranteed to call init after the servlet object is constructed and before any request is handled. The init method is handed a ServletConfig object that can be used to obtain initialization parameters.

All servlet engines provide for defining initialization parameters to be passed to a given servlet. The conventions by which the server administrator can set these parameters vary between servlet engines, but the basic idea remains the same. A parameter name is associated with a text value. Programmers familiar with Java applets will note the parallel with the way in which an applet container (the browser) provides named parameters to an applet. `Servlet-Config` provides three methods:

getInitParameter(String name)   This method returns a `String` corresponding to the name or returns null if no such parameter exists.

getInitParameterNames()   This method returns an `Enumeration` over all the names in the set of parameters.

getServletContext()   This method gets the `ServletContext` that the servlet is operating in.

In general, I feel that if you have more than one or two parameters that a servlet needs for initialization, you should store them in a file of properties and use an initialization parameter to point to that file. The `java.util.Properties` class provides very convenient methods for loading a properties file into memory and recovering data from it.

Listing 1.10 shows an example of code used in an `init` method to load properties data from a path specified in an initialization parameter. The `Properties` class is an extension of the `java.util.Hashtable` class that handles the details of loading a `Hashtable` from a file.

Listing 1.10: A code fragment from an init method

```
public static Properties statusProp ;

public void init( ServletConfig config )
   throws ServletException {
  String workDir = config.getInitParameter("workdir");
  if( workDir == null ){
     System.err.println("Failed to find workdir");
     workDir = defaultWorkDir ;
  }
  statusProp = new Properties();
  File f = new File( workDir, "Status.properties");
  FileInputStream fis = null ;
  try {
    statusProp.load( fis = new FileInputStream( f ));
    statusProp.list(System.out); // for debugging
    fis.close();
  }catch(IOException e){
     System.err.println("Status.properties file err:" + e);
  }
  // more initialization goes here
}
```

When you're creating a file to be loaded by a `Properties` object, you use a plain ASCII text editor and write one name-value pair per line. Note that because the lines will be read as Java `String` objects, you need to escape special characters such as the backslash as used in Windows paths. Here are some example lines from a properties file to illustrate this point:

```
maxSearchTime=5000
Ft6.dat=F\:\\FTEXT6\\
logEnable=ON
portN=2980
```

Note that the `Properties` class has a convenient `list()` method that you can use to show all the properties as they have been read for debugging purposes. Because `Properties` is based on `Hashtable`, the order in which the items are listed will probably not be the same as the original file order.

The Http Request Service Methods

As discussed earlier, the standard methods in the HTTP 1.1 protocol are OPTIONS, GET, HEAD, POST, PUT, DELETE, TRACE, and CONNECT. Although practically all servlets deal with only the GET and POST methods, the service method in the `HttpServlet` class can dispatch requests to doOptions, doGet, doHead, doPost, doPut, doDelete, and doTrace methods.

Although parameters in a GET request are parsed out of the URL, and parameters in a POST method are parsed out of the body of the request, the `HttpServletRequest` object does not distinguish between them. So typical `doGet` and `doPost` methods have similar sequences of action:

1. Examine the request and determine what to do.
2. Set the response content type.
3. Create the appropriate output stream.
4. Perform the desired function and create the response content.

Methods in the ServletRequest Interface

Although you will typically be working with a `HttpServletRequest` object, the most commonly used methods are defined in the `ServletRequest` interface. I discuss these commonly used methods here and relegate discussion of the less frequently used methods to an appendix.

BufferedReader getReader() A `BufferedReader` would be used if you want to read and parse the request body text line by line instead of using the parsed parameters.

ServletInputStream getInputStream() The `ServletInputStream` class is an extension of `InputStream` that is capable of reading binary data.

String getContentType()   The String returned gives the MIME (Multipurpose Internet Mail Extensions) type of the content.

int getContentLength()   The int value returned is the number of bytes in the body of the request. You might use this as a preliminary verification that the content is what you expect. For instance, excessively long input might be due to a hacker attempting to overload the server.

Enumeration getParameterNames()   The names of parameters parsed out of the request are made available as an Enumeration rather than a String array because the name–value pairs are stored in a Hashtable, and Hashtable objects return the list of all keys as an Enumeration.

String getParameter(String name)   This method returns the String value corresponding to a parameter name or returns null if the name does not appear in the request. It is a wise precaution to always check the returned value versus null. If there may be more than one parameter with the same name, this method returns only the first one in the request.

String[] getParameterValues(String name)   If there may be more than one value associated with a particular name, this method should be used. The String array that is returned preserves the original order of the parameters. If no parameter with this name exists, null is returned.

Methods Added by HttpServletRequest

This interface extends ServletRequest and adds a number of useful methods, most of which are related to getting at information in the HTTP header that precedes the body of the request. The GET methods that access the header information by name are not sensitive to case.

String getMethod()   A call to getMethod() returns a String indicating the HTTP method used in the request, such as GET or POST. You would use this if you were implementing your own version of the service method.

Cookie[] getCookies   Cookies are chunks of text sent from a server to a Web browser that the browser can return on subsequent transactions. Cookie data contained in a request are parsed into Cookie objects that are available as an array. The method returns null if the request contains no cookie data.

String getHeader(String name)   This method returns the String value associated with a header name. For example, the request shown in Listing 1.2 would return the String "localhost" when called with the name "Host." The method returns null if the name does not appear in the request header.

Enumeration getHeaderNames()   This returns an Enumeration over all the header names in the request as uppercase strings. For example, the request shown in Listing 1.2 would return all these names: ACCEPT, ACCEPT-LANGUAGE, ACCEPT-ENCODING, USER-AGENT, HOST, and CONNECTION. However, not all servlet engines support this method, so it may return a null.

I have found at least one engine that returns an Enumeration of names that *might* appear in a header rather than those that actually do appear. Therefore, you should always test a value returned by getHeader or getHeaderNames for null before using it.

String getQueryString()   This method returns the original query String that was present in the URL of a GET request. When working with this String, remember that many special characters get encoded by HTTP conventions.

HttpSession getSession()   HttpSession objects are used to maintain state information between transactions with a particular user. The servlet engine can maintain sessions for the programmer automatically and provide the object associated with a given user with this method. We will be exploring this capability in Chapter 3.

MIME Content Types

A servlet response is always characterized by a MIME content type. As the name implies, content type was originally developed to facilitate transmission and interpretation of non-text data in e-mail. The concept proved so useful that it is widely used in other areas. For example, Java can use MIME types in cut-and-paste operations. A content type string takes the form type/sub-type, which results in a very flexible format. Many MIME types are in use on the Internet; a good starting point for more details is RFC2045. Here are just a few MIME types to give you the idea:

image/gif   An image in the 256-color gif format.

image/jpeg   An image in the more flexible JPEG format.

text/html   Normal HTML.

text/plain   Straight ASCII text.

application/pdf   Used for Adobe Acrobat.

application/java-archive   Used for Java JAR files.

application/x-zip-compressed   Used for ZIP format archives.

application/octet-stream   Used for arbitrary binary data.

Methods in the ServletResponse Interface

All the data returned to a client in response to a request is managed by a single response object created by the servlet engine and passed to your servlet. Although you will typically be working with a `HttpServletResponse` object, the most commonly used methods are defined in the `ServletResponse` interface.

void setContentType(String type) The response type will be one of the MIME types and may optionally include character encoding information. For example, the type for html in the "Latin-4" character set for Northern European languages would be "text/html; charset=ISO-8859-4." If the character set is not specified, the default of ISO-8859-1 (ASCII) will be used. You should set the content type before getting a text output stream because the `PrintWriter` class encodes the characters.

void setContentLength(int len) This sets the number in the Content-Length header line and must be called before any content is actually sent. Use of this method is optional. In order to use it, you must know the exact length of the body the servlet is going to send.

ServletOutputStream getOutputStream() The `ServletOutputStream` returned by this method is suitable for output of binary data. It is an extension of `java.io.Output-Stream` and can be used to create specialized output streams such as `ObjectOutputStream` or `ZipOutputStream`.

PrintWriter getWriter() This returns a `PrintWriter` that will encode the output stream according to the content type set earlier. It is important to remember that bytes are buffered by both `PrintWriter` and `ServletOutputStream` and are not sent as soon as they are written. You can call the `flush()` method to force the data out. The `close()` method must be called when your servlet has finished writing output, or the client may never receive anything.

Methods Added by HttpServletResponse

Most of the time, you will work with an object implementing the `HttpServletResponse` interface. This interface adds some useful methods specific to HTTP output and also defines a bunch of constants corresponding to the response status codes such as the infamous "404 – page not found" message. Here are some of the most commonly used methods in this interface:

void addCookie(Cookie c) Adds the content of an individual cookie to the response. This method can be called multiple times, but note that browsers may accept only 20 cookies from a given source or may be set to refuse all cookies.

void addHeader(String name, String value) and void setHeader(String name, String value) These two methods may be used to create or modify a line in the response header.

void sendRedirect(String newurl) This method redirects the user's browser to a new URL. Calling this method effectively terminates the response.

void sendError(int ecode)   This method sends a header with one of those annoying error codes that are defined as constants in the **HttpServletResponse** interface.

Working with Cookies

Cookies were introduced by Netscape to store a limited amount of information on the user's system so that it can be returned to the server in subsequent transactions. Cookies are the basis for Amazon's "one-click" shopping and sites that "remember" your password. The cookie mechanism will return cookie information to only the host that originated it, subject to various restrictions. Cookies have the following properties:

Version   Only two values are possible, version "0" is the original Netscape style, and version "1" is defined in RFC2109.

Domain   The domain controls the range of servers to which the cookie is sent. By default, it is only returned to the originating domain such as **www.sybex.com**, but setting the domain to **.sybex.com** will allow the return of the cookie to servers such as **www2.sybex.com** or **ftp.sybex.com**.

Max-Age   This numeric property should be used to avoid clogging up a browser with outdated information. The browser is expected to delete cookies that are older than this age in seconds. The server can force a browser to expire a cookie at once by setting Max-Age to zero. Setting a negative value instructs the browser to keep the cookie for the duration of the session but not to save the cookie when it exits.

Path   This variable restricts the paths on the server to which the cookie is returned. This is the path as seen by external clients, not the file system path. A setting of "/" would allow it to be returned to all paths on a server, whereas a setting of "/servlets" would restrict visibility of the cookie to URLs starting with "servlets," including all subdirectories.

Secure   If the Secure attribute is present, the browser should send the cookie only if the communication channel is secure.

Name   All cookies must have a name.

Value   This is the text that is returned to the server.

The **javax.servlet.http.Cookie** API provides methods for setting and getting all these properties. A **Cookie** is always constructed with a name and value **String** and is then modified as necessary. Programming with **Cookie** objects is discussed in Chapter 3.

The destroy Method

The **destroy()** method is called when a servlet engine is about to discard the servlet object, either to recover the memory or as part of an orderly shutdown. Typically you would use the **destroy** method to close files or database connections and generally save any state information.

The servlet engine will not call `destroy` if any `Thread` objects are using it. You are guaranteed that after `destroy` has been called, no more requests will be sent to the servlet. Note that just like all Java objects, the `finalize()` method will be called after the servlet object has been selected for garbage collection.

Setting Up a System for Servlet Development

All the major Java integrated development environments (IDEs) now support servlet programming and some support servlet debugging. If you are using a commercial Java IDE, it probably already supports servlet development.

You do not need to have multiple machines and a network to develop servlets and JavaServer Pages, provided your development machine has enough memory. If you already have a Web server such as Microsoft's PWS or IIS on a Windows system, all you have to do is install a server add-on module.

Commercially Available Servlet Engines

Sun maintains a list of commercially available and open-source products for running Java servlets and JavaServer Pages. As of this writing, there were 28 servers and 6 add-on products on the list at:

```
http://java.sun.com/products/servlet/industry.html
```

Add-on products can add servlet capability to all major server brands very simply. At the present time, the major vendors of add-on engines supporting both servlets and JavaServer Pages include the following:

Allaire   This major vendor sells JRun, one of the most commonly used servlet engines. In addition to commercial versions, they provide a free version entirely suitable for small-scale Web sites. JRun can be a standalone Web server or an add-on to Windows and some UNIX-based servers.

New Atlanta   This company provides free evaluation copy downloads of the ServletExec add-on engine and server, which includes debugging facilities. Systems supported include Windows, Mac, and UNIX.

Configuration and Administration

Unfortunately, configuration and administration follow no set pattern, so you must depend on the product documentation for details. A general trend is to use XML-encoded files to set up system parameters. One reason for this is the extensive use of XML in Sun's Java 2 Enterprise Edition (J2EE) framework for application servers.

Combined Web Server and Servlet Engine Installation

Due to the rapidly changing market, these products undergo frequent upgrades. Therefore, you should always consult the latest installation instructions for a particular product. However, we can make the following generalizations about decisions you will have to make during installation:

Connecting an Add-On When a servlet engine is an add-on to an existing server, some special steps have to be taken to set up the server so it will pass servlet and JSP requests to the add-on.

JDK Support Although some servlet engines ship with their own Java Virtual Machine and standard libraries, in most cases you will have to have the JDK installed.

Aliases In practically all cases, you will want to refer to servlets by an alias rather than by the full servlet class name. Your servlet engine will have to be configured to associate an alias with the complete servlet class name.

Other Environment Paths Other settings will let you configure the directory used for log files.

The Official Reference Implementation

To encourage software developers to experiment with Java programming, Sun has created "reference implementation" versions of many Java technology systems. A reference implementation is supposed to be working code that demonstrates a potential application but is not a polished commercial product. Prior to December 1999, the JavaServer Web Development Kit (JSWDK) 1.0.1 was Sun's official development kit for servlets and JSP. As of December, 1999, Sun turned over all source code for the reference implementation of servlets and JSP to the Apache organization.

The informal group of developers who created the Apache Web server that runs more than half the world's Web sites have now created a formal organization. Here is that organization's statement of purpose as displayed at the primary Web site `http://www.apache.org`:

> *"The Apache Software Foundation exists to provide organizational, legal, and financial support for the Apache open-source software projects. Formerly known as the Apache Group, the Foundation has been incorporated as a membership-based, not-for-profit corporation in order to ensure that the Apache projects continue to exist beyond the participation of individual volunteers, to enable contributions of intellectual property and funds on a sound basis, and to provide a vehicle for limiting legal exposure while participating in open-source software projects."*

Several Java-related projects are going on through the Apache Software Foundation, including the JServe servlet add-on for the Apache Web server and the Cocoon project for a totally XML-based server. The servlet and JSP project is called Jakarta, and the reference implementation is code-named Tomcat. The primary Web site for Tomcat information is:

```
http://jakarta.apache.org/tomcat
```

As of this writing, the Tomcat server is still under development. The installation procedure improves with every iteration, but it is still not as polished as the commercial servlet engines.

CHAPTER 2

The Basic JSP API

- The Role of JavaServer Pages

- The Relation of the Servlet API to JavaServer Pages

- How a JavaServer Pages Page Is Handled by a Server

- The Tags Used in JavaServer Pages

- The Relation of JavaServer Pages to XML

As Web servers have expanded into application servers over the last few years, there has been a great interest in special scripting languages that add functionality to plain Web pages. Many proprietary languages, such as Microsoft's ASP (Active Server Pages) and Netscape's Server-Side JavaScript, have been created. With JSP and other languages, the intent for scripting in Web pages is to permit the separation of presentation from content generation, thus giving Web designers great flexibility while minimizing the need for involving a programmer with presentation design issues.

The Role of JavaServer Pages

In the emerging picture of the Java-powered Internet, JavaServer Pages (JSP) and servlets occupy a central position between Web-enabled clients and application servers. You can think of JSP and servlets as working in the environment of a *Web container* that provides connections and services. By means of these connections, JSP and servlets control the presentation of data derived from operations on databases to network-connected clients. This central role is suggested in Figure 2.1.

FIGURE 2.1

The central position of JSP and Java servlets in Web applications

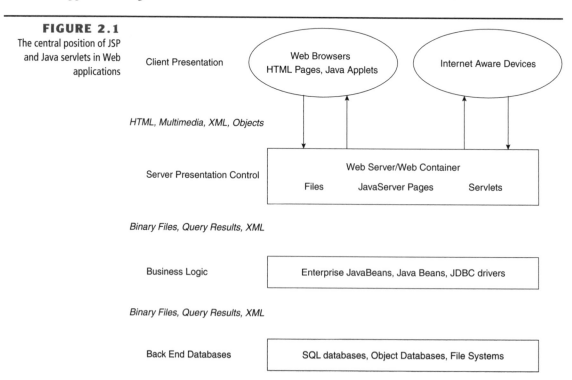

As part of Sun Microsystems' attempt to make sense out of the proliferation of Java application programming interfaces (APIs) and various other initiatives in the "application server" market, the company created Java 2 Enterprise Edition (J2EE). This package brings together the toolkits and APIs needed to create large-scale commercial applications with Java. Both servlets and JSP are as much an essential part of J2EE as Enterprise JavaBeans.

However, you don't have to use expensive application server hardware and software to take advantage of JSP. The basic software technology is available in free or low-cost implementations and can run on modest hardware.

It is important to note that JSP is not limited to generating Hypertext Markup Language (HTML) pages. The technology generates content with Extensible Markup Language (XML) markup or Extensible HTML (XHTML) formatting equally well. Some people feel that serving XML documents to browsers that then format the data according to separate style sheets is the future of the Web.

NOTE   Complete coverage of XML developments is beyond the scope of this book. A great compact reference publication is *XML Pocket Reference*, 1999, by Robert Eckstein, ISBN 1-565-92709-5, published by O'Reilly & Associates. A more complete book is *Mastering XML*, 1999, by Ann Navarro, Chuck White, and Linda Burman, ISBN 0-782-12266-3, published by Sybex, Inc.

Other people have their own visions of the best way to create dynamic Web applications, many of which involve custom tag systems and specialized application servers. However, at the present time, the industry seems to be moving rapidly to support for Java in the form of servlets and JSP, with or without additional specialized toolkits. By permitting the use of custom tag libraries, the JSP 1.1 version may allow the industry to have both the advantages of a common platform and the capability of specialized toolkits.

Sun's Web Application Vision

In the 2.2 version of the Java Servlet Specification, Sun uses the term *Web application* for a collection of servlets, JSP pages, HTML files, image files, and other resources that exist in a structured hierarchy of directories on a server. The idea is that descriptive information in a standard XML-based format will support administration of this application in a consistent way. Distribution of a Web application can be accomplished in a single Web Application Archive file that will run under any server meeting the standard. These archives use the Java Archive (JAR) format but with a file type of `.war` to indicate the intended purpose.

NOTE   Creating a complete application to fit this vision is considerably beyond the scope of this book. As Web developers, we have to walk before we try to fly. I only mention this vision because some of the servlet and JSP functionality we explore in this book is aimed at making it feasible.

Creators of application servers are rapidly adopting the use of XML as a flexible tool for administering server engines because it is more flexible and easier to understand than previous approaches. However, it is not yet clear whether the industry as a whole will go with Sun's approach.

How JSP Is Related to Servlets

As discussed in Chapter 1, a Web server essentially receives a client request and creates a response. In the servlet processing model, the request is translated into a request object, which is passed to the appropriate servlet method. The server also provides a response object that the servlet uses to create a complete response to the client.

That is exactly the model used in processing JSP, except that instead of a servlet written entirely by a Java programmer, the servlet is written by the server engine, based on the contents of a JSP page. A JSP page looks very much like a standard HTML page, and in fact may contain nothing but standard HTML tags. A JSP page may also consist of nothing but JSP tags, but most commonly has both HTML and JSP.

You might think of a server handling a JSP request as a "page compiler," combining template text with Java code directed by JSP elements into a single servlet that implements the `HttpJspPage` interface. The `_jspService` method in this servlet is executed to create the response. Although parsing and compiling takes a fair amount of time the first time the JSP is executed, after that, the servlet can be executed directly. Here are the steps involved:

1. A request naming a JSP page is directed to the JSP engine by the Web server.
2. The JSP engine looks for the corresponding servlet based on the page name. If the servlet exists and is up to date, the request is passed to the servlet `_jspService` method using `HttpServletRequest` and `HttpServletResponse` objects just like with a regular servlet.
3. If the source page has been changed or has never been compiled, the page compiler parses the source and creates the equivalent Java source code for a servlet, extending `HttpJSPServlet`.
4. This code is then compiled, and the new servlet is executed. The servlet object can stay in memory, providing a very fast response to the next request.

The request and response objects are exactly the same ones used in normal servlets; the difference in this situation is that the service method is created by the JSP engine.

JSP and Components

The potential for JSP is very much enhanced by the ease of using software components in building a page. The idea of software components that would be as easy to connect as electronic components are has been kicked around programming circles for quite a while. Microsoft's Visual Basic is probably the most successful software component architecture in recent years, thus demonstrating that you don't have to use a true object-oriented language to use software components.

Java has two kinds of components: JavaBeans and Enterprise JavaBeans. Enterprise Java-Bean (EJB) components are an essential part of Sun's J2EE vision and depend on specialized server services, whereas JavaBean components are simpler.

If you are using a modern development environment for Java, it probably provides for building graphical user interfaces (GUIs) with JavaBeans, but JavaBeans are not restricted to GUI components. A JavaBean is simply a Java class that meets the following criteria:

- The class must be public.
- The class must have a no-arguments constructor.
- The class must provide `set` and `get` methods to access variables.

If the JavaBean class is serializable, the JSP programmer has the option of either creating a new object from the class file or reading in a serialized object with variables already set.

JSP and Java Version History

Trying to keep track of the Java revolution has been quite a wild ride over the last few years. A glance back at Java history will help to orient us. First, the following are important dates for the Java language:

May, 1995   First public announcement of Java 1.0 alpha.

January, 1996   Production release of JDK 1.0.

December, 1996   Production release of JDK 1.1 with many changes and improvements.

1997   Many APIs are undergoing development by Sun and industry partners.

1998   Continued development of many APIs.

December, 1998   Production release of JDK 1.2.

1999   Java 2 Enterprise Edition brings together many lines of development. Servlets and JSP are an essential part.

Developments that would eventually become the Servlet API started in 1996 with work at Sun to create a totally Java Web server. The following are some of the landmarks in the development:

June, 1997   The Servlet API 1.0 is finalized.

April, 1998   Servlet API 2.0 is released with the Java Servlet Development Kit (JSDK).

October, 1999   Sun turns over all Servlet 2.2 and JavaServer Pages 1.1 code to the Apache organization, which will manage open source development of future reference implementations of pure Java servlet and JSP engines. Apache calls this server the Tomcat project.

December, 1999   The Servlet API 2.2 is part of the J2EE final release.

JSP Version 0.92

Development of the JavaServer Pages API has been somewhat slower than that of the Servlet API, because changes in the basic Java language and the Servlet API had to be incorporated into the JSP mechanism. Version 0.92 was used in the JRun product until recently, and many Web sites are still running this version.

JSP Version 1.0

Many aspects of JSP changed with the 1.0 release. This version is compatible with the 2.1 servlet specification and includes many tag revisions. There is no compatibility between version 0.92 and version 1.0 JSP pages; for example, the `<%@ include` directive replaces a technology known as Server Side Includes (SSI).

Other major changes include making all tags case sensitive for compatibility with XML and XHTML and the addition of many new directives. The final release of the 1.0 specification occurred in September 1999, but many vendors had been working on preliminary versions. As of this writing, most vendors support version 1.0 and are working on support for the next version.

JSP Version 1.1

The final release of the 1.1 specifications was in December 1999, so it clearly was prepared in parallel with the 1.0 specification. At the present time, many application server providers are concentrating on achieving compatibility with the 1.0 specification, but it is obvious that they all intend to eventually support the 1.1 version. The following are the main differences between the 1.0 and 1.1 specifications:

- The 1.1 specification was based on the Servlet 2.2 specification.
- The classes `JspException` and `JspError` were added to better unify exception reporting.
- The 1.1 specification provided for tag extensions with the `taglib` mechanism. This is intended to foster creation of portable toolkits.
- The 1.1 specification clarified the relationship between JSP pages and JSP containers.

Although the basic Java language release has now reached JDK 1.3, the servlet and JSP APIs are compatible with the JDK 1.1 release and are likely to remain so. For information on the current status of the reference implementation of servlets and JSP by the Apache organization, visit their Web site at:

```
http://jakarta.apache.org/
```

Creating JSP Pages

What you create when working with JSP is, not surprisingly, a page of text that looks like plain text with HTML markup tags using the familiar angle bracket (<>) symbols in conjunction with other punctuation. A JSP engine can process a page with only text and HTML markup, a page with nothing but JSP tags, or a mixture of both. Listing 2.1 shows a simple page with a single JSP tag embedded in HTML.

Listing 2.1: A Java expression embedded in HTML with a JSP tag

```
<HTML>
<HEAD><TITLE>JRun Date Demo</TITLE></HEAD>
<BODY>
<H2>Date And Time <%= new Date().toString() %></H2>
<hr>
</BODY>
</HTML>
```

The example in Listing 2.1 uses what we might call the original style of JSP tag, in which the tag starts with special punctuation and ends with the "%>" character sequence. We discuss XML-compatible tags in the section titled "XML Compatibility Style Tags," later in this chapter.

Table 2.1 shows all the JSP tags that use this style.

TABLE 2.1: JSP tags in the original style

Tag	Used for	Example
<%-- --%>	Comments	<%-- this is never shown --%>
<%= %>	Expressions (evaluated as String)	<%= new Date() %>
<%! %>	Declarations	<%! Date myD = new Date() ; %>
<% %>	Code Fragments	<% for(int i = 0 ; i < 10 ; i++ { %>
<%@ %>	Directives	<%@ page import="java.util.*" %>

Here is a quick summary of how these tags are used, followed by greater details:

Comments   Text inside the <%-- to --%> comment tags is not processed by the JSP compilation process.

Expressions   The Java expression inside the tags is evaluated as a String and is written to the output stream.

Declarations   A declaration declares a variable or method that can be used in the page.

Code Fragments   A code fragment can contain any valid Java code. It is executed when the request is processed.

Directives   The page, include, and taglib directives are discussed in the section titled "Directives," later in this chapter.

Comments in JSP

Several different forms of comments are actually possible in a JSP page. These styles let you control where the comment can be seen.

<%-- jsp comment text %>   This text appears in the original JSP page but is skipped over by the page compiler, so it does not appear in the resulting Java code.

<% /* java comment */ %> or <% // java comment %>   These standard Java comments enclosed in code fragment tags will appear in the Java code created by the page compiler but not in the output page.

<!-- html comment -->   An HTML style comment can be used anywhere in the template data; it will be transmitted with the output page but not displayed. You can generate an HTML comment that includes text generated by Java expressions.

Declarations and Member Variables

Declarations define variables and methods that will be members of the servlet that the page compiler creates and will be available in the entire page. Listing 2.2 shows an example declaration of a String, a Vector, and a jspInit method that reads a text file into the Vector. Note that we override the jspInit method but call the parent class method in case it has to do any implementation-specific actions.

Listing 2.2: An example of declaring variables and methods with declaration tags

```
<%!
  String listPath = "E:\\scripts\\errata\\errcatISBN.txt";
  Vector ertLines = new Vector() ;

  public void jspInit(){
    super.jspInit();
    File f = new File( listPath );
```

```
    try {
      BufferedReader br = new BufferedReader( new FileReader(f));
      String tmp = br.readLine();
      while( tmp != null ){
        if( ! tmp.startsWith(":") ){
          ertLines.addElement( tmp );
        }
        tmp = br.readLine();
      }
      br.close();
    }catch(IOException e){
    }
  }
%>
```

The Implicit Variables

Every JSP page contains reference variables pointing to objects, called *implicit objects*, that are always defined. You can use implicit variables inside your code. Many of the classes these objects implement have already been described in Chapter 1; the rest are discussed later in this chapter in the section titled "The JSP Packages." Table 2.2 summarizes the variable names and uses. Note that the exception variable is defined only if the page is declared an error page.

TABLE 2.2: The implicit JSP page variables

Variable name	Type	Used for
request	A descendent of javax. servlet.ServletRequest	Represents the user's request
response	A descendent of javax. servlet.ServletResponse	Creates the output response
pageContext	A javax.servlet.jsp. PageContext object	Contains attributes of this page
session	A javax.servlet.http. HttpSession	Contains arbitrary variables attached to this user's session
application	A javax.servlet. ServletContext object	Contains attributes for the entire application; affects the interpretation of several other tags
out	A javax.servlet. jsp.JspWriter object	The output stream for the response
config	A javax.servlet. ServletConfig object	Contains servlet initialization parameter name value pairs and the ServletContext object
page	An object reference pointing to *this*	The current servlet object
exception	A java.lang.Throwable object	Only pages designated as error pages in the page directive have this object

Scope of Variables

Some of the implicit variables have a scope beyond that of a single JSP page. In addition to page scope, a variable can have request, application, or session scope.

Request Scope   A request can actually be processed by several pages because of the forwarding mechanism. The request object can carry additional objects with it.

Application Scope   Sun uses the term "Web application" to refer to the collection of servlets, JSP, and other resources installed in a particular server address space. The Servlet-Context class is intended to let all of these resources share information by means of mutually accessible stored objects in "application scope." The application scope affects the interpretation of relative URL specifications. However, version 1.0 of the JSP API provides only a small fraction of the functions planned for ServletContext in version 1.1.

Session Scope   As we will see in Chapter 3, servlets and JSP pages can save information specific to a user in an HttpSession object managed by the servlet engine. Objects stored this way are said to have "session" scope.

Code Fragments

Code fragments are chunks of Java code that will end up being compiled into the _jspService method of the servlet that the page compiler writes. The order in which code fragments appear in the page is the order in which they appear in the method. You may also see code fragments referred to as "scriptlets." Each code fragment must be a legal Java code element, but it can be mixed in with template text, as shown in Listing 2.3.

Listing 2.3: Code fragment tags mixed with normal text

```
<% for( int j = 1 ; j <= 10 ; j++ ){
%>  count = <%= j %> <br>
<% }
%>
```

The Java code produced by the JSP engine from these tags is shown in Listing 2.4.

Listing 2.4: The Java statements created from Listing 2.3

```
for( int j = 1 ; j <= 10 ; j++ ){
        out.print("  count = ");
        out.print(j );
        out.print(" <br>\r\n");
}
```

The ability to mix code fragments with literal text is very powerful, but it also means there are a number of different ways of combining tags with literal text to create a given output. As we will see in later examples, JSP allows the possibility of writing very hard-to-understand code.

Directives

There are three kinds of directives: `page`, `include`, and `taglib`. The `page` and `include` directives define conditions for the entire JSP page, whereas a `taglib` directive acts at a particular place in the page.

Page Directive

The `page` directive defines attributes that apply to an entire JSP page. A typical use would be

```
<%@ page language="java" import="java.util.*,java.io.*" %>
```

which informs the JSP processor that the language of the code on the page will be Java, as well as declaring the packages that will be imported. At present, Java is the only language defined for JSP, but obviously the designers wanted to leave open the possibility of using other languages. Note that the value of an attribute must be enclosed in quotation marks. Table 2.3 shows the attributes that may appear in a `page` directive.

TABLE 2.3: Attributes appearing in the page directive

Attribute	Used for	Note
language	Defines the language used in code fragments.	Currently always Java.
extends	Defines the parent of the resulting servlet.	Use with caution.
import	Defines a list of classes to be imported, separated by commas.	The list becomes Java import statements.
session	Determines whether a session object will have to be defined.	Value is either "true" or "false," default is true.
buffer	Controls the size of the response output buffer.	Value can be either "none" or a size such as "12kb"; the default is "8kb."
autoFlush	If set "false," an overflow of the buffer causes an exception. If set "true," the buffer will be flushed to the output stream when full. The default value is "true."	Must not be set to "false" when the buffer value is "none."
isThreadSafe	When set "false," the JSP container must allow only one request to be processed at a time. When set "true," more than one request Thread can run at the same time.	Default is "true."
info	Defines a String value that can be accessed in the code using the getServletInfo() method.	
errorPage	If present, the value defines a URL of a resource that will be sent any Exception or Error object that is not caught in the Java code of this page.	The JSP engine will provide a default errorPage.
isErrorPage	If set "true," the current page is the target of another page's errorPage URL.	If "true," this page will have an "exception" variable defined.
contentType	This value gives the MIME content type and character encoding of the page as used in the ServletResponse setContentType method.	The default is "text/html: charset=ISO-8859-1" character encoding.

Include Directive

The include directive tells the engine to include text or output from a specified resource. The format uses the relative URL specified above. For example, the following tag would be useful to ensure that the same copyright message is included on every page:

```
<%@ include file="/JSPbook/copyright.txt" %>
```

When this tag is encountered, the text in the file will be read and processed. It can be anything that can legally appear in a JSP page.

Relative URLs for Resources

When tags refer to resources, such as servlets or JSP files, they can use relative URLs that are based on the ServletContext or the current JSP page location. Consider the following examples of the include directive:

1. `<%@ include file="/JSPbook/copyright.txt" %>`
2. `<%@ include file="copyright.txt" %>`

In line 1, the leading "/" character indicates that the system should look for the file in this path relative to the ServletContext. In line 2, the system would look for the file in the same directory as the current JSP page.

This design lets each Web application live in its own address space. It is intended to make it easy to install a new application in a server with a minimum of fiddling with the file system by allowing resources to be addressed relative to the application.

Taglib Directive

The `taglib` directive allows you to define a library of custom action tags that will be used in the page. This is a very powerful concept that will enable you to use specialized toolkits as easily as you use the standard tags. Custom tags use interfaces and classes in the `javax.servlet.jsp.tagext` package. Due to the complexity of defining your own tag library, I discuss this directive in detail in Chapter 11.

XML Compatibility Style Tags

You have no doubt noticed that Web applications are all turning to XML and XML-related ideas for many functions. Java applications are no exception, but this created a problem for the further development of JSP because the original tags are not compatible with the XML standard. This incompatibility would prevent use of JSP tags in pages using the new XHTML standard, which was clearly not acceptable.

XHTML is the standard that many developers hope will finally rationalize HTML markup. The latest recommendations for XHTML are to be found at:

```
http://www.w3.org/TR/
```

To be compatible with XHTML, Sun created a complete alternate set of tags that satisfy the XML requirement for formatting. Adopting XML namespace conventions also makes JSP much more flexible and powerful because it allows you to create your own library of custom tags or to buy a custom toolkit for particular purposes.

Before the advent of JSP, many application server vendors created their own custom tag systems, such as ColdFusion for HTML markup. These vendors may now be able to fit their specialized tags into the general JSP framework as tag libraries, which will allow for wider acceptance.

Table 2.4 shows the XML equivalent tags for the basic "<%" style tags. The "jsp:" at the start of the tag identifies the namespace that the tag belongs to, in this case the standard JSP namespace. This XML convention ensures that JSP tags can be interpreted separately from other XML tags in the data. Naturally, being able to use a named tag makes this style a lot easier to use than the punctuation-based tag style.

TABLE 2.4: The XML equivalent for JSP tags

Tag	jsp tag	Used for	Example
<%!	<jsp:declaration>	declaration	<jsp:declaration> String ver = "version 1.0"; </jsp:declaration>
<%=	<jsp:expression	expression	<jsp:expression> </jsp:expression>
<%	<jsp:scriptlet>	Java code fragment	<jsp:scriptlet> for(int i = 0 ; i < 10 ; i++) { </jsp:scriptlet>
<%@	<jsp:directive	directives	<jsp:directive.page language="java" />

There are two styles of elements in XML markup; Table 2.5 shows both kinds. The code fragment markup uses an opening and a closing tag to enclose text. On the other hand, the directives tag style has all data enclosed in a single "<" – "/>" pair and contains named attributes that give values in quotation marks. This style is called "empty."

Tags are also divided into directives and actions. Directives are messages to the JSP engine that do not produce any output. Actions such as an expression modify the output stream and create, use, or modify objects.

TABLE 2.5: XML-style JSP tags

jsp tag	Used for	Example
<jsp:include />	Incorporates bulk text from a file	<jsp:include page="copyright.htm" />
<jsp:forward />	Forwards the request to a servlet, another JSP, or ?	<jsp:forward page="someURL.jsp" />
<jsp:param />	Used inside a forward, include, or plugin to add or modify a parameter in the request object	<jsp:param name="user" value="newName" />
<jsp:getProperty />	Gets the value of a Bean property by name	<jsp:getProperty name="nameOfBean" property="nameOfProperty"/>
<jsp:setProperty />	Sets the value of a Bean property	<jsp:setProperty name="nameOfBean" property="nameOfProperty" value="somevalue" />
<jsp:useBean />	Locates or creates a Bean with the specific name and scope	See Chapter 11
<jsp:plugin />	Provides full information for a download of a Java plugin to the client Web browser	See Chapter 12

The XML Equivalent of a JSP Page

Sun and its industry partners are so convinced that XML will play a big role in the future of Web applications that the JSP 1.1 specification includes a section on JSP pages as XML documents. The feeling is that as improved authoring tools become available, XML provides the best way to store an accurate representation of a JSP page. Present JSP engines are not required to create an XML representation; the designers are thinking ahead to future releases of the standard.

One reason people are thinking that XML is vital to the future of the Web is the potential for Internet connectivity for devices other than a basic desktop computer. For example, the wireless access protocol (WAP) that is being pushed as a standard for connecting digital telephones and pocket organizers to the Net is based on content transformations using XML.

Although JSP engines are not required to do so, the JRun servlet engine does create an XML representation along with the Java source code when compiling a JSP page. This gives us a chance to look at what may be the future of JSP as an XML generator. Listing 2.5 shows a JSP page that has only two elements: one that outputs a String showing the current date and time and one that includes a copyright message.

Listing 2.5: A simple JSP page to show current time

```
<HTML>
<HEAD>
  <META NAME="GENERATOR" CONTENT="JSPbook Chapt02" >
  <TITLE>A Simple Page</TITLE>
</HEAD>
<BODY>
<%@ page language="java" %>
<%= new Date() %>
<br><hr>
<%@ include file="/JSPbook/copyright.txt" %>
</BODY>
</HTML>
```

Listing 2.6 shows this page translated into XML by the JRun JSP page compiler. The original was in only two lines of text that have been split along logical lines for this listing.

Listing 2.6: XML representation of the page created by JRun

```
<?xml version="1.0" ?>
<jsp:root xmlns:jsp="http://java.sun.com/products/jsp/dtd/jsp_1_0.dtd"
    package="jsp.JSPbook.Chapt02" name="TimeNow">
  <jsp:directive.dependency resource="/JSPbook/Chapt02/TimeNow.jsp"/>
    <![CDATA[\r\n<HTML>\r\n
    <HEAD>\r\n  <META NAME=\"GENERATOR\"
        CONTENT=\"JSPbook Chapt02\" >\r\n  <TITLE>A Simple Page</TITLE>\r\n
    </HEAD>\r\n<BODY>\r\n]]>
  <jsp:directive.page language="java" /><![CDATA[\r\n]]>
  <jsp:expression><![CDATA[new Date()]]>
  </jsp:expression>
  <![CDATA[\r\n<br><hr>\r\n]]>
  <jsp:expression>
  <![CDATA["<i>Copyright &#169; 2000, LANWrights, Inc., Austin, TX</i><br>"]]>
  </jsp:expression>
  <![CDATA[\r\n]]><jsp:directive.dependency resource="/JSPbook/copyright.txt"/>
  <![CDATA[\r\n</BODY>\r\n</HTML>\r\n]]>
</jsp:root>
```

This listing gives us an excellent chance to see XML concepts in action. Here are some important points:

The `<?xml version="1.0" ?>` line gives the XML version.

The `<jsp:root` tag and the corresponding `</jsp:root>` tag at the end of the page provide the required enclosing tag or *root* for the document. The starting tag has attributes that give the document type definition (DTD) the document follows, the name of the class that will be generated, and the package the class will belong to.

The `<jsp:directive page` tag specifies the language attribute as called for in the JSP 1.1 API.

The <jsp:directive dependency> tags give the names of resources involved in generating the page. This information could be used by the JSP engine to determine whether or not the generated Java class is out of date. However, note that a dependency directive is not part of the JSP 1.1 API. Presumably, it is a JRun extension.

The template data of the original JSP page end up as chunks of text enclosed in tags that start with <![CDATA[and end with]]>. XML treats this as literal character data to be written out without XML processing. Because this is data to be written by a Java servlet, you will find escaped special characters (such as the string "\r\n" that stands for carriage return) and line feed control characters.

The original JSP tag <%= is turned into <jsp:expression> with the Java statement enclosed as a CDATA section followed by a closing tag of </jsp:expression>.

The original JSP <%@ include tag caused the text of the copyright.txt file to be brought into the XML as CDATA and enclosed in a <jsp:expression> </jsp:expression> tag pair plus a dependency notation.

After looking at that, you will probably agree that the XML representation of the page would be a lot harder to edit by hand than the JSP version. However, Java provides some nice tools for parsing and manipulating XML documents, as you will see in Chapter 6.

Finally, Listing 2.7 shows the Java source code generated for this JSP page by the JRun page compiler. Some long lines have been split for this listing.

Listing 2.7: The Java code generated by JRun for the TimeNow page

```java
package jsp.JSPbook.Chapt02;

import java.io.*;
import java.util.*;
import java.net.*;
import java.beans.*;

import javax.servlet.*;
import javax.servlet.http.*;
import javax.servlet.jsp.*;

public class TimeNow extends com.livesoftware.jsp.HttpJSPServlet implements
    com.livesoftware.jsp.JRunJspPage, HttpJspPage
{

    public void _jspService(HttpServletRequest request,
        HttpServletResponse response) throws ServletException, IOException
    {
        ServletConfig config = getServletConfig();
        ServletContext application = config.getServletContext();
        Object page = (Object) this;
```

```
        PageContext pageContext =
            JspFactory.getDefaultFactory().getPageContext(this, request,
                response,  null, true,8192, true);
        JspWriter out = pageContext.getOut();
        HttpSession session = request.getSession(true);
        response.setContentType("text/html; charset=ISO-8859-1");

        out.print("\r\n<HTML>\r\n<HEAD>\r\n  <META NAME=\"GENERATOR\"
                CONTENT=\"JSPbook Chapt02\" >\r\n  <TITLE>A Simple Page</TITLE>
                \r\n</HEAD>\r\n<BODY>\r\n");
        out.print("\r\n");
        out.print(new Date());
        out.print("\r\n<br><hr>\r\n");
        out.print(
            "<i>Copyright &#169; 2000, LANWrights, Inc., Austin, TX</i><br>");
        out.print("\r\n");
        out.print("\r\n</BODY>\r\n</HTML>\r\n");
        out.flush();
    }
    private static final String[][] __dependencies__ = {
        {"/JSPbook/Chapt02/TimeNow.jsp", "953159826000" },
        {"/JSPbook/copyright.txt", "952623990000" }, };

    public String[][] __getDependencies()
    {
        return __dependencies__;
    }

    public String __getTranslationVersion()
    {
        return "5";
    }
}
```

The JSP Packages

Two packages with classes are related to JSP. Both are considered standard extensions closely related to servlets, so the package names start with `javax.servlet` in both cases.

The javax.servlet.jsp Package

This package contains all the interfaces, classes, and exceptions used by standard JSP pages. I am going to discuss the most commonly used methods in these interfaces and classes in detail; however, I will relegate discussion of the less frequently used methods to an appendix.

The javax.servlet.jsp.JspPage Interface

When the JSP engine creates a servlet to handle a page, this interface defines two of the methods it must provide. JspPage extends the servlet interface, and these methods are an obvious parallel to the `init` and `destroy` methods in that interface.

public void jspInit()   This method is the first one called by the server when the JSP-created servlet is loaded. At this point, the programmer can call the `getServletConfig` method to access initialization parameters.

public void destroy()   This method is called just before the server destroys the servlet object. This is the programmer's chance to close files and generally release any resources held by the servlet.

The javax.servlet.jsp.HttpJspPage Interface

This extension of the `JspPage` interface defines the `_jspService` method that the JSP compiler must produce. The method parameter list is the same as that of the `doGet` and `doPost` methods in the `HttpServlet` interface.

```
public void _jspService( HttpServletRequest request, HttpServletResponse➡
response )
```

The JspEngineInfo Class

Each JSP engine should provide an extension of this abstract class to provide information about itself. At the present time, the only required method is

```
public String getSpecificationVersion()
```

which returns a String giving the version of the JSP API that the engine implements. This String is in "Dewey decimal" style format, such as "1.1.2," where the left digit is most significant. It is anticipated that future versions will provide information such as the vendor's name and the engine's title.

The JspFactory Class

Each JSP engine implements an extension of this abstract class to control creation of instances of the various objects needed to support the servlet. You can think of this class as a parallel to the java.awt.Toolkit class used in AWT-based graphic applications.

public static JspFactory getDefaultFactory()   This static method simply returns the current default `JspFactory`.

public static void setDefaultFactory(JspFactory fac)   This method is for use by creators of JSP servers only.

public JspEngineInfo getEngineInfo()   The JspEngineInfo object returned here presently can only be used to determine the JSP API version the engine implements. Future APIs are expected to expand the role of this object.

public void releasePageContext(PageContext pc)   This method is typically called just before the _jspService method exits. The purpose is to release any resources held by the PageContext.

public PageContext getPageContext(Servlet thisServ, ServletRequest sreq, ServletResponse sresp, String errorPageURL, boolean needSession, int buffer, boolean autoflush)   The getPageContext method initializes a PageContext object with the various reference variables and parameters that characterize the processing of a request. It is typically called early in the _jspService method constructed by the JSP engine so that JSP programmers don't have to create the call.

Listing 2.8 shows a bit of Java code from a generated servlet to illustrate how JspFactory and the getPageContext method are used.

Listing 2.8: The start of a service method generated by JSP

```
public void _jspService(HttpServletRequest request, HttpServletResponse➥
response) throws ServletException, IOException
{
    ServletConfig config = getServletConfig();
    ServletContext application =
        config.getServletContext();
    Object page = (Object) this;
    PageContext pageContext =
        JspFactory.getDefaultFactory().getPageContext(this,
            request, response,  null, true,8192, true);
    JspWriter out = pageContext.getOut();
```

The JspWriter Class

An instance of this class, called out, is created automatically in the _jspService method from a PageContext as shown in the preceding code listing. A JspWriter object is similar to a java.io.PrintWriter object in that it writes a character stream with a specific encoding. However, there is a significant difference in that a JspWriter output method can throw an IOException. In the PrintWriter class, an IOException is handled internally, and the programmer has to call checkError() to determine if an exception was thrown.

The capability to throw an IOException is essential for managing the buffering behavior of the JspWriter. Recall that the *page* directive lets you set two attributes named buffer and autoFlush. A buffer of "8kb" and the value autoFlush = true are the defaults. With these settings, output goes to the buffer, and the buffer is flushed to the response output stream when it is full. If the buffer attribute is set to "none," all output immediately goes to the response output stream. The `JspWriter` class has three important methods related to buffer behavior.

public void clear()   This discards the current buffer contents, but if the buffer has already been flushed, it throws an `IOException` to warn you that some output has already been sent.

public void clearBuffer()   This method discards the buffer contents but will never throw an `IOException`.

public void flush()   The `flush` method immediately sends the buffer contents.

To see why use of the `clear()` method might be necessary, suppose your JSP page consists of these three sections:

- Introductory text
- Table generated from a database query
- Concluding text

If an error occurs in accessing the database, you can `clear()` the introductory text and write a completely different message to the response. Naturally, you must set a large enough buffer to accommodate the introductory text.

If autoFlush is false, overflowing the buffer causes an `IOException` to be thrown. I suspect this capability exists to prevent a runaway process from writing an endless stream of text.

In addition to the `print( String s )` method, `JspWriter` provides a full set of methods to output primitives, including output from all or part of an array of type `char`. These methods are similar to those in the `PrintWriter` class.

The PageContext class

The `PageContext` class is used to organize references to all of the objects involved in creating a JSP page and provide a number of utilities. As shown in Listing 2.8, the JSP compiler generates a call to the `getPageContext` method of the default `JspFactory` to create an instance of `PageContext` named `pageContext` in the `_jspService` method.

The `PageContext` class has many utility methods. Table 2.6 summarizes those that provide convenient access to the implicit objects and configuration information objects in a typical JSP.

TABLE 2.6: Some utility methods in the PageContext class.

Method	Returned reference type	The implicit object reference returned
getOut()	JspWriter	out
getException()	Exception	exception
getPage()	Servlet	page
getRequest()	ServletRequest	request
getSession	HttpSession	session
getResponse()	ServletResponse	response
getServletConfig()	ServletConfig	config
getServletContext()	ServletContext	-

Normally, the JSP engine writes the code that obtains the implicit objects from the pageContext, so you don't have to worry about that. However, many more objects are accessible through the pageContext. Unfortunately, the method names are rather similar and easily confused:

findAttribute(String name)   Searches all of the contexts—page, request, session, and application—and returns any object that has been stored under this name.

getAttribute(String name)   Looks only in the pageContext and returns any object that has been stored under this name.

getAttribute(String name, int scope)   Searches a scope defined by the scope constant that must be one of those defined in the PageContext class, PAGE_SCOPE, REQUEST_SCOPE, SESSION_SCOPE, or APPLICATION_SCOPE.

There are also methods that place named objects in the various scopes:

setAttribute(String name, Object obj)   Stores the object in the pageContext with page scope.

setAttribute(String name, Object obj, int scope)   Stores the object in the scope indicated by the constant.

The combination of these methods allows the various parts of an application to communicate by means of stored objects. For example, if one page locates a file name, it can be stored in the SESSION_SCOPE context and later retrieved by another page.

The pageContext object is responsible for forwarding or including, as directed by the <jsp:forward> or <jsp:include> tags. The JSP engine normally takes care of writing this code for you.

The `pageContext` object is also responsible for handling exceptions that occur in the `_jspService` method if the *page* directive gives an *errorPage*. This is illustrated in Listing 2.9, which shows a code fragment from the end of a `_jspService` method that catches all exceptions.

Listing 2.9: The pageContext object handles an exception

```
    } catch (Exception ex) {
      if (out.getBufferSize() != 0)
            out.clear();
            pageContext.handlePageException(ex);
    } finally {
            out.flush();
            _jspxFactory.releasePageContext(pageContext);
    }
```

The JspException Class

This is a generic exception for reporting errors in JSP processing, which was added in the 1.1 API. JSP engines will presumably extend this class for specific purposes. Presently, only certain methods in the tag extension package throw a `JspException`.

The JspError Class

The `JspError` class descends from `JspException` and is used to report errors in JSP processing that are unrecoverable. Note that in spite of the name, this class descends from `java.lang.Exception` and not `java.lang.Error`. The JSP engine must forward the exception to the error page where it has the default name `exception`.

The javax.servlet.jsp.tagext Package

Tagext stands for Tag Extension. Classes in this package are intended to provide a method for extending JSP capabilities with new tags and to support authoring systems for JSP pages. The `tagext` package is new with the 1.1 Servlet API and thus is supported by only a few experimental servers at this time. Tag extensions are sure to become very popular, but I am going to postpone detailed discussion of the `tagext` package to Chapter 11.

Design Considerations

Today's Web designers face a tremendous number of choices. There are so many powerful technologies, and some, like JavaServer Pages and Java servlet technology, are so new that standard design techniques have not really evolved.

The basic philosophy, which you will hear frequently, is that JSP pages let you separate data from presentation. In Sun's view of the Java-powered application server, JSP and servlets handle presentation, whereas JavaBeans and Enterprise JavaBeans handle business logic. However, it seems all too easy to create a page that mixes presentation logic and data logic.

Too Many Alternatives?

Some serious commentators on the Java scene have suggested that the JSP approach offers too many alternatives and too many ways to write bad code. Jason Hunter, co-author of one of the first books about Java servlets, has posted an essay on this issue on his Web site that deserves your consideration:

```
http://www.servlets.com/soapbox/problems-jsp.html
```

Design for Debugging

Unfortunately, there are many ways for a JSP page to go wrong and produce hard-to-understand results or no output at all. Remember, for a JSP page to work, several levels of technology must cooperate, and there is a chance for error at every level.

Debugging in this environment is so complex that the subject deserves a chapter by itself. However, I am sure you are going to be trying some projects of your own before we get to that chapter, so keep these basic principles in mind.

Build from Working Parts   For example, check the layout of a page in HTML before you add JSP elements. Check the workings of a JavaBean in a simple test program before adding it to a JSP page.

Use Logging   Statements that write to System.out or a log file can let you know what is going on. Learn to use the logging facilities your JSP engine offers.

Catch Those Exceptions   Java's Exception mechanism can be a big help.

A Simple JSP Example

As you start programming JSP pages, you will probably be struck by the fact that there is a tremendous number of ways to accomplish the same output. This is due to the fact that the programmer can combine HTML, JSP, Java servlets, and other Java technologies.

As I see it, the JSP programmer must actively strive to develop a style that produces clear, easily debugged, and easily maintained code. It is too easy to whip out something that does the job but will be incomprehensible when you look at it later.

For the purposes of this example, assume we need to create an online demonstration of the workings of the Java shift operators for a beginning Java class. The student will enter an integer into a form, click a button, and view a table that shows the number in decimal, hex, and binary form, as acted on by the different shift operators. Figure 2.2 shows the desired result.

FIGURE 2.2

A table in an HTML page, showing the result of applying Java shift operators

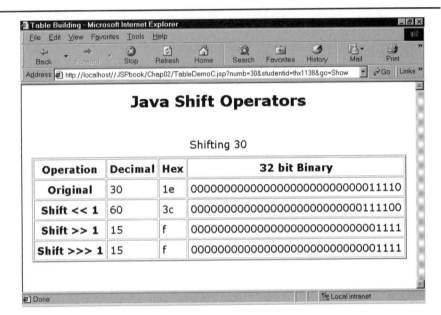

The Input Form

Input is simple enough; we just need a plain HTML page with a form that sends a request to a JSP page. Listing 2.10 shows the page text.

Listing 2.10: A simple input form to get a number

```
<HTML>
<HEAD>
<TITLE>Shift Demo Number Entry</TITLE>
</HEAD>
<BODY BGCOLOR="#FFFFFF" TEXT="#000000">
<FONT FACE=VERDANA>
<H2 ALIGN=CENTER>
    Welcome to the Shift Operator Demo
</H2><BR>
<form action="TableDemo.jsp" method="GET">
```

```
Enter Number to be shifted: <input name="numb" type="text" size="10">
<input type="submit" value="Show" name="go" ><br>
</form>
</BODY>
</HTML>
```

One Approach to Presentation

This approach takes what you might call the direct approach to creating the desired table. Essentially, the complete page is developed in HTML, and then code fragments are plugged into the table values as shown in Listing 2.11. It isn't elegant, but it does the job at the cost of a lot of JSP tags.

Listing 2.11: Building the table directly in JSP

```
<HTML>
<HEAD>
<TITLE>Table Building</TITLE>
</HEAD>
<BODY BGCOLOR="#FFFFFF" TEXT="#000000">
<FONT FACE=VERDANA>
<H2 ALIGN=CENTER>Java Shift Operators
</H2><BR>
<%@ page language="java" errorPage="/JSPbook/Chap02/whoops.jsp" %>
<%!
public String padBinary( int n ){
    String tmp = "00000000000000000000000000000000"
        + Integer.toBinaryString( n );
    return tmp.substring( tmp.length() - 32 );
}
%>
<%
String numbS = request.getParameter( "numb" );
int x = Integer.parseInt( numbS ) ;
int n = x ;
%>

<table align="center" border="2" cellpadding="5" >
<caption><%= "Shifting " + x + "<br>\r\n" %></caption>
<tr><th>Operation</th><th>Decimal</th><th>Hex</th><th>32 bit Binary</th></tr>
<tr><th>Original</th><td><%= n %></td>
        <td><%= Integer.toHexString(n)%></td>
        <td><%= padBinary( n ) %></td></tr>
<% n = x << 1 ; %>
<tr><th>Shift &lt;&lt; 1</th><td><%= n %></td>
        <td><%= Integer.toHexString(n)%></td>
        <td><%= padBinary( n ) %></td></tr>
<% n = x >> 1 ; %>
<tr><th>Shift &gt;&gt; 1</th><td><%= n %></td>
        <td><%= Integer.toHexString(n)%></td>
        <td><%= padBinary( n ) %></td></tr>
</tr>
```

```
<% n = x >>> 1 ; %>
<tr><th>Shift &gt;&gt;&gt; 1</th><td><%= n %></td>
         <td><%= Integer.toHexString(n)%></td>
         <td><%= padBinary( n ) %></td></tr>
</TABLE>
</BODY>
</HTML>
```

Debugging with this approach was rather time consuming. The only way to test it was to try to submit a number through a browser and see what happened. Because JSP parsing has to proceed without error to create a Java servlet, a single missed tag syntax tended to produce the dreaded "HTTP 500 - Internal server error" message. Every time that happened, I had to examine the JSP engine log to locate the error.

The resulting Java servlet code was not particularly elegant either. There were dozens of little out.print() statements.

The JavaBean Approach

As discussed earlier, in the section titled "JSP and Components," a JavaBean is a way of creating a software component that has simple provisions for setting and getting parameters. A JSP page can get an instance of a bean with the simple <jsp:useBean tag and can later refer to it by name. This is illustrated in Listing 2.12, where all the table-creating functions have been delegated to the tableBean bean, resulting in a much more compact JSP page.

Listing 2.12: A JSP page to create the table using a bean

```
<HTML>
<HEAD>
<TITLE>Table Building</TITLE>
</HEAD>
<BODY BGCOLOR="#FFFFFF" TEXT="#000000">
<FONT FACE=VERDANA>
<H2 ALIGN=CENTER>Java Shift Operators
</H2><BR>
<%@ page language="java" errorPage="/JSPbook/Chapt02/whoops.jsp" %>
<jsp:useBean id="tableBean" scope="page" class="JSPbook.Chapt02.ShiftTable" >
</jsp:useBean>
<jsp:setProperty name="tableBean" property="*" />
<%= tableBean.getTable() %>
</BODY>
</HTML>
```

It is particularly interesting to note how easy it is to transfer the input parameter from the request to the bean in the <jsp:setProperty tag. The syntax property="*" means that for every named value in the request, the servlet will try to locate a set method in the bean and call it with the matching value. Listings 2.13 through 2.15 show the service method that the JSP engine creates from the page in the preceding listing.

Listing 2.13: The _jspService method created from the JSP in Listing 2.12

```
    public void _jspService(HttpServletRequest request, HttpServletResponse
response)
    throws ServletException, IOException
{
    ServletConfig config = getServletConfig();
    ServletContext application = config.getServletContext();
    Object page = (Object) this;
    PageContext pageContext = JspFactory.getDefaultFactory().getPageContext(this,
        request, response, "/JSPbook/Chapt02/whoops.jsp", true,8192, true);
    JspWriter out = pageContext.getOut();

    HttpSession session = request.getSession(true);
    response.setContentType("text/html; charset=ISO-8859-1");

    try {
    out.print("<HTML>\r\n<HEAD>\r\n<TITLE>Table Building</TITLE>\r\n➥
    </HEAD>\r\n<BODY BGCOLOR=\"#FFFFFF\"
    TEXT=\"#000000\">\r\n<FONT FACE=VERDANA>\r\n➥
    <H2 ALIGN=CENTER>Java Shift Operators\r\n</H2><BR>\r\n");
    out.print("\r\n");
    JSPbook.Chapt02.ShiftTable tableBean=null;
    tableBean = (JSPbook.Chapt02.ShiftTable) ➥
    pageContext.getAttribute("tableBean",
        pageContext.PAGE_SCOPE);
```

The last statement attempts to recover the `tableBean` object by name from the `pageContext`. A `PageContext` instance acts as a sort of repository of objects for a particular JSP page. If no `tableBean` is already defined, we proceed to create one.

Listing 2.14: The _jspService method continued

```
    if(tableBean == null) {
        tableBean = new JSPbook.Chapt02.ShiftTable();
        pageContext.setAttribute("tableBean", tableBean,  pageContext.PAGE_SCOPE);
        out.print("\r\n");
    } // end useBean initialization
    out.print("\r\n");
    com.livesoftware.jsp.JSPRuntime.setBeanProperties( tableBean, "tableBean", ➥
    request);
```

The call to `setBeanProperties` transfers the values of all request parameters that have names matching properties defined by the bean by means of the `set` methods. In this example, this means that the text from the input text field named "numb" will be used to call a `setNumb` method in the bean.

After all the work of setting up the `tableBean`, generating the actual output involves a single call to the `getTable` method.

Listing 2.15: The _jspService method continued

```
    out.print("\r\n");
    out.print(tableBean.getTable());
    out.print("\r\n</BODY>\r\n</HTML>\r\n");
    out.flush();
    }
    catch(Throwable __exception__) {
      ((com.livesoftware.jsp.JRunPageContext) ➥
      pageContext).handlePageException(__exception__);
    }
  }
```

Note that any error or exception thrown during the operation—such as a NumberFormatException that might occur if the user enters text that can't be converted to an integer in the setNumb method—is handed to the designated error handling page. Because the output stream is buffered by default, nothing is written to the response until the out.flush() statement is executed, and only then if no exceptions or errors are thrown. This means that the only text displayed in the event of an error will be that generated by the error page.

The error page for our example gets the error or exceptions as the default variable exception. It can test the type of exception and respond accordingly, as shown in Listing 2.16.

Listing 2.16: The whoops.jsp error handling page

```
    <HTML>
    <HEAD>
    <TITLE>Database Testing Entry</TITLE>
    </HEAD>
    <BODY BGCOLOR="#FFFFFF" TEXT="#000000">
    <FONT FACE=VERDANA>
    <H2 ALIGN=CENTER>
        Shift Operator Demo Error
    </H2><BR>
    <%@ page language="java" isErrorPage="true" %>
    <% if( exception instanceof NumberFormatException ){
    %> Only numeric characters may be entered.<br>
    <% } else { %>
    <%= exception %>
    <% } %>
    </form>
    </BODY>
    </HTML>
```

In a complicated application, you should consider creating a custom exception type rather than carry detailed information to the error page.

The Table Building Bean

As mentioned previously, the requirements for a JavaBean are easily stated:

- The class must be public.

- The class must have a no-arguments constructor.

- The class must provide set and get methods to access variables.

For the purposes of our example, I created a simple bean having methods to set a variable named numb and get a variable named table. Note that the JavaBean naming conventions require that the method names use the variable name but with an initial uppercase character, so the methods end up named setNumb and getTable. Listing 2.17 shows the complete bean source code.

Listing 2.17: A Java class to create an HTML table

```java
// simple JavaBean to create a table building String
package JSPbook.Chapt02;

public class ShiftTable extends java.lang.Object
{
  protected int numb;
  public ShiftTable(){ }

  public void setNumb(String s )
  {
    this.numb = Integer.parseInt( s ) ;
  }

  public String padBinary( int n ){
    String tmp = "00000000000000000000000000000000"
      + Integer.toBinaryString( n );
    return tmp.substring( tmp.length() - 32 );
  }

  void buildRow( StringBuffer sb, String hdr, int n ){
    sb.append("<tr><th>");
    sb.append( hdr );
    sb.append("</th><td>");
    sb.append( Integer.toString(n) );
    sb.append("</td><td>");
    sb.append( Integer.toHexString(n));
    sb.append("</td><td>");
    sb.append( padBinary( n ));
    sb.append("</td></tr>\r\n");
  }
```

```java
public java.lang.String getTable()
{ StringBuffer sb = new StringBuffer();
  sb.append("\r\n\r\n<table align=\"center\" border=\"2\"" +
      "cellpadding=\"5\" >\r\n<caption>");
  sb.append("Shifting " + numb + "<br>\r\n");
  sb.append("</caption>\r\n<tr><th>Operation</th><th>Decimal</th>" +
      "<th>Hex</th><th>32 bit Binary</th></tr> \r\n" );
  buildRow( sb, "Original", numb );
  buildRow( sb, "Shift &lt;&lt; 1", numb << 1 );
  buildRow( sb, "Shift &gt;&gt; 1", numb >> 1 );
  buildRow( sb, "Shift &gt;&gt;&gt; 1", numb >>> 1);
  sb.append("</TABLE>\r\n");
  return sb.toString() ;
  }
}
```

The convention for the base of the directory where the JSP engine looks for bean classes depends on the individual engine.

Future Developments

To some extent—this is speculation on my part—I think we will see further development of the JSP standard in the following directions:

- Expanded support for custom tag creation
- Standard tags that provide better support for HTML and XHTML
- Integration of XML support with the standardization of XML support in the Java language

In the area of open source development, Sun has turned over all source code for the Java Servlet Development Kit to the Apache organization. In addition to the all Java Web server project, code-named Tomcat, Apache is rapidly integrating servlet, JSP, and XML technology into the widely used Apache source Web server.

The Apache organization is also working on the cocoon project, a Java Web server driven entirely by XML coded files. For the current status of these and other projects by the Apache organization, visit:

```
http://www.apache.org/
```

Session Tracking

- Using Hidden Form Variables for Session Tracking

- Using Cookies for Session Tracking

- Using Java's HttpSession Objects

- Understanding the Session Life Cycle

- Managing Persistence Data

One of the basic characteristics of the Hypertext Transfer Protocol (HTTP) request-response transaction is that it is *stateless*, which is another way of saying that the Web server doesn't remember a thing. Each transaction appears to be independent of all that has gone before. This is the great simplifying assumption that makes fast Web servers and Web surfing possible, but it creates a serious problem when we want to do more than serve up static Web pages.

Because HTTP transactions are stateless, special measures must be taken so a server can continue to identify and remember a particular user during a series of transactions. The Java servlet library provides the Session application programming interface (API) for this purpose, but you can also create your own.

This chapter covers the following topics:

The Example Application

To explore how to keep track of a single user in an application based on HTTP transactions, this chapter uses a single basic example of session tracking implementation in several different ways. The example is a "chat" system that can be extended to become a discussion group.

You may wonder why I have not chosen the typical "shopping cart" example for this discussion. The reason is that, in addition to the basic concepts that can easily be used in a shopping cart, the chat application has another requirement that illustrates interesting points. Each user's contributions must be visible to other users of the system while remaining uniquely identifiable.

Application Requirements

Let's summarize the attributes we want this system to have:

- It should maintain several separate discussion areas.
- Once a user has established an identity, that identity must be maintained as long as the user stays connected.
- Each user's contributions must be visible to other users of the system while remaining uniquely identifiable.
- It must be able to handle a reasonable number of simultaneous users without Thread conflicts.
- It must provide for management to prevent the bulk of messages from growing too large.

To keep this example simple, we are not going to implement such embellishments as accounts with password protection, moderator control, or naughty word filtering.

User Interface

This application will present a simple user interface. As shown in Figure 3.1, the initial entry will present a list of chat "rooms" available and a field for entering your desired "handle" while in the system.

FIGURE 3.1
The chat entry page as an HTML form

One way to create this entry page is as a plain Hypertext Markup Language (HTML) page, as shown in Listing 3.1. This is simple, but the disadvantage is that when you want to change the list of rooms, the page must be re-edited.

Listing 3.1: The HTML to generate the entry page
```
<html>
<head><title>Chat Entry Page</title>
</head>
<body BGCOLOR="#FFFFFF" TEXT="#000000">
<font FACE=VERDANA>
<h2 ALIGN=CENTER>Welcome to Chat</h2><br>
<center>Select a Chat area, enter a Handle and click the Enter Chat button
<br>
<form METHOD="post" ACTION="http://localhost/servlet/ChatServ" >
```

```
<input TYPE=hidden VALUE="entry page" name="hidden" >
<select name="room">
<option value="jsp" >JavaServer Pages Technology
<option value="xml" >Java And XML Technology
</select><br>
Your Handle: <input TYPE="TEXT" VALUE="" name="handle" ><br>
<input TYPE="submit" VALUE="Enter Chat" name="chatgo" >
</form></center><hr>
</body>
</html>
```

Within the system, the user interface consists of the following:

- A text area presenting the recent discussion
- A text area for the user to type in
- A set of option buttons

The options allow a user to send a message to the room, refresh the discussion display while preserving the message being composed, and exit the system gracefully. Figure 3.2 shows a screen shot of what the user sees while in the chat system. The following sections discuss variations of the code that generates this display, starting with a servlet version that uses hidden form variables.

FIGURE 3.2

The user interface as it appears while the user is in a chat room

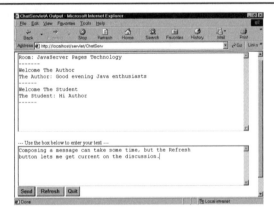

Tracking with Hidden Form Variables

The great benefit of hidden form variables is that they work with browsers that have cookies turned off. The principle is simple: Every time the servlet generates the chat page display, it inserts hidden variables into the HTML form that includes the option buttons. These variables are then read from the request when the user clicks one of the options. Listing 3.2 shows the text of a page similar to that shown in Figure 3.2, which was generated by the servlet discussed in this section.

Listing 3.2: Complete text of a page using hidden variables

```
<HTML>
<HEAD><TITLE>ChatServletA Output</TITLE></HEAD>
<BODY>
<form><textarea rows="12" cols="72" >
Room: JavaServer Pages Technology
-------
Welcome The Student

</textarea></form>
<form METHOD="post" action="http://localhost/servlet/ChatServ" >
<input type=hidden value="The Student" name="handle" >
<input type=hidden value="jsp" name="room" >
--- Use the box below to enter your text ---<br>
<textarea rows="6" cols="72" name="msg" >
</textarea><br>
<INPUT TYPE="SUBMIT" value="Send" name="action" >
<INPUT TYPE="SUBMIT" value="Refresh" name="action" >
<INPUT TYPE="SUBMIT" value="Quit" name="action" >
</form><br>
</BODY>
</HTML>
```

NOTE Note that two forms are defined on this page. The first contains only a `<textarea>` that displays the current chat content. Without a method or a submit control, the first form cannot generate a request.

The second form is declared to use a `post` method and has an `action` linking it to a servlet. The `servlet/ChatServ` is an alias for the servlet class that both wrote the page and will process any requests. Two hidden variables—handle and room—are attached to the form.

Chat Application Design

Before getting into the details of how the hidden variable example works, let's take a minute to look at the overall application organization. We need the following elements:

- Analysis of user request
- Creation of the response as an HTML-formatted page
- Tracking of chat room content

We are going to create several variations on items 1 and 2, but item 3 will be a constant. The basic entry of chat room content is a ChatItem object that holds three pieces of data: the author, the message, and a timestamp. Listing 3.3 shows the code for the ChatItem class. We thought ahead a little and made the class implement Serializable in case we later want to save ChatItem objects to a file.

Listing 3.3: The ChatItem class

```java
// a object to represent a single chat entry   ChatItem.java
package com.JSPbook.Chap03;

import java.io.*;

public class ChatItem implements java.io.Serializable
{
  String author ;
  String content ;
  long timestamp ;

  public ChatItem( String handle, String msg ){
    author = handle ; content = msg ;
    timestamp = System.currentTimeMillis();
  }

  public String toString()
  {
    return author + ": " + content + "\r\n------\r\n" ;
  }
}
```

The contents of a single chat room will be handled by an instance of the ChatRoom class, and management of all chat rooms in the system will be handled by static methods in that class. The source code for ChatRoom begins in Listing 3.4 with the static variables and methods.

Listing 3.4: Static members of the ChatRoom class

```java
// the static methods handle a collection of ChatRoom objects
// a single ChatRoom object tracks a single chat room

package com.JSPbook.Chap03;
import java.util.* ;

public class ChatRoom extends java.lang.Thread
{
  static int MIN_SB = 1000 ;
  static Hashtable rooms ; // ChatRoom objects keyed by short name
  static Hashtable roomTitles ; // ChatRoom Titles keyed by short name
    // format of a string to set up a chat room is
    // code,full title,## where ## is the number of messages to keep
```

```
public static void initChatRooms( String[] list ){
  if( rooms != null ) return ;
  rooms = new Hashtable();
  roomTitles = new Hashtable();
  for( int i = 0 ; i < list.length ; i++ ){
    int p = list[i].indexOf(',');
    String key = list[i].substring(0,p).trim() ;
    String title = list[i].substring(p + 1).trim();
    roomTitles.put( key , title);
  }
}
```

Data to establish the chat rooms is passed as an array of String to the initChatRooms method. Encoded in a String, each chat room has a unique code, a title, and a number of chat items to keep in memory. The following is an example:

```
jsp,JavaServer Pages Technology, 20"
```

The code is used as a key in the rooms and roomTitles Hashtable objects. Note that the initChatRooms method creates the rooms object only; we don't create ChatRoom objects until they are needed in order to keep memory requirements down.

Listing 3.5 gives the static method getRoomsAsSelect. This method builds a long String that contains the HTML code needed to build a form input list box using the <select> tag. Each <option> has a chat room code for a value and is followed by the chat room title. By doing all of the construction in a StringBuffer, we avoid unnecessary String object formation.

Listing 3.5: ChatRoom code continued

```
  // returns HTML code to build a room selection list
  public static String getRoomsAsSelect(){
    StringBuffer sb = new StringBuffer();
    sb.append("<select name=\"room\">");
    Enumeration e = roomTitles.keys();
    while( e.hasMoreElements()){
      String key = (String)e.nextElement();
      sb.append("<option value=\"" ); sb.append( key );
      sb.append("\" >");
      String title = (String)roomTitles.get(key);
      int p = title.lastIndexOf(',');
      if( p > 0 ) title = title.substring(0,p).trim();
      sb.append( title );
      sb.append("\r\n");
    }
    sb.append("</select>");
    return sb.toString();
  }
```

In Listing 3.6, we have the method that returns a ChatRoom object corresponding to a code. If the object has already been created, we simply return it; otherwise, we create a new ChatRoom object using the code, title, and number of items to keep that was defined in the initChat-Rooms method.

Listing 3.6: ChatRoom continued

```
public static ChatRoom getChatRoom( String room ){
   ChatRoom ch = (ChatRoom)rooms.get( room );
   if( ch != null ) return ch ;
   String title = (String)roomTitles.get( room );
   if( title == null ) return null ;
   // message limit is in title string after ,
   int p = title.lastIndexOf(',');
   if( p < 0 ) return null ;
   int nch = 10 ;
   try {
      nch = Integer.parseInt( title.substring(p+1).trim());
   }catch(NumberFormatException e){
      System.err.println("Bad chat limit in " + title );
   }
   title = title.substring(0,p);
   ch = new ChatRoom( room, title, nch );
   rooms.put( room, ch );
   return ch ;
}
```

In Listing 3.7, we address the ChatRoom instance variables and methods. We use a Vector named msgs to store the messages that have been added to the ChatRoom rather than an array because it is convenient to be able to add new messages to the tail of the Vector and trim messages from its front. A Vector is also convenient because we can add any kind of object to it. There is a Hash-table named users in which we keep user information keyed by the user's handle.

NOTE Note that the ChatRoom constructor is private because creation of ChatRoom objects must be done in the static getChatRoom method. ChatRoom objects are created with a room code, a title, and a number that is used to limit the number of messages stored in memory. The constructor adds the first message to the Vector—a String giving the room title. When we later trim messages from the msgs Vector, we will remove the message at position 1, leaving the room title String in place.

Trimming old messages from msgs is an option controlled by the msgLimit variable. If this number is greater than 1, the Thread (remember, ChatRoom extends Thread) has its priority set and is started. In the run method, which appears in a later listing, the Thread spends most of the time sleeping but wakes up to check the size of the msgs collection.

Listing 3.7: ChatRoom continued

```java
//---- ChatRoom Instance Variables
Vector msgs ; // mixture of String and ChatItem objects
int msgLimit = 10 ; //

Hashtable users ;
String roomName, roomTitle ;
int sizeEst = MIN_SB ;

  // private constructor - all access through static method
private ChatRoom( String room, String title, int lim ){
    roomName = room ; roomTitle = title ;
    msgLimit = lim ;
    msgs = new Vector();
    msgs.addElement("Room: " + roomTitle + "\r\n-------\r\n");
    users = new Hashtable();
    // only start maintenance Thread if limit is > 1
    if( lim > 1 ){
        setPriority( Thread.MIN_PRIORITY);
        start();
    }
}
```

Listing 3.8 provides the methods that add and remove users. For this example, the object that is stored in the users Hashtable is simply a Long containing the entry time. An obvious improvement would be to make this a special User object that might hold a password or other specialized data. The addUser and removeUser methods insert a message into the chat room contents when a user arrives or leaves.

Listing 3.8: ChatRoom continued

```java
public synchronized int addUser( String handle ){
  users.put( handle, new Long(System.currentTimeMillis() ));
  msgs.addElement("Welcome " + handle + "\r\n" );
  return users.size();
}

public synchronized int removeUser( String handle ){
  Object obj = users.remove( handle );
  String time = "unknown" ;
  if( obj instanceof Long ){
    int del = (int)(( System.currentTimeMillis() - ➡
    ((Long)obj).longValue() )/1000);
    time = Integer.toString( del ) + " second " ;
  }
```

```
      String msg = "User " + handle + " leaves " + roomName +
         " after " + time + " stay.\r\n";
      msgs.addElement( msg );
      System.out.println( msg );
      return users.size();
   }
```

Listing 3.9 gives two methods that deal with messages. The addMsg method creates a new ChatItem and adds it to the Vector. The getCurrent method creates a single String with the current chat contents using a StringBuffer to concatenate all the String and ChatItem objects. The reason for using the sizeEst variable to set the original StringBuffer size and for increasing sizeEst if the actual character count is larger is that adding to a String-Buffer is most efficient if you don't exceed the starting size.

Listing 3.9: ChatRoom continued

```
      // add message with handle and separator
      public void addMsg(String handle, String msg ){
        msgs.addElement( new ChatItem( handle, msg ) );
      }

      // create a formatted String from accumulated chat
      public synchronized String getCurrent(){
        StringBuffer sb = new StringBuffer( sizeEst );
        int ct = 0 ;
        Enumeration e = msgs.elements();
        while( e.hasMoreElements() ){
          String msg = e.nextElement().toString();
          ct += msg.length();
          sb.append( msg );
        }
        if( ct > MIN_SB ) sizeEst = ct ;
        return sb.toString();
      }
```

Now we come to the data maintenance section. There are several reasons to limit the total message collection. The getCurrent method formats all the msgs data for presentation in the user's Web page, so this amount of text must be kept to a manageable level. Also, if we didn't trim messages from the collection, the application would eventually use excessive amounts of memory. The doUpkeep method in Listing 3.10 simply discards the message at position 1 in the msgs Vector. A reasonable alternative would be to write each one to a file for archival storage.

> **Listing 3.10: ChatRoom continued**

```
    // we will use the run method for various upkeep tasks
    public void run()
    { while( true ){
        try{ sleep( 10000 ) ; // 10 seconds
        }catch(InterruptedException e){
        }
        doUpkeep();
      }
    }

    public void doUpkeep(){
      while( msgs.size() > msgLimit && msgs.size() > 1 ){
        msgs.removeElementAt(1)  ; // leave first msg = title
      }
    }
    // this should be called from the servlet destroy method
    public void destroy()
    { // here is where we would save files, etc. if necessary
    }

    // handy for debugging
    public String toString()
    { StringBuffer sb = new StringBuffer("ChatRoom object " );
      sb.append("code "); sb.append( roomName );
      return sb.toString() ;
    }

}
```

Now that we have defined the ChatRoom and ChatItem classes, it is time to start looking at alternative ways to provide the functions of carrying out client transactions. The first one we will look at uses a servlet.

Tracking Hidden Variables with a Servlet

The first servlet version we explore locates the handle and room variables in the request object. On initial entry, these variables have been set in a form (like that shown in Figure 3.1) from user input. In subsequent requests, the variables have been hidden in a form on a page like that shown in Figure 3.2.

In Listing 3.11, we see the start of a typical servlet class. To keep this example compact, I have directly coded the alias and roomData variables. In a functioning system, it would be better to bring this data in from a properties file.

Listing 3.11: The start of the ChatServletA class

```
// ChatServlet - version A, using hidden form variables  ChatServletA
package com.JSPbook.Chap03;

import java.io.*;
import java.util.* ;
import javax.servlet.*;
import javax.servlet.http.*;

public class ChatServletA extends HttpServlet
{
  // in a real installation these could be read from a
  // properties file in the init method but we fake it here
  static String alias = "http://localhost/servlet/ChatServ" ;
  static String[] roomData = {
    "jsp,JavaServer Pages Technology, 20",
    "xml,Java And XML Technology,20"
  };
  static String chatRows = "12" ;
  static String chatCols = "72" ;
  static String inputRows = "6" ;
  static String inputCols = "72" ;

  public void init(ServletConfig config) throws ServletException
  {
    super.init(config);
    ChatRoom.initChatRooms( roomData );
  }

  public void destroy()
  { // here is where we would close any open files
    super.destroy();
  }

  public String getServletInfo() {
      return "A simple chat servlet";
  }
```

Next, we come to the doGet method in Listing 3.12. This method would not be activated if
the user were to enter through a pure HTML page such as that shown in Listing 3.1 because
that page uses the post method. However, it would run if the user directly addressed the servlet with a URL such as this:

```
http://localhost/servlet/ChatServ
```

In such a case, it would generate a form showing the available chat rooms as in the pure
HTML page. This precaution allows the user to bookmark the servlet address without causing problems.

Listing 3.12: ChatServletA continued

```
    // the only GET is the initial entry
public void doGet(HttpServletRequest req, HttpServletResponse resp)
  throws ServletException, IOException
{
    resp.setContentType("text/html");
    PrintWriter out = new PrintWriter(resp.getOutputStream());
    out.println("<HTML>");
    out.println("<HEAD><TITLE>ChatServletA Output</TITLE></HEAD>");
    out.println("<BODY>");
    out.println("<h2 ALIGN=CENTER>Welcome to Chat</h2><br>");
    out.print( getRoomsAsForm() );
    out.println("</BODY>");
    out.println("</HTML>");
    out.close();
}

public String getRoomsAsForm(){
    StringBuffer sb = new StringBuffer(1000);
    sb.append("<center>Please select a chat room,<br>");
    sb.append("enter a Handle, and click the Enter button<br>");
    sb.append("<form method=\"post\" action=\"" + alias + "\" > ");
    sb.append( ChatRoom.getRoomsAsSelect() );
    sb.append("<br>");
    sb.append("Handle: <input TYPE=\"TEXT\" VALUE=\"\"" );
    sb.append(" name=\"handle\"><br>\r\n");
    sb.append("<input TYPE=\"submit\" VALUE=\"Enter Chat\"" );
    sb.append(" name=\"chatgo\">\r\n");
    sb.append("</form></center><hr>\r\n");
    return sb.toString();
}
```

The normal entry to the servlet is through the doPost method, as shown in Listing 3.13. A parameter named "chatgo" is used to detect initial entry requests by a new user; otherwise, the request is assumed to come from a user who has already selected one of the options on the chat page, as shown in Figure 3.2. The three possible actions and our desired responses are described here:

Send   The user's input is added to the chat room, the chat page is regenerated with the new messages, and the user's input text area is cleared.

Refresh   The chat page is regenerated with the current contents, but the user's input is preserved and restored to the text area.

Quit   The user is removed from the ChatRoom object, and a goodbye message is generated.

This method also handles the special condition of the user's handle entry being unsatisfactory for some reason.

Listing 3.13: ChatServletA continues with doPost

```java
// request from chat is always a post
public void doPost(HttpServletRequest req, HttpServletResponse resp)
  throws ServletException, IOException
{
  resp.setContentType("text/html");
  PrintWriter out = new PrintWriter(resp.getOutputStream());
  String action = req.getParameter( "chatgo" ); // initial entry
  String handle = "" ;
  String room = "" ;
  String error = "" ;
  ChatRoom chatR = null ;
  int phase = 0 ;
  if( action != null ){
     // here is where a password check would go
     handle = req.getParameter( "handle" );
     if( handle == null || handle.length() < 4 ){
        phase = 8 ;
     }
     room = req.getParameter("room");
  }
  else { // not initial entry
     // action should be either "Send" "Refresh" or "Quit"
     action = req.getParameter("action");
     handle = req.getParameter( "handle" );
     room = req.getParameter("room");
     if( handle == null || room == null || action == null ){
        error = "handle, room or action missing "; phase = 9 ;
     }
     else {
        if( action.equals("Send"))phase = 1 ;
        if( action.equals("Refresh")) phase = 2 ;
        if( action.equals("Quit")) phase = 3 ;
     }
  }
  if( room == null ){ error = "null value for room"; phase = 9 ;
  }
  else {
    chatR = ChatRoom.getChatRoom( room );
  }
     // chatR now valid or its an error
  out.println("<HTML>");
  out.println("<HEAD><TITLE>ChatServletA Output</TITLE></HEAD>");
  out.println("<BODY>");
  try {
    switch( phase ){
      case 0 : // new entry
        chatR.addUser( handle );
        sendInitialPage( out, handle, chatR );
        break ;
```

```
          case 1 : // "Send" - entry with text to be added
            sendPlusPage( req, out, handle, chatR );
            break ;
          case 2 : // "Refresh" - don't add text
            sendRefresh( req, out, handle, chatR );
            break ;
          case 3 : // "Quit"
            sendQuit( out, handle, chatR );
            break ;
          case 8 : // user failed to enter usable handle
            badHandleMsg( out, handle ); break ;
          case 9 : // parameters not found, serious problem
            out.println("<h2>Serious problem - " + error +
                " notify operator.</h2>" );
            break ;
          default :
            out.println("Unknown phase " + phase );
        }
      }catch(Throwable et){
          out.print("Serious Problem<br>\r\n");
          et.printStackTrace( out );
      }
      out.println("</BODY>");
      out.println("</HTML>");
      out.close();
    }
```

In Listing 3.14, we come to the methods that handle initial entry and the three different actions on the chat page. The HTML page with forms (shown in Figure 3.2) is generated by the sendAll method, and we simply call it with different parameters according to the action required.

Listing 3.14: ChatServletA continued

```
    // send recent text and a form for text entry
  public void sendInitialPage( PrintWriter out, String handle, ChatRoom r ){
      sendAll( out, handle, r, r.getCurrent() , "" );
  }

    // req has textarea contents as msg elements
  public void sendPlusPage(HttpServletRequest req,
      PrintWriter out, String handle,ChatRoom r ){
    r.addMsg( handle, getMsg( req ) ); // add msg to room
    sendAll( out, handle, r, r.getCurrent(), "" );
  }

    //"Refresh" - don't add text to room chat but restore it to textarea
  public void sendRefresh(HttpServletRequest req,
      PrintWriter out, String handle,ChatRoom r ){
      sendAll( out, handle, r, r.getCurrent(), getMsg( req ) );
  }
```

```
    // chat = potentially large String of chat session
    // wrk = refresh contents of working textarea or blank
 private void sendAll( PrintWriter out, String handle, ChatRoom r,
      String chat, String wrk ){
    String room = r.roomName ;
    out.println("<form><textarea rows=\"" + chatRows +
             "\" cols=\"" + chatCols + "\" >");
    out.println(chat);
    out.println("</textarea></form>");
    out.println("<form METHOD=\"post\" action=\"" + alias + "\" >" );
    out.println("<input type=hidden value=\"" +
       handle + "\" name=\"handle\" >" );
    out.println("<input type=hidden value=\"" +
       room + "\" name=\"room\" >" );
    out.println("--- Use the box below to enter your text ---<br>");
    out.println("<textarea rows=\"" + inputRows    +
             "\" cols=\"" + inputCols + "\" name=\"msg\" >" );
    out.print(wrk);
    out.println("</textarea><br>");
    doButton( out,"action","Send");
    doButton( out,"action","Refresh");
    doButton( out,"action","Quit");
    out.println("</form><br>");
 }

 public void sendQuit( PrintWriter out, String handle,ChatRoom r){
     // notify room and remove handle from active use
     r.removeUser( handle );
     out.println("<h2>Goodbye " + handle + "</h2><br><hr>");
 }

 public String getMsg(HttpServletRequest req){
    String s = req.getParameter("msg");
    if( s == null ) return "" ;
    return s ;
 }
```

Finally, two utility methods are shown in Listing 3.15. The doButton method simply writes the HTML markup to create a button with the designated name and label. The badHandleMsg method demonstrates how you would notify the user that the handle entered is unusable and prompt for a different one. The only error the ChatServletA code detects is a handle shorter than four characters.

Listing 3.15: The last of the ChatServletA code

```
    // convenient utility
    public void doButton( PrintWriter out, String name, String value){
       out.println("<INPUT TYPE=\"SUBMIT\" value=\"" +
          value + "\" name=\"" + name + "\" >" );
    }
```

```
    public void badHandleMsg( PrintWriter out, String handle ){
      out.println("<center><h2>The handle you entered is not usable</h2>");
       // switch here for various reasons
      out.println("<h2>" + handle + " is too short </h2></center>" );
      out.print( getRoomsAsForm());
    }
  } // end of ChatServletA
```

We have created a base case in which tracking uses hidden parameters in a form. The most important limitation of this method is that every response to the user must include a form that has the hidden parameters, and every user request must use this form.

Tracking with Cookies

Netscape pioneered the idea of cookies to allow browsers to keep track of state information in their exchanges with Web servers. Cookies are small chunks of text created in headers sent from a server to a client and stored on the client system. Under the appropriate conditions, these chunks of text are repeated back to a server.

Cookie Standards in HTTP

To refine and standardize the idea introduced by Netscape, an industry working group created the document known as RFC 2109. The following is a quote from the February 1997 version:

"There are, of course, many different potential contexts and thus many different potential types of sessions. The designers' paradigm for sessions created by the exchange of cookies has these key attributes:

- *Each session has a beginning and an end.*
- *Each session is relatively short-lived.*
- *Either the user agent or the origin server may terminate a session.*
- *The session is implicit in the exchange of state information."*

The Set-Cookie Header from the Server

A server sends one or more of these headers to a client. Each may contain one or more cookies. Each cookie starts with its name and value in the format name="value." The javax.servlet.http.Cookie class is used in servlets and JavaServer Pages (JSP) to set and read cookie contents. Cookie objects can be attached to an HttpServletResponse and read from an `HttpServletRequest`. As you learned in Chapter 1, `Cookie` objects are created with a name and value and have methods for setting and reading the following parameters:

Value   A text string.

Comment   A (hopefully) informative text string.

Domain   The domain for which the cookie is valid; defaults to the originating domain.

MaxAge   The `set` method uses cookie lifetime in seconds. The value sent is a date. If the value is –1 or not specified, the cookie is discarded when the browser exits. A value of 0 causes the cookie to be discarded at once.

Path   Controls the path inside the domain for which the cookie is valid.

Version   Distinguishes between original Netscape behavior "0" and RFC2109 behavior "1."

Secure   Does not have a value. If present, the cookie should be sent only if the channel is secure.

Note that text strings cannot be completely arbitrary, so a production version of the `ChatServlet` program would check the handle entered by the user for punctuation that would interfere with cookie operation. The `ChatServletB` class uses cookies instead of hidden form variables to save state information. The only portion of the code already reported in Listing 3.13 that has to be modified is shown in Listing 3.16. Note that we specify that the version is 1 to be compatible with RFC 2109.

Listing 3.16: Chat server doPost code modified to use cookies

```
if( action != null ){
        // here is where a password check would go
        handle = req.getParameter( "handle" );
        room = req.getParameter("room");
        if( handle == null || handle.length() < 4 || room == null ){
          phase = 8 ;
        }
        else {
          Cookie hC = new Cookie( "handle", handle );
          hC.setMaxAge( 600 ); hC.setVersion( 1 );
          Cookie rC = new Cookie( "room", room );
          rC.setMaxAge( 600 ); rC.setVersion( 1 );
          resp.addCookie( hC );
          resp.addCookie( rC );
        }
    }
    else { // not initial entry
      // action should be either "Send" "Refresh" or "Quit"
        action = req.getParameter("action");
        Cookie[] cks = req.getCookies();
      for( int i = 0 ; i < cks.length ; i++){
```

```
            if( cks[i].getName().equals("handle")) {
               handle = cks[i].getValue() ;
            }
            if( cks[i].getName().equals("room")){
               room = cks[i].getValue();
            } // reset the time limit
            cks[i].setMaxAge( 600 ); cks[i].setVersion( 1 );
            resp.addCookie( cks[i] );
         }
         if( handle == null || room == null || action == null ){
            error = "handle, room or action missing "; phase = 9 ;
         }
         else {
            if( action.equals("Send"))phase = 1 ;
            if( action.equals("Refresh")) phase = 2 ;
            if( action.equals("Quit")) phase = 3 ;
         }
      }
```

Listing 3.17 shows an example set of headers sent by the cookie using version 1 of the chat server. Apparently, this servlet engine (JRun 2.3) tries to send cookies in both version 0 and version 1 styles in spite of the fact that the code set is version 1. Notice that, in the Set-Cookie lines, the MaxAge parameter has been turned into a date string based on Greenwich Mean Time (GMT), whereas in the Set-Cookie2 lines, MaxAge is used. The header line that starts with "Expires:" gives a date in the past to prevent the browser from caching the entire page, thus circumventing the desired cookie expiration.

Listing 3.17: Headers from ChatServletB using Set-Cookie

```
HTTP/1.0 200 OK
Server: Microsoft-PWS/2.0
Date: Tue, 28 Mar 2000 21:46:40 GMT
Expires: Thu, 01 Dec 1994 16:00:00 GMT
Cache-Control: no-cache="set-cookie,set-cookie2"
Set-Cookie: handle=Author; expires=Tue, 28-Mar-2000 21:56:40 GMT
Set-Cookie: room=jsp; expires=Tue, 28-Mar-2000 21:56:40 GMT
Set-Cookie2: handle=Author; version=1; MaxAge=600
Set-Cookie2: room=jsp; version=1; MaxAge=600
Content-Type: text/html
```

I think all programmers will breathe a sigh of relief when all browsers support the RFC 2109 cookie standard.

Cookie Management by the Client

You can think of the client as a Web browser, although RFC 2109 talks about a "user-agent." Given the rapidity with which Web access is spreading into smaller appliances, such as Web-capable telephones, you should not assume a large-capacity browser is on the other end of your application.

As you know, if you have ever examined your browser's cookie file, a regular browser can have a huge collection of cookies. The RFC 2109 recommendations suggest that a browser should be able to track at least 300 cookies with a maximum size of 4096 bytes per cookie. However, for a particular site, the browser is required to store only 20 cookies. The RFC also mentions limited-capacity browsers that are expected to hold 20 cookies of 4096 bytes each. In general, you should use the fewest and smallest cookies possible.

The browser is required by RFC 2109 to keep all the information sent by the server in a cookie or to discard the whole thing. The browser decides to send a cookie with a request based on these factors:

- The host it is sending to must match the cookie.

- The path on the host must match the cookie path or be a sub-path.

- The date time limit must not have expired.

The client sends only name, value, and version number in a request to the cookie-using chat server, as shown in Listing 3.18. Note that the Host has 9000 as a port number—this is because I had to run the request and response through a debugging tool in order to capture the headers. This tool will be discussed in greater detail in Chapter 5.

Listing 3.18: The headers in the client request

```
POST /servlet/ChatServ HTTP/1.1
Accept: application/msword, application/vnd.ms-excel, image/gif, ➥
image/x-xbitmap, image/jpeg, image/pjpeg, */*
Referer: http://localhost:9000/servlet/ChatServ
Accept-Language: en-us
Content-Type: application/x-www-form-urlencoded
Accept-Encoding: gzip, deflate
User-Agent: Mozilla/4.0 (compatible; MSIE 5.0; Windows NT; DigExt)
Host: localhost:9000
Content-Length: 59
Connection: Keep-Alive
Cookie: handle=Author; room=jsp
```

As you can see, although the browser is supposed to keep all the information it receives in a cookie, when it sends a cookie, it sends only name and value.

Tracking with Session Objects

One problem with cookies is the limited amount of information they store. Our simple chat example does not create a problem, but suppose you need to keep track of a shopping cart—hopefully loaded with items. The obvious solution is to keep the bulky data on the server and have the browser store only a unique key as a cookie.

The Servlet API provides the `HttpSession` interface to implement this storage function. The servlet engine can create an object implementing this interface, automatically creating a unique key and attaching it to the response. By default, a JSP always has an `HttpSession` implementing object named "session," so we will refer to this object as `session`. Note that you can use an attribute in the page directive to turn off session generation if your JSP does not need it.

The servlet engine is responsible for storing the session, tracking its age, and retrieving it as needed by a servlet. A `session` object must have a lifetime so that the engine can discard it.

NOTE   Note that because a browser may make multiple requests to the same host, more than one servlet or JSP on a server may have access to the session at the same time. It is the programmer's responsibility to ensure that conflicts are avoided when servlets interact with the session.

Methods in the HttpSession Interface

Note that these are Servlet API 2.2 versions, and there have been significant upheavals in the methods and naming conventions since version 2.1. For example, instead of `getValue( String name )`, we now should be using `getAttribute(String name )`. In the following, deprecated methods have a trailing * and are grouped with the preferred method.

```
Enumeration getAttributeNames()
String[] getValueNames() *
```

The Enumeration that is returned has a String object name for each object added to the session.

```
long getCreationTime()
```

Returns the creation time of the session object in the base used by the `System.current-TimeMillis` method, milliseconds since the start of January 1, 1970, GMT.

```
long getLastAccessedTime()
```

Returns the time this session object was last used for anything in the same base as used by `getCreationTime`.

```
int getMaxInactiveInterval()
```

Returns the current setting for this session parameter; the time is in seconds.

```
String getId()
```

Returns the unique String name that the engine generated for this session.

```
HttpSessionContext getSessionContext() *
```

This method is deprecated as a security risk and will be removed entirely in a future version of the API.

```
Object getAttribute( String name )
Object getValue( String name ) *
```

This returns the `Object` reference stored in the session with this name, or it returns null if the name is not in use. Remember that you will have to cast this reference to the correct type before using.

```
void invalidate()
```

This is the method to use when you are sure you won't be needing the session anymore. The session releases all object references and will be discarded by the servlet engine.

```
boolean isNew()
```

A session is considered new until it has been accepted by the client (browser), as detected by the ID being returned as a cookie or as part of a URL. In other words, if `isNew` returns true, you should not assume that the browser is correctly tracking the state of the application.

```
void removeAttribute( String name )
void removeValue( String name ) *
```

The object attached to the session with this name is discarded.

```
void setAttribute( String name, Object val )
void putValue( String name, Object val ) *
```

This object is attached to the session using this name. Any previous object using this name is discarded. Note that any attempt to attach an object to an invalid session throws an `Illegal-StateException`.

```
void setMaxInactiveInterval( int seconds )
```

Session Listeners

Because you can attach or *bind* a reference to any object to a session by name, any servlet in the same `ServletContext` can get access to that object. If your object needs to keep track of the sessions that it has been attached to, you can have it implement the `HttpSessionBindingListener` interface. This interface requires two methods:

valueBound(HttpSessionBindingEvent evt)   Called when an object implementing the interface is attached to an `HttpSession` object using the `setAttribute` method.

valueUnbound(HttpSessionBindingEvent evt)   Called when the object reference is removed using `removeAttribute`.

The `HttpSessionBindingEvent` class has two methods:

getName()   This returns the String that was used to bind the object to the session.

getSession()   This returns a reference to the `HttpSession` object involved.

Example of JSP Using Sessions

This example rewrites the chat application as JSP pages and uses a session to store the user's handle and room variables. Listing 3.19 shows the JSP page used to get the user's room selection and handle. As with the earlier servlet-based example, we are initializing the static ChatRoom variables with hard-coded Strings and using the static getRoomsAsSelect method to generate the room selection list box.

Listing 3.19: EnterChat.jsp

```
<html>
<head>
<meta name="GENERATOR" CONTENT="JSPbook Chapt03" >
<title>Chat Entry Page</title>
</head>

<body BGCOLOR="#FFFFFF" TEXT="#000000">
<font FACE=VERDANA>
<%@ page language="java" import="com.JSPbook.Chap03.*" %>
<%! // String constants to create rooms
    String[] rmStr = {
        "jsp,JavaServer Pages Technology, 20",
        "xml,Java And XML Technology,20"
    } ;
%>
<h2 ALIGN=CENTER>Welcome to Chat
</h2><br>
<center>Enter a Handle and click the Enter button
<br>
<form METHOD="post" ACTION="/JSPbook/Chap03/Chat.jsp" >
Please select a chat room and enter your desired handle.<br>
<%  ChatRoom.initChatRooms( rmStr ); %>
<%= ChatRoom.getRoomsAsSelect() %><br>
<input TYPE="TEXT" VALUE="" name="handle" ><br>
<input TYPE="submit" VALUE="Enter Chat" name="chatgo" >
</form></center>
<hr>
</body>
</html>
```

The JSP page that generates the chat page is very similar in structure to the doPost method in the servlet version. The main difference is that we use the implicit session variable generated automatically by the code written by the JSP engine to save the user's handle and room selections. Listing 3.20 shows the headers that Chat.jsp sends to the browser on the first entry. Notice that the Set-Cookie line sets a cookie named jrunsessionid with a value of a unique long string of digits. The servlet API does not specify how the session ID is to be generated or named, only that the server must keep track of them. This example was obtained with the JRun servlet engine.

Listing 3.20: The server sends headers setting a jrunsessionid

```
HTTP/1.0 200 OK
Server: Microsoft-PWS/2.0
Date: Thu, 30 Mar 2000 23:35:54 GMT
Content-Length: 746
Connection: Keep-alive
Expires: Thu, 01 Dec 1994 16:00:00 GMT
Cache-Control: no-cache="set-cookie,set-cookie2"
Set-Cookie: jrunsessionid=954459354734154404; path=/
Content-Type: text/html; charset=ISO-8859-1
```

Listing 3.21 shows the complete Chat.jsp text. The HTML page generated is essentially the same as that generated by the servlet shown in Listing 3.11.

Listing 3.21: The JSP Chat page using a session

```
<html>
<head>
<meta name="GENERATOR" CONTENT="JSPbook Chapt03" >
<title>Chat </title>
</head>
<body BGCOLOR="#FFFFFF" TEXT="#000000">
<font FACE=VERDANA>
<%@ page language="java" import="com.JSPbook.Chap03.*,java.util.*" %>
<%!
  static String[] roomData = {
    "jsp,JavaServer Pages Technology, 20",
    "xml,Java And XML Technology,20"
  };
  static String chatRows = "12" ;
  static String chatCols = "72" ;
  static String inputRows = "6" ;
  static String inputCols = "72" ;

  public void _jspInit(){
    ChatRoom.initChatRooms( roomData );
  }
    // convenient utility
  public void doButton( JspWriter out, String name, String value)
    throws IOException {
    out.println("<INPUT TYPE=\"SUBMIT\" value=\"" +
      value + "\" name=\"" + name + "\" >" );
  }

  // chat = potentially large String of chat session
  // wrk = refresh contents of working textarea or blank
  private void sendAll( JspWriter out, String chat, String wrk )
    throws IOException {
    out.println("<form><textarea rows=\"" + chatRows +
             "\" cols=\"" + chatCols + "\" >");
```

```
        out.println(chat);
        out.println("</textarea></form>");
        out.println("<form METHOD=\"post\" action=\"Chat.jsp\" >" );
        out.println("--- Use the box below to enter your text ---<br>");
        out.println("<textarea rows=\"" + inputRows    +
                "\" cols=\"" + inputCols + "\" name=\"msg\" >" );
        out.print(wrk);
        out.println("</textarea><br>");
        doButton( out,"action","Send");
        doButton( out,"action","Refresh");
        doButton( out,"action","Quit");
        out.println("</form><br>");
    }
%>
<%  String room = "" ;
    String handle = "" ;
    String err = "unknown error" ;
    String tmp, msg = "" ;
    ChatRoom cr ;
    int phase = 9 ; // default is error report
    // HttpSession session is an implicit variable
    tmp = request.getParameter("chatgo");
    if( tmp != null ){ // must be initial entry
      room = request.getParameter("room");
      handle = request.getParameter("handle");
      session = request.getSession( true );
      session.putValue( "room", room );
      session.putValue( "handle",handle);
      phase = 0 ;
    }
    else {
      tmp = request.getParameter("action");
      if( session.isNew() ){ // not chatgo, stay in phase 9 for error
        err = "In order to participate, your browser must allow cookies!" ;
      }
      else {  // session is old, get attached information
        room = (String)session.getValue("room");
        handle = (String)session.getValue("handle");
        msg = request.getParameter("msg") ;
        tmp = request.getParameter("action");
        if( "Send".equals( tmp ) )phase = 1 ;
        if( "Refresh".equals( tmp )) phase = 2 ;
        if( "Quit".equals( tmp )) phase = 3 ;
      }
    }
    cr = ChatRoom.getChatRoom( room );
    switch( phase ) {
      case 0 : // new entry
        cr.addUser( handle );
        sendAll( out, cr.getCurrent() , "" );
        break ;
```

```
     case 1 : // "Send" - entry with text to be added
       cr.addMsg( handle, msg ); // add msg to room
       sendAll( out, cr.getCurrent(), "" );
       break ;
     case 2 : // "Refresh" - don't add text
       sendAll( out, cr.getCurrent(), msg );
       break ;
     case 3 : // "Quit"
       cr.removeUser( handle );
       session.invalidate();
%><%= "<h2>Goodbye " + handle + "</h2><br><hr>" %>
<%        break ;
     case 8 : // user failed to enter usable handle
%><%= "<center><h2>The handle you entered is not usable</h2>" +
      "<h2>" + handle + " is too short </h2></center>" %>
   <center>Please select a chat room,<br>
   enter a Handle, and click the Enter button<br>
<%= "<form method=\"post\" action=\"Chat.jsp\" > " +
    ChatRoom.getRoomsAsSelect() +
    "<br>Handle: <input TYPE=\"TEXT\" VALUE=\"\"" +
    " name=\"handle\"><br>\r\n" +
    "<input TYPE=\"submit\" VALUE=\"Enter Chat\"" +
    " name=\"chatgo\">\r\n</form></center><hr>\r\n" %>
<%
           break ;
         case 9 :
%> <%= "<h2>" + err + "</h2><br>" %> <%
   } // end switch
%>
<hr>
</body>
</html>
```

Do-It-Yourself Session Tracking

If you are a hands-on type of programmer who likes to know exactly what is going on in applications, it is relatively easy to write your own session tracking code. You need to provide for the following:

Unique ID   This might be a user ID that you assign only to paying users or an ID generated randomly. The Java Hashtable class is ideal for storing data under a key and determining whether a proposed key is unique.

Saving State   As shown in Listing 3.4, static methods of a class can hold data to be shared between users and associated with sessions. To save data over periods when the server is shut down, you would have to add a destroy method that writes the stored data to a file as serialized objects. The init method would have to look for the serialized object file and rebuild the static data storage. This is really quite simple if all objects involved implement the Serializable interface.

Controlled Expiration   You don't want your session tracking code to accumulate data forever, so some sort of time-out mechanism is needed to remove unused objects. An example is shown in the ChatRoom class in Listing 3.10.

Scaling Up to Server Farms

All the approaches we have discussed in this chapter work well when the Web server is a single machine running a single version of the server program. However, using increasingly faster servers to handle higher throughputs eventually won't keep up with increasing request rates, so you have to consider using multiple servers.

The problem with multiple servers is that each one will have its own Java Virtual Machine, so sharing data between users and maintaining session data is no longer as simple as using static class methods. Instead, there must a way for all servers to share session data in a reliable way, either by duplicating sessions across all servers or by having multiple session repositories.

Sun's Java 2 Enterprise Edition specifications address these problems by stating the kind of support that Web containers must provide. The complexities of handling this sort of problem accounts for the high price of scalable Web servers.

Generating Other Types of Content

- Directing Graphics Files to HTML Pages

- Creating Graphics On-the-Fly

- File Compression on Demand

- Creating Sound Files On-the-Fly

- General Principles for Any Data Type

So far in this book, we have been generating plain HTML pages, but great Web applications demand all sorts of other content. Using Java servlets and JavaServer Pages (JSP), your application can serve up just about any kind of content. As Internet connectivity spreads beyond the desktop to Internet appliances and wireless devices, the demand for specialized content is bound to increase. For example, your Internet-connected car could make good use of sound synthesized on-the-fly or a custom-generated map image.

HTML and Media Types

Originally, Multipurpose Internet Mail Extensions (MIME) type standardization was a standard only for describing attachments to e-mail and was restricted to a very few types that client mail programs were expected to understand. With the birth of the Web, these types were adopted to describe formats that Web browsers were expected to handle. Because programmers wanted to use more different types of data on the Web, these standards had to be generalized and made more flexible. MIME types are now used in the Java clipboard-related classes to describe data types, so they have come a long way from simple beginnings.

The Hypertext Markup Language (HTML) standards now define allowed media types in terms of six discrete top-level media types that are further subdivided. The rules for using MIME types are described in a series of RFC documents, RFC2045 through RFC2049. Registration of new MIME types is accomplished by the Internet Assigned Numbers Authority (IANA), available on the Web at **www.iana.org**. The following top-level types are used to organize MIME types:

text   Textual information. Commonly used subtypes are "plain" and "html." A typical content-type header using text is:

```
Content-type: text/plain; charset=iso-8859-1
```

image   Image data. This data requires a graphical display or printer to view the information. Subtypes are defined for two widely used image formats: JPEG and GIF.

audio   Audio data. Audio requires an audio output device, such as a sound card and speaker. The subtype "basic" is a very simple format: single-channel audio encoded using 8-bit Integrated Services Digital Network (ISDN) mu-law encoding at a sample rate of 8000Hz. If you have done any work with Java sound in applets, you will recognize this as the sound format supported by the applet `play()` method.

video   Video data. Video requires the capability to display moving images. The subtype "mpeg" is defined in RFC2046 for video coded according to the Motion Picture Experts Group (MPEG) standard. Some other common subtypes are "avi" and "quicktime."

model　3D model data. This data requires a specific rendering engine to present a 3D model. The subtype "vrml" is a well-known standard.

application　Other data. This is used for data that is to be passed to a plug-in or specialized application. Some example subtypes are "pdf," "x-compressed," "java-archive," and "msword." The subtype "octet-stream" is used for binary data. A browser that receives data of type "octet-stream" should simply offer to write the information into a file for the user.

message　Message data. This is used for e-mail and related data.

sr　Used for encryption.

In general, Web servers decide how to set the content type of a response based on the file type of a static resource. When using a servlet or JSP to generate a response, it is up to the programmer to set the right content type. In this chapter, we discuss MIME types that are well known and standardized, but in the "Vendor Specific Formats" section, we get into more unusual data types.

Sending Images

Naturally, the first thing you will want to do to jazz up your Web application is to include some graphics. You have plenty of options here; for static images, a plain <img> tag has the virtue of simplicity. Let's review the commonly used attributes of an image tag in HTML 4.0 as shown in Table 4.1. According to strict HTML standards, both an src and alt attribute are required although you frequently see img tags without any alt text. The purpose of alt text is to provide a usable label if the Web browser has image loading turned off. Web browsers for visually impaired users read an alt tag out loud. If height and width are specified, the browser will stretch or shrink the image data to fit. If height and width are not specified, the original dimensions of the image are used.

TABLE 4.1: Attributes used in <img> tags

Attribute	Use	Example
src	Uniform Resource Identifier (URI) of the image source	src="mydog.jpg"
alt	Text description	alt="picture of my dog"
height	Image height in pixels or percent	height="200"
width	Image width in pixels or percent	width="65%"

Listing 4.1 shows a JSP page that generates a random number between 0.0 and 1.0 and sets up the Uniform Resource Locator (URL) that creates a request to a servlet. Note that the browser request for the image URL is a separate action from the request that gets the JSP page. The servlet looks at the request and then selects and transmits a random image based on the number.

Listing 4.1: A JSP page getting a random image

```
<html>
<head>
<meta name="GENERATOR" CONTENT="JSPbook Chapt04" >
<title>A Random Dog Picture</title>
</head>
<body BGCOLOR="#FFFFFF" TEXT="#000000">
<font FACE=VERDANA>
<%@ page language="java" import="com.JSPbook.Chap04.*,java.util.Random" %>
<%! // create a random number generator
 Random ran = new Random();
%>
<h2 ALIGN=CENTER>Welcome To The Random Basset Page
</h2><br>
<%
   String ranStr = "" + ran.nextFloat() ; // between 0.0 and 1.0
%>
<table align="CENTER" border="5" width="80%" ><tr>
<td>A Basset hound may <br>be the dog for you!</td>
<td><img src="/servlet/ImgServ?RandomImage=<%= ranStr %>" ➥
alt="random dog picture" ></td>
</tr></table>
</center>
<hr>
</body>
</html>
```

The ImgServ servlet name used in the JSP page is an alias for the actual ImgServA servlet whose code starts in Listing 4.2. This example was executed in the Tomcat Web server so the creation of the servlet alias was done in the web.xml file. Other servlet engines use different approaches to setting servlet alias and initialization parameters.

Listing 4.2: The random image serving servlet

```
// Random image server
package com.JSPbook.Chap04;

import java.io.*;
import javax.servlet.*;
import javax.servlet.http.*;

public class ImgServA extends HttpServlet
{
  static String basePath = "c:\\tomcat\\webapps\\Root\\JSPbook\\Chap04\\images";
  static String[] pics = {
    "Minnie.gif", "Charmer.gif","Frieda.gif", "Rufus.gif", "Vita.jpg"
  };

  static String errorPic = "Sorry.gif";
```

```
public void init(ServletConfig config) throws ServletException    {
  super.init(config);
  System.out.println("ImgServ initialized");
  // In a real application, we would read in the picture file list
}
```

Because a Web browser requests <img> tag data with a GET operation, the servlet must implement either the `service` or the `doGet` method as shown in Listing 4.3. The random number from the JSP page is turned into an index into the array of `String` image file names. To simplify the example, I used a static list of files. In a real application, the list of images could come from a variety of sources.

Listing 4.3: The random image serving servlet continued

```
public void doGet(HttpServletRequest req, HttpServletResponse resp)
throws ServletException, IOException
{
  ServletContext sctx = getServletContext();
  String path = req.getPathInfo();
  String que = req.getQueryString();
  int select = -1 ;
  float ranf ;
  String image = req.getParameter("RandomImage");
  try {
    ranf = new Float( image.trim() ).floatValue();
    select = (int)(ranf * pics.length ); // 0 - n-1
  }catch(Exception e0 ){
      select = 0 ;
  }
  File f = new File( basePath, pics[select] );
  int sze = 0;
  byte[] buf ;
  try {
    sze = (int)f.length(); // throws IOException if no file
    if( sze < 1 ){
        f = new File( basePath, errorPic );
        sze = (int)f.length();
    }
    buf= new byte[ sze ];
```

Now that we have located the image file to be sent and created a buffer to hold the image data, we come to the code that sets the header information in Listing 4.4. This is an essential part of serving non-text data because the headers control how the browser interprets the data. Note that setting the content length is not required in this case, but it does help the browser estimate the percentage of completion of the image.

Listing 4.4: The random image serving servlet continued

```
      String type = "image/gif" ;
      if( f.getAbsolutePath().endsWith("jpg")) type = "image/jpg";
      resp.setContentType( type );
      resp.setContentLength( sze );
      OutputStream out = resp.getOutputStream();
      RandomAccessFile raf = new RandomAccessFile( f, "r" );
      raf.read( buf );
      raf.close();
      out.write(buf);
      out.close();
    }catch(Exception ex ){
      System.err.println("ImgServletA throws " + ex );
      ex.printStackTrace( System.err );
    }
  }
}
```

The resulting HTML page display is shown in Figure 4.1. Because the JSP page wrote the
<img> tag without specifying height and width, the browser uses the original image size. Basset lovers will be glad to know that this dog was adopted shortly after the picture was taken.

FIGURE 4.1

The RandomDog.jsp
page display

Creating Images

In the previous example, the transmitted image was from a static file. Java provides excellent facilities for creating images on-the-fly, allowing you to create striking Web page presentations. To demonstrate these capabilities, we will use a well-known board game. Go is a two-player game played on a 19 x 19 grid; each player places "stones" on the board to control territory. Figure 4.2 shows an example display with a game in progress.

FIGURE 4.2

The dynamically generated game board display

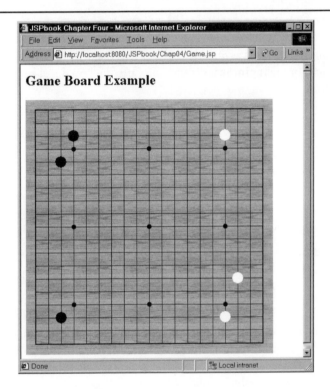

The JSP page that was used to generate Figure 4.2 is shown in Listing 4.5. A playable Go interface would require a much more complex presentation of user options, but for purposes of this demonstration, we are using this simple page.

Listing 4.5: A JSP page to show the Go board

```
<HTML>
<HEAD>
  <META NAME="GENERATOR" CONTENT="JSPbook Chapt04" >
  <TITLE>JSPbook Chapter Four</TITLE>
</HEAD>
```

```
<BODY>
<h2>Game Board Example</h2>
<%@ page language="java" %>
<%
    session.setAttribute("player","Author");
%>
<img src="/servlet/GoBoard" >
</BODY>
</HTML>
```

The servlet that responds to the `<img>` tag request uses the Java 2D application programming interface (API) classes. The original graphics classes in the 1.0 version of Java were extremely limited, and it was quickly realized that major enhancements would be required. However, development proceeded slowly because the Java development team at Sun didn't really have a background in graphics.

The Java 2D classes were created by involving graphics experts from Sun's industry partners. The details of working with these classes are far beyond the scope of this book. A good starting point for further study of the Java 2D API is the tutorial at:

```
http://java.sun.com/products/java-media/
```

The basic steps in this example servlet would be found in any servlet for dynamically creating dynamic images. The `init` method is used to get resources and create a reusable background image. The `doGet` method has to accomplish the following tasks:

- Use session data to locate the current game data for this player.
- Create an image in memory by combining the standard background with current game information.
- Encode the memory image into the JPEG format and send it.

Our review of the `GoBoard` source code starts with Listing 4.6, which shows some static variables and the `init` method. Note that in the `init` method, we create a `java.awt.Frame` object. This object is not displayed, it is simply used to force the Java Virtual Machine (JVM) to load the graphics toolkit. Due to this Java peculiarity, this servlet could not be run on a system that does not have Java graphics capability.

The woodgrain effect for the background board image is created from a small JPEG file that is repeatedly drawn over the board. A simpler alternative would be to create the entire board image with an offline paint program, but I opted to use this method to illustrate how you could build up complex images such as a war game map by assembling small images. The `init` method loads the `Woodgrain.jpg` file and then calls the `drawBoard` method to create the board image.

Listing 4.6: The GoBoard servlet source code

```
package com.JSPbook.Chap04 ;

import java.io.*;
import javax.servlet.*;
import javax.servlet.http.*;

import java.awt.*;
import java.awt.font.*;
import java.awt.geom.*;
import java.awt.image.*;
import com.sun.image.codec.jpeg.*;

public class GoBoard extends HttpServlet
{
  static String bkgFileName = "c:\\MultiMedia Files\\Images\\Woodgrain.jpg";
  static int bkgW, bkgH ;
  static BufferedImage bareGoBoard ;
  static int[] xGrid, yGrid ;
  static int WIDTH = 490, HEIGHT = 490 ;
  static int stoneDiameter = 22 ;

  public void init(ServletConfig config) throws ServletException
  {
      super.init(config);
      File f = new File( bkgFileName );
      Image bkg = null ;
      if( f.exists() ){
        Frame dummy = new Frame() ; // this frame is never shown
        dummy.addNotify();  // forces JVM to get graphics context
        Toolkit tk = Toolkit.getDefaultToolkit();
        bkg = tk.createImage( bkgFileName );
        MediaTracker mt = new MediaTracker( dummy );
        mt.addImage( bkg, 0 );
       try {
         mt.waitForID( 0 );
         System.out.println("Read " + bkgFileName );
         bkgW = bkg.getWidth( dummy );
         bkgH = bkg.getHeight( dummy );
       }catch(InterruptedException ex){
         bkg = null ;
       }
      }
      else { System.out.println("File not found");
      }
      drawBoard( bkg );
  }
```

In the `drawBoard` method shown in Listing 4.7, we first calculate the grid positions found on a Go board. Then `BufferedImage` is created and tiled with the woodgrain texture image. Next, we draw the grid lines that define the points where stones can be played in Go. Certain locations that are used for handicapping are emphasized with dots. Note the call to the Graphics2D method, `setRenderingHint`, which requests antialiasing to be used to minimize the jagged edge effect.

Listing 4.7: The GoBoard servlet listing continues with the drawBoard method

```java
static private void drawBoard( Image bkg ){
    xGrid = new int[19]; yGrid = new int[19];
    int ulX = 19, ulY = 19 ;
    int delX = 25, delY = 25 ;
    int x1, y1, x2, y2 ;
    int i,j ;
    for( i = 0 ; i < 19 ; i++ ){ // create grid
        xGrid[i] = ulX + (i * delX );
        yGrid[i] = ulY + (i * delY );
    }
    BufferedImage img =
        new BufferedImage(WIDTH,HEIGHT,
                          BufferedImage.TYPE_INT_RGB);
    Graphics2D g2 = img.createGraphics();
    g2.setBackground(Color.yellow);
    g2.clearRect(0,0,WIDTH,HEIGHT);
    if( bkg != null ){
      x1 = 0 ; y1 = 0 ; // prepare to tile the background
      while( y1 < HEIGHT ){
        while( x1 < WIDTH ){
          g2.drawImage( bkg , x1, y1, null );
          x1 += bkgW ;
        }
        y1 += bkgH ; x1 = 0 ;
      }
    }
    g2.setRenderingHint(RenderingHints.KEY_ANTIALIASING,
                        RenderingHints.VALUE_ANTIALIAS_ON);
    g2.setColor(Color.black);
    // make thick outer border
    g2.drawRect( ulX - 1, ulY - 1, 2 + (18 * delX),2 + (18 * delY));
    for( i = 0 ; i < 19 ; i++  ){
      x1 = ulX ; x2 = xGrid[18] ;
      y1 = y2 = yGrid[i] ;
      g2.drawLine( x1,y1,x2,y2 );
    }
    for( i = 0 ; i < 19 ; i++  ){
      x1 = x2 = xGrid[i] ;
      y1 = ulY ; y2 = yGrid[18] ;
      g2.drawLine( x1,y1,x2,y2 );
    }
```

```
for( i = 3 ; i <19 ; i += 6 ){
  for( j = 3 ; j < 19 ; j += 6 ){
    x1 = xGrid[ i ] - 4 ;
    y1 = yGrid[ j ] - 4 ;
    g2.fillOval( x1, y1, 9, 9 );
  }
}
//
bareGoBoard = img ;
g2.dispose(); // essential to conserve resources
}
```

For the purpose of this demonstration, I have included white and black stone positions as static data. In a real game, these arrays could be stored in a session object or database. Note that in Listing 4.8, both x and y indices are packed in a single short value.

Listing 4.8: The GoBoard servlet continued

```
// this is fake data for demo purposes,
// x and y positions use indexes 1 - 19
// packing x * 100 + y = result
static short[] blackStones = {317, 403, 305};
static short[] whiteStones = {1603,1617,1714};
// instance methods below this
```

The paintStones method shown in Listing 4.9 paints over the board image by drawing a circle for each of the stones. A more elegant effect could be accomplished by using a small image for white and black stones to show the shading you would see on a real Go board.

Listing 4.9: The GoBoard servlet continued

```
void paintStones( Graphics2D g2, short[] bS, short[] wS ){
  g2.setColor( Color.black );
  if( bS == null || wS == null || bS.length == 0 ) return ;
  int x, y ;
  int del = stoneDiameter / 2 ;
  for( int i = 0 ; i < bS.length ; i++ ){
    x = bS[i] /100   ;
    y = bS[i] % 100 ;
    g2.fillOval( xGrid[x - 1] - del, yGrid[y - 1] - del ,
            stoneDiameter,stoneDiameter);
  }
  g2.setColor( Color.white );
  for( int i = 0 ; i < wS.length ; i++ ){
    x = wS[i] /100   ; // 1 based
    y = wS[i] % 100 ;
    g2.fillOval( xGrid[x - 1] - del, yGrid[y - 1] - del ,
            stoneDiameter,stoneDiameter);
  }
}
```

The doGet method in Listing 4.10 provides for recovering the state of the game and initializing a BufferedImage in memory by drawing the bareGoBoard image into it. After the paintStones method has drawn in the playing pieces, we create a JPEGImageEncoder object to encode and send the image.

Note that we call the Graphics class dispose method on the Graphics2D object that was obtained by getGraphics. Depending on the JVM implementation, Graphics objects may use system resources that might be in short supply on some operating systems, so it is best to specifically release these resources.

Listing 4.10: The doGet method of the GoBoard servlet

```java
public void doGet(HttpServletRequest request,
                  HttpServletResponse response)
    throws ServletException, IOException
{
    response.setContentType("image/jpeg");
    HttpSession session = request.getSession( false );
    short[] bStone = null, wStone = null ;
    if( session != null ){
      String player = (String)session.getAttribute("player");
      if( player != null ){// recover moves - fake it here
        // in real game, would recover from session or database
        bStone = blackStones ;
        wStone = whiteStones ;
      }
    }
    // create current image
    BufferedImage img = new BufferedImage(WIDTH,HEIGHT,
                    BufferedImage.TYPE_INT_RGB);
    Graphics2D g2 = img.createGraphics();
    g2.drawImage( bareGoBoard, 0, 0, null );
    paintStones( g2, bStone, wStone );
    // now send image
    OutputStream out = response.getOutputStream();
    JPEGImageEncoder encoder = JPEGCodec.createJPEGEncoder(out);
    JPEGEncodeParam param = encoder.getDefaultJPEGEncodeParam(img);
    param.setQuality(1.0f,true);
    encoder.encode(img,param);
    out.close();
    g2.dispose();
}

public String getServletInfo()
{
    return "GoBoard presentation servlet";
}
}
```

Creating Zip Files

Although the number of users with high-speed Internet connections is increasing, there will always be a demand for compression techniques to reduce download time. Although some formats used in Internet applications already incorporate optimized compression, many file formats have a lot of redundancy. The example in this section demonstrates how Java can create compressed data files on-the-fly with maximum flexibility.

The Compression Classes

The standard Java library includes the `java.util.zip` package that contains the classes we will use in this example. This package provides generalized classes for performing the most popular compression algorithms, but because it is sufficiently flexible in design, better algorithms can be plugged in to the general classes. The `java.util.jar` package that Java uses extensively for packaging class files and other resources is based on the zip package classes. Table 4.2 summarizes the main classes in the zip package.

TABLE 4.2: Some classes in the java.util.zip package

Class	Function
Adler32	Class to compute a checksum.
CheckedInputStream	An InputStream that keeps a running checksum of input data bytes.
CheckedOutputStream	An OutputStream that keeps a running checksum of output data bytes.
CRC32	Class to compute a checksum.
Deflater	Implements a general-purpose compression algorithm.
DeflaterOutputStream	The parent of GZIPOutputStream and ZipOutputStream classes.
GZIPInputStream	Implements the GZIP file format for input.
GZIPOutputStream	Implements the GZIP file format for output.
Inflater	Reverses the compression created by Deflater.
InflaterInputStream	The parent of GZIPInputStream and ZipInputStream classes.
ZipEntry	Each file in a zipped collection is represented by a ZipEntry object.
ZipFile	Used when reading the contents of zipped files in random order.
ZipInputStream	Reads the contents of a PKZip formatted zipped file in sequence.
ZipOutputStream	Writes PKZip formatted zipped data to a stream.

A Zip File Creating Servlet

This servlet uses the `ZipOutputStream` class to compress one or more files and send the compressed result as a response with the MIME type used for compressed files. Utilities to unzip this format are very common.

This version writes compressed data to an in-memory byte array first so that the final size of the data can be determined and sent in a content-length header before the data is written to the response. Thus, it is fast but limited to file sizes that are small relative to available memory. To use it with any file size, you would have to write the compressed data to a temporary disk file, close the file, determine the resulting size, and then set the headers and send the file.

All the action takes place in the `service` method, as shown in Listing 4.11. The list of files to be compressed is in a `Vector` attached to the `session` object with the name "filelist." Each item in the `Vector` is a `String` giving the absolute path for a file.

> **NOTE**   Note the commented out `println` method calls that are typical of statements used during debugging of a servlet; debugging will be discussed in more detail in Chapter 5.

Listing 4.11: The ZipUtility servlet

```
package com.JSPbook.Chap04;

import java.io.*;
import java.util.* ;
import java.util.zip.* ;
import javax.servlet.* ;
import javax.servlet.http.*;

public class ZipUtility extends HttpServlet
{
  public String getServletInfo()
  {
    return "Collects and zips multiple files";
  }

  public void service(HttpServletRequest req, HttpServletResponse res)
     throws ServletException, IOException
  {
    HttpSession session = req.getSession();
    ServletContext context = getServletConfig().getServletContext();
    Vector vf = (Vector)session.getAttribute("filelist");
    // filenames are in absolute context
    // System.out.println("starting service in ZipUtility");
    if( vf == null ) { context.log("ZipUtility - session is empty");
        return ;
    }
```

```java
    int chct = 0 ;
    if( vf.size() == 0 ) return ;
    Vector files = new Vector( vf.size() ) ;
    //
    Enumeration e = vf.elements();
    while( e.hasMoreElements() ){
      String tmp = (String)e.nextElement();
      // System.out.println( tmp );
      File f = new File( tmp );
      if( f.exists() ) {
        if (f.canRead()) {
          files.addElement( f );
            chct += (int) f.length();
        }
        else { context.log("canRead fails for " + tmp );
        }
      }
      else { context.log("exists fails for " + tmp );
      }
    }
    if( files.size() == 0 ){
        context.log("ZipUtility - No files verified");
        return ;
    }
// now files contains a valid File object for each
    // chct = total character count without compression
    int estSize = chct / 3 ;
    int bRead ;
    byte[] buf = new byte[ 4096 ];
    ByteArrayOutputStream baos = new ByteArrayOutputStream( estSize );
    ZipOutputStream zip = new ZipOutputStream( baos );
    zip.setMethod( ZipOutputStream.DEFLATED );
    zip.setLevel( Deflater.BEST_COMPRESSION );
    context.log("Zip est size in memory " + estSize );
      e = files.elements();
      while( e.hasMoreElements() ){
        File f = (File)e.nextElement();
        String fname = f.getAbsolutePath();
        int p = fname.lastIndexOf( File.separatorChar );
        ZipEntry zentry = new ZipEntry( fname.substring( p + 1 ) );
        zip.putNextEntry( zentry );
        FileInputStream fis = new FileInputStream( f );
        while( (bRead = fis.read( buf )) != -1 ){
            zip.write( buf, 0, bRead );
        }
        fis.close();
        // System.out.println( fname.substring( p + 1 ));
      } // loop over all files
```

```
            zip.close() ;
            // System.out.println("Zipped size " + baos.size() );
            res.setContentType("application/x-zip-compressed");
            res.setContentLength( baos.size() );
            OutputStream out = res.getOutputStream() ;
            baos.writeTo( out );
            out.close();
    }
}
```

A Sample File Zipping Application

The Web server directory setup for this application includes the following:

- A plain HTML file selection page in a base directory. This page shows a form listing the available files with check boxes.

- A JSP page in the base directory that processes the selected file list.

- A subdirectory named "data" containing the downloadable files.

- The ZipUtility servlet class. The exact location of this class depends on the conventions of the servlet engine in use.

In this example, when I selected the three HTML files that total about 225KB, they were compressed to 66KB, or about 30 percent of the original size. This is pretty typical for text files and means that downloading the zipped file would take less than one-third of the time required to download the uncompressed files individually.

Some file formats, such as Adobe's Portable Document Format (PDF) and the JPEG image format are already compressed. Zipping these files would not yield any advantage in downloading time.

Figure 4.3 shows the list of downloadable files in a form created by the HTML page shown in Listing 4.12.

FIGURE 4.3
Presenting the file list in
a form

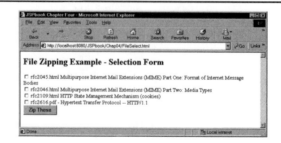

Listing 4.12: The HTML used to create the form

```
<html>
<head>
  <meta name="GENERATOR" content="JSPbook Chapt04" >
  <title>JSPbook Chapter Four</title>
</head>
<body>
<h2>File Zipping Example - Selection Form</h2>
<form method="POST" action="FileZip.jsp" >
<input type="checkbox" name="sel" value="rfc2045.html" >
    rfc2045.html Multipurpose Internet Mail Extensions (MIME) Part One:
    Format of Internet Message Bodies<br>
<input type="checkbox" name="sel" value="rfc2046.html" >
    rfc2046.html Multipurpose Internet Mail Extensions (MIME) Part Two:
    Media Types<br>
<input type="checkbox" name="sel" value="rfc2109.html" >
    rfc2109.html HTTP State Management Mechanism (cookies)<br>
<input type="checkbox" name="sel" value="rfc2616.pdf" >
    rfc2616.pdf - Hypertext Transfer Protocol -- HTTP/1.1<br>
<input type="submit" value="Zip These" name="action" >
</form>
</body>
</html>
```

When the "Zip These" button is clicked, the JSP page shown in Listing 4.13 gets the request. The first thing this code does is get the Web server URL that the JSP page lives in using the getServletPath method on the request object. This is combined with the "data" subdirectory and the selected file name, and the absolute file path is obtained with the getRealPath method of the ServletContext. This method of getting an absolute file path is more complex than just hard-wiring in a file name as I did in the image examples, but it has the advantage of being more flexible.

The String objects containing the file paths are stored in a Vector. This Vector is attached to the session object with the name "filelist" as required by the ZipUtility servlet.

Listing 4.13: The JSP page that processes the form

```
<HTML>
<HEAD>
  <META NAME="GENERATOR" CONTENT="JSPbook Chapt04" >
  <TITLE>File Zipping Example</TITLE>
</HEAD>
<BODY>
<h2>File Zipping Example</h2>
This page processes input from the file selection page.<br>
<%@ page language="java" import="java.util.*" %>
<%
  Vector files = new Vector(); // to hold absolute paths
```

```
String path = request.getServletPath();
int p = path.lastIndexOf( '/' );
path = path.substring( 0, p + 1 );
// we trimmed off the jsp page name to get directory alias
String[] selected = request.getParameterValues("sel");
if( selected != null ){
  // now get the real path and add to the data
  for( int i = 0 ; i < selected.length ; i++ ){
    String tmp = application.getRealPath(path + "data/" + selected[i] );
    if( tmp != null ) files.addElement(tmp );
  }
  // attach the Vector to the session
  session.setAttribute("filelist",files);
  } // selected != null test
  if( files.size() > 0 ) {
%>
<a HREF="/servlet/ZipUtility?usename=/files.zip" >
  Click here to download your <%= files.size() %> files in zipped format.➡
  </a><br>
<% }
  else { %>
  No files were selected.<br>
<% } %>
</BODY>
</HTML>
```

Figure 4.4 shows the browser page created by the JSP in Listing 4.13. If the user does not choose to click on the active area, the session object holding the file list will eventually be discarded by the servlet engine after the prescribed amount of time has passed.

FIGURE 4.4

Presenting the download link

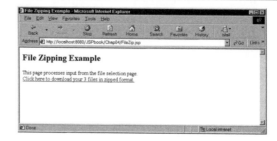

Sound On-the-Fly

Sun has released the Java Media Framework (JMF), an API for incorporating sound files from a huge variety of formats into Java applets and applications. Unfortunately, the JMF is way too complicated for use in simple servlets. If you want more information, go to the current Web page:

```
http://java.sun.com/products/java-media/jmf/index.html
```

By far, the simplest form of sound data transmission on the Web has the MIME type audio/basic and the characteristic file type of ".au." This is the format used in the Java applet play and getAudioClip methods.

The au format actually can provide for both mono and stereo recording and a variety of compression techniques. However, only the "u-law" encoding single-channel format encoded at 8000 samples per second can be used by Java applets. This is certainly low-fidelity, but it is compact. A file in this format consists of only three parts: a header of six int values, a variable length information field, and a block of data. These are 32-bit int values in the normal Java (high byte first) order. Table 4.3 shows more detail on these headers.

TABLE 4.3: The headers in an ".au" format sound file

Byte positions	Field name	Used for
0 – 3	magic number	The ASCII characters ".snd"
4 – 7	data offset	Point to the start of sound data
8 – 11	data size	The number of bytes in the data block
12 – 15	encoding	The data encoding format; Java understands only type 1
16 – 19	sample rate	Samples per second; always 8000 for Java
20 – 23	channels	The number of interleaved channels; always 1 for Java

The use of a 4-byte "magic number" at the start of the file is fairly common in file formats intended for delivery over the Internet. A receiving application can use these bytes to verify that it is receiving the expected format. (Incidentally, the magic number for Java class files is "CAFEBABE" when rendered in hexadecimal notation.)

The space from byte 24 to the data offset is available to be used for ASCII information. I found that the Goldwave utility I used to record the example sounds stores the characters "GW!" in this spot.

A Sound Demonstration Project

Because synthesizing sound on-the-fly would probably get us only boops and beeps, I have elected to create custom sounds by stitching together small chunks. The demonstration servlet will be able to "speak" an arbitrary number sequence, but the principle can be applied to create any sound sequence from small chunks in the .au format.

I used the Goldwave sound utility program to record myself saying the numbers from one to nine. After using Goldwave to filter out hum and noise, I cut the resulting recording into single digit sound bite files. I also recorded a few tenths of a second of silence in the same format. Figure 4.5 shows cutting a single word out of the recorded speech.

FIGURE 4.5

Using Goldwave to copy the word "five"

Goldwave is an exceptionally powerful shareware sound-manipulating program that can be downloaded from www.goldwave.com. You will need some sort of editing and filtering utility if you decide to work with sound applications because of the limitations of the typical office recording environment.

The NumberSoundServ Servlet

This servlet will get a request that has a string of numbers as a parameter, stitch together the required sound segments, and return the result as if it was reading an .au format file. Storing an individual sound clip is accomplished with the AUfileData class, as shown in Listing 4.14 and following listings. We start with the two constructors. The first reads an entire disk file into a byte array and then interprets the header information. The second constructor makes a complete copy of another AUfileData object.

Listing 4.14: The AUfileData class

```
package com.JSPbook.Chap04;

import java.io.* ;
import java.util.* ;

public class AUfileData
{
  byte[] buf ; // raw data buffer
  int[] header = new int[6] ;
```

```
AUfileData( File f ) throws IOException{
  int ct = (int)f.length();
  FileInputStream fis = new FileInputStream( f );
  buf = new byte[ ct ];
  fis.read( buf );
  fis.close();
  bufToHeader();
}

// constructor to copy existing data
public AUfileData( AUfileData orig ){
  buf = new byte[ orig.buf.length ];
  System.arraycopy( orig.buf, 0, buf, 0, orig.buf.length ); // copy data
  bufToHeader() ; // set header
}
```

The main work of the class is accomplished by the addAU method, which concatenates the data from another AUfileData object onto the data of the current object as shown in Listing 4.15. This method returns the current object, rather like the StringBuffer append method.

Listing 4.15: The AUfileData class continues with the addAU method

```
// append data from another AUfileData object
// return reference to this
public AUfileData addAU( AUfileData au ){
  int ct = au.header[ 2 ];
  int off = au.header[ 1 ] ;
  int sz = buf.length + ct ; // current size + new data
  byte[] nb = null ;
  nb = new byte[ sz ];
  // src, offset, dest, offset, bytect
  System.arraycopy( buf, 0, nb, 0, buf.length ); // current data
  // now nb has data from 0 to buf.length - 1 from original
  // add new data from buf.length to end of buf
  System.arraycopy( au.buf, off, nb, buf.length, ct );
  header[ 2 ] += ct ; // new count
  buf = nb ; // replace this buffer
  updateBuf(); // set header data correctly w new count
  return this ;
}
```

Finally, in Listing 4.16, we have some utility methods that copy the header array int values in and out of the byte array buffer, as well as utility methods useful for debugging.

Listing 4.16: Utility methods in the AUfileData class

```
void bufToHeader(){
  int p = 0 ;
  for( int i = 0 ; i < 6 ; i++){
    int n = 0xFF & buf[p++];
```

```
      n = (n << 8) + (0xFF & buf[p++]);
      n = (n << 8) + (0xFF & buf[p++]);
      n = (n << 8) + (0xFF & buf[p++]);
      header[i] = n ;
    }
  }
  //  header values to buf
  void updateBuf( ){
    int p = 0 ;
    for( int i = 0 ; i < 6 ; i++ ){
      int n = header[i];
      buf[p++] = (byte)( 0xFF & ( n >>24 )) ; // high byte
      buf[p++] = (byte)( 0xFF & ( n >>16 )) ; //
      buf[p++] = (byte)( 0xFF & ( n >>8 )) ; //
      buf[p++] = (byte)( 0xFF &  n ) ; // low byte
    }
  }
// useful for debugging
  public void write( File f )throws IOException {
    FileOutputStream fos = new FileOutputStream( f );
    fos.write(buf);
    fos.close();
  }

  // another handy debug item - format a header value in hex
  public String headerStr(int n ){
    return Integer.toString( header[n] ) + " -0x"
      + Integer.toHexString( header[n] ) ;
  }

  public String toString()
  { StringBuffer sb = new StringBuffer("AUfileData size:");
    sb.append( Integer.toString( buf.length ) );
    return sb.toString();
  }
}
```

In this demonstration servlet, the base path and names of the sound clip files are hard coded. A more flexible version would read this data in as initialization parameters. The init method, shown in Listing 4.17, creates an AUfileData object from each file to fill the static numFiles array.

If you wanted to synthesize a phrase or sentence from a vocabulary of spoken words, you could use the Hashtable class to retrieve the AUfileData object corresponding to an input word. At approximately 8K per second of speech, you could store a pretty good basic vocabulary in a few megabytes.

Listing 4.17: The start of the NumberSoundServ class

```
package com.JSPbook.Chap04;

import java.io.*;
import javax.servlet.*;
import javax.servlet.http.*;

public class NumberSoundServ extends HttpServlet
{
  static String basePath = "c:\\Multimedia Files\\SoundEffects" ;
  static String[] numFiles = { "zero.au","one.au","two.au","three.au",
    "four.au", "five.au","six.au", "seven.au","eight.au", "nine.au",
    "deadair.au"
  } ;
  static AUfileData[] nAU = new AUfileData[11];

  public void init(ServletConfig config) throws ServletException
  {
    super.init(config);
    ServletContext context = config.getServletContext();
    for(int i = 0 ; i < numFiles.length ; i++ ){
      try{
        File f = new File( basePath, numFiles[i] );
        nAU[i] = new AUfileData( f );
       // System.out.println("Loaded: " + i + " " + numFiles[i] );
      }catch(Exception e){
        System.out.println("init " + e.toString());
        context.log("NumberSoundServ.init err: " + e.toString() );
      }
    }
  }

  public String getServletInfo(){
    return "Stitches AU sound files together";
  }
```

Responding to a request is done in the doGet method, as shown in Listing 4.18. Note the commented out calls to System.out.println–these statements were used to debug the servlet. Because the output of the servlet is a binary data file, we don't have the opportunity of sending debugging data to the browser; therefore, we have to record it in servlet engine logs. Debugging servlets and JSP will be covered in more detail in Chapter 5.

The servlet expects to find a parameter named "digits" in the request that contains a sequence of ASCII digit characters. These characters are turned into indexes to the nAU array of AUfileData objects. Characters out of the number range are turned into the index of the deadair.au sound clip. The starting AUfileData object is a copy of the sound clip for the first digit, and subsequent digits, if any, are added to it.

Listing 4.18: The doGet method of the NumberSoundServ servlet

```java
public void doGet(HttpServletRequest req, HttpServletResponse resp)
throws ServletException, IOException
{
  String digits = req.getParameter("digits");
//  System.out.println("got digits:" + digits );
  if( digits == null || digits.length() == 0 )return ;
  int[] dig = new int[ digits.length() ];
  for( int i = 0 ; i < dig.length ; i++ ){
    int n  = digits.charAt(i) - '0' ;
    if( n < 0 || n > 9 ) n = 10 ;
    dig[i] = n ;
//System.out.println("result dig[ " + i + " ] = " + dig[i] );
  }
  try {
      // copy first one to build on
    AUfileData wrk = new AUfileData( nAU[ dig[0] ]);
    for( int n = 1 ; n < dig.length ; n++ ){
      wrk = wrk.addAU( nAU[ dig[n] ] );
    }
    resp.setContentType("audio/basic");
    resp.setContentLength( wrk.buf.length );
    OutputStream out = resp.getOutputStream();
    out.write( wrk.buf );
    out.close();
    //System.out.println("Sent " + wrk.buf.length + " bytes" );
  }catch(Exception e){
      System.out.println("NumberSoundServ " + e );
      e.printStackTrace( System.out );
  }
 }
}
```

Note that we set the response content type to "audio/basic" and set the content length before sending the response with an `OutputStream`.

Next let's look at various ways of using sound on the client side.

The Talking Applet

There are two ways to make an applet sound off: the single-shot `play` method and storing sound data in an `AudioClip` object. The `java.applet.Applet` class offers two versions of `play`. In both, the sound is played by a new `Thread` that opens the URL and starts playing while the `Thread` that executed the `play` method continues separately. These are the two versions of `play`:

public void play(URL url)   The URL must describe a complete path to a sound resource. In typical applications, the source is a file, but in our example, it will be the servlet just described.

public void play(URL url, String file)   In this case, the URL describes a server location, and the String gives the file name.

The AudioClip approach uses the getAudioClip method in the Applet class or the AppletContext class to create an object implementing the AudioClip interface. This object keeps all the sound data in memory and can play the sound on demand or in a continuous loop. For this demonstration applet, I will use the play method.

The SoundAp applet simply presents a text field and a button. Any text entered in the text field is made part of the URL used to execute the play method, as shown in Listing 4.19. Incidentally, the reason the inner class that implements ActionListener is named SymAction is that I used Symantec's Visual Cafe Interactive Development Environment (IDE) to create the applet.

Listing 4.19: Start of the SoundAp applet listing

```java
import java.awt.*;
import java.applet.*;
import java.net.* ;

public class SoundAp extends Applet
{
  public void init()
  {
    setLayout(null);
    setSize(426,76);
    add(textField);
    textField.setBounds(36,12,216,40);
    button1.setLabel("Say It");
    add(button1);
    button1.setBackground(java.awt.Color.lightGray);
    button1.setBounds(276,12,132,36);
    SymAction lSymAction = new SymAction();
    button1.addActionListener(lSymAction);
  }

  java.awt.TextField textField = new java.awt.TextField();
  java.awt.Button button1 = new java.awt.Button();

  class SymAction implements java.awt.event.ActionListener
  {
    public void actionPerformed(java.awt.event.ActionEvent event)
```

```
    {
      Object object = event.getSource();
      if (object == button1)
        button1_ActionPerformed(event);
    }
  }
```

Listing 4.20 shows the method executed when the button is clicked. It takes any text entered in the text field and builds a request to the `NumberSoundServ` servlet using the `saynumb.au` alias. The reason I used this alias will become apparent in the next section.

Listing 4.20: The SoundAp applet continued

```
    void button1_ActionPerformed(java.awt.event.ActionEvent event)
    {
      try {
        String say = textField.getText();
        if( say.length() == 0 ) return ;
        String pro = getDocumentBase().getProtocol();
        String host = getDocumentBase().getHost();
        int port = getDocumentBase().getPort();
        String fname = "/servlet/saynumb.au?digits=" + say ;
        URL url = new URL(pro,host,port,fname);
        this.play( url );
      } catch (Exception e) {
        System.out.println("Play : " + e.toString());
      }
    }
  }
```

Playing Sounds with JavaScript

After a lot of experimentation, I found a fairly reliable way to get Web pages with JavaScript to play sounds created by the servlet in both the Microsoft Internet Explorer (MSIE) and Netscape Navigator browsers. One trick was to use the `saynumb.au` alias for the servlet. Apparently, some browsers use the file type to decide that the resource is a sound file, ignoring other tags that are supposed to set the resource type.

Listing 4.21 shows a page that uses a JavaScript function and a plain HTML approach to playing a sound on demand. Activating the servlet as a hypertext link has worked in both MSIE and Netscape browsers, but the `onMouseover` code was not detected with Netscape.

Listing 4.21: An HTML page showing two ways to play a sound

```
    <html>
    <head>
    <meta name="GENERATOR" CONTENT="JSPbook Chapt04" >
```

```
<title>Sound Function Test</title>
<SCRIPT language="JavaScript">
<!--
    function playSound(snd){
     window.location = "http://localhost/servlet/saynumb.au?digits="+ snd  ;
    }
//-->
</SCRIPT>
</head>
<a HREF="http://localhost/servlet/saynumb.au?digits=321"
   >Click here to play sound as location.</a>

<H3 onMouseover='playSound("1987"); status="start" ; return true ;'
               onMouseOut="status='stop';">
   Play a sound using JavaScript on mouseover.</H3><br>
<br>
</body>
</html>
```

Vendor-Specific Formats

If you want to create or serve data files in formats specific to various vendors' products, you need two kinds of information: details of the file format and the MIME type associated with that format. Although the RFC2048 document formally outlines the correct way to formulate and register a new MIME type, some vendors create types without regard to this specification.

The IANA at www.iana.org acts as a central registry for MIME types. In addition, the following sites offer useful compilations of information about MIME types created by various vendors:

```
http://www.qnx.com/~chrish/Be/info/mime-types.html
```

```
http://www.ltsw.se/knbase/internet/mime.htp
```

To determine the file format used by various applications, you may be able to get information from the manufacturer, but in some cases, software companies don't release details of file formats. In such cases, you might have to depend on sites such as "Wotsit's File Format Site" located at

```
http://www.wotsit.org/
```

In any case, you can apply the general principles we used in this chapter to serve up just about any kind of data with Java servlets and JSP.

Debugging

- Debugging Hints for Browser Settings
- Snooping on Browser Requests and Server Responses
- Common Server Installation Problems
- Hints for Debugging JSP
- Designing for Ease in Debugging
- Making the Most of Exceptions
- Monitoring Memory Leaks

or many programmers, working with servlets and JavaServer Pages will be their first contact with multi-tier applications. Because servlets and JSP applications involve so many cooperating parts, there are many places for bugs to reside. Further complicating things is the fact that working applications are usually multithreaded and have many simultaneous activities. Debugging these complex applications involves techniques that must be adapted especially for this complex environment.

Anything That Can Go Wrong Will

The first rule of debugging is to be methodical, so I am going to start with a diagram (see Figure 5.1) of things that can go wrong between the client and the servlet engine. Later sections tackle debugging inside servlets.

FIGURE 5.1
Some bug locations
between client and servlet

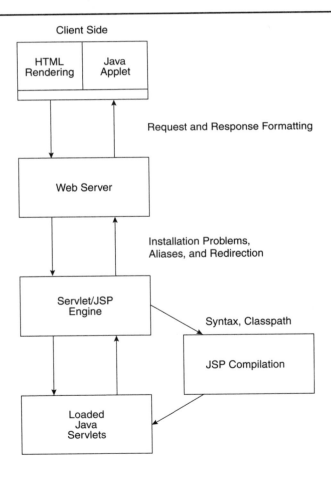

Let's consider things that can go wrong at the very top of the diagram—the typical Web browser. There are several things to watch out for at the browser level:

Web Page Caching   Many programmer hours are wasted because browsers use cached pages instead of loading your newly modified page. When debugging, make sure your browser is doing minimal caching and checks for newer versions of a page with every visit. It is helpful to have your JSP or servlet write a version number as part of the page output. (Of course, you do, however, have to remember to change the version number with every source code change.)

Cookie Security   Naturally, if your application needs to use cookies or sessions, you should make sure your browser allows them.

Proxy Caching   If your browser communicates with the Web server through a proxy, make sure the proxy is not caching pages or applet classes.

Proxy Blocking   A proxy or firewall may block certain kinds of content, causing strange behavior in your Web application.

Applet Class Reloading   If your application involves an applet on the client side, beware of browsers that do not reload applets when the Web page is reloaded. Try closing all instances of the browser and restarting if you get strange behavior by applets. I like to incorporate a statement writing the version number to System.out in an applet. That way you can look at the browser's Java console or javalog.txt file to verify that an old version has not been cached.

Requests to a Web server may be formulated by the browser interface or by an applet. With an applet, you can print the request line to System.out to examine it, but with forms on HTML pages and with JavaScript methods, it is hard to determine exactly what is being sent. I have written a Java application to spy on both requests and responses; that application is discussed in the following sections.

Responses from a Web server can be very uninformative and frustrating, as anybody who has gotten a "404 File Not Found" message is aware. The HTTP standard defines a number of standard error numbers for responses that are summarized in Appendix A. Your servlet or JSP code can send an error message with the sendError method in the HttpServletResponse class. Unfortunately, when your browser gets one of these codes, you frequently can't tell if it is coming from the Web server or from a servlet.

Spying on Requests

Because communication between a client and a Web server is conducted with streams and sockets, it is possible to create a Java utility that can intercept and monitor both request and response. In this section, I describe one simple utility that captures the client request and server responses (as long as they are in text form).

The UtilSnoop Application

The UtilSnoop program takes advantage of the fact that browser requests are directed at both a specific host and a specific port. In the example I am using, the Tomcat server listens on port 8080. The utility listens for browser requests on port 9000 and redirects lines of text to Tomcat while copying the lines to a display area. Responses coming to the utility are both sent to the client on port 9000 and copied to another display area. Figure 5.2 summarizes this data flow.

FIGURE 5.2
The Snoop utility sits between the client and Web server.

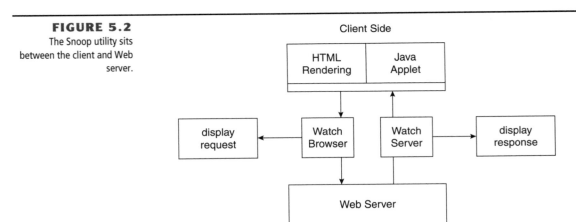

The program is implemented as a Java AWT graphic application. Figure 5.3 shows it in action: The top text area is the request from the browser, and the bottom shows the start of the server response. This particular request was for the JSP page named snoop.jsp that is one of the standard examples usually shipped with JSP engines.

FIGURE 5.3
Snoop utility display

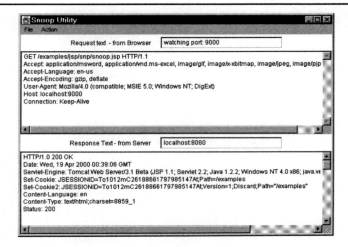

Many interesting points about interactions between a browser and a server are revealed by snooping on the headers, as shown in Figure 5.3. For example, you can see that the server has sent both "Set-Cookie" and "Set-Cookie2" headers to set a session ID. Note that the path for these cookies has been set to the "/examples" directory; this means that these cookies will only be sent with future requests to pages based at that directory.

You can copy the text in the utility displays to the Windows Clipboard by highlighting the text with the mouse and pressing Ctrl+C. However, a better solution would be to provide an option for saving the text in a file, but this is left as an exercise for the student.

Figure 5.4 shows the browser's display for this request. The snoop.jsp page formats request parameters in an easy-to-read list. Directing your browser to this page is a good way to verify that a JSP engine is working correctly.

FIGURE 5.4
The browser results

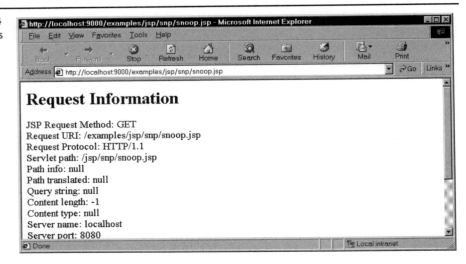

How UtilSnoop Works

UtilSnoop is a Java graphical application that uses the AWT graphical user interface (GUI) classes. The following menu options are provided:

File—Load Properties   Brings up a file dialog box so that the default settings can be changed via a properties file.

File—Exit   Simply exits immediately.

Action—Clear   Clears the text areas.

Action—Start   Opens sockets and starts threads, ready for the next request and response.

Action—Stop   Sets a flag that will eventually stop the threads.

Listing 5.1 shows the start of the UtilSnoop class source code. Note that there are instance variables with default values for the host name and the ports involved. These can be replaced in the setProp method by values read in from a properties file.

Listing 5.1: Start of the UtilSnoop class listing

```
import java.awt.*;
import java.io.* ;
import java.util.* ;
import java.net.* ;
```

```
public class UtilSnoop extends java.awt.Frame implements java.lang.Runnable {
  String host = "localhost" ;
  int browserPort = 9000 ;
  int hostPort = 80 ;

  Vector fromBrowser, fromServer ;
  boolean running = false ;

  PrintWriter toBrowser ;
  Socket browserSocket ;
  ServerSocket ssok ;

  PrintWriter toServer ;
  Socket serverSocket ;

  private void setWatchTF(){
    requestTF.setText("watching port: " + browserPort );
    responseTF.setText( host + ":" + hostPort );
  }

  // set from properties file
  private void setProp( Properties p ){
    try {
      String tmp = p.getProperty("host") ;
      if( tmp != null ) host = tmp ;
      tmp = p.getProperty("hostport");
      if( tmp != null ){
        hostPort = Integer.parseInt( tmp );
      }
      tmp = p.getProperty("browserport");
      if( tmp != null ){
        browserPort = Integer.parseInt( tmp );
      }
    }catch( Exception e){
      System.out.println("Setting Propeties " + e );
    }
  }
}
```

When the Start menu item is selected, the method shown in Listing 5.2 is executed. This method creates new Vector objects to store the String objects received from browser and server, and then it starts two Thread objects attached to anonymous inner classes, one to execute the watchBrowser method and one for the watchServer method. Finally, it starts the Thread that executes the run method in the UtilSnoop class itself.

Listing 5.2: The method that starts snooping

```java
void startMI_ActionPerformed(java.awt.event.ActionEvent event){
  // note: every start creates new Vectors and Threads
  fromBrowser = new Vector();
  fromServer = new Vector();
  running = true ;
  Thread t1 = new Thread( new Runnable() {
    public void run(){
      while( running ){
        System.out.println("watchBrowser start");
        try{   watchBrowser();
          System.out.println("watchBrowser returns");
        }catch(Exception e1){
          System.out.println("watchBrowser " + e1 );
        }
      }
      System.out.println("exit watchBrowser Thread");
    } // end run method
  });
  t1.setPriority( Thread.MIN_PRIORITY );
  Thread t2 = new Thread( new Runnable() {
    public void run(){
      while( running ){
        System.out.println("watchServer start");
        try { watchServer();
          System.out.println("watchServer returns");
        }catch(Exception e2){
          System.out.println("watchServer " + e2 );
        }
      }
      System.out.println("exit watchServer Thread");
    }
  });
  t2.setPriority( Thread.MIN_PRIORITY );
  t1.start() ;
  t2.start() ;
  new Thread( this ).start();
}

void stopMI_ActionPerformed( java.awt.event.ActionEvent event){
  running = false ;
  System.out.println("running stop");
}
```

The run method belonging to the UtilSnoop class (see Listing 5.3) watches both Vector objects for String objects received from the browser or server and sends them to the correct destination. It also adds them to their respective TextArea displays. Recall that the adding and removing methods in the Vector class are synchronized, so there can be no conflict between the different threads.

Listing 5.3: The UtilSnoop class run method

```
    // this Thread handles received data from both sides
    public void run() {
      String tmp = null ;
      int errCt = 0 ;
      System.out.println("main run method starts");
      while( running ){
        try {
          while( fromBrowser.size() > 0 ){
            tmp = (String)fromBrowser.firstElement();
            toServer.print( tmp ); toServer.print("\r\n");
            toServer.flush();
            requestTA.append( tmp ); requestTA.append("\n");
            fromBrowser.removeElementAt(0);
          }
          while( fromServer.size() > 0 ){
            tmp = (String)fromServer.firstElement();
            toBrowser.print( tmp ); toBrowser.print("\r\n");
            toBrowser.flush();
            responseTA.append( tmp ); responseTA.append("\n");
            fromServer.removeElementAt(0);
          }
          Thread.sleep( 80 );
        }catch(Exception e){
            e.printStackTrace( System.out );
            if( ++errCt > 10 ) break ; ;
        }
      }
      System.out.println("main run stop");
    }
```

Recall that the watchBrowser and watchServer methods (see Listing 5.4) are executed by two separate Thread objects using two anonymous inner classes. Although the watch-Browser method normally runs without interruption, the watchServer method throws an IOException every time the server closes the socket. Obviously, a busy Web server can't afford to keep sockets open for very long, even if the client has requested a "Keep-Alive" connection. The watchServer method gets a null value from reading the DataInputStream when the server socket closes. The inner class run method simply restarts the watchServer method so it is ready for the next response. Any IOException that might be thrown is treated the same way.

Listing 5.4: The watchBrowser and watchServer methods

```
    void watchBrowser() throws IOException {
      if( ssok == null ){
        ssok = new ServerSocket( browserPort );
        requestTF.setText("watching port: " + browserPort );
      }
```

```
    browserSocket = ssok.accept();
    System.out.println("watchBrowser got socket");
    OutputStream os = browserSocket.getOutputStream();
    InputStream is = browserSocket.getInputStream();
    toBrowser = new PrintWriter( os );
    BufferedReader br = new BufferedReader( new InputStreamReader( is ));
    String tmp = br.readLine();
    while( running && tmp != null ){
      fromBrowser.addElement( tmp );
      tmp = br.readLine();
    }
}

void watchServer() throws IOException {
    serverSocket = new Socket( host, hostPort );
    responseTF.setText( host + ":" + hostPort );
    OutputStream os = serverSocket.getOutputStream();
    toServer = new PrintWriter( os );
    InputStream is = serverSocket.getInputStream();
    DataInputStream dis = new DataInputStream( is );
    // an alternative would be to use a BufferedReader here
    // instead of DataInputStream
    System.out.println("watchServer got socket");
    String tmp = dis.readLine();
    while( running && tmp != null ){
      fromServer.addElement( tmp );
      tmp = dis.readLine();
    }
}
```

Note that the compiler objects to the deprecated `DataInputStream` class `readLine` method, so you could substitute a `BufferedReader` in `watchServer`. The advantage of the `DataInputStream` class is that `readLine` doesn't perform any Unicode translations; thus, you could switch from reading character lines to reading binary data.

Listing 5.5 shows the constructor for `UtilSnoop`. Because this utility was put together using Visual Cafe, there are some extra comment lines with special formats that the IDE uses to locate certain chunks of code. Essentially, the application shows two panels, one for data from the browser on top and the other for data from the server. Each panel has a `TextArea` object for the message text and a `TextField` used to display the port information. Because `TextArea` objects in Windows systems are limited to about 32kb of character data, this limits the amount of text that can be shown.

Listing 5.5: The UtilSnoop constructor

```
public UtilSnoop()  {
  //{{INIT_CONTROLS
  setLayout(new GridLayout(2,1,0,0));
  setSize(600,400);
```

```
        setVisible(false);
        reqPanel.setLayout(new BorderLayout(0,0));
        add(reqPanel);
        reqPanel.setBounds(0,0,20,40);
        requestTA.setEditable(false);
        reqPanel.add("Center",requestTA);
        requestTA.setBounds(0,0,405,305);
        reqTopP.setLayout(new FlowLayout(FlowLayout.CENTER,5,5));
        reqPanel.add("North",reqTopP);
        reqTopP.setBounds(0,0,20,40);
        label1.setText("Request text  - from Browser");
        reqTopP.add(label1);
        label1.setBounds(0,0,100,40);
        requestTF.setEditable(false);
        reqTopP.add(requestTF);
        requestTF.setBounds(0,0,100,40);
        respPanel.setLayout(new BorderLayout(0,0));
        add(respPanel);
        respPanel.setBounds(0,0,20,40);
        respTopP.setLayout(new FlowLayout(FlowLayout.CENTER,5,5));
        respPanel.add("North",respTopP);
        respTopP.setBounds(0,0,20,40);
        label2.setText("Response Text - from Server");
        respTopP.add(label2);
        label2.setBounds(0,0,100,40);
        responseTF.setEditable(false);
        respTopP.add(responseTF);
        responseTF.setBounds(0,0,100,40);
        respPanel.add("Center",responseTA);
        responseTA.setBounds(0,0,100,40);
        setTitle("Snoop Utility");
        //}}

        //{{INIT_MENUS
        menu1.setLabel("File");
        menu1.add(loadPropMI);
        loadPropMI.setLabel("Load Properties");
        menu1.add(separatorMenuItem);
        separatorMenuItem.setLabel("-");
        menu1.add(exitMI);
        exitMI.setLabel("Exit");
        mainMenuBar.add(menu1);
        menu2.setLabel("Action");
        menu2.add(clearMI);
        clearMI.setLabel("Clear");
        menu2.add(startMI);
        startMI.setLabel("Start");
        menu2.add(menuItem1);
        menu2.add(stopMI);
        stopMI.setLabel("STOP");
        mainMenuBar.add(menu2);
```

```
    //$$ mainMenuBar.move(0,312);
    setMenuBar(mainMenuBar);
    //}}

    //{{REGISTER_LISTENERS
    SymWindow aSymWindow = new SymWindow();
    this.addWindowListener(aSymWindow);
    SymAction lSymAction = new SymAction();
    exitMI.addActionListener(lSymAction);
    clearMI.addActionListener(lSymAction);
    loadPropMI.addActionListener(lSymAction);
    startMI.addActionListener(lSymAction);
    stopMI.addActionListener(lSymAction);
    //}}
  }

public UtilSnoop(String title)  {
  this();
  setTitle(title);
}

public void setVisible(boolean b)  {
  if(b){
    setLocation(50, 50);
  }
  super.setVisible(b);
}
```

The listings continue with the main method and some of the utility methods used to initialize the application. Listing 5.6 also includes the declarations of the GUI components in the Visual Cafe format.

Listing 5.6: The UtilSnoop main method

```
static public void main(String args[])  {
  try  {
      (new UtilSnoop()).setVisible(true);
  }  catch (Throwable t)  {
    System.err.println(t);
    t.printStackTrace( System.err );
    //Ensure the application exits with an error condition.
    System.exit(1);
  }
}

public void addNotify()  {
  // Record the size of the window prior to calling parents addNotify.
  Dimension d = getSize();
  super.addNotify();
  if (fComponentsAdjusted)return;
```

```java
      // Adjust components according to the insets
      setSize(getInsets().left + getInsets().right + d.width,
          getInsets().top + getInsets().bottom + d.height);
      Component components[] = getComponents();
      for (int i = 0; i < components.length; i++)
      {
        Point p = components[i].getLocation();
        p.translate(getInsets().left, getInsets().top);
        components[i].setLocation(p);
      }
      fComponentsAdjusted = true;
   }

   // Used for addNotify check.
   boolean fComponentsAdjusted = false;

   //{{DECLARE_CONTROLS
   java.awt.Panel reqPanel = new java.awt.Panel();
   java.awt.TextArea requestTA = new java.awt.TextArea();
   java.awt.Panel reqTopP = new java.awt.Panel();
   java.awt.Label label1 = new java.awt.Label();
   java.awt.TextField requestTF = new java.awt.TextField(30);
   java.awt.Panel respPanel = new java.awt.Panel();
   java.awt.Panel respTopP = new java.awt.Panel();
   java.awt.Label label2 = new java.awt.Label();
   java.awt.TextField responseTF = new java.awt.TextField(30);
   java.awt.TextArea responseTA = new java.awt.TextArea();
   //}}

   //{{DECLARE_MENUS
   java.awt.MenuBar mainMenuBar = new java.awt.MenuBar();
   java.awt.Menu menu1 = new java.awt.Menu();
   java.awt.MenuItem loadPropMI = new java.awt.MenuItem();
   java.awt.MenuItem separatorMenuItem = new java.awt.MenuItem();
   java.awt.MenuItem exitMI = new java.awt.MenuItem();
   java.awt.Menu menu2 = new java.awt.Menu();
   java.awt.MenuItem clearMI = new java.awt.MenuItem();
   java.awt.MenuItem startMI = new java.awt.MenuItem();
   java.awt.MenuItem menuItem1 = new java.awt.MenuItem("-");
   java.awt.MenuItem stopMI = new java.awt.MenuItem();
   //}}

   class SymWindow extends java.awt.event.WindowAdapter
   {
     public void windowClosing(java.awt.event.WindowEvent event)
     {
       Object object = event.getSource();
       if (object == UtilSnoop.this)
         System.exit(0);
     }
   }
```

Menu selections are handled by the method shown in Listing 5.7.

Listing 5.7: Menu event handling in UtilSnoop

```
class SymAction implements java.awt.event.ActionListener
{
  public void actionPerformed(java.awt.event.ActionEvent event)
  { Object obj = event.getSource();
    if (obj == exitMI)
      exitMI_ActionPerformed(event);
    if (obj == clearMI)
      clearMI_ActionPerformed(event);
    if (obj == loadPropMI)
      loadPropMI_ActionPerformed(event);
    if (obj == startMI)
      startMI_ActionPerformed(event);
    if (obj == stopMI)
      stopMI_ActionPerformed(event);
    }
}

void exitMI_ActionPerformed(java.awt.event.ActionEvent event)  {
  System.exit(0);
}

void clearMI_ActionPerformed(java.awt.event.ActionEvent event)
{ requestTA.setText("");
  responseTA.setText("");
}
```

Finally, we come to the method used to show a file dialog box and open a properties file (see Listing 5.8). Having a properties file to set the host name and port values makes it easy to use the utility for many different configurations.

Listing 5.8: The method that reads a property file

```
void loadPropMI_ActionPerformed( java.awt.event.ActionEvent event)
{
  FileDialog fd = new FileDialog(this,"Load Properties",
      FileDialog.LOAD );
  fd.show();
  String path = fd.getDirectory();
  String fname = fd.getFile();
  if( path == null || fname == null )return;
  File f = new File( path, fname );
  try{
    FileInputStream fis = new FileInputStream( f );
    Properties p = new Properties();
    p.load( fis );
    setProp( p );
  }catch(IOException e){
```

```
            System.out.println( e.toString());
        }
    }
}
```

The properties file is very simply formatted, with only three variables as shown in Listing 5.9. Note that the `Properties` class reads lines starting with the pound sign (#) as comments and ignores them.

Listing 5.9: A properties file for UtilSnoop

```
# Chapter 5 snoop utility properties
host=localhost
browserport=9000
hostport=8080
```

Here are some possible extensions to the snoop utility that could make it even more useful:

- Saving the recorded text to a file.

- Sending a request that emulates a browser. You could create a text file containing an example request and add a menu command to read and send the file. This would give you an easily repeatable test case.

- Providing for the capture of binary data. The `watchServer` method could look for Content-Type and Content-Length headers and read the data into a byte array. Note that you would have to change the reading method from `readLine` to one of the byte array reading methods.

Web Server Errors

At the Web server/servlet/JSP engine level of organization, a number of things can go wrong. Hopefully, by the time you read this, Tomcat—the official "reference" implementation of servlets and JSP—will have a detailed set of installation instructions and an online FAQ system for installation problems. Here are some of the reasons people have not been able to get Tomcat running (commercial systems have similar problems):

Out of Date JDK Installation   There have been reports of problems with JDK 1.2.0 and 1.2.1, so make sure you have the most recent compiler and standard library files.

Leftover Jar or Class Files   If you have been working with the earlier Sun JSDK version, make sure you remove all traces of the previous jar or class files.

Out of Date Linking Software   If you are using a servlet engine as an add-on to a commercial server such as IIS, be sure you have the latest DLL or other software that links the Web server to the servlet engine.

Log Files

It is good debugging practice to have a servlet record progress messages to a log file. Unfortunately, there does not appear to be any standardization among servlet engines as to where log files are stored. For example, the JRun 2.3 servlet engine has the rather complex directory structure summarized in Listing 5.10. There are eight different directories named *logs* within this structure. Fortunately, if you are using this engine, you will usually be concerned with only two of these log directories.

Listing 5.10: Schematic diagram of the JRun directory structure

```
|
|-- bin
|-- classes
|-- connectors
|-- examples
|-- jre
|-- jsm-default
|       |-- logs (stdout.log, error.log)
|       |-- properties
|       |-- services
|       |       |
|       |       |-- jcp
|       |       |-- jse
|       |       |    |-- logs (servlet log method, JSP logs)
|       |       |    |-- servlets (JSP compiled classes)
|       |       |
|       |       |-- jws
|       |            |
|       |            |-- htdocs
|-- lib
|-- properties
|-- servlets (general servlets directory root)
```

Whichever servlet engine you choose, use your early testing of the installation to get familiar with the location and use of log files. Don't jump into doing your own projects until the examples provided by the vendor work as expected and you understand where the log files are written.

Application Locations and Alias Settings

There is no particular uniformity about the installation and setup of the current generation of Web servers and Java servlet/JSP engines. However, the Servlet 2.2 API documentation makes some clear statements about this subject, so the commercial products might become more uniform.

Sun has whole-heartedly adopted XML for the purpose of configuring applications in the J2EE (Java 2 Enterprise Edition) and the Servlet 2.2 API. This makes for configuration files that are bulky but very easy to read and parse. Still, many users have problems in the configuration area.

Applications have two effective locations: the location as seen by the Web server and the location as seen by the native file system. The Web server converts between request URLs and real files by means of aliases that you, the operator, have to set up. If you get the dreaded "404 - File Not Found" error when trying to access your JSP file, this is the place to start looking. Because different commercial servers have different conventions, I am going to concentrate on the Tomcat server.

Locating HTML and JSP Pages

The Tomcat server uses the TOMCAT_HOME environment variable plus context information from the server.xml file to locate HTML and JSP files. Listing 5.11 shows the xml-coded text that sets up three separate contexts for URLs, and Table 5.1 shows how the Tomcat server converts URLs using this information plus the TOMCAT_HOME value of "c:\tomcat" to create an absolute path. Note that file paths in configuration files use forward slashes—even if your server is running under Windows—to ensure that the files are portable. Java automatically handles path separator differences between platforms.

Listing 5.11: Example Tomcat context settings from server.xml

```
<Context path="/examples" docBase="webapps/examples"
    debug="0" reloadable="true" >
</Context>
<Context path="" docBase="webapps/ROOT" debug="0" reloadable="true" >
</Context>
<Context path="/training" docBase="c:/InetPub/wwwroot/training"
    debug="1" reloadable="true" >
</Context>
```

TABLE 5.1: URL to file path conversion

URL	Resulting path
http://localhost/index.htm	c:\tomcat\webapps\ROOT\index.htm
http://localhost/JSPbook/Chap04/Game.jsp	c:\tomcat\webapps\ROOT\JSPbook\Chap04\Game.jsp
http://localhost/examples/jsp/source.jsp	c:\tomcat\webapps\examples\jsp\source.jsp
http://localhost/training/signin.htm	c:\InetPub\wwwroot\training\signin.htm

In Table 5.1, note that when the server does not have a specific context for a path (as with the "JSPbook/Chap04" URL), the ROOT value is used as a starting point. When the context specifies a complete path (as with the "training" context), the server uses that instead of building one based on TOMCAT_HOME.

The other parameters in each context shown in Listing 5.11 are also significant for debugging. The debug value of "0" minimizes the amount of information the server writes for applications in this path, whereas values up to "9" are more prolific. When you are debugging a new application, if you put it in a separate server context, you can set the level of debugging messages high for this application alone. That way you won't have to wade through debugging messages from other applications.

The reloadable attribute should be set "true" if you want Tomcat to check the timestamp on servlet classes and reload them if a new class file has appeared. This is the normal setting for debugging, but it does take extra time for the engine to check the timestamp with every use.

Locating Servlets

Locating Java servlets follows a convention based on the servlet package. No matter how a servlet engine selects a root directory for servlets, the class file location must use the package naming convention. Let's consider the NumberSoundServ servlet we created in Chapter 4. The Tomcat server will expect to find the servlet class at this absolute path

```
c:\tomcat\webapps\ROOT\WEB-INF\classes\com\JSPbook\Chap04\NumberSoundServ.class
```

which is created by concatenating the following information:

c:\tomcat   This comes from the TOMCAT_HOME environment variable.

webapps\ROOT   This comes from the context setting (Listing 5.11).

Web-inf\classes   This comes from the Sun standard application layout specification.

com\JSPbook\Chap04\NumberSoundServ   This comes from the package and servlet class name.

The client Web browser requests the URL as follows:

```
http://localhost/servlet/saynumb.au?digits=123
```

and the Tomcat server looks up "saynumb.au" using configuration data provided by the programmer in the web.xml file for this application, as shown in Listing 5.12. This configuration data gives the complete package and class name.

⤵ **Listing 5.12: Configuration data in Web.xml for a servlet**

```
<servlet>
    <servlet-name>saynumb.au</servlet-name>
    <servlet-class>com.JSPbook.Chap04.NumberSoundServ</servlet-class>
        <init-param>
            <param-name>basepath</param-name>
            <param-value>c:\\tomcat\\webapps\\Root\\JSPbook\\Chap04\\sounds
            </param-value>
        </init-param>
</servlet>
```

If and when you distribute your application in a jar file, that file will have to be in the Web-inf/lib directory instead of the Web-inf/classes directory.

JSP Debugging Problems

In the Tomcat implementation, JSP pages are handled by a servlet that has its own log file, called "jasper.log" by default. However, because the JSP servlet is run by the normal servlet engine, errors during compilation presently end up in the main "tomcat.log" file. If you are using another servlet and JSP engine, it will probably have different log file conventions. Therefore, the most important advice I can give on JSP debugging is that you should become very familiar with all the logging capabilities of your chosen platform.

JSP Syntax Errors

A JSP page has to go through both translation to a Java servlet and compilation of the servlet before you even get to make runtime errors. You are probably going to be chasing a lot of simple syntax problems. An example that seems to occur a lot has to do with escaping quotation marks in JSP expression statements. The JSP code in Listing 5.13, an example from Chapter 3, gets translated into a single Java out.write statement that writes part of a <form> tag in HTML. Because the <form> tag requires quoted values, a mind-boggling number of escaped quotation marks is required; missing any one of these could cause a translation error, a compilation error, or an error in the resulting HTML page.

⤵ **Listing 5.13: A JSP expression involving many escaped quotation marks**

```
<%= "<form method=\"post\" action=\"Chat.jsp\" > " +
    ChatRoom.getRoomsAsSelect() +
    "<br>Handle: <input TYPE=\"TEXT\" VALUE=\"\"" +
    " name=\"handle\"><br>\r\n" +
    "<input TYPE=\"submit\" VALUE=\"Enter Chat\"" +
    " name=\"chatgo\">\r\n</form></center><hr>\r\n" %>
```

When debugging a statement like this, you have to be very methodical. It also helps to examine the Java code produced by the JSP translation.

Importing Classes

Due to the way JSP pages mix HTML and Java, it is easy to forget to import required classes. The JSP translator creates the necessary import statements based on the code it writes, but you have to provide your own for the code you write. When writing the memory.jsp code used later in this chapter, I got the compilation error shown in Listing 5.14. Note that the error message is formulated in XML, a design decision by Sun that will make creation of more advanced tools for JSP much easier.

If you wade through the verbiage, you can see that the compiler error is reported as an inability to find the `Date` class in the Java class with the astonishingly long name that Tomcat makes up when translating JSP pages.

Listing 5.14: An example JSP compilation error

```
<l:ctx path="" ><b>Internal Servlet Error:</b><br>
<pre>
org.apache.jasper.JasperException: Unable to compile class for JSPC:\tomcat➡
\work\localhost_8080\_0002fJSPbook_0002fChap_00030_00035_0002fmemory➡
_0002ejspmemory_jsp_0.java:87: Class JSPbook.Chap_00030_00035.Date not found.
                out.print( new Date().toString() );
                               ^
1 error

  at org.apache.jasper.compiler.Compiler.compile(Compiler.java:240)
  at org.apache.jasper.runtime.JspServlet.loadJSP(JspServlet.java:414)
  at org.apache.jasper.runtime.JspServlet$JspServletWrapper.loadIfNecessary➡
(JspServlet.java:149)
  at org.apache.jasper.runtime.JspServlet$JspServletWrapper.service➡
(JspServlet.java:161)
  at org.apache.jasper.runtime.JspServlet.serviceJspFile(JspServlet.java:261)
  at org.apache.jasper.runtime.JspServlet.service(JspServlet.java:369)
  at javax.servlet.http.HttpServlet.service(HttpServlet.java:853)
  at org.apache.tomcat.core.ServletWrapper.handleRequest➡
(ServletWrapper.java:492)
  at org.apache.tomcat.core.ContextManager.service(ContextManager.java:558)
  at org.apache.tomcat.service.http.HttpConnectionHandler.processConnection➡
(HttpConnectionHandler.java:160)
  at org.apache.tomcat.service.TcpConnectionThread.run➡
(SimpleTcpEndpoint.java:338)
  at java.lang.Thread.run(Thread.java:479)
</pre>
</l:ctx>
```

This bug was cured by adding the `java.util` class to the page directive statement as shown here:

```
<%@ page language="java" import="java.util.*" %>
```

After that fix, the JSP translation proceeded without error. It is instructive to look at the `import` statements produced, as shown in Listing 5.15. Some of the imported classes were not used in the actual servlet produced. Apparently, the JSP translator has a set of `import` statements that it automatically uses.

Listing 5.15: Import statements in the Memory.jsp Java code

```
import javax.servlet.*;
import javax.servlet.http.*;
import javax.servlet.jsp.*;
import javax.servlet.jsp.tagext.*;
import java.io.PrintWriter;
import java.io.IOException;
import java.io.FileInputStream;
import java.io.ObjectInputStream;
import java.util.Vector;
import org.apache.jasper.runtime.*;
import java.beans.*;
import org.apache.jasper.JasperException;
import java.util.*;
```

Design for Debugging

An alternate name for this section would be "Design for Testing," because the basic idea is that if you plan your Java classes so they can be tested in a controlled environment, there will be fewer bugs when the classes are used in a Web server environment. This principle is one reason Sun emphasizes the use of JavaBeans in JSP and servlet applications.

Tools for Beans

As we discussed in Chapter 2, a JavaBean is simply a Java class that meets the following criteria:

- The class must be public.
- The class must have a no-arguments constructor.
- The class must provide `set` and `get` methods to access variables.

The JavaBean component architecture has been around for several years, and many vendors of IDEs and toolkits have adapted their products to work with JavaBeans. Although most of these tools emphasize JavaBeans as GUI components, they also work with beans used in servlets. The central Sun home Web page for JavaBeans and related technology is at:

```
http://java.sun.com/beans/
```

One of the tools available at that site is the "BeanBox," a tool that is mainly intended for use with GUI components but could be used with any bean. If the JavaBean class is serializable, the JSP programmer has the option of either creating a new object from the class file or reading in a serialized object with variables already set.

Catch That Exception!

When working with JSP, remember that you can designate your own custom error page by specifying it in the page directive tag as in this example from Chapter 2.

```
<%@ page language="java" errorPage="/JSPbook/Chapt02/whoops.jsp" %>
```

Any JSP page that is designated as the error page must include a tag similar to the following:

```
<%@ page language="java" isErrorPage="true" %>
```

which sets the isErrorPage parameter. This ensures that the page will have a default variable named exception that will refer to the actual error or exception.

When working with a servlet, it frequently makes sense to enclose most of the statements in the doPost or doGet method with a try - catch block structure. However, remember that your variable declarations should be made before the try block starts; otherwise, they will be out of scope in the catch block. Listing 5.16 shows a skeleton of a doGet method. Note that it takes advantage of the fact that when the JVM is trying to find a handler for an exception, it will use the first catch statement that fits the hierarchy. This allows us to provide special handling for IOException and MyCustomException exceptions while ensuring that every exception is caught.

Listing 5.16: Outline of a doGet method

```
public void doGet(HttpServletRequest req, HttpServletResponse resp)
    throws ServletException, IOException
{
  resp.setContentType("text/html");
  PrintWriter out = new PrintWriter(resp.getOutputStream());
  // various other variable declarations
  out.println("<HTML>");
   .. // outputof page start
```

```
    try { //  do main calculations
        .. // normal output
    } catch( IOException ioe ){
        ... // output debugging related to IO exceptions
    } catch( MyCustomException mce ){
        ... // output specialized debugging information
    } catch( Exception ex ){
        ex.printStackTrace( out );
        out.println("<br>\r\n");
    } finally {
        out.println("</BODY>");
        out.println("</HTML>");
        out.close();
    }
}
```

Custom Exceptions

Writing your own extension of a standard library Exception class to fit your particular application is an excellent way to get more information than the normal exception provides. Your
custom exception class can have several different constructors reflecting different possible
problems. If you don't want the compiler to force you to write exception handling code, your
custom class should descend from RuntimeException.

Using Assertions

Although Java does not have assertion capability built in, it is easy to add. The purpose of an
assertion statement is to verify that certain conditions are true before the program is allowed
to proceed. It serves as a single statement shorthand for logic that would otherwise be
expressed with an if statement. For example, if a program required a non-null reference
named userName, you could code it like this:

```
if( userName == null ){
    throw new IllegalArgumentException("bad user name");
}
```

Or using the Assertion class, you could code it like this:

```
Assertion.assert( userName != null, "bad user name");
```

Note that with the assertion, the logic test is expected to yield a value of true under normal
conditions. If the test yields false, an AssertionException is thrown. Listing 5.17 shows
the Assertion class source code, and Listing 5.18 shows the code for the AssertionException class.

Listing 5.17: The Assertion class has only static methods

```java
public class Assertion {
   public static boolean ASSERTION_ON = true ;
   private Assertion() {} ; // no public constructor
   // method without a message
   public static void assert( boolean validFlg )
         throws AssertionException {
     if( ASSERTION_ON && !validFlg ) {
        throw new AssertionException();
     }
   }

   // method with a message
   public static void assert( boolean validFlg, String msg )
        throws AssertionException {
     if( ASSERTION_ON && !validFlg ) {
        throw new AssertionException(msg);
     }
   }
}
```

Listing 5.18: The AssertionException class

```java
public class AssertionException extends RuntimeException {
    // this constructor assures that there will always be a message
   public AssertionException(){
     super("AssertionException");
   }

   public AssertionException(String msg ){
     super( msg ) ;
   }
}
```

You may reasonably ask, why use a special class when the same logic could be accomplished with an if statement? One answer is that using assertions makes the purpose of the logic very clear. You can tell at a glance that the program would be interrupted at that point if the condition is not met, whereas an if statement could be used for any purpose.

If you use assertions correctly, so that the program does not depend on a result caused by an assertion statement, then you can confidently remove the assertion statements when you are sure that the program is running correctly. Personally, I prefer to comment out the assertion statements so that they stay in the source code as a reminder of what was checked during program development.

Monitoring

Well, you got your application running in your `localhost` test system. It gives the right results and doesn't throw exceptions, so you must be finished with debugging, right? Wrong, there are still plenty of bugs that can become apparent only after it has been running a while.

For example, you might have a memory leak due if objects are being put into a `Vector` or `Hashtable` and are never removed. If each object is only a hundred bytes, it will take many requests to finally kill the server with a memory error. Your first inkling of a problem may come when you notice that the server is getting slower and slower due to excessive paging of memory.

A `Thread` leak might occur if every request creates a `Thread` to carry out some task but you have neglected to provide a way for the `Thread` to exit the `run` method and die normally. After a few thousand `Thread` objects have accumulated, the application may get very odd.

What you need for this kind of debugging is a way to remotely monitor memory and Thread usage in a running server. That way you can look in from time to time and watch for trends that might indicate a bug. Listing 5.19 shows `memory.jsp`, a simple JSP that can display the current servlet engine `Thread`s and Java Virtual Machine memory usage.

Listing 5.19: The memory.jsp source

```
<HTML><HEAD>
<TITLE>Memory Usage Monitor</TITLE>
</HEAD>
<BODY BGCOLOR="#FFFFFF" TEXT="#000000"><FONT FACE=VERDANA>
<H2 ALIGN=CENTER>
    Thread And Memory Status
</H2><BR>
<%@ page language="java" import="java.util.*" %>
<%! String brcrlf = "<br>\r\n"; %>
<%
    ThreadGroup tg = Thread.currentThread().getThreadGroup();
    Thread[] thrds = new Thread[ tg.activeCount() ] ;
    tg.enumerate( thrds ); // fills array
%><h3> Active Thread Count:
<%= thrds.length + brcrlf %></h3>
<ul>
<%
    for( int i = 0 ; i < thrds.length ; i++ ){
        out.print("<li>");
        out.print( thrds[i].toString() );
        out.print( brcrlf );
    }
%>
```

```
</ul><h3>Memory Usage</h3>
<%
    Runtime rt = Runtime.getRuntime();
    out.print("Total memory: " + rt.totalMemory() + brcrlf +
              " Free memory: " + rt.freeMemory() + brcrlf );
%>
<%= new Date().toString() %><br>

</BODY>
</HTML>
```

This page uses the fact that all `Thread` objects created in a servlet engine typically belong to the same `ThreadGroup`. The `toString` method displays the name of the `Thread`, its priority, and the name of the `ThreadGroup` it belongs to. Example output from the Tomcat Web server using this JSP is shown in Figure 5.5.

FIGURE 5.5

Output from memory.jsp on a Tomcat server

Note that some of the `Thread` objects shown in Figure 5.5 are named "StandardManager" and some are named "Thread-*n*" where *n* is a sequence number. The sequence number naming style is the default for `Thread` objects created without a programmer-supplied name. If your application creates any `Thread` objects, you should name them so that they will stand out in this listing.

Custom Logging

The main thing to remember when writing a custom logging facility is that there may be many `Threads` executing the same servlet, so log writing methods must be synchronized on the stream object used to write the log. For example, suppose you wanted to add logging to the `ChatRoom` class created in Chapter 3. The code in Listing 5.20 can be added to the `init-ChatRooms` static method to open the log file in the append mode.

Listing 5.20: Adding a log file to the ChatRoom class

```
try {
    FileOutputStream fos = new FileOutputStream( "chat.log" , true );
    chatLog = new PrintWriter( fos );
}catch(IOException e){
    System.err.println("Unable to create chat.log");
}
```

At a minimum, a custom log should provide for logging a simple message and for logging an exception with a message as shown in Listing 5.21. Note that a call to the `flush` method is needed because `PrintWriter` streams do not flush output by default.

Listing 5.21: Static log writing methods for the ChatRoom class

```
public static void log(String msg ){
   if( chatLog == null ) return ;
   synchronized( chatLog ){
     chatLog.println( msg );
     chatLog.flush();
   }
}

public static void log( String msg, Exception e){
   if( chatLog == null ) return ;
   synchronized( chatLog ){
     chatLog.println( msg );
     e.printStackTrace( chatLog );
     chatLog.flush();
   }
}
```

Miscellaneous Notes

This section contains some debugging hints that I could not figure out a way to categorize. Therefore, I list them here:

- Note that log buffering by the servlet engine means that if you look at the log while the engine is still running, you may not see the latest messages.

- A frequent source of mysterious runtime errors in servlets occurs when the programmer forgets to include a call to `super.init()` in an `init()` method.

- As a precaution, if your servlet does all its work in a `doPost` method, have your `doGet` call `doPost`. That way, if the servlet is ever addressed directly, you will at least get something back instead of seeing a "page not found" error.

- If a program works right the first (n) times but crashes on subsequent tries, look for a resource such as a database connection that has not been released.

- If a JSP or servlet works fine every time you try it, but certain users can never get it to work, the first thing to ask is "does your browser have cookies turned on?"

- When building a Web page with a JSP or servlet, you can avoid confusion about the location of static resources such as image files by using a <base> tag in the <head> tag area of the HTML document. This establishes a base URL for the location of resource files.

CHAPTER 6

Servlets, JSP, and XML

- XML Basics

- Document Type Definitions

- Programming with the Document Object Model (DOM)

- Programming with the Simplified API for XML (SAX)

- Alternatives to SAX and DOM

This chapter discusses a combination of the hottest topics in the world of the Internet, XML, and Java. XML (Extensible Markup Language) is the latest incarnation of an idea that has been kicked around for a while, namely, documents that can describe their own contents. The first major attempt to find a way to allow a document to describe itself was SGML (Standard Generalized Markup Language). HTML (Hypertext Markup Language), the language of the Web, is a vastly simplified version of SGML. Programmers' experience with the complexity of SGML and the imprecise and inflexible nature of HTML led to the development of the less complex, but more precise and flexible XML.

Because Java is the ideal medium for portable programs, and XML is the medium for portable data, obviously the Java-XML combination is a marriage made in heaven. In this chapter, I cover the basics of using XML-formatted data in Java programs.

XML Basics

The world of XML can look a little intimidating, especially with all the new acronyms flying around. Don't worry, you don't have to swallow the whole thing at one sitting. Here is a quick review of the characteristics of XML:

XML allows you to put structured data in a text file.   This can be the deep and complex structure of a complete book or the shallow and repetitive structure of a spreadsheet.

XML looks like HTML but isn't the same.   HTML tag usage is fixed, but XML users can make up their own tags. HTML rendering browsers are forgiving and can usually display something usable even if tags are not used correctly. XML parsers are unforgiving about errors.

XML is readable text.   This makes it easy for experts to edit and modify XML files, but it is not intended to be read by end users.

XML has spawned a whole family of related technologies.   Some of these have reached the stage of stable specification, but many are still works in progress.

XML files are bulky, but don't worry about it.   In the early days of computing, storage was expensive and transmission speeds were slow, leading to compact but inflexible data formats. With XML, we can take advantage of cheap storage and fast transmission to gain flexibility and more nearly universal formats.

XML is open.   Nobody owns the idea, and free resources are everywhere. This has a lot of appeal in the modern world of ill-advised software patents and lawsuits. The authority for XML is a consensus "recommendation" published by the World Wide Web Consortium (W3C). (See `http://www.w3.org` for the official documents.)

NOTE The world of XML and related technology is changing so fast that there will be many new features by the time this chapter sees print. You will have to use the Web to find out the current status. Some good starting points are `http://www.xml.com` and `http://xmlhack.com`.

The Parts of XML

One of the reasons XML has become so popular is that the rules for composition of a document are relatively simple and very similar to HTML. In fact, HTML can be made to conform to XML specifications without too much trouble, resulting in XHTML (Extensible HTML). Here are some of the important characteristics of XML documents:

- Documents are made up of one or more *elements* that can have only two forms. The first form for an element is an opening tag, content text, and a closing tag:

  ```
  <p>
  Paragraph text.
  </p>
  ```

- A closing tag must match the name of an opening tag exactly, with the addition of a '/' character as a prefix. The content may contain other markup elements or simply text.

- The other form for an element is an *empty element* in which only one tag appears, as in the following:

  ```
  <br />
  ```

- Note that the empty element uses a "/>" at the end of the tag.

- A document always has a single *root* element. For example, an HTML document always has the `html` root.

- Elements may contain *attributes*, each of which must have a name and a value enclosed in quotation marks. Either single or double quotation marks may be used, but the start and end must match, as in this example:

  ```
  <Book isbn="1576102912" >
  ```

- Leading and trailing white space will be trimmed from attribute values by parsers. Four characters are treated as white-space: the ASCII space, linefeed, carriage return, and tab.

- XML documents are required to be *well formed*. Element tags must nest correctly, with closing tags occurring in the reverse order of opening tags. For example:

  Well formed: `<b><i> some text </i></b>`

  Not well formed: `<b><i> some text </b></i>`

- Although Web browsers frequently manage to render HTML that fails the "well formed" test, XML parsers will detect the error. Note that Microsoft Word is notorious for creating incorrect tag sequences when saving documents as HTML.

- XML tag names are case sensitive. Note that the XHTML standard calls for all HTML formatting tags to be lowercase.

- XML tag names must start with a letter or an underscore and can then have any number of letters, numbers, hyphens, periods, or underscores. Names cannot contain spaces.

- Names starting with "xml" in any combination of upper- and lowercase letters are reserved for further expansion of the standard.

Starting an XML File

A well-formed XML document starts with a prolog that declares that this is an XML document and that (optionally) describes the XML version, the character encoding, and whether or not a Document Type Definition (DTD) is provided. The standalone="no" in the following example indicates that a DTD will be provided:

```
<?xml version="1.0" encoding="us-ascii" standalone="no" ?>
<!DOCTYPE BookErrata SYSTEM "BookErrata.dtd">
```

In the example, the `<!DOCTYPE>` tag specifies a few things:

- The name of the *root-element*, in this case "BookErrata."

- A reference to the DTD. In this case, the word SYSTEM means that the DTD is in a local file. Alternatively, the word PUBLIC would imply that the document follows a publicly available DTD and that the statement includes a name and a URL for that DTD. For example, here is the correct form for the beginning of XML documents following the "Open eBook" format for electronic publishing in which the root-element name is html:

```
<?xml version="1.0"?>
<!DOCTYPE html PUBLIC
        "+//ISBN 0-9673008-1-9//DTD OEB 1.0 Document//EN"
        "http://openebook.org/dtds/oeb-1.0/oebdoc10.dtd">
```

- If a DTD is specified, a parser may verify that the document conforms to the DTD. Because verification is time consuming, many applications do not actually verify a document against the DTD even if one is specified. Frequently, a program switch is provided to control verification.

XML Entities

Entities are used to substitute one series of characters for another series of characters in a document. This lets you include characters that would otherwise be part of markup in documents. You have probably seen this idea in use in HTML pages where the `&lt;` and `&gt;` sequences are rendered as < and > characters by the browser. The `&lt;` sequence is called an *entity reference* for the < entity. An entity reference starts with the ampersand character and ends with a semicolon.

XML recognizes five predefined entity references as substitutes for markup characters:

`&lt;`	<
`&gt;`	>
`&amp;`	&
`&quot;`	"
`&apos;`	'

You can also define entity references by using a hexadecimal constant in the sequence `&#xHH;` in which the HH represents a hexadecimal number. For example, `&#xA9;` is a reference for the copyright character.

A DTD can declare an arbitrary entity character sequence and its corresponding entity reference, either entirely inside the DTD or as an *external entity*. An external entity points to another document that is included in its entirety in an XML document wherever the entity reference appears.

The CDATA and PCDATA Content Types

All text in an XML document that is not markup constitutes the character data of the document. An XML processor can treat character data in two ways, as parsed or unparsed, which is indicated in a DTD with #PCDATA and CDATA respectively.

In a DTD, these element declarations

```
<!ATTLIST Book isbn CDATA #IMPLIED>
<!ELEMENT Title (#PCDATA)* >
```

would be interpreted to mean that the isbn attribute of the Book element consists of unparsed character data, whereas the Title element contents are parsed.

A special form of CDATA can be used to enclose text that will not be interpreted by the XML parser. The start sequence is `<![CDATA[`, and the end sequence is `]]>`. The main use for CDATA sections is to enclose text that uses special characters such as < and &, which might otherwise be interpreted as XML markup. Once the start sequence is recognized, the only thing the parser can do is look for the end sequence, ignoring all other text.

Processing Instructions and Comments

Two kinds of text can be contained in a document but are ignored by XML parsers: comments and processing instructions. Comments follow the form you are probably familiar with from HTML:

```
<!-- this is a comment -->
```

Comments can occur anywhere except the first line of an XML document but may not be embedded inside tags.

Processing instructions use the <? start and ?> end characters to enclose text that provides special instructions to your application. Note that the instructions that start with <?xml are reserved for use by the XML processor. For other instructions, it is up to the programmer to interpret the contents. Processing instructions may not be embedded inside tags.

Namespaces

As more programmers embrace XML, it has become obvious that many tag names, such as "Book," will be duplicated. The concept of a namespace has been added to XML to provide for unique tag naming. An example tag with the namespace added would be <Sybex:Book> where the ID characters before the colon create the namespace. You can declare a namespace in effect within an element by using an attribute that starts with xmlns: combined with the ID and having as a value a unique identifier such as a corporate URI (universal resource identifier), as in the following example:

```
<Sybex:Book xmlns:Sybex="http://www.sybex.com" >
    <!-- various Book elements -->
</Sybex:Book>
```

At the present time, exactly how namespaces will be standardized and used appears to be a matter of controversy. The main reason for mentioning them here is so you can recognize them when you see them in use.

XML and DTD Examples

We have very handy examples of using an XML and a DTD in the configuration files used by the Tomcat Web server. The complete files are rather long, so I am showing only sections. Listing 6.1 shows the DTD for the server.xml file.

Listing 6.1: The server.dtd used by Tomcat

```
<?xml version="1.0" encoding="ISO-8859-1"?>
<!ELEMENT Server (ContextManager+)>
<!ATTLIST Server adminPort NMTOKEN "-1"
                 workDir CDATA "work">
<!ELEMENT ContextManager (Context+, Interceptor*, Connector+)>
<!ATTLIST ContextManager port NMTOKEN "8080"
    hostName NMTOKEN ""
    inet NMTOKEN "">
<!ELEMENT Context EMPTY>
<!ATTLIST Context
    path CDATA #REQUIRED
    docBase CDATA #REQUIRED
    defaultSessionTimeOut NMTOKEN "30"
    isWARExpanded (true | false) "true"
    isWARValidated (false | true) "false"
    isInvokerEnabled (true | false) "true"
    isWorkDirPersistent (false | true) "false">
<!ELEMENT Interceptor EMPTY>
<!ATTLIST Interceptor
    className NMTOKEN #REQUIRED
    docBase   CDATA #REQUIRED>
<!ELEMENT Connector (Parameter*)>
<!ATTLIST Connector
    className NMTOKEN #REQUIRED>
<!ELEMENT Parameter EMPTY>
<!ATTLIST Parameter
    name CDATA #REQUIRED
    value CDATA "">
```

Listing 6.2 shows part of a server.xml file that controls a Tomcat installation. This example uses the <Context> tag to create "/training" as a server alias for a real disk path. Note that not all the attributes listed in the DTD are set in the tag. Although path and docBase are required, the others have default values.

Listing 6.2: Part of a server.xml file

```
<Context path="/training" docBase="c:/InetPub/wwwroot/training"
    debug="1" reloadable="true" >
</Context>
```

Listing 6.3 shows part of Tomcat's web.dtd file that defines the <servlet> element contents. Note that the comment that starts the listing is used to provide extra information.

Listing 6.3: Part of the web.dtd used by Tomcat

```
<!-- The servlet element contains the declarative data of a
servlet. If a jsp-file is specified and the load-on-startup element is
present, then the JSP should be precompiled and loaded. -->

<!ELEMENT servlet (icon?, servlet-name, display-name?,
    description?, (servlet-class|jsp-file), init-param*,
    load-on-startup?, security-role-ref*)>

<!-- The servlet-name element contains the canonical name of the
servlet. -->

<!ELEMENT servlet-name (#PCDATA)>

<!-- The servlet-class element contains the fully qualified class name
of the servlet. -->

<!ELEMENT servlet-class (#PCDATA)>
```

An example of configuring a servlet according to the web.dtd is shown in Listing 6.4. The data in the `<init-param> .. </init-param>` area defines the parameter name and value as passed to the `init` method in the servlet.

Listing 6.4: Part of the web.xml configuration file

```
<servlet><servlet-name>saynumb.au</servlet-name>
<servlet-class>com.JSPbook.Chap04.NumberSoundServ</servlet-class>
  <init-param>
    <param-name>basepath</param-name>
    <param-value>c:\\tomcat\\webapps\\Root\\JSPbook\\Chap04\\sounds➥
    </param-value>
  </init-param>
</servlet>
```

The DOM and SAX Programming Models

The orientation of SGML is a complete document, so it is hardly surprising that XML started out thinking in Document Object Model (DOM) terms. All DOM processing assumes that you have read and parsed a complete document into memory so that all parts are equally accessible. This approach is shown symbolically in Figure 6.1.

FIGURE 6.1
Document Object Model
processing

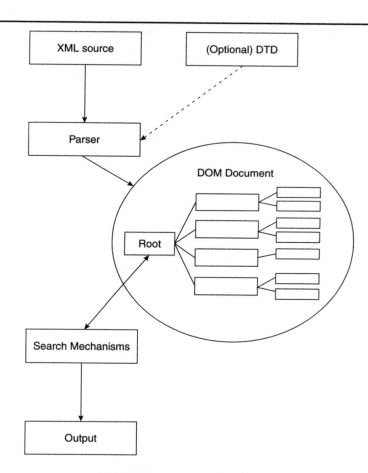

As people started programming with the DOM, they found it was pretty clumsy if all you wanted to do was pick out a few elements. Furthermore, the memory requirements could get restrictive—if not downright impossible. Thus, the Simplified API for XML (SAX) was born of necessity. Both the DOM and SAX specify application programming interfaces that have been implemented in a number of languages in addition to Java.

As shown in Figure 6.2, a SAX parser makes a single pass through an XML file, reporting what it has parsed by calling various methods in the application code. The SAX documentation uses the term *event* for what happens when the parser decides it has identified an element in the XML document, so these methods are called *event handlers*. When the parser reaches the end of the document, the only data in memory is what your application saved.

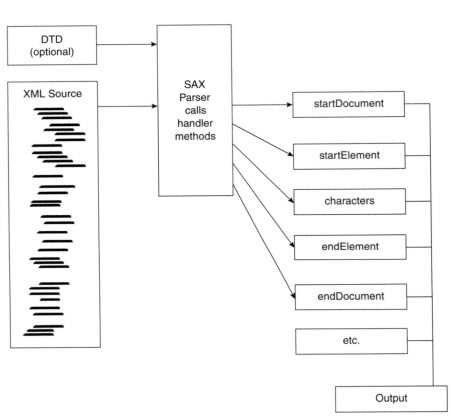

FIGURE 6.2
Simplified API for XML
processing

The reason both figures show input from a DTD as optional is that XML is frequently parsed without a DTD. In that case, the parser can determine that the XML is well formed but not whether it is valid.

Both models can be useful for servlet and JavaServer Pages (JSP) programming, as I will demonstrate in the examples. First, however, let's look at the Java tools for both the DOM and SAX. These are tools for the "level 1" DOM and version 1 of the SAX. Just to keep things complicated, version 2.0 of the SAX 2.0 and DOM level 2 are currently in the works.

Programming with the DOM

The definitive API for working with the DOM is provided by the `org.w3c.dom` package, a recommendation of the W3C. This API consists entirely of interface definitions plus a single exception class. The basic idea is that an XML document is turned into a DOM consisting of Java objects that implement these interfaces. Every part of the document becomes an object, and the connections between the objects reflect the hierarchy of the document.

Parsing XML to Create a DOM

From the programmer's standpoint, creating a DOM is simplicity itself because all the work is done by the parser. All the programmer has to do is create an input stream, select a parser, and stand back. Listing 6.5 shows a skeleton of a method to read from a file using utility classes from the `com.sun.xml.parser` package and return a `com.sun.xml.tree.XmlDocument` object. The `XmlDocument` class implements the `Document` interface as specified in the W3C recommendation.

If you were using parser utilities from a different supplier, the names would be different, but the general flow control would be similar. This particular example uses classes released by Sun as "Java Project X" and currently used in the Tomcat servlet engine. However, note that the Tomcat project will eventually use whatever Sun's current parser is.

An astonishingly large number of different XML parsers have been created in the last few years, but only a few are completely compliant with the W3C DOM recommendations. The most recent compliance tests as of this writing indicate that the Sun parser has the highest compliance rating.

Listing 6.5: A skeleton of a method to create an XmlDocument

```
public XmlDocument exampleDOM(String src ) {
  File xmlFile = new File( src ) ;
  try {
    InputSource input = Resolver.createInputSource( xmlFile );
    // ... the "false" flag says not to validate
    XmlDocument doc = XmlDocument.createXmlDocument (input, false);
   return doc ;
  }catch(SAXParseException spe ){
    // handle parse exception here
  }catch( SAXException se ){
    // handle other SAX exceptions here
  }catch( IOException ie ){
    // handle IO exceptions here
  }
  return null ;
}
```

Once you have a DOM in memory, you manipulate it using methods provided in the DOM interface recommendation embodied in the `org.w3c.org` package plus additional methods provided by the available toolkit.

The Java Objects in a DOM

In the following discussion, when I speak of objects of various types, you should understand this to mean objects belonging to classes that implement the named interfaces. You don't really need to know the actual class names because they vary from parser to parser.

The primary set of methods for the entire package is provided by the **Node** interface. There are 13 sub-interfaces derived from **Node** to represent various parts of a document. Although they all extend **Node**, certain methods don't make any sense in some sub-interfaces. Table 6.1 summarizes the **Node** methods. Note that the interpretation of the `nodeName` and `nodeValue` return values depends on the type of node, as shown in Table 6.2.

TABLE 6.1: The Node methods

Method	Returns	Value is used for
getNodeName	nodeName (see Table 6.2)	The String name of the node; interpretation depends on type.
getNodeValue	nodeValue (see Table 6.2)	The String value of the node; depends on type.
setNodeValue	void	
getNodeType	short	A code defined in the Node interface, representing the node type.
getParentNode	a Node reference	The parent of this node in the document hierarchy. Not all types have parents.
getChildNodes	a NodeList reference	NodeList objects provide for accessing an ordered list of Node references.
getFirstChild	a Node reference	The first child of this Node, or null if none exists.
getLastChild	a Node reference	The last child of this Node, or null if none exists.
previousSibling	a Node reference	The node immediately preceding this one, or null if none exists.
nextSibling	a Node reference	The node immediately following this one, or null if none exists.
getAttributes	a NamedNodeMap reference	NamedNodeMap methods provide for access to attributes by name. Returns null if the node has no attributes.
getOwnerDocument	a Document reference	The Document this Node belongs to, or null if this Node is a Document.

Table 6.2 shows how nodeName and nodeValue (refer to Table 6.1) are interpreted. Each Node type is an interface name. Each one also has a unique code defined in the Node interface.

TABLE 6.2:   Interpretation of returned values

Node type	nodeName	nodeValue	Comments
Element	tag name	null	Most document objects are Elements.
Attr	name of attribute	value of attribute	
Text	#text	text content of node	
CDATASection	#cdata-section	text content	
EntityReference	name of the entity referenced	null	
Entity	entity name	null	
ProcessingInstruction	target	all other text in the tag	Processing instruction tags start with <? and end with ?>.
Comment	#comment	text content of the comment	Comment tags start with <!-- and end with -->.
Document	#document	null	
DocumentType	document type name	null	The name of the document root element from the DTD, if any.
DocumentFragment	#document-fragment	null	
Notation	notation name	null	Notations provide information for unparsed entities.

Manipulating the DOM

Given that you have in memory an object having the Document interface, you have several possible ways to search and traverse it. The NodeList interface in the org.w3c.dom package defines ways to manipulate an ordered collection of Node references. Here is how you would obtain a NodeList with all elements named "Book" in a document:

```
Element E = doc.getDocumentElement();
NodeList vlist = E.getElementsByTagName( "Book" );
```

NodeList provides two methods: length() returns the number of Nodes in the collection, and item(int n) returns the *n*th Node in the collection.

Another approach uses the method `getFirstChild()` to get the first `Node` below the root element of the document. From that `Node`, you can use `nextSibling` to find the next `Node` at the same level in the document hierarchy.

If, on the other hand, you continued to look for child nodes, you would be conducting a *depth-first* traversal of the DOM. The Sun `com.sun.xml.tree` package has a `TreeWalker` class that provides convenient methods for depth-first traversal of any `Node`.

Another convenient interface is the `NamedNodeMap`. This is typically used to manipulate collections of nodes by name, similar to the way you would use a `Hashtable`. A typical use would be to get the attributes attached to an `Element Node`. Just as with a `Hashtable`, there is no particular order in a `NamedNodeMap` collection.

Although the interfaces of the `org.w3c.dom` package offer many methods for modifying objects contained in a DOM, the various implementers of XML toolkits in Java typically provide methods of their own. Generally speaking, you can get and set the character contents of any `Node` using `getData()` and `setData( String data )`.

Programming with SAX

The following list summarizes the basic steps required to process an XML document with SAX:

- Create one or more custom classes to handle the "events" that the SAX parser detects.
- Create an object to provide an input stream of characters.
- Create a parser from one of the toolkits.
- Attach the event handling classes to the parser.
- Attach the input stream to the parser and start parsing.
- Handle all the events in your custom classes to capture the data you are interested in, detect errors, and so on.

As you can see, SAX processing of XML involves a programming philosophy that is completely different from using the DOM. Deciding which approach to use for a particular application is your most important design decision. Table 6.3 summarizes the important considerations.

TABLE 6.3: Comparison of DOM and SAX programming

Programming factor	DOM style	SAX style
Memory requirements	May be quite large	Only as large as the items retained in memory
Startup time	Slower because every element is parsed	Faster, especially if the elements of interest are easy to locate
Repeated search time	Faster because everything is in memory	Slower because every search involves a new parsing run
Modification capability	Very flexible	Limited to writing a new XML document with every pass

Interfaces for Event Handlers

Interfaces in the org.xml.sax package define methods that an application writer will typically implement to receive information from the parser about parser decisions. The documentation speaks of these decisions as events, but note that these are parser events and are not related to Java Event class objects. Essentially, when the parser decides that it has detected a particular element in the XML data stream, it calls one of these methods.

DocumentHandler Interface

Classes implementing the DocumentHandler interface must provide the following methods. The HandlerBase is the utility class that implements all these methods and is typically used as the base for custom classes.

startDocument( )   This method is called once when the parser starts. This is a good place to put initialization code.

endDocument()   When this method is called, the parser has finished due to the end of input or an unrecoverable error.

startElement(String name, AttributeList atr)   Called when a starting element and accompanying attributes have been parsed.

endElement(String name)   Called when the parser reaches an end attribute.

characters(char[] buf, int start, int count)   Called with a chunk of character data. This may be only a portion of the data in a character data block, or it may be the entire chunk. The method should read from the buffer only in the range specified.

ignorableWhitespace(char[] buf, int start, int count)   This method lets a parser report non-printing characters that are not legally part of XML data. Validating parsers are required to call this method, but it is optional for non-validating parsers.

processingInstruction(String target, String data)   Called when the parser encounters a processing instruction. The target is the name immediately following the opening <?, and the data String is all of the remaining text.

setDocumentLocator(Locator loc)   Supplies a Locator object reference that the parser will be using. The Locator can be used to obtain additional information about where the parser is in the XML document text. A typical use would be to determine the location that caused an exception.

DTDHandler Interface

This interface defines notationDecl and unparsedEntityDecl methods that report the SAX parser's progress in processing a DTD. To receive these method calls, an application has to register with the parser specifically. If a handler is registered, the parser will call these methods after startDocument has been called but before any calls to startElement.

EntityResolver Interface

This interface defines the resolveEntity method. It essentially creates an input stream of characters as a replacement for an entity reference. Your application needs to implement this method only if your XML has external entities that require custom handling.

ErrorHandler Interface

This interface is used if you want to substitute specialized error handling in place of having the SAX parser throw an exception. Your class implementing the interface must register with the parser before it is started. There are three levels of error handling methods: warning, error, and fatalError. The input to each is a SAXParseException reference.

Interfaces for SAX Parsers

To give the maximum freedom to designers of SAX parsers, the specifications define interfaces for classes that a complete parser package must provide.

Locator Interface

A SAX parser may provide an object implementing this interface to assist your application in interpreting events. Parsers are not required to implement this function, but it is strongly suggested.

The methods getColumnNumber and getLineNumber return an int value indicating the column and line in the XML text that the parser read when it generated a particular event.

AttributeList Interface

An object implementing the AttributeList interface is used to communicate a list of attributes found in an element to the startElement method. Attributes have a name, a value, and a type (all String objects), and this interface provides for retrieval both by name and by position in the list.

getLength()   Returns the number of attributes (possibly zero) found in the element.

getName(int i)   Returns the String name of an attribute by position in the list.

getType(int i)   Returns the type of an attribute in the list. Possible types are the constants CDATA, ID, IDREF, IDREFS, NMTOKEN, NMTOKENS, ENTITY, ENTITIES, or NOTATION.

getType(String name)   Returns the type of an attribute by name.

getValue(int i)   Returns the String value of an attribute by list position.

getValue(String name)   Returns the String value by the attribute name.

Classes for Parsers

Most of the elements in the org.w3c.dom and org.xml.sax packages are specified as interfaces. Presumably this was done to allow parser writers maximum flexibility.

Exception Classes

The SAXException class provides the general error reporting mechanism for XML parsers. Any exception occurring in a SAX parser must be wrapped in a SAXException before being thrown to the enclosing application. This design decision means that every exception thrown by a parser will be a SAXException or a class derived from SAXException.

The SAXParseException class provides methods, as in the following list, that can be used as indicators of the location of the cause of a parsing exception. These are the same methods that the Locator interface calls for:

- The getColumnNumber and getLineNumber methods return an int value indicating the position in the XML document where the parser decided it had an error.

- The getPublicID method returns a String containing the public identifier of the entity the parser was working on when the error occurred.

- The getSystemID method returns a String with the system identifier where the exception occurred. This could be a file name or URL.

A SAX Example

As an example of programming with SAX, I am going to use a practical problem experienced by publishers like my company, LANWrights, Inc. That problem relates to creating, updating, and presenting errata errors in a book that are found after the book is published. We need these errata lists so that subsequent printings can be corrected and so that readers can correct their own copies.

Technical publishing companies vary considerably in their approach to errata. Sometimes you are lucky if a Web page gets updated every six months. We took the approach of creating a Web page on-the-fly every time a query is made, using a list of errata that can be updated by an online editor. Originally, the list used a simple and compact format that was processed by a Perl script to generate the page, but now we are converting to XML to take advantage of the flexibility it provides.

The XML Document for Errata

A single Web page is provided for all access to errata. The interface lets a user select a book and specify the following criteria:

- *Seriousness of the error.* The options are major, major plus moderate, or all errors including minor typos.

- *Printing number the error appears in.* This is needed because errors are frequently corrected in subsequent editions, but new errors may be introduced.

- *The date after which the error note was created or modified.* With this parameter, a truly methodical user could search for errata that are new or have changed since the last visit.

These criteria are related to the XML elements and attributes as shown in Table 6.4.

TABLE 6.4: Elements and attributes of the errata XML system

Item	Type	Used for
Title	element	Cover title of the book
isbn	attribute	The universally accepted book identification
Errata	element	Encapsulates a single errata report that has identifying attributes plus descriptive text
page	attribute	Identifies the page the error starts on; may be a page number or some other text
printing	attribute	List of printings the error occurs in
significance	attribute	Classification of the error in terms of how serious it is
author	attribute	Identifies the person who put the error in the system
datemod	attribute	When the error was entered or modified

In addition to the elements and attributes described in Table 6.4, the DTD also includes HTML formatting codes used to present the text. For example, code listings use the <pre> and <tt> tags, and quotation marks frequently appear in the error text. An alternative to providing for these elements in the DTD would have been to enclose the bulk text in the special <![CDATA[.....]]> tags so it would not be examined for markup characters, as shown in Listing 6.6.

Listing 6.6: The DTD for errata

```
<!ELEMENT BookErrata (Title|Errata)* >
<!ATTLIST BookErrata isbn CDATA #IMPLIED>
<!ELEMENT Title (#PCDATA)* >
<!ELEMENT Errata (#PCDATA|br|A|TT|B|I|PRE)* >
<!ATTLIST Errata page CDATA #IMPLIED>
<!ATTLIST Errata printing CDATA #IMPLIED>
<!ATTLIST Errata significance CDATA #IMPLIED>
<!ATTLIST Errata author CDATA #IMPLIED>
<!ATTLIST Errata datemod CDATA #IMPLIED>
<!ELEMENT br EMPTY >
 <!ELEMENT A (#PCDATA)* >
<!ATTLIST A HREF CDATA #IMPLIED>
<!ELEMENT TT (#PCDATA|br)* >
<!ELEMENT B (#PCDATA)* >
<!ELEMENT I (#PCDATA)* >
<!ELEMENT PRE (TT)* >
<!ENTITY quot "&quot;" >
```

I chose to implement the code that selects and presents errata as a JavaBean so that the class could be used by a servlet, a JSP page, or an applet. Because queries for errata at our Web site are infrequent, using the SAX model instead of DOM is the best way to minimize memory use by the server. Queries from users may also select only recent additions or the most significant errors so there is no good reason to keep the entire structure in memory.

A single errata entry is shown in Listing 6.7. The page attribute value "CS" stands for "Cram Sheet," a special book insert.

Listing 6.7: A single errata entry

```
<Errata page="CS" printing="1,2" significance="1"
author="WBB" datemod="990603">Cram Sheet item 16 should state:<br/>
Division by zero in floating point arithmetic: No exception occurs; instead ➦
the result is one of the special values, <b>NaN, NEGATIVE_INFINITY</b> or ➦
<b>POSITIVE_INFINITY</b> defined in the <b>Float</b> and <b>Double</b> ➦
wrapper classes.
</Errata>
```

The ErrataParserBean Class

The ErrataParserBean class is an extension of the HandlerBase convenience class in the org.xml.sax package. HandlerBase extends java.lang.Object and implements the SAX interfaces EntityResolver, DTDHandler, DocumentHandler, and ErrorHandler. This bean gets search criteria from a form submission and scans the XML file for a particular book, creating formatted output from each entry that matches the criteria.

Listing 6.8 shows the class declaration and the static variables and methods. The parser-Class variable is provided in case you decide to experiment with parsers other than the default Sun parser.

Listing 6.8: The start of the ErrataParserBean source code

```
import java.io.* ;
import java.util.* ;
import org.xml.sax.* ;
import org.xml.sax.helpers.ParserFactory ;
import com.sun.xml.parser.Resolver ;

public class ErrataParserBean extends HandlerBase
{
  static public String parserClass = "com.sun.xml.parser.Parser" ;
  static public String crlf = "\r\n" ;
  // these provide default formatting tags
  static public String[] bookTitle = {"<h2>", "</h2>"};
  static public String[] bookISBN = {"<b>ISBN ", "</b>" };

  // these relate the elements that represent xhtml to the output
  static String[] tagnames = { "br","tt","b","i","pre"  };
  static String[] startT = { "<br />", "<tt>","<b>","<i>","<pre>"};
  static String[] endT = {  "", "</tt>","</b>","</i>","</pre>" };

  static String[] monthstr = {
"Jan", "Feb", "Mar", "Apr", "May", "Jun", "Jul", "Aug", "Sep", "Oct", "Nov", ➡
"Dec"};
  static String[] monthnum = {
"01", "02", "03", "04", "05", "06", "07", "08", "09", "10", "11", "12" };

  // hashtables providing fast lookup for various functions
  static public Hashtable startHash, endHash, monthHash, signifHash ;
  static { // static initialization block
    startHash  = new Hashtable();
    endHash    = new Hashtable();
    monthHash  = new Hashtable();
    signifHash = new Hashtable();
    for( int i = 0 ; i < tagnames.length ; i++ ){
      startHash.put(tagnames[i], startT[i] );
      endHash.put(  tagnames[i], endT[i]   );
```

```
    }
    for( int n = 0 ; n < 12 ; n++ ){
      monthHash.put( monthstr[n], monthnum[n] );
    }
    signifHash.put("1","Major errors only");
    signifHash.put("2","Major and moderate errors");
    signifHash.put("3","All errors");
  }
```

Listing 6.9 continues the class with the instance variables that are parsed out of each <Errata> tag by the startElement method and the search criteria variables that are set by a query.

Listing 6.9: The ErrataParserBean code continues with instance variables

```
// values taken from <Errata tag attributes as they are parsed
  String page ;
  String printing ;
  String significance ;
  String author ;
  String datemod ; // yymmdd - 991231 is followed by A00101
  boolean match ;
  // title and ISBN
  String title ;
  boolean lookForTitle ;
  String isbn ;

  String href ; // as found with <A tag elements

  // search criteria
  String prntSC = "Any" ;
  String signifSC = "3" ; // default = all
  String datemodSC = "970101" ; // compact format of search date
  String yearSC = "1997" ;
  String monSC = "Jan" ;
  String daySC = "01" ;
  int hitCt = 0 ;
  // Input source
  String srcFile, srcPath ;
  InputSource input ;
  StringWriter swrite ;
  PrintWriter out ;
```

Next, we have the constructor in Listing 6.10, which must be a no-arguments style constructor because the object will be created as a bean. This is followed by the access methods that follow the bean syntax that permits use of the JSP setProperty tag using this syntax

```
<jsp:setProperty name="errataParserBean" property="*" />
```

which automatically associates named parameters from a form input with bean variables. For example, the form variable named dtyr will be associated automatically with the setDtyr method to set the `yearSC` search criteria `String`. Note that the `setWriter` method lets the calling JSP or servlet pass an object to receive the bean output.

Listing 6.10: The ErrataParserBean code continues

```java
// as a Bean, must have a no-args constructor
public ErrataParserBean(){}

public void setWriter( PrintWriter pw ){out = pw; }
public void setErrataPath(String s){ srcPath = s ; }

// these set methods correspond to form variable names
public void setErrataFile(String s){ srcFile = s ; }
public void setPrver(String s ){ prntSC = s ; }
public void setSignif(String s){ signifSC = s ; }
public void setDtyr( String s ){ yearSC = s ; }
public void setDtmo( String s ){ monSC = s ; }
public void setDtdy( String s ){
  if( s.length() == 1 ) daySC = "0" + s ;
  else daySC = s ;
}
```

In Listing 6.11, we have the `checkForMatch` method, which compares the attributes of an errata entry with the search criteria values. This is followed by the `setDateMod` method that converts the year, month, and day search criteria into the compact form used in the XML.

Listing 6.11: The ErrataParserBean code continues

```java
// return true if this set of parameters match search criteria
boolean checkForMatch(){
  boolean ret = true ; //assume true and disqualify
  int n = datemodSC.compareTo(datemod);
  if( n > 0 ) return false ;
  if( !prntSC.equals("Any")){ // prntSC will be a short string
    if( printing.indexOf( prntSC ) < 0 ) return false ;
  }
  n = signifSC.compareTo( significance );
  if( n < 0 ) ret = false ;
  return ret ;
}

// turn search criteria dates into compact format
void setDateMod(){
  int yr = 1997 ;
  String yrstr = null ;
  try{ yr = Integer.parseInt( yearSC );
  }catch(NumberFormatException ne){}
  if( yr < 2000 ) yrstr = yearSC.substring( 2 ); // 97 - 99
  else yrstr = "A" + yearSC.charAt( 3 ); // A0 - A9
  String mostr = (String) monthHash.get( monSC );
```

```
      if( mostr == null ) mostr = "00" ;
      datemodSC = yrstr + mostr + daySC ;
   }
```

The process of scanning an XML file is carried out by the getErrata method as shown in Listing 6.12. I have provided two alternatives for output of formatted text. If the calling JSP or servlet calls setWriter to provide an output stream, it will be used; otherwise, a String-Writer object is created, and the entire formatted output is returned as a String by the getErrata method. Note that the code catching a SAXParseException provides for determining the line and column causing the error.

Listing 6.12: The getErrata method

```java
// This is the main method that accomplishes parsing.
// It traps all Exceptions and creates an error msg output.
// If out has not been set, it creates a StringWriter and
// uses that for output, returning the result as a String
public String getErrata(){
    Parser parser ;
    hitCt = 0 ;
    try {
      File f = new File( srcFile );
      input = Resolver.createInputSource( f );
      if( out == null ){
        swrite = new StringWriter( );
        out = new PrintWriter( swrite );
      }
      parser = ParserFactory.makeParser( parserClass );
      parser.setDocumentHandler( this );
      System.out.println("Start parse");
      parser.parse( input );
    }catch(SAXParseException spe){
        StringBuffer sb = new StringBuffer( spe.toString() );
        sb.append("\n  Line number: " + spe.getLineNumber());
        sb.append("\nColumn number: " + spe.getColumnNumber() );
        sb.append("\n Public ID: " + spe.getPublicId() );
        sb.append("\n System ID: " + spe.getSystemId() + "\n");
        return sb.toString();
    }catch(Exception e){
        return e.toString();
    }
    if( swrite != null  ){
        return swrite.getBuffer().toString();
    }
    return ""; // out must have been set elsewhere
}
```

Now we come to the methods that get called as the SAX parser detects various parsing events, starting in Listing 6.13.

Listing 6.13: The methods called by the SAX parser

```java
// the following are required by DocumentHandler interface
public void startDocument(){
  setDateMod();
  System.out.println("Start Document");
  out.print("<br>"); out.print(crlf);
}
public void endDocument(){
  System.out.println("End Document");
  out.print("<br>");
  out.print("Total errata found = ");
  out.print( Integer.toString( hitCt ));
  out.print("<br>"); out.print(crlf);
  out.flush();
}

public void startElement( String name, AttributeList attrib)
    throws SAXException
{
  if( "BookErrata".equals( name )){
     isbn = attrib.getValue("isbn");
     return ;
  }
  if( "Title".equals( name )){
      lookForTitle = true ; return ;
  }
  if( "Errata".equals( name ) ) {
    int ct = attrib.getLength();
    page = attrib.getValue("page");
    printing = attrib.getValue("printing");
    significance = attrib.getValue("significance");
    author = attrib.getValue("author");
    datemod = attrib.getValue("datemod");
    match = checkForMatch() ;  // determine if this matches criteria
    if( !match ) return ; // not a match
    hitCt++ ;
    out.print( exStartStr() );
    return ;
  }
  if( !match ) return ;
  // if we are in a matching item, need to process special tags <b <a etc.
  name = name.toLowerCase();
  String stag = (String) startHash.get( name );
  if( stag == null ){
    if( name.equals("a")){    // A tag gets special handling
      out.print("<a href=\"");
```

```
            href = attrib.getValue("HREF");
            if( href == null ) href = attrib.getValue("href");
            out.print( href );
            out.print("\" >");
        }
    }
    else out.print( stag );
    return ;
} // end startElement()

public void endElement(String name ){
    if( "Title".equals( name )){
        outputTitle(); return ;
    }
    if( !match ) return ;
    if( "Errata".equals( name )) {
        out.print("</p><br>"); out.print( crlf ); return ;
    }
    name = name.toLowerCase();
    String etag = (String)endHash.get( name );
    if( etag == null ){
        if( name.equals("a")){
            out.print( "</a>" );
        }
        return ;
    }
    out.print( etag );
} // end endElement

// only print if we are in a matching errata item
public void characters( char[] buf, int start, int count ){
    if( lookForTitle ){
        title = new String( buf, start, count );
        // must be at start, output title and isbn
        lookForTitle = false ;
    }
    if( !match ) return ;
    out.write( buf, start, count );
}
```

Listing 6.14 gives methods that create HTML formatting for errata entries. Significance is indicated by the color applied.

Listing 6.14: Methods that supply HTML formatting of errata entries

```java
// the following are formatting methods

// assumes attributes have been set - displays significance and page
// in start of <p> paragraph
private String exStartStr(){
  StringBuffer sb = new StringBuffer(100);
  sb.append("<p><b><FONT COLOR=\"" );
  switch( significance.charAt(0)){
     case '1' : sb.append("red\">"); break ;
     case '2' : sb.append("blue\">");break ;
     default : sb.append("teal\">"); // case 3 and unknown
  }
  // page can be CS, a roman numeral or a page number
  if( page.equals("CS")){
     sb.append("On Cram Sheet ") ;
  }
  else {
     sb.append("On page "); sb.append( page );
  }
  // superscript printing numbers in angle braces
  sb.append("<sup>");
  StringTokenizer st = new StringTokenizer( printing,",");
  while( st.hasMoreTokens()){
    sb.append("&lt;"); sb.append( st.nextToken()); sb.append("&gt;");
  }
  sb.append( "</sup></font></b>, ");
  return sb.toString() ;
}

// writes title, isbn and selection criteria
void outputTitle(){
  out.print(bookTitle[0]); out.print(title);out.print(bookTitle[1]);
  out.print(bookISBN[0]); out.print( isbn);out.print(bookISBN[1] );
  out.print("<br>");
  out.print(crlf);
  out.print("<p>Errata selected for ");
  out.print( signifHash.get( signifSC ));
  out.print("   Printing = "); out.print( prntSC );
  out.print(" and errata entered on or after ");
  out.print( yearSC ); out.print(" ");
  out.print( monSC  ); out.print(" ");
  out.print( daySC  ); out.print("</p>"); out.print(crlf);
}
```

```
    // general debug
    public String toString()
    { StringBuffer sb = new StringBuffer("ErrataParserBean ");
      return sb.toString() ;
    }

}
```

As I discussed in Chapter 5, "Debugging," the complex environment of a Web server is not the ideal place to debug Java code because so many things can go wrong. It is faster and a lot less frustrating to test as much of your code as possible in a controlled environment. In the case of the `ErrataParserBean`, I debugged parsing and formatting functions with a simple graphical user interface (GUI) test rig. This test program, shown in Figure 6.3, was built using `java.awt.Choice` widgets to simulate the HTML form that will be used in an actual Web server. Formatted output goes to a `java.awt.TextArea` so that it can be examined in detail.

FIGURE 6.3
The program used to test
the ErrataParserBean

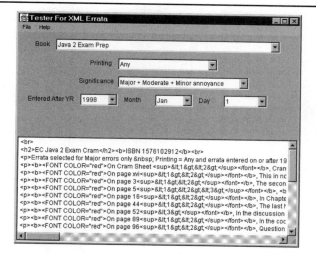

Figure 6.4 shows formatted output as rendered by a Web browser.

FIGURE 6.4
HTML output from the
ErrataParserBean rendered
in a Web browser

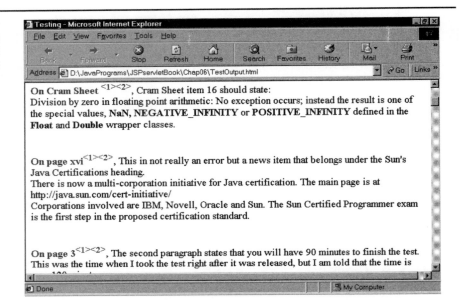

A DOM Example

The example I use to illustrate DOM programming is a requirement on a Web site to display items from a list of publications in a variety of formats. This application is characterized as described here:

- The list of publications is accessed frequently.
- The total list size is less than 100kb of text.
- The XML list is maintained and validated offline.
- Several different forms of output are desired.
- The ability to search for and sort items must be provided.
- New items are added only occasionally.

These requirements are all best met by a DOM approach because that keeps the entire set of entries in the server memory.

The Publications DTD

The DTD devised for this application is shown in Listing 6.15. There are two primary kinds of entry, Book and Article, which have many common attributes. Naturally, there are also some attributes unique to each, such as Cdrom for Book and Pages for Article.

Listing 6.15: The Publications DTD used in the example

```
<!ELEMENT Publications (Book|Article)* >
<!ATTLIST Publications date CDATA #IMPLIED>
<!ELEMENT Book
    (Title|Author|Edition|DatePublished|Publisher|Press|
    Series|Size|Topic|Cover|Errata|BriefDescription|Cdrom)* >
<!ATTLIST Book isbn CDATA #IMPLIED>
<!ELEMENT Title (#PCDATA)* >
<!ELEMENT Author (#PCDATA)* >
<!ELEMENT Edition EMPTY >
 <!ATTLIST Edition edition CDATA #IMPLIED>
<!ELEMENT DatePublished EMPTY >
 <!ATTLIST DatePublished year CDATA #IMPLIED>
<!ATTLIST DatePublished month CDATA #IMPLIED>
<!ELEMENT Publisher (#PCDATA)* >
<!ELEMENT Press (#PCDATA)* >
<!ELEMENT Series (#PCDATA)* >
<!ELEMENT Size EMPTY >
 <!ATTLIST Size pp CDATA #IMPLIED>
 <!-- Size is total book length -->
<!ELEMENT Cover EMPTY >
 <!ATTLIST Cover img CDATA #IMPLIED>
<!ELEMENT Topic (#PCDATA)* >
<!ELEMENT Errata EMPTY >
 <!ATTLIST Errata code CDATA #IMPLIED>
<!ELEMENT BriefDescription (#PCDATA)* >
<!ELEMENT Cdrom EMPTY >
 <!ELEMENT Article
 (Title|Author|Publisher|DatePublished|Pages|Topic|BriefDescription)* >
<!ELEMENT Pages EMPTY >
 <!ATTLIST Pages pp CDATA #IMPLIED>
 <!-- Pages is used to give an article page range -->
```

An example entry for a single book is shown in Listing 6.16. Notice the <Topic> elements, because one of the program examples demonstrates extracting the text from these elements for presentation using a JavaBean.

Listing 6.16: A single Book element

```
<Book isbn="1576102912" >
<Title>Java 2 Exam Cram</Title>
<Author>Bill Brogden</Author>
<Edition edition="1" />
<DatePublished year="1999" />
<Publisher>The Coriolis Group</Publisher>
<Press>Certification Insider Press</Press>
<Series>Exam Cram</Series>
<Size pp="388"/>
<Cover img="images/j2ec.gif" />
<Topic>Java</Topic>
<Topic>Certification</Topic>
<Topic>Exam 310-025</Topic>
<Topic>Certified Programmer for the Java 2 Platform</Topic>
<Topic>Study Guide</Topic>
<Errata code="ecj2" />
<BriefDescription>This compact study guide concentrates on the topics covered ➥
in Sun's Java 2 programmer certification exam.
Numerous questions similar to those on the real exam are presented and ➥
discussed.
</BriefDescription>
</Book>
```

A DOM Library Function

As I suggested in Table 6.3, the DOM approach is ideal if you need access to all the elements of an XML document, as long as the size is reasonable to keep in memory. Given the computational expense involved in creating a DOM, it is wise to keep it in memory if there is a reasonable chance it will be reused. However, keeping track of the uses of a particular DOM object requires some management functions that I have implemented in the DOMlibrary class as an example that you could expand to fit your own situation.

The DOMlibrary class follows the "singleton" design pattern in which static variables and methods are used to ensure that only one instance of the class is created. The reason we want to use an instance rather than all static methods and variables is that the management functions require a separate Thread; so DOMlibrary implements the Runnable interface. Listing 6.17 shows the import statements and the static variable and method that manage the single instance. Note that the getLibrary function is synchronized so that there is no way that multiple instances could be created.

Listing 6.17: A class to manage DOM objects

```
package com.JSPbook.Chap06 ;

import java.io.* ;
import java.util.* ;
import com.sun.xml.tree.* ;
import com.sun.xml.parser.Resolver ;
import org.xml.sax.* ;
import org.w3c.dom.* ;

public class DOMlibrary implements java.lang.Runnable
{
  private static DOMlibrary theLib ;
  public synchronized static DOMlibrary getLibrary(){
    if( theLib == null ) theLib = new DOMlibrary();
    return theLib ;
  }
```

The constructor and instance variables are shown in Listing 6.18. The main instance variables are two Hashtable objects, one to hold Document objects and the other to hold management information. The Thread that is created in the constructor to execute the run method is given minimum priority.

Listing 6.18: The DOMlibrary instance variables and constructor

```
// instance variables below this
private Hashtable domHash, timestampHash ;
boolean running ;
private String lastErr = "none" ;
// private constructor to ensure singleton
private DOMlibrary(){
  domHash = new Hashtable();
  timestampHash = new Hashtable();
  Thread upkeep = new Thread("DOMlibrary upkeep");
  upkeep.setPriority( Thread.MIN_PRIORITY );
  running = true ;
  upkeep.start();
}
```

In this approach, XML documents are located in the getDOM method shown in Listing 6.19 by a String giving an absolute path to a file. The path is used to retrieve the document object from a Hashtable or to read it in if it isn't available in memory.

Probably a better approach would be to have a properties file relating the document title to the file location. That would let you download files via a URL in addition to local files.

Every time a document is retrieved, the current time is stored in the `timestampHash` Hashtable as a `Long` object. This timestamp could be used to choose relatively unused documents to be discarded from memory. An alternative would be to create an object specifically to track usage.

Note that if the `loadXML` method encounters an error, it stores a `String` with error information in the `Hashtable`. When `getDOM` finds a `String` in the `domHash`, it returns null. This means that the library will not repeat an attempt to read a document if it contains an error. It is up to the programmer to fix the error and call `reloadDOM` to recover from this condition.

Listing 6.19: The DOMlibrary class listing continues

```
// either return the doc or null if a problem
public Document getDOM( String src ){
  Object doc = domHash.get( src );
  if( doc == null ){
      loadXML( src );
      doc = domHash.get( src );

  }
  if( doc instanceof Document ) {
     timestampHash.put( src, new Long( System.currentTimeMillis()));
     return (Document) doc ;
  }
  return null ; // error was encountered
}

// call this to force a reload after src is modified
public Document reloadDOM( String src ){
  if( domHash.get( src ) != null ){
    domHash.remove( src );
  }
  return getDOM( src );
}

private synchronized void loadXML(String src ) {
  File xmlFile = new File( src ) ;
  try {
    InputSource input = Resolver.createInputSource( xmlFile );
// ... the "false" flag says not to validate
    Document doc = XmlDocument.createXmlDocument (input, false);
    domHash.put( src, doc );
  }catch(SAXParseException spe ){
      StringBuffer sb = new StringBuffer( spe.toString() );
      sb.append("\n  Line number: " + spe.getLineNumber());
      sb.append("\nColumn number: " + spe.getColumnNumber() );
      sb.append("\n Public ID: " + spe.getPublicId() );
      sb.append("\n System ID: " + spe.getSystemId() + "\n");
      lastErr = sb.toString();
```

```
        domHash.put( src, lastErr );
        System.out.print( lastErr );
    }catch( SAXException se ){
       lastErr = se.toString();
       System.out.println("loadXML threw " + lastErr );
       domHash.put( src, lastErr );
       se.printStackTrace( System.out );
    }catch( IOException ie ){
       lastErr = ie.toString();
       System.out.println("loadXML threw " + lastErr +
         " trying to read " + src );
       domHash.put( src, lastErr );
    }
  } // end loadXML
```

Because this chapter is already getting pretty long and we have a lot more to cover, I have not included any upkeep functions in the run method shown in Listing 6.20.

Listing 6.20: The run method and some utility methods

```
    // run is used for upkeep, not reading XML
    public void run()
    { while( running ){
         try{ Thread.sleep( 100000 );
         // place upkeep code here
         }catch(InterruptedException e){
         }
       }// end while
    }

    public String getLastErr(){ return lastErr ; }

    public String toString()
    { StringBuffer sb = new StringBuffer("DOMlibrary contains ");
      int ct = domHash.size();
      if( ct > 0 ){
          sb.append(Integer.toString( ct ) );
          sb.append( " DOM objects ");
      }
      else { sb.append("no DOM objects");
      }
      sb.append(" Last error: " );
      sb.append( lastErr );
      return sb.toString();
    }
  }
```

The BookDOMbean Class

Now that we have the DOMlibrary class as a general way to create DOM documents in memory, the next thing we need is a class to pull information out of the document for presentation on a Web page. Listing 6.21 shows the import statements, the required no-arguments constructor, and the setSource method that gets a Document read in.

Listing 6.21: Start of the BookDOMbean class

```
package com.JSPbook.Chap06 ;

import java.io.* ;
import java.util.* ;
import com.sun.xml.tree.* ;
import com.sun.xml.parser.Resolver ;
import org.xml.sax.InputSource;
import org.xml.sax.SAXException;
import org.xml.sax.SAXParseException;
import org.w3c.dom.* ;

public class BookDOMbean
{
  Document doc ;

  public BookDOMbean(){}

  public void setSource(String src ){
    DOMlibrary lib = DOMlibrary.getLibrary();
    doc = lib.getDOM( src );
  }
```

Now we are ready for some methods to search the document and return data for use in presentation of HTML forms. The first one we will look at can be used to collect all the unique <Topic> text in a publications.dtd (refer to Listing 6.15) formatted XML file. The collectValues method shown in Listing 6.22 locates all Elements with the specified name and collects the text associated with the Element. To avoid keeping duplicate String values, we just store them temporarily in a Hashtable. The values from the Hashtable are put in an array and sorted.

Listing 6.22: The collectValues method in BookDOMbean

```
    // object is to collect the text associated with elements having s name
    // from the entire list and produce an array of unique values
    public String[] collectValues( String s ){
      Hashtable hash = new Hashtable();
      Element E = doc.getDocumentElement();
      NodeList vlist = E.getElementsByTagName( s );
      String tmp = null ;
```

```
      int n, i, ct = vlist.getLength();
      for( i = 0 ; i < ct ; i++ ){
        Node en = vlist.item( i );
        if( en.getNodeType()== Node.ELEMENT_NODE ){
          NodeList clist = en.getChildNodes();
          int nch = clist.getLength();
          if( nch > 0 ){
            for( n = 0 ; n < nch ; n++ ){
              Node cn = clist.item(n);
              if( cn.getNodeType() == Node.TEXT_NODE ){
                tmp = cn.getNodeValue();
                hash.put( tmp, tmp );
              }
            }
          }
        }
      } // loop over vlist
      ct = hash.size(); // number of unique values
      String[] ret = new String[ ct ];
      Enumeration e = hash.keys();
      n = 0 ;
      while( e.hasMoreElements() ){
          ret[n++] = (String)e.nextElement();
      }
      if( ct > 1 ) shellSort( ret );
      return ret ;
    }
```

In the publications DTD, International Standard Book Number (ISBN) numbers are an attribute found in the <Book> tag. Getting at attributes by name requires another version of the collectValues method, as shown in Listing 6.23.

Listing 6.23: A version of collectValues to collect attributes

```
  // similar except select element el and collect values of attribute attrib
  // from the entire document
    public String[] collectValues( String el, String attrib ){
      Hashtable hash = new Hashtable();
      Element E = doc.getDocumentElement();
      NodeList nlist = E.getElementsByTagName( el );
      String tmp = null ;
      int n, i, ct = nlist.getLength();
      for( i = 0 ; i < ct ; i++ ){
        Node en = nlist.item( i );
        if( en.getNodeType()== Node.ELEMENT_NODE ){
          tmp = ((Element)en).getAttribute( attrib );
          if( tmp != null && tmp.length() > 0 ){
              hash.put( tmp, tmp );
          }
          else hash.put("unknown","unknown");
        }
```

```
    } // loop over nlist
    ct = hash.size(); // number of unique values
    String[] ret = new String[ ct ];
    Enumeration e = hash.keys();
    n = 0 ;
    while( e.hasMoreElements() ){
        ret[n++] = (String)e.nextElement();
    }
    if( ct > 1 ) shellSort( ret );
    return ret ;
}
```

Listing 6.24 continues the class with some utility methods to retrieve String values from a given Element by name. The getText method is used for elements that have associated text, whereas the getAttributeText locates attributes by name.

Listing 6.24: BookDOMbean continued

```
// from the nd Element
// get the text associated with child nodes having name
public String getText(Element nd, String name ){
  StringBuffer sb = new StringBuffer();
  NodeList tlist = nd.getElementsByTagName( name );
  int ct = tlist.getLength();
  if( tlist.getLength() > 0 ){
    for( int i = 0 ; i < ct ; i++ ){
      Node en = tlist.item(i); // text is a child of Element node
      NodeList clist = en.getChildNodes();
      sb.append( clist.item(0).getNodeValue() );
      if( ct > 1 && i < (ct - 1) ){
        sb.append(", ");
      }
    }
  }
  else sb.append("not available");
  return sb.toString();
}

// from the Element nd, get the text from attributes named attrib
// from child nodes of type name
public String getAttributeText(Element nd, String name, String attrib ){
  StringBuffer sb = new StringBuffer();
  NodeList tlist = nd.getElementsByTagName( name );
  int ct = tlist.getLength();
  if( tlist.getLength() > 0 ){
    for( int i = 0 ; i < ct ; i++ ){
      Node en = tlist.item(i); // text is a child of Element node
      if( en instanceof Element ){
        sb.append(((Element)en).getAttribute( attrib ) );
```

```
                 if( ct > 1 && i < (ct - 1) ){
                    sb.append(", ");
                 }
              }
           }
        }
        else sb.append("not available");
        return sb.toString();
     }
```

Listing 6.25 shows a simple method that does a little formatting of the title and ISBN number of a <Book> Element.

Listing 6.25: BookDOMbean continued

```
     // shortest output format Title and ISBN
     public String shortTitle(Element nd ){
       StringBuffer sb = new StringBuffer();
       NodeList tlist = nd.getElementsByTagName( "Title" );
       if( tlist.getLength() > 0 ){
         Node en = tlist.item(0); // should have only one title per book
         NodeList clist = en.getChildNodes();
         sb.append( clist.item(0).getNodeValue() );
       }
       else sb.append("No Title Available");
       sb.append(" isbn:");
       String isbn = nd.getAttribute("isbn");
       if( isbn != null ) sb.append( isbn );
       else sb.append( "No ISBN found");
       return sb.toString();
     }
```

Finally, in Listing 6.26, we have some utility methods. The toString method returns some information about the state of the object, and the shellSort method sorts an array of String objects.

Listing 6.26: Utility methods in BookDOMbean

```
     public String toString()
     { StringBuffer sb = new StringBuffer("BookDOMbean ");
        if( doc == null ) sb.append(" DOM not loaded");
        else {
           sb.append("Document: " );
           sb.append( doc.getDoctype().getName() );
        }
        return sb.toString();
     }

     public  void shellSort ( String[] items ) {
        // h is the separation between items we compare.
        int h = 1;
```

```
    while ( h < items.length ) {
        h = 3 * h + 1;
    }
    // now h is optimum
    while ( h > 0 ) {
        h = (h - 1)/3;
        for ( int i = h; i < items.length; ++i ) {
            String item = items[i];
            int j=0;
            for ( j = i - h;
                  j >= 0 && item.compareTo( items[j] ) < 0;
                  j -= h ) {
                items[j+h] = items[j];
            } // end inner for
            items[j+h] = item;
        } // end outer for
    } // end while
} // end sort
}
```

Using BookDOMbean in a JSP Page

To exercise the BookDOMbean, I created the code shown in Listing 6.27. It uses the two collectValues methods to create forms with selectable lists of topics and ISBN numbers.

Listing 6.27: The BookTopics.jsp page

```
<html>
<head>
<title>Topics List</title>
</head>
<body BGCOLOR="#FFFFFF" TEXT="#000000">
<font FACE=VERDANA>
<h2 ALIGN=CENTER>Demonstrating DOM access to Books
</h2><br>
<%@ page language="java" errorPage="/JSPbook/Chapt06/whoops.jsp" %>
<jsp:useBean id="bookBean" scope="page"
       class="com.JSPbook.Chap06.BookDOMbean" >
</jsp:useBean>
<jsp:setProperty name="bookBean" property="source"
     value="c:\\InetPub\\wwwroot\\JSPbook\\pubs.xml" />
<%! String[] topics, isbns ;
%>
<%
  topics = bookBean.collectValues("Topic") ;
  isbns  = bookBean.collectValues("Book", "isbn" );
%>
<center>
<table border="4" bordercolor=gray cellpadding="8" >
<tr><td align="center">
<form METHOD="post" ACTION="/JSPbook/Chap06/ShowBooks.jsp" >
```

```
Please select a topic.<br><br>
<select name="topic" >
<%
  for( int i = 0 ; i < topics.length ; i++ ){
    out.print( "<option value=\"" + topics[i] + "\" >" + topics[i] + "\r\n" );
  }
%>
</select><br><br>
<input TYPE="submit" VALUE="Show" name="seltopic" >
</form></td>
<td align="center">
<form METHOD="post" ACTION="/JSPbook/Chap06/ShowBooks.jsp" >
Please select an ISBN number.<br><br>
<select name="isbn" >
<%
  for( int i = 0 ; i < isbns.length ; i++ ){
    out.print( "<option value=\"" + isbns[i] + "\" >" + isbns[i] + "\r\n" );
  }
%>
</select><br><br>
<input TYPE="submit" VALUE="Show" name="seltopic" >
</form>
</td></tr>
</table></center>
</body>
</html>
```

The presentation created by this form is shown in Figure 6.5.

FIGURE 6.5
Displaying the
BookTopics.jsp page

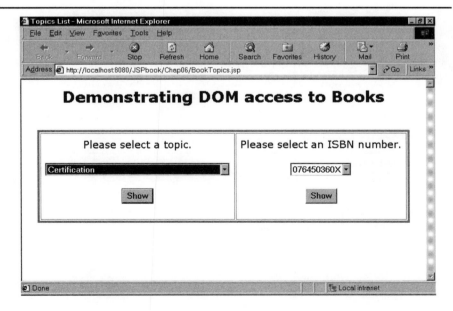

Alternatives to SAX and DOM

The perceived complexity of processing XML with the SAX and DOM approaches seems to have set off a flurry of experimentation with alternatives. Some of these approaches have reduced the functionality of parsers to achieve speed while keeping essential functions.

Java Document Object Model (JDOM)

Jason Hunter, co-author of the widely used *Java Servlet Programming* book, maintains a Web site at:

```
http://www.servlets.com
```

In spite of, or perhaps in consequence of, his familiarity with the DOM and SAX approaches, this Web site contains the following quotation introducing his proposed JDOM API for working with XML.

> *"There is no compelling reason for a Java API to manipulate XML to be complex, tricky, unintuitive, or a pain in the neck. JDOM^{TM} is both Java-centric and Java-optimized. It behaves like Java, it uses Java collections, it is a completely natural API for current Java developers, and it provides a low-cost entry point for using XML."*

Development of the JDOM follows an open-source approach similar to the Apache project. As of this writing, the JDOM code is still beta. For the current status of this project, visit `http://jdom.org/`.

Related Technology

The XML idea has really caught on; various schemes and technologies related to XML are popping up like mushrooms after a rain. Table 6.5 presents some technologies that seem to me to have some chance of being significant to the world of Java servlets and JSP.

TABLE 6.5: XML-related technology

Acronym	Stands for	Use
SOAP	Simple Object Access Protocol	Communication between programs.
SVG	Scalable Vector Graphics	A scalable vector graphic format based on XML.
XHTML	Extensible Hypertext Markup Language	A standard resulting from applying XML 1.0 rules to HTML 4.0.
Xlink	XML Linking Language (also known as XLL)	The rules for adding hyperlinks to XML documents.

TABLE 6.5: XML-related technology *(continued)*

Acronym	Stands for	Use
XLL	XML Linking Language (also referred to as XLink)	See Xlink.
XMI	XML Metadata Interchange Format	A standard of the OMG for exchanging data about data.
XPath		Rules for addressing internal elements in an XML document.
XQL	Extensible Query Language	Used for addressing and filtering the elements and text of XML documents.
XSL	Extensible Stylesheet Language	A stylesheet format for XML documents.
XSLT	Extensible Stylesheet Language Transformations	A language used to transform the structure of XML documents.
XUL	Extensible User-Interface Language	A standard for creating the user interface for a cross-platform application. See the Mozilla project at http://www.mozilla.org.

CHAPTER 7

Using Enterprise JavaBeans

- Sun's Vision of Large Scale Web Applications
- Do You Really Need EJB?
- EJB Technology Survey
- The Uses of Entity Beans
- The Uses of Session Beans
- Understanding the EJB Life Cycle

The Enterprise JavaBean (EJB) API is the foundation of the new generation of application Web servers. This chapter surveys the basic technologies used in EJB and discusses how servlets and JSP can use them.

Web Application Server Architecture

So far, the environments for Java servlets and JSP that we have discussed have been fairly simple. However, a Web server with a servlet engine living on a single CPU can handle only a limited amount of traffic. For large scale applications, the various software components may be distributed over a variety of systems.

Sun's vision of the ideal large scale application server is expressed in the Java 2 Enterprise Edition (J2EE) APIs and packages. The J2EE model is expected to bring the following advantages to application development:

- A standardized platform to ensure that applications developed on one server are portable to others.
- Standardization promotes competition between application vendors within the open standard to bring out the best implementation.
- Standardization creates a market for toolkits and utilities to support applications.

The Enterprise JavaBean (EJB) programming model is considered to be the essential core technology for J2EE. The programming model is as much about the services provided by the container for EJB as it is about the EJB internals. The EJB standard has gone through several cycles of change with extensive input from Sun's software industry partners. The current EJB API is version 1.1, and the next version (2.0) is in the public comment stage.

The topic of programming EJBs is much too large to cover here (the 2.0 specification is 525 pages). The purpose of this chapter is to acquaint you with the basic principles of EJBs in the J2EE environment. Hopefully, this chapter will help you decide if your particular servlet and JSP applications will require an EJB solution.

Thinking about Containers

Thinking about an application in terms of the relation between components and a *container* may seem an odd approach if your programming experience has been confined to desktop applications, but it is a very fruitful way of looking at Web-based applications. A container is responsible for providing an execution context and services for certain types of components. There are three containers in a J2EE Web application:

- The Web browser provides simple container services to a Java applet by managing URLs and TCP/IP connections, display graphics, and user events.

- The Web server container for Java servlets and JSP provides services that include managing Internet connections, threads, sessions, and contexts for page, session, and application.

- The Enterprise JavaBean container supports components for business logic, persistence, and connections to enterprise data sources. The EJB container has nothing to do with presentation.

Figure 7.1 shows this architecture diagrammatically. Separating functions this way allows a Web application to be distributed across as many systems as are required to do the job. The following list generalizes the communication between the parts:

Client with Web Server   Clients and web servers communicate with TCP/IP controlled streams of data in the familiar request/response form used by servlets and JSP. In addition to HTML and other forms of text, transmission of arbitrary binary data such as images and serialized objects can be expected.

Servlets with EJB Containers   Servlets always treat EJBs as remote objects accessed by network methods indirectly through connections mediated by the EJB container.

Servlets and JSP Direct with Databases   As an alternative to communicating with an EJB container, servlets can communicate with databases directly by using the JDBC standards or proprietary methods. With this approach, the servlets must manage database connections and persistence of database objects.

EJB with Databases   The Java Database Connectivity (JDBC) standard is the most practical form for this communication because JDBC drivers exist for most commercial databases, and a converter from JDBC to ODBC format is available from Sun.

FIGURE 7.1

The three containers in a Web application

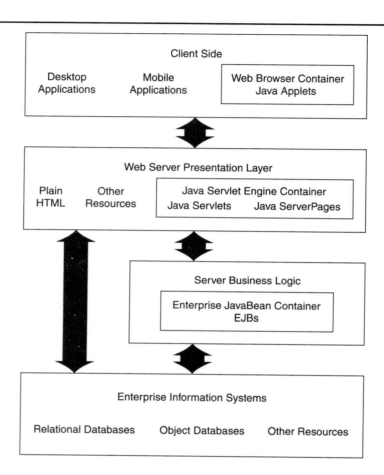

When Is It Appropriate to Use EJB?

An EJB solution is not necessarily the best way to handle all application server designs. Here are some of the points to consider:

Scaling Up   When an application has to be scalable to a networked environment with multiple computers, use of the J2EE architecture and EJBs gets your application online much sooner. On the other hand, if you are sure your application will stay within the capacity of a single server, EJBs may be overkill.

Heterogeneous Systems The J2EE architecture supports industry standards for communication between systems by different manufacturers. If all your application components come from the same vendor, you may not need this capability.

Security An EJB container can enforce security restrictions on access to data based on the class of users. If your application does not deal with sensitive data or you would prefer to create your own security, you may not need this EJB feature.

Transactions An EJB container can provide management of transactions so that equipment failure cannot corrupt a database. If your application does not involve database transactions, or if an occasional lost transaction is not a cause for alarm, you may not need this capability. For example, the danger of losing a single message in a chat server would certainly not justify an EJB solution.

Persistence An EJB container can provide for storing and restoring the vital data of an EJB object, giving the effect that the object is always available. Of course, there are other techniques for accomplishing this effect, such as an object-oriented database. Visit `http://www.odmg.org/`, the Web site of the Object Data Management Group, for an overview of object-oriented databases.

Toolkits As the J2EE standard becomes more widely accepted, numerous companies are creating toolkits that simplify creating and interfacing to EJB components. It may be that the functionality you need is available off the shelf, although possibly at a high price.

Alternatives

In the software business, there are always alternative ways to solve a problem. Here are some approaches for multi-tier applications that don't use J2EE and EJBs.

Direct JDBC Connections Your Java servlets and JSP can connect directly to databases with the JDBC standard. Classes that can improve the performance of this model by maintaining pools of database connections are widely available. Servlets using JDBC directly are discussed in Chapter 8.

The JavaSpaces Model of Distributed Objects The JavaSpaces approach to distributed objects has been developed in connection with Sun's JINI project. It is a more recent development and is less mature than EJB, but it has the virtue of simplicity. In this approach, the distributed components of applications are loosely coordinated by a JavaSpaces server that provides for storage and retrieval of Java objects. An object might represent a request for a particular database search, which a database server could use to locate and perform a search. I explore this use of distributed objects in Chapter 11.

Remote Method Invocation The standard Java library package, java.rmi, and related packages can be used to create an application composed of distributed objects without the extra overhead of EJB. Of course, this only works if you are entirely in a Java environment.

Direct Socket Communication   Servlets can use sockets to communicate with other programs on the network such as database interfaces. This requires some standardization of port numbers and other details, but it has the virtue of low overhead. Chapter 9 explores some of these possibilities.

Essential EJB Technology

Many of the Java packages and techniques used in working with EJBs will be unfamiliar to you if you have worked only with programs executing on a single computer in a relatively simple environment. This section reviews each of the essential technologies.

One of the hazards of trying to keep up with J2EE and EJB technology is the state of the various standard releases. For example, we have tried to use the latest (2.2) servlet and (1.1) JSP API terminology, but the servlet standard has introduced new terms such as WAR files that have not yet filtered down to the J2EE standard documentation.

Object Serialization

An object is serializable when it can be written to a byte stream format from one Java Virtual Machine and reconstructed intact in another Java Virtual Machine. This ability is absolutely essential to Remote Method Invocation (RMI) and the operation of Java programs in a distributed application.

The interfaces and classes essential to object serialization are found in the `java.io` package. The `Serializable` interface is used as a marker to indicate that an object can be written to a stream using the `ObjectOutputStream` class. Most standard library classes including `String` and primitive arrays are `Serializable`. `Serializable` objects must provide a no-arguments constructor.

When an object is serialized, all the objects that it has references to must also be serialized at the same time in order to permit reconstruction of the complete original object. For example, if object A contains a `Hashtable`, all the key and contents objects in the `Hashtable` will be serialized when object A is serialized. This can lead to a very time and memory consuming process, so it pays to keep an object that is to be serialized as simple as possible.

If your class needs to use a custom method of serializing itself, you can implement the `Externalizable` interface and provide your own methods for serializing your object's data. In order to reduce the bulk of a serialized object, you can use the `transient` modifier on all instance variables that do not have to be stored (for example, `String` objects that are built for temporary use).

As a simple collection of bytes, a serialized object can be stored in a database or written to a file and reconstituted as needed. Rebuilding an object from the byte stream requires that the JVM have access to the class file or files that define the object.

As you can readily imagine, an object built with one version of the class and serialized cannot be reconstituted with a new version of the class file if the new version uses different variables. When writing out an object, the `ObjectOutputStream` class computes a 64-bit version number based on the class file and attaches it to the object. The object reconstruction stream compares this version number to the one computed from its current copy of the class file and throws an exception if there is no match.

Because even the slightest change to a class can alter this computed version number, this can be very annoying during software development. You can override the computed version number process by creating your own version number as a `final static long` variable named `serialVersionUID`. As long as you don't change the names, order, and type of the instance variables, you can alter the methods and still recover serialized objects from earlier versions of the class.

CORBA

CORBA stands for Common Object Request Broker Architecture, a widely supported standard created by the Object Management Group, a software industry consortium. This standard enables communication between software objects written in different languages and running on different platforms. EJB architecture has a lot in common with CORBA, and EJB objects can communicate with software objects written in other languages using CORBA.

RMI and RMI IIOP

Remote Method Invocation (RMI) provides for essentially transparent communication between processes that may or may not reside on separate hardware. Internet Inter-ORB Protocol (IIOP), where ORB stands for Object Request Broker, is a standard for communication between objects. The combination of Java's RMI and IIOP provides a reliable means of communication between objects across networks.

The main Java toolkit for enabling RMI is the `java.rmi` package. For objects to be accessible for remote communication, you must implement the `Remote` interface. This interface has no methods but simply serves as an indicator. When you create methods that are open to RMI, they must be defined in a custom interface that extends `Remote`.

To permit your servlet to call methods in remote objects as if they were local objects, Java has to provide a way of handling exceptions generated in the remote object. This is accomplished with the `RemoteException` class or one of its descendents. When an exception is thrown by a remote method, it is encapsulated in a `RemoteException` for return to the calling method.

Communication between objects in separate processes requires a method for object A to locate object B; a simple method is provided by the RMI registry function. The Java SDK provides the rmiregistry.exe utility program that can be run from a command line. It listens at an established port for remote objects to register themselves as available and provides a way for other objects to locate remote objects by name. A more advanced location service is performed by the JNDI interface.

JNDI

The Java Naming and Directory Interface (JNDI) is used to locate Java components, EJBs, and other resources across a network. It is an extension of the RMI system that provides greater flexibility. In the EJB 1.1 API, all EJB containers are required to support JNDI.

JMS

The Java Message Service is implemented in the `javax.jms` package. It provides for asynchronous passage of messages between separate Java processes, a much more loosely coupled method of communication than RMI. Messages are passed correctly even if the intended recipient is temporarily offline. A message can consist of text or a variety of binary data types including serialized objects. The 1.2 version of the J2EE specification does not require support for JMS, but subsequent versions are expected to require that EJB containers provide this service.

Deployment Descriptor

Much effort in the design of J2EE and EJBs has gone into making it easy for a packaged application to be deployed on a new server. In the first version of EJB, a developer had to create a deployment descriptor class that accompanied the EJB class files in a jar file.

As of the EJB 1.1 and Java servlet 2.2 APIs, deployment descriptors are to be provided as XML formatted files. This is a much more flexible technique because parameters can be changed with a simple editor rather than by compiling Java code. Elements in the deployment descriptor include the names of all the classes and interfaces, indicators of the bean type (session or entity), and other parameters that the EJB container requires to build an environment to house the bean.

WAR and EJB-Jar Files

In the J2EE vision of portable Web applications, the goal is to be able to distribute a single file containing all the resources used by the application. The Java servlet API version 2.2 defines a WAR (Web Application Resource) file as a jar format file containing Java classes, JSP files, and static resources such as HTML pages and images. It also contains a web.xml file that serves as a deployment descriptor. The jar format is the familiar zip format and can be created by a command line utility in the Java Development Kit.

Ideally, to add a new servlet/JSP-based application to your servlet engine, you just create a new directory, drop in a WAR file, tell the server about it, and stand back. It is the responsibility of the server to unpack the files and place them in the correct directories. Because this requirement appeared only in the 2.2 servlet specification, commercial servlet engines still implement their own directory conventions.

As expressed in the Java servlet 2.2 specifications, a Web application has a single root directory that has certain required subdirectories. Static resources that are served directly to the client (such as HTML pages, Java applet class files, and JSP page files) are based in the root directory. Resources used on the server to create servlets and JSP are based in the WEB-INF directory attached to the root directory. As a security measure, the Web server is forbidden to serve any file directly from the WEB-INF directory. This directory organization is suggested by the following diagram:

```
Application Root
   |
   +- WEB-INF  <- the web.xml deployment descriptor file
      |
      +- lib   <- .jar files with Java classes
      |
      +- classes <- servlet and utility class files
```

On the EJB container side of an application server, the 1.1 EJB specification uses ejb-jar files as a similar packaging system. An ejb-jar file contains Java class files for the actual EJB and for the home and remote interfaces. It also must contain a deployment descriptor file in XML format. The goal of the designers of the EJB API is the separation of the functions of designing an EJB from the functions of configuring a working application.

EJB with JSP and Servlets

A Java servlet or JSP can only communicate with an EJB indirectly. Communication is accomplished through a set of interfaces known as the Home, Remote, and Metadata interfaces. The following interfaces in the `javax.ejb` package are used:

EJBHome   The home interface is used to obtain an initial connection to a particular EJB from the EJB container and also to create or remove a bean. This interface may include methods related to initializing instances of the EJB class.

EJBObject   A remote interface for each EJB is created by the EJB designer, extending `EJBObject`. This interface exposes the methods provided by the EJB to carry out useful work.

EJBMetaData   The metadata interface can be used to look up the capabilities that an EJB provides. This interface is primarily used by development tools.

Figure 7.2 shows a diagram of the indirect communication between a servlet and an EJB. The EJB container is responsible for creating a home object that exposes the bean's home interface, an extension of `EJBHome`. In addition to implementing the home interface, this object contains many details that are specific to the particular container and network configuration.

Generating the code for the home object is the responsibility of the EJB container, not the creator of the actual EJB. This separation of functionality frees an EJB designer from all details of the EJB container and network communication implementation.

When a servlet requests the home interface from the container, it gets a "stub" object that is RMI capable and communicates transparently with the EJB container. Creating the code for this stub is also the responsibility of the EJB container.

Using the home interface, the servlet can request one or more instances of objects that implement the remote interface as extensions of the EJBObject interface. The objects that the servlet gets are of course instances of a class created by the EJB container, implementing the user interface for the EJB object and also aware of the communication configuration.

The result of all of this indirection is that the servlet can call methods in the EJB and get back results as if it were a local object. All the details of communication are carried out transparently by the intervening objects.

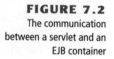

FIGURE 7.2

The communication between a servlet and an EJB container

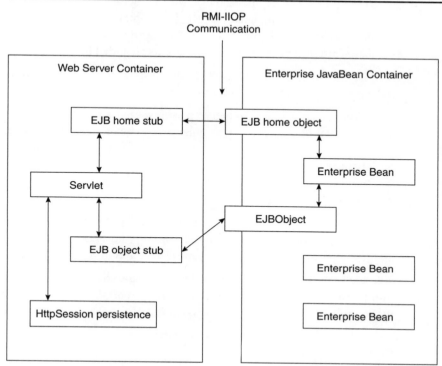

Basically, two types of EJB objects are defined in the 1.1 standard: entity and session objects. The 2.0 standard, which is in draft form as of this writing, adds a third type: message driven objects. The basic classes and interfaces are defined in the `javax.ejb` package.

Entity Beans

Entity bean objects are typically used to provide a Java object representation of data in a database or data provided by another application. They are characterized by a long lifetime and can be reconstructed from persistent storage every time the server is restarted. There are two models for relating persistent storage to an entity bean: "container-managed persistence" and "bean-managed persistence."

In container-managed persistence, the deployment descriptor for the bean lists the variables that are to be initialized, and the EJB container creates the necessary classes to perform the database queries required. This has the advantage of making the bean independent of database variation between vendors but puts an added burden on the deployment mechanism.

In bean-managed persistence, the EJB designer provides the complete mechanism for initializing a bean from a database or other application.

Entity beans must be designed to permit shared access by multiple users. EJB containers can use a pool of objects of a particular bean type to facilitate a high rate of transactions. In general, EJB containers must provide a scalable runtime environment to manage a large number of entity beans.

Session Beans

In Chapter 3, we discussed the use of `HttpSession` objects to preserve session information for a particular Web user between request-response transactions in the context of Java servlets and JSP. A session type EJB has a similar function in the context of an EJB container.

A session bean is always associated with a single client and typically maintains state information between client transactions. A session bean may assist in a transaction and update information in a database, but it depends on entity beans for database representations.

The EJB standard also provides for stateless session beans that are used for various auxiliary functions.

Outline of EJB Usage

This section outlines the typical sequence of events by which a servlet would make use of EJBs. Let us assume that the application is a fairly typical online catalog and shopping cart application.

Servlet init Method

In the `init` method, the servlet locates working parameters for contacting the JNDI services. References to the home interfaces of entity EJBs representing permanent system resources, such as the product catalog and shipping cost calculator, are typically obtained at this time.

First User Request

On initial entry to the servlet, the product catalog bean is used to create an ordering form. A session bean representing the "shopping cart" can be created and stored in the corresponding `HttpSession` at this time. Note that this is a "stateful" session bean because it records the state of the user's order.

Subsequent Requests

Subsequent requests have to process possible user actions such as changing the selection quantities or proceeding to checkout. Selection changes are all made by calling shopping cart bean methods as defined in the custom remote interface, an extension of EJBObject. The ordering form is then re-created showing the current selections.

If the user has decided to check out, the entity bean representing shipping cost calculation is called to compute shipping charges that are added to the shopping cart bean.

The Future of EJB

Enterprise JavaBean support is now widely available in application servers and appears to be widely accepted in the industry. However, the technology may not be the best solution to every server problem. I hope the overview in this chapter will aid you in deciding whether or not to jump into using EJBs.

CHAPTER 8

Servlets, JSP, and JDBC Connections

- Relating Java Variable Types to SQL
- Understanding the JDBC API
- Creating a Database Query in a Servlet
- Extracting Data from a Query Response

In the early days of computing, each database system had a query language that was completely different from all other systems, which made it very difficult to move an application between databases. However, a great push for standardization produced SQL (Structured Query Language), which is widely supported as a common database language. Java provides the JDBC (Java Database Connectivity) toolkit for Java programs to use for connecting with relational databases using SQL.

Practically all major relational database products now provide a JDBC style interface. This chapter will discuss the various considerations Java programmers must take into account when connecting a servlet or JSP to a database using JDBC.

Introduction to JDBC

The Java Database Connectivity API is designed to give Java programmers a consistent set of classes and methods for access to a wide variety of databases. Commercial databases use many different file structures and algorithms, so creating a unified set of access methods is not a trivial task. At the present state of development, the JDBC API offers access to the most commonly used functions of commercial relational databases. This is possible only because of a degree of convergence and standardization in the database management industry on relational database structure and the Structured Query Language (SQL) for expressing database operations.

The SQL standard is defined by the ISO (International Organization for Standardization) and ANSI (American National Standards Institute). Major releases of the standard are known as SQL86, SQL89, SQL92, and SQL99. Just to confuse things, SQL99 is also known as SQL3. Due to the large number of features that were added to SQL92, it has three levels of feature conformance known as entry-level, intermediate, and full. Most commercial products support the entry-level functionality and provide varying support for the higher levels.

There are two major versions of JDBC: 1.0 and 2.0. JDBC 1.0 has been part of the Java standard library since JDK 1.1. JDBC 2.0, which arrived with the release of Java 2, supports all JDBC 1.0 features and adds many improvements. The `java.sql` package contains the Java classes supporting the JDBC API at version 1.0 and most of the version 2.0 additions. The `javax.sql` package is considered a standard extension and contains additional classes added for JDBC 2.0.

Relational Databases

The basic idea of a Relational Database Management System (RDBMS) is that any database structure can be represented as one or more *tables* consisting of rows and columns. A single table looks like a flat-file database where each row is a single record, and the position of data within the row indicates what the data type is and how it is interpreted. For example, in

Table 8.1, the first column is an alphanumeric code, followed by three columns of text, followed by a logical entry, and an integer. Many discussions of RDBMS use the term "record" when speaking of a row and "field" when speaking of a column.

TABLE 8.1: An example row in a table

ID	Email	Last name	First name	Married	Birth year
124c41	Wbrogden@bga.com	William	Brogden	yes	1939

If another table in this database had rows corresponding to book purchase invoices, it would have to have a unique identifier for the customer in each invoice row in order for you to locate all book purchases by a particular customer. A relational database works by *relating* the data in separate tables based on data that is common between them, such as the customer ID.

Each table in an RDBMS must have at least one column or a combination of columns that has a unique value for each row. This column or combination of columns is the *primary key* for that table. When a value that is a primary key in one table appears in another table, it is said to be a foreign key.

When adding data or creating queries, you can address tables by name. Data columns can be addressed by name or by column position in the table. A large database system may consist of many tables, not all of which may be required for a particular job. A working group of table and variable names is called a database schema.

Other Database Designs

Many approaches to representing the structure of a database have been tried, including hierarchical trees and networks. For example, XML documents such as those discussed in Chapter 6 create a hierarchy with a single root element. It can be shown that these other structures can be turned into relational databases without loss of data, but potentially with a great loss of efficiency. For this reason, relational databases have not completely taken over all database jobs.

Talking SQL to Databases

Java programmers enjoy complete standardization of variable types between platforms. We know that an `int` is going to be a signed 32-bit integer whether it is on a mainframe or a Palm Pilot. Unfortunately, this degree of standardization does not exist in the SQL world, but there is enough standardization to make most Java applications portable.

The most widely supported SQL standard is known as SQL-92. A new standard called SQL-99 (also known as SQL3) is intended to better support object oriented programming.

The first step in accomplishing communication between a Java program and a database is the creation of a connection using a Java driver that is specific to the particular database. JDBC uses `java.sql.Connection` objects to represent a connection once it has been created by the `DriverManager` class through the `getConnection` method.

Communication between a program and a database once a connection has been established is accomplished by constructing and executing SQL statements and receiving results from the database. By convention, SQL keywords are written in uppercase, although this is not required. For example, a command to receive all the contents of a table named Address would look like the following, where `SELECT` and `FROM` are SQL keywords:

```
SELECT * FROM Address
```

Java commonly uses the `java.sql.Statement` interface to handle the transmission of text from an SQL statement to a database. `Statement` objects are always obtained through a method of the `Connection` class and are specific to a particular connection. In addition to `Statement`, the `java.sql` package also defines `PreparedStatement` and `CallableStatement`. `PreparedStatement` objects offer improved performance, and `CallableStatement` objects allow access to SQL procedures stored in a database.

SQL Statement Types

SQL statements or commands fall into three primary categories:

- *Creating and modifying entities.* These are the commands that create tables and other database entities, as distinct from the data the entities contain.

- *Creating, modifying, and retrieving data.* Commands such as `INSERT`, `UPDATA`, and `DELETE` modify data but not the table structure. Retrieval is based on `SELECT` commands.

- *Controlling user permissions.* These commands relate user roles to privileges.

Discussion of the details of SQL commands is well beyond the scope of this chapter. A good recent reference is *Mastering SQL*, by Martin Gruber, ISBN 0-7821-2538-7, published by Sybex. There is also considerable variation between commercial databases once you get away from the most common commands, so you may need documentation specific to a particular product.

While I am mentioning books, the definitive guide to JDBC is *JDBC API Tutorial and Reference, Second Edition*, by Seth White et al., ISBN 0-201-63459-7, published by Addison Wesley. This massive (1,060 page) book is the current official Sun guide to JDBC 2.0.

SQL Datatypes

One of the significant steps in creating an SQL database and designing a Java program to talk to it is working out the equivalence between SQL datatypes and Java datatypes. The Java class `java.sql.Types` has a list of constants that are used in Java programs to indicate SQL datatypes. The following is a quick survey of the relation of SQL datatypes to Java.

SQL Numeric Types

Here is a list of SQL numeric datatypes as defined in the SQL-92 standard and as they are named in SQL statements with a discussion of the usage and Java equivalents. Terms in parentheses are allowed alternatives.

INTEGER (INT)   A signed integer with unspecified precision. In practice, databases use at least a 32-bit integer, so it is usual to map INTEGER to Java's *int* primitive.

SMALLINT   A signed integer with implementation-specific size that uses less space than INTEGER. In practice, this is typically implemented as a 16-bit integer that maps to Java's `short` primitive.

TINYINT   An unsigned 8-bit integer. Apparently, this is not supported widely at present in commercial databases. Because Java's 8-bit primitive is signed, the cautious programmer will map this to the `short` primitive.

NUMERIC   This is a signed decimal having precision that is set when the programmer creates a NUMERIC variable. A typical use would be as a currency value. Because of the arbitrary precision, the recommended Java mapping is the `java.math.BigDecimal` class rather than `float` or `double` primitives.

DECIMAL   This is very similar to NUMERIC except that it may store a higher degree of precision using more decimal places.

REAL   A floating point number roughly equivalent to Java's `float` primitive.

DOUBLE PRECISION (DOUBLE)   A floating point number roughly equivalent to Java's `double` primitive.

SQL Character Types

The character-storing SQL92 types shown below generally can be treated as Java String objects. An exception might be the case in which LONGVARCHAR is used to store really large character sequences, in which case JDBC provides for reading the variable as a stream.

CHAR (CHARACTER)   A character variable with a fixed length set by the database creator. Java String variables stored in a CHAR will be padded with spaces or truncated to the fixed length. CHAR variables up to 254 characters in length are typically supported.

VARCHAR (CHARACTER VARYING)   Similar to CHAR except that String variables are not padded to the fixed length. Typically limited to 254 characters or less.

LONGVARCHAR   Similar to VARCHAR except that Strings can be much longer.

SQL Binary Types

There are three SQL datatypes that store byte sequences as binary data—data that the database does not attempt to interpret as characters or numbers. JDBC and SQL use the same name for BINARY and VARBINARY but different databases use non-standard names for long arrays of bytes. All of these types may be mapped to Java byte arrays, but in the event of really long variables of type, reading as a byte stream is more practical.

BINARY   Similar to CHAR, the number of bytes is fixed when the variable is created. Typically limited to 254 bytes.

VARBINARY   Similar to VARCHAR, an array of bytes with variable length up to 254. This is implemented on only a few databases.

Long arrays   There is no SQL standard name, but JDBC uses the LONGVARBINARY name and translates as required to the particular database. The maximum size depends on the vendor.

Advanced JDBC Datatypes

JDBC 2.0 attempts to keep up with new datatypes introduced with the SQL99 (also known as SQL3) standard. Two of these provide the basis for using a database with really large chunks of data because they allow a database entry to point to a data source using a data type called a *Locator* rather than including bulk data in database files. Obviously, transmitting large chunks of data across a network in response to a query would be extremely inefficient. By providing indirect access, these datatypes remove barriers that had prevented SQL databases from being complete solutions in typical Web applications. The following list describes these new datatypes:

BLOB   Short for Binary Large Object, this data type provides for efficient storage and retrieval of large chunks of binary data. Rather than containing the data, a retrieved BLOB points to the data source. This is the data type to use for images, audio files, and other multimedia.

CLOB   Similar to BLOB but for character data. A typical use is storage and retrieval of Web pages.

ARRAY   Another approach to accessing large blocks of data is provided by this data type. The corresponding JDBC Array object does not necessarily store all the data in memory, but it provides for addressing individual elements of the array stored in the database. Methods are also provided for bringing the entire array into memory if extensive manipulation is needed.

Obviously, the capability to store arbitrarily large binary data can be combined with Java's object serialization capabilities to store data in the form of Java objects. JDBC 2.0 provides the JAVA_OBJECT data type for this usage.

SQL99 also provides for stored procedures—that is, objects in the database that perform operations using SQL and other languages. This kind of flexibility so obviously fits in with Java's portable byte codes that an industry group has created SQLJ, a standard for incorporating Java into stored procedures.

The Four Types of JDBC Drivers

All JDBC drivers fall into one of four types. You might be forced to decide which type to use based on the necessity of connecting with a particular database. If you are fortunate, you can choose according to your needs for efficiency. Most database vendors now supply information and driver software to assist you in connecting to their systems.

Type 1 Drivers

This type, illustrated in Figure 8.1, communicates with databases that have an ODBC (Open Database Connectivity) interface. This widespread industry standard interface is available on many commercial databases. Sun created JDBC-to-ODBC bridge software as part of the Java standard library. Each standard JDBC database operation is translated into an ODBC operation for submission to the database, and returned results go through another translation stage. Because the database's native interface may not exactly correspond to ODBC standards, another translation process might be necessary. Naturally these extra translations take time, and not all JDBC operations can be supported this way.

FIGURE 8.1
Connecting to a database
with a type 1 driver

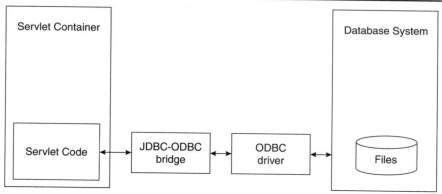

Type 2 Drivers

In this case, the JDBC driver interface is implemented in custom classes and native methods so that it can communicate directly with the database API. There is only one stage of translation from JDBC method calls to the database format and one stage of translation with returned data. However, because native code is involved, you may be giving up Java features such as garbage collection. A type 2 connection is shown in Figure 8.2.

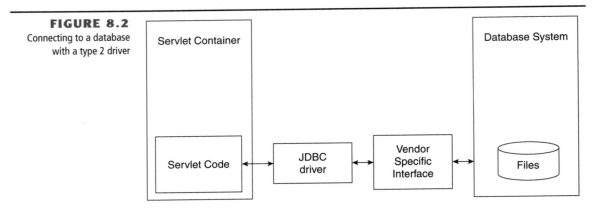

FIGURE 8.2
Connecting to a database with a type 2 driver

Type 3 Drivers

With type 3 drivers, an all-Java middle-tier application serves as an access point on the network for JDBC applications. This application can receive JDBC calls from clients and translate them to the required type 1 or type 2 access used by the actual database. This architecture is particularly suited to clients that are applets. Figure 8.3 shows a type 3 connection.

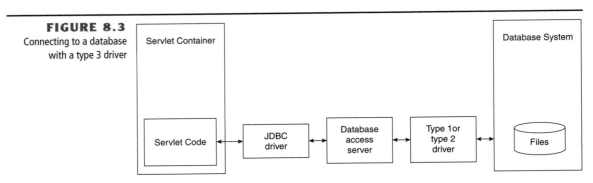

FIGURE 8.3
Connecting to a database with a type 3 driver

Type 4 Drivers

The type 4 driver (see Figure 8.4) provides an all-Java solution with a JDBC driver that can speak directly to the database interface. This is the most efficient solution because it requires no translation steps and a minimum of network connections. Most commercial database makers now provide type 4 drivers.

FIGURE 8.4

Connecting to a database
with a type 4 driver

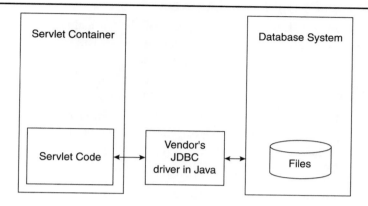

Finding a Database Engine

If you already have a relational database engine on your system, you can skip this section. Although a commercial RDBMS can be extremely expensive, we are fortunate that there is strong open-source support for SQL-capable database servers. Several of these projects have been so successful that commercial support organizations have been formed, thus eliminating the worry that you won't be able to find technical support with an open source system.

The MySQL Engine

An estimated half million servers around the world run the MySQL package because it provides an incredible amount of database power and the stability needed to operate a Web site. The database engine is written in C and C++ and was designed from the beginning to operate in a multi-threaded environment, which is an important consideration for working with servlets.

The developers of MySQL have released MySQL under the General Public License (GPL). Progress Software, which is supporting the further development of MySQL with a significant cash contribution, has formed NuSphere to distribute and support the NuSphere MySQL open source database. This switch in approach from selling the software to giving away the software and offering commercial support and training services for an open source database seems to be catching on in the industry. The status of this project can be found at the following Web site:

www.nusphere.com

The PostgreSQL Engine

PostgreSQL is a relatively sophisticated relational DBMS oriented toward the UNIX operating system. It supports almost all SQL constructs, including transactions and user-defined types and has some object-oriented extensions. It is generally considered to be more advanced than MySQL in terms of the number of SQL functions it supports. In 1999, PostgreSQL received the LinuxWorld Editors Choice Award for the best database management system.

This is an open source database, but there are also commercial operations, PostgreSQL, Inc., and GreatBridge, that can supply support and training. Visit these Web sites for more information:

```
http://www.postgresql.org/
http://www.greatbridge.com/
```

The HyperSQL Engine

One attraction of the Hypersonic SQL package is that it is 100% implemented in Java and comes with complete source code. This gives the student an excellent chance to look at the program underpinnings for JDBC. It has standard SQL syntax and a standard JDBC interface. Furthermore, it is free to use and redistribute. It is also extremely compact and supports a large number of SQL functions (but not all those required for the complete JDBC API). The home page for this open source project is located at:

```
http://hsql.oron.ch/
```

Examples are provided in the Hypersonic SQL package for servlets, applets, and standalone database server applications. This is an excellent starting package if you want to learn SQL and JDBC. Figure 8.5 shows one of the applications included in the package, a simple database manager implemented as an applet. The left panel shows the database schema composed of a number of simple tables. The top-right panel shows an SQL query that has been executed to create the data table shown in the bottom-right panel.

FIGURE 8.5
The Hypersonic SQL
Database Manager
demonstration

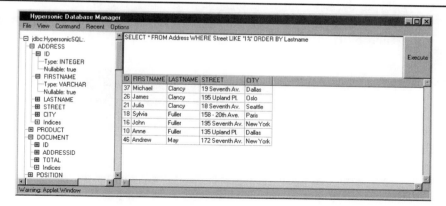

JDBC Database Creation

As my example program for this chapter, I have chosen to rework the XML-based `Errata-ParserBean` example from Chapter 6. The first thing we have to do is convert the XML data file into a database table. Creating a table with JDBC involves these steps:

1. Loading a Java driver class for the particular database
2. Obtaining a `Connection` using the `DriverManager` class
3. Getting a `Statement` object from the `Connection`
4. Using the `Statement` object to dispatch commands to the database

The initial steps 1, 2, and 3 can be as deceptively simple as the following statements that I used for a simple example:

```
Class.forName("org.hsql.jdbcDriver");
Connection conn = DriverManager.getConnection(
        "jdbc:HypersonicSQL:Errata","sa","" );
Statement stmt = conn.createStatement();
```

Getting a Connection

In general, the greatest amount of difficulty people have in getting started with JDBC is just locating the right driver and specifying the input to the `DriverManager getConnection` method. The `Class.forName` statement forces the JVM to load the specified Java class.

Typically, static initialization code in the class registers a new instance with the JDBC DriverManager class. For example, the following is a static initializer block in the Hypersonic SQL jdbcConnection class:

```
static {
  try {
    DriverManager.registerDriver(new jdbcDriver());
    if(Trace.TRACE) Trace.trace(PRODUCT+" "+MAJOR+"."+MINOR);
  } catch(Exception e) {
    if(Trace.TRACE) Trace.trace(e.getMessage());
  }
}
```

When the correct driver has been registered, you use the getConnection method in the DriverManager class to get a Connection object. These are the three String parameters to this getConnection method:

url   A database URL String is composed of several elements that indicate the connection type and the database source. In the above example, "jdbc:HypersonicSQL" matches the driver type, and "Errata" is the database name. If you were using Sun's JDBC-ODBC bridge driver, the URL would be "jdbc:odbc."

username   Exactly how username and password are used depends on the particular database. In this case, I am using the default for the Hypersonic SQL database.

password   As with username, the way this String is used depends on the database.

Other forms of getConnection use just the URL or the URL plus a Properties object. A Properties object would be expected to contain a property entry for "user" and one for "password."

Using a Statement to Send Commands

With an object implementing the Statement interface obtained from the Connection, you issue commands in the form of a String. The basic syntax for table creation is

```
CREATE TABLE tablename ( columnname datatype,..);
```

where CREATE and TABLE are SQL keywords, "tablename" is provided by the programmer, and the "columnname datatype" pair is repeated as needed. The tablename and columnname must not contain any spaces because spaces are considered separators. The datatype is one of the SQL datatypes, in some cases modified with other SQL commands. Some datatypes are declared with a decimal number in parentheses indicating their size. CHAR variables are always specified with a size, as shown here:

```
CREATE TABLE customer (
  lastname CHAR(25), firstname CHAR(20), emailadr CHAR(100) );
```

In Java, it is convenient to store frequently used SQL commands as arrays of `String` objects. Listing 8.1 shows the declaration of an array with two `String` objects that I use in this example program to create a table that will hold errata data.

Listing 8.1: Commands to create a table

```
static String[] creCmds = {
    "DROP TABLE errsql",
    "CREATE CACHED TABLE errsql(SEQ INTEGER PRIMARY KEY," +
    "isbn CHAR(12),Page CHAR(4),Printing INTEGER," +
    "Significance INTEGER, Author VARCHAR(10),Datemod CHAR(10)," +
    "Text VARCHAR )"
} ;
```

The DROP command discards any pre-existing version of the table. The line starting with CREATE creates a new table with the same name and having the variables shown in Table 8.2. The word CACHED is specific to the Hypersonic SQL database and forces the completed database structure to be written to a disk file. This table uses the CHAR, INTEGER, and VARCHAR datatypes. Recall from the SQL datatypes discussion that INTEGER is the equivalent of a Java `int`, and the character types are the equivalent of Java `String` objects.

TABLE 8.2: The variables for the errsql table

SQL variable	Type	Used for
SEQ	integer	Provides a unique key and preserves the order of the original data.
isbn	char	Identifies a book.
Page	char	We have to use char instead of a page number due to the presence of inserts, roman numeral page numbers, and other book elements that don't get a decimal number.
Printing	integer	The printing number is typically in the 1 - 10 range, but it could be higher.
Significance	integer	A numeric code where 1 is the highest significance, 2 is moderate, and 3 is a minor error.
Author	char	The person who created the errata entry (not the book author); this is used for quality control.
Datemod	char	Date last modified, as represented in the XML format.
Text	variable length char array	A complete HTML-formatted string of characters that could be several hundred bytes long.

The `ErrataToSQL` constructor shown in Listing 8.2 creates the table by executing the command `String` objects. The `Statement` method `executeUpdate` is called with each `String`, and any failure will cause an `SQLException`. And, because the DROP command will fail if there is not a pre-existing table, we need the try-catch block inside the loop so that the CREATE command will be executed even if DROP fails.

Listing 8.2: The first part of this constructor creates a table and adds data

```
ErrataToSQL( String srcFile )throws Exception{
    try {
        Class.forName("org.hsql.jdbcDriver");
        DriverManager.registerDriver( new org.hsql.jdbcDriver());
        System.out.println("Registered");
        conn = DriverManager.getConnection(
          "jdbc:HypersonicSQL:Errata","sa",""
        );
        stmt = conn.createStatement();
        System.out.println("Connection obtained");
        for(int i = 0 ; i < creCmds.length ; i++ ){
            try {
                stmt.executeUpdate( creCmds[i] );
                System.out.println("Executed " + creCmds[i] );
            }catch(SQLException se){ // ignore err from drop table
                System.out.println("creCmds " + se );
            }
        }
    }
```

At this point in the constructor, a new empty table has been created. Now we are going to add rows generated by running an XML parser. Creating the code to do this involves only a small change from the ErrataParserBean example. We still start a SAX style parser and respond to the various parser events, but now instead of output of formatted text when a single <Errata> element is parsed, we will write a row of data into the database table.

To insert data into the table, we could use the Statement object named stmt that we used to create the table. However, JDBC provides a more efficient way to perform repetitive operations in the PreparedStatement class. Furthermore, use of a PreparedStatement avoids a serious problem related to the format for an SQL command that inserts data. The command to insert a new row of data into a table follows a format that looks like this:

```
INSERT INTO tablename VALUES( value-1, value-2,... )
```
Character sequence variables are set off by single quotation marks so that data can have spaces and commas that won't be confused with the command parameters. Thus, a command inserting my information into a customer database might look like this:

```
INSERT INTO customer VALUES( 'William', 'Brogden','wbrogden@bga.com' )
```
The problem is that the text of an errata entry could contain just about any character sequence, including single quotation marks. A PreparedStatement effectively precompiles an SQL command while reserving space for changing variable values. Furthermore, no restrictions are placed on the characters that can appear in a variable. A PreparedStatement object is created using a String that sets a pattern for the actual data insertions, as in this example:

```
String pattern = "INSERT INTO errsql VALUES( ?,?,?,?,?,?,?,? );" ;
```

Using a `PreparedStatement` created with that pattern, you can set the value that replaces a "?" by referring to a position number. Following the SQL convention rather than the Java convention, position numbers start with 1.

Having established all that, we now continue with the `ErrataToSQL` class constructor method in Listing 8.3. The code creates a `PreparedStatement` named `prep` and then starts the parsing process. The parser object is created using the `com.sun.xml.parser.Parser` class. As you will recall from Chapter 6's discussion of the `ErrataParserBean` class, all the action takes place in methods that the SAX style parser calls in the `ErrataToSQL` class.

Listing 8.3: The ErrataToSQL constructor continues

```
        stmt.close();
        prep = conn.prepareStatement( pattern );
        System.out.println("create table done");
    }catch(Exception e){
        System.out.println("Startup error " + e );
        throw e ;
    }
    try {
      File f = new File( srcFile );
      input = Resolver.createInputSource( f );
      parser = ParserFactory.makeParser( parserClass );
      parser.setDocumentHandler( this );
      System.out.println("Start parse");
      parser.parse( input );
      System.out.println("Exit parse, ct= " + itemCt );
    }catch(SAXParseException spe){
        StringBuffer sb = new StringBuffer( spe.toString() );
        sb.append("\n  Line number: " + spe.getLineNumber());
        sb.append("\nColumn number: " + spe.getColumnNumber() );
        sb.append("\n Public ID: " + spe.getPublicId() );
        sb.append("\n System ID: " + spe.getSystemId() + "\n");
        System.out.println( sb.toString());
    }
}
```

Because most of the code that parses and formats the errata data as it is located by the XML parser is the same as in the `ErrataParserBean` of Chapter 6, I am not going to reproduce it here. If you are interested, the complete code is on the CD that accompanies this book. The key differences are outlined here:

- There is no selection; all `<Errata>` items are used.
- A separate table entry is created for each printing.
- The `text` variable contains a complete HTML formatted item.

The parser action that signals the end of an <Errata> item is a call to the endElement method. When this occurs, all the variables that characterize an errata entry have been formatted. The endElement method now calls the doInsert method, as shown in Listing 8.4. This method calls the prepInsert method once for each printing value. The prepInsert method uses the PreparedStatement object named prep to insert a row into the table.

Listing 8.4: The methods that create table entries

```
void doInsert()throws SQLException {
    StringTokenizer st = new StringTokenizer( printing,"," );
    while( st.hasMoreTokens() ){
      int prn = Integer.parseInt( st.nextToken());
      prepInsert( prn );
    }
}

void prepInsert( int prnt )throws SQLException{
  prep.clearParameters();
  prep.setInt( 1, seq++ );
  prep.setString( 2, isbn );
  prep.setString(3, page );
  prep.setInt( 4, prnt );
  prep.setInt( 5, significance);
  prep.setString(6, author );
  prep.setString(7, datemod );
  prep.setString(8, text );
  int ret = prep.executeUpdate();
  // uncomment to see the returned value
  //System.out.println( "prep returns " + ret );
}
```

Note that the prepInsert method uses setInt to put an integer value into the Prepared-Statement and setString to put in a String value. The PreparedStatement class has a long list of methods, one for each Java type, so it is a very general-purpose class. The value that is returned by executeUpdate is an integer that tells how many table rows were altered by the command.

In addition to executeUpdate, which is used for commands that modify a table, Pre-paredStatement also has executeQuery and execute methods. As you would expect, exe-cuteQuery is used for queries that return results. The execute method will execute any command, but it is primarily used for commands that are more complex than a simple update or query.

The other major modification to the ErrataParserBean code is that the endDocument method now closes the PreparedStatement and the database Connection object as shown in Listing 8.5.

Listing 8.5: The endDocument method

```java
public void endDocument(){
    try{
        prep.close();
        conn.commit();
        conn.close();
    }catch(SQLException se ){
        System.out.println("endDocument " + se );
    }
    System.out.println("End Document");
    System.out.println("Total errata found = " + itemCt + " Longest text "
        + longest );
}
```

The program just described creates an SQL table using the JDBC interface. Next we are going to look at what it takes to execute a query that searches this table.

Servlets with JDBC

Creating servlet output derived from a database using JDBC classes typically follows this sequence:

1. Obtain a `Connection` object for the database.
2. Create a `Statement` object.
3. Create a command `String` expressing a query.
4. Call the Statement `executeQuery` method and get a returned `ResultSet` object.
5. Use methods in the `ResultSet` class to convert retrieved values to Java primitives and objects.
6. Format the output.

Let's look at these steps in detail. The example code I will be using is `ErrataSQLbean`, a simple example that works with the "Errata" database and "errsql" table created in the previous section. To keep things simple and make it easier to debug, I am using a short console-style program to exercise the `ErrataSQLbean` code. This program, as shown in Listing 8.6, takes a database name on the command line, creates an `ErrataSQLbean` object, and runs a simple query.

Listing 8.6: The TestSQLBean program

```java
import java.sql.* ;
import java.io.* ;
import java.util.* ;
```

```
public class TestSQLBean
{
  public static void main(String[] args ){
    if( args.length == 0 ){
      System.out.println("Expects database name on cmd line");
      System.exit(0);
    }
    try {
      System.out.println("Try to create ErrataSQLbean with " + args[0]);
      ErrataSQLbean esb = new ErrataSQLbean( args[0]);
      System.out.println("Bean created ");
      esb.setIsbn("1576102912");
      esb.setSignificance( "1" );
      esb.setPrinting("1");
      esb.doOutput( System.out );
    }catch(SQLException se ){
      while( se != null ){
        System.out.println( "msg: " + se.getMessage() );
        System.out.println( "state: " + se.getSQLState() );
        System.out.println( "err: " + se.getErrorCode() );
        se = se.getNextException();
      }
    }catch(Exception e){
        e.printStackTrace( System.out );
    }
    // this just waits for a keypress
    try { System.in.read();
    }catch(Exception ex){
    }
    System.exit(0);
  }

}
```

Obtaining a Connection

Listing 8.7 shows the start of the ErrataSQLbean code with the import statements, instance variables, and constructor. The constructor gets a Connection with the simplest possible approach.

Listing 8.7: The start of the ErrataSQLbean code

```
import java.sql.* ;
import java.io.* ;
import java.util.* ;

public class ErrataSQLbean
```

```
{
  private String isbn ;
  private int significance ;
  private int printing ;
  String dbString ;
  String errStr = "" ;
  private Connection conn ;

  ErrataSQLbean( String db ) throws Exception {
    Class.forName("org.hsql.jdbcDriver");
    DriverManager.registerDriver( new org.hsql.jdbcDriver());
    //System.out.println("driver registered");
    dbString = "jdbc:HypersonicSQL:" + db ;
    //System.out.println("Try for connection:" + dbString );
    // parameters are URL, User id, password
    conn = DriverManager.getConnection( dbString , "sa","" );
    System.out.println("Got connection " );
  }
```

Unfortunately, this simple example has a lot of deficiencies. For one, creating a connection is a rather time-consuming process. Even with the database and test program on the same machine, my system takes almost three seconds to create a connection. If you have to access the database over a network, it can take even longer.

Another problem is that commercial database programs may limit the number of simultaneous connections according to the terms of your license. If you have ever shopped for databases, you have undoubtedly noticed that costs go up sharply if you want the capability of a large number of connections. Connections are also expensive objects in terms of system resources, such as memory and threads.

This brings us to the topic of "connection pooling," a very significant aspect of using databases with servlets and JSP. The basic idea is that because connections are expensive, you should create only a few of them and reuse them. Instead of creating a connection directly, your program has to obtain one from a pool manager, and if no connection is available, your program has to wait.

A number of programmers have worked up connection pool approaches that can be used with JDBC version 1.0. One example is DbConnectionBroker, which is located at:

www.javaexchange.com

JDBC 2.0 has implemented new classes and interfaces to provide connection pooling. These are found in the java.sql standard extension package. When using any of these connection pool approaches, you obtain a Connection object indirectly. However, for the purposes of my demonstration program, I am going to stick to the simple and direct approach.

Creating and Executing a Query

The example ErrataSQLbean has three parameters that must be set for any query. These correspond to the table entries isbn, Printing, and Significance. Each one has a matching setXxx method that takes a String, following the bean convention, as shown in Listing 8.8.

Listing 8.8: The set methods in ErrataSQLbean

```
// 1 = major, 2 = major + med, 3 = all including minor tyops
  public void setSignificance(String s ){
    try {  significance = Integer.parseInt( s ) ;
    }catch(Exception e ){
      errStr += " setSignificance " + e.toString();
      significance = 3 ; // to get all
    }
  }

  // typically 1 - 10
  public void setPrinting( String s ){
    try{ printing = Integer.parseInt( s );
    }catch( Exception e ){
      errStr += " setPrinting " + e.toString() ;
      printing = 1 ;
    }
  }

  public void setIsbn(String s ){ isbn = s ; }
```

Now that we have a Connection object and search parameters, we can create a Statement object and send a query command as shown in Listing 8.9. The query String requests only the text field; because it is completely formatted, we don't need the other fields to create output. With the test parameters, the resulting query is this:

```
SELECT Text FROM errsql WHERE isbn = '1576102912' AND Significance <= 1 AND
printing = 1
```

I am using the <= operator with the Significance parameter to allow for the selection of all errata of a given or greater significance. Note that this version of doOutput is intended to work with the test program shown in Listing 8.6 so it does output to a PrintStream. When installed in a JSP or servlet, the output would have to be to a PrintWriter instead.

Listing 8.9: The doOutput performs the search

```
public void doOutput( PrintStream ps ) throws SQLException {
    Statement st = conn.createStatement();
    String query = "SELECT Text FROM errsql WHERE " +
        "isbn = '" + isbn + "' AND Significance <= " +
        significance + " AND printing = " + printing ;
```

```
        ResultSet rslt = st.executeQuery( query );
        ResultSetMetaData rmd = rslt.getMetaData();
        while( rslt.next()){ ctrec++ ;
          ps.println( rslt.getString(1));
          // note SQL column addressing convention based on 1
        }
    // the following is a debug statement to examine ResultSetMetaData
    //  ps.println("Meta: " + rmd.getColumnCount() );
        ps.println( toString() );
        }
    int ctrec = 0 ; // count output records
```

The **executeQuery** call returns an object implementing the **ResultSet** interface, and you use the methods of this interface to extract data from the query results. The **ResultSet** interface specifies a huge list of methods to get Java primitives or objects.

Working with the ResultSet

You can think of the results of a query as a temporary table containing the variables you specified in the SELECT statement as columns, and containing the database elements matching the query logic as rows. A **ResultSet** has the **next** method that acts rather like the **nextElement** method of an **Enumeration**. Every time you call **next**, the **ResultSet**'s *cursor* moves to the next row of the result table. The **next** method returns **true** as long as the cursor points to a valid row.

Extracting Data from a ResultSet

Within a row, you can extract Java data with either an index number or a variable name. In Listing 8.9, I used **rslt.getString(1)**, but I could just as easily have used **rslt.get-String("Text")**. In the example, the data from the SQL table field defined as a VARCHAR is turned into a **String** object. Practically all SQL datatypes can be retrieved as a **String**, similar to the way Java variables are automatically converted to a **String** in print statements.

As defined in the JDBC, the methods in **ResultSet** are very flexible in terms of being able to convert SQL datatypes to Java primitives. For instance, you *could* use **getByte** on a BIG-INT data type. Obviously, you are well advised to stick to the **get** methods that most closely match Java and SQL types.

All the **ResultSet** methods can throw an **SQLException** that should contain a message, an SQL state code, and an error code specific to the database vendor. An **SQLException** object can be linked to another **SQLException** so your method to catch an exception should look to see if there are additional chained exceptions, as shown in the **TestSQLBean** code in Listing 8.6.

ResultSetMetaData

As shown in Listing 8.9, you can get an object implementing the `ResultSetMetaData` interface from a `ResultSet` (metadata is data about data). Metadata for a `ResultSet` includes information on the characteristics of the datatypes in the retrieved data on a column-by-column basis. For example, the `getColumnType` method returns an `int` value corresponding to the various JDBC constants in the `java.sql.Types` class.

The JDBC API offers a powerful set of classes and methods for flexible access to relational databases. Programs using JDBC are largely portable between different operating systems. However, because not all databases support all methods called for in the JDBC and SQL standards or have minor differences in the way they support methods, developing programs with JDBC involves a lot of testing. Database programming has not yet reached the Java goal of write once, run anywhere.

CHAPTER 9

Connecting to Custom Database Servers

- Managing Socket Connections in Java

- Communicating with Object Serialization

- Communicating with Remote Method Invocation

The previous chapter dealt with connections to databases using the JDBC API. There are many applications for which writing your own custom database is simpler and more efficient than trying to make SQL and a relational database do the work. However, you then have the problem of fitting your custom database into the Web server environment with its requirements for scalability. This chapter discusses some efficient alternatives for connecting servlets to custom database programs.

Using Sockets in Java

Sockets are the underlying technology for communication between processes in Java. The socket mechanism allows programs on the same machine or connected by a network to reliably send one another packages of bytes. All the details of transmitting and receiving these packets are handled by layers of software in the operating system so that all the programmer has to do is provide basic information to identify the processes involved.

Java's `Socket` and `ServerSocket` classes provide your interface to the actual operating system socket implementation. The provider of the JVM for your system has to create a class extending `SocketImpl` that provides the actual implementation for your particular system.

The classes you need to know about first are in the `java.net` package. Here is a summary of the major classes and their uses.

Socket   A `Socket` object is one end of a communication channel between two programs. The client side of a client-server configuration creates a `Socket` using a network address and a port and attempts to establish a connection with a `ServerSocket`.

ServerSocket   A `ServerSocket` listens on a particular port for a request to establish a TCP/IP connection. A Java `Thread` has to be dedicated to the listening process. When a connection is established, a `Socket` is created with a port assigned by the operating system, and subsequent communication between client and server proceeds with Socket objects.

InetAddress   This class represents the network address of a particular computer. A given computer may have many addresses. Network addresses can be expressed in text form or in numeric form. For example, by default, your computer has the name "localhost" and the numeric address "127.0.0.1".

DatagramSocket   A simpler and faster form of communication is the User Datagram Protocol (UDP). This protocol also uses IP to address packets of data, but it does not have the error-checking and handshaking overhead of TCP. Java implements UDP with the `DatagramSocket` and `DatagramPacket` classes. Due to the unreliable nature of UDP, you would not use it to carry out critical communication.

Sockets and Streams

Socket communication is well integrated into the Java classes for dealing with input and output in terms of streams. I feel that the flexibility of Java's IO classes is an excellent example of the virtues of object oriented programming. Let's review some of the basic stream-related classes in the `java.io` package.

InputStream   This abstract class is the parent class for all stream input classes. It defines basic methods for reading a single byte or array of bytes. The `available` method returns the number of bytes, which can be read from the stream without blocking. The `close` method closes the stream and releases any system resources associated with it.

OutputStream   This abstract class is the parent for all stream output classes. It defines methods for writing a single byte or an array of bytes. Because operating systems buffer many forms of output, `OutputStream` includes the `flush` method to flush any buffers. Failing to `flush` an output stream is the cause of many hard-to-find bugs.

ByteArrayInputStream   This class lets you turn an array of bytes into an input stream that behaves just like any other.

ByteArrayOutputStream   Writing to this stream fills a byte array in memory.

FilterInputStream   This class serves as a base for classes that perform some sort of "filtering" operation on an input stream and provide the filtered bytes via the `InputStream` methods. A `FilterInputStream` is never created directly; it provides the base that is extended by a number of useful classes.

FilterOutputStream   Similar to `FilterInputStream`, this class is the base for classes that perform some filtering operation on bytes written to them. Examples of filtering operations include buffering, compression, and encryption.

DataInputStream   A subclass of `FilterInputStream`, this class provides for reading Java primitives as written by a `DataOutputStream`.

DataOutputStream   This subclass of `FilterOutputStream` provides methods for writing Java primitive values in an operating system independent format. The byte order is most significant byte (MSB) first, the opposite of the order in which primitive values are written in Windows, but the standard for network transmission.

ObjectInputStream   This class provides for reading one or more objects from a stream written by `ObjectOutputStream`. In order to reconstruct an object, an `ObjectInputStream` must have access to the appropriate version of the class files that define the objects. Recreating an object from an input stream is sometimes called *deserialization*.

ObjectOutputStream An `ObjectOutputStream` can be created with any `Output-Stream` and can write any Java object that meets certain criteria. The object must implement the `java.io.Serializable` or the `java.io.Externalizable` interface and have a no-arguments constructor. Writing multiple objects to a stream is made easier by the fact that Java arrays and collection classes such as `Vector` are all serializable, so writing an array of `String` objects or a collection of miscellaneous objects can be done in a single call to `writeObject`.

Character-Oriented Streams

The classes just discussed are all byte oriented, but there is a major group of classes in the `java.io` package devoted to character streams. These classes correctly handle conversion between character encoding such as ASCII and the Unicode that Java uses internally.

These character streams were not present in the initial version of Java, which relied on byte-oriented streams. The `PrintStream` class was the standard for writing text streams, and the `DataInputStream` was used for reading a line of text at a time. However, as Sun tried to improve on the international alphabet capabilities of Java, it was found that altering the original classes to make them behave correctly would introduce too much complexity. So a completely new set of character-oriented classes was created.

Unfortunately, the use of `PrintStream` classes for the standard `System.out` and `System.err` objects made it impossible to get rid of `PrintStream` entirely, so we are left with a mixture of byte- and character-oriented classes used for text input and output. Fortunately, the character stream classes behave well with plain ASCII text. Here is a quick survey of the some of the more useful character stream classes in the `java.io` package:

Reader The abstract parent class for all character stream reading classes.

Writer The abstract parent class for all character stream writing classes.

BufferedReader This class provides improved performance in some cases by filling a buffer from the stream. This is the preferred class for reading text one line at a time, replacing the `DataInputStream` `readLine` method, which is deprecated.

BufferedWriter Provides buffering for output of characters to a stream.

StringReader Creates a `Reader` interface in which the character source is a `String`.

StringWriter Provides a `Writer` interface in which output goes to an internal `String-Buffer` that automatically expands as needed. When closed, you can get the resulting `String`.

PrintWriter Provides many convenient methods parallel to those in `PrintStream`. Handles ASCII characters well but also correctly handles Unicode characters.

Socket Class Methods

Once you have `Socket` objects on both the client and server ends of a connection, you use the `getInputStream` and `getOutputStream` methods of the `Socket` class to get references to the objects that you can use to build a communication system.

getInputStream Returns a reference to an object implementing the `InputStream` methods. The internal details of this object depend on the socket implementation, but you don't have to worry about this.

getOutputStream Returns a reference to an object implementing the `OutputStream` methods.

TIP Closing either the input or output stream obtained from a `Socket` closes the socket and, therefore, the other stream. I have wasted a lot of time tracking bugs related to this fact. Java 1.3 adds the methods `shutdownInput` and `shutdownOutput` that get around this problem.

Here are some of the `Socket` class methods that may be useful in servlet-to-custom database communication. These methods should be called before you obtain an input or output stream:

setsoTimeout(int millisec) Normally, any read of a `Socket`-based input stream will block until some input appears or the socket is closed. This method sets the longest time a `Socket` will wait for input before it creates an `InterruptedException`. The input stream stays open so you can try for input again later.

setReceiveBufferSize(int ct) The value of `ct` is passed to the underlying socket implementation software as a "hint," not an absolute requirement. You can call `getReceiveBufferSize` to see what the system is actually providing.

setSendBufferSize(int ct) As with the `receive` buffer, this sets a "hint" for the underlying socket implementation. In general, the default values provide reasonable results, but you might be able to use knowledge about the typical size of messages your application sends to optimize network performance.

Socket Communication Examples

For a simple but complete example of socket communication between a servlet and a database, I have chosen to revise the chat servlet created in Chapter 3. As you may recall, in that example, the history of messages in various chat "rooms" was maintained by static and instance methods of the `ChatRoom` class residing in the same JVM as the chat servlet.

All the data required to create a user's view of a particular chat room can be represented as an array of String objects. Likewise, all messages from the servlet to the application maintaining the chat rooms can be represented as an array of String objects. Therefore, I investigated the various ways of transmitting String arrays between a client and a server using sockets.

Socket Communication Test Case

The test case used a simple program that simulated chat users by creating Runnable objects in which the Thread sleeps for 0.5 seconds and then sends a small array of String objects and receives an array of String objects from the server. On the server side, a ServerSocket used accept to get connections and then passed them off to ChatThread objects. For each test of a communication method, ChatThread implemented a different approach.

Listing 9.1 shows the code involved in creating a ServerSocket, accepting new connections, and passing them off to a ChatThread. Note that the ChatThread is given a lower priority than the thread that runs the ServerSocket accept method to ensure that the ServerSocket has a minimum downtime. Just to demonstrate the capability, I had the ServerSocket timeout set for one second. When the accept method is interrupted, it just increments a counter and goes back to accepting new connections.

Listing 9.1: The server test case program run method

```
public void run(){
  try {
      srvSok = new ServerSocket( port );
      srvSok.setSoTimeout( 1000 ); // effecive interrupt every sec
  }catch(SocketException se){
      System.out.println("Unable to set socket timeout " + se );
      return ;
  }catch(IOException x2){
      System.out.println("Unable to create socket " + x2 );
  }
  while( running ){
    try {
        Socket wrk = null ;
        wrk = srvSok.accept(); // blocks here
        ChatThread ct = new ChatThread( wrk );
        ct.setPriority( Thread.NORM_PRIORITY - 1 );
        ct.start();
        recCt++ ;
        //  note that wrk.close(); is executed by ChatThread
    }catch(InterruptedIOException ie){
        ticCt++ ;
```

```
        }catch(IOException ioe ){
            System.out.println("Unplanned " + ioe);
            ioe.printStackTrace(System.err );
            running = false ;
        }
    } // end while
}
```

Directly Writing Strings

One obvious way to transmit a series of String objects is to simply create a PrintStream or PrintWriter from the OutputStream obtained from a Socket and then output each String using println. The problem with this approach turns out to be that the receiving application needs to know when the last String has been received so it can process the input. Sending the ASCII end-of-file control code (0x1A or Ctrl-Z) is used in the example code shown in Listing 9.2.

Listing 9.2: Sending and receiving Strings using an eof character

```
public String[] doChatStr(Socket wrk){
    int i ;
    try {
        InputStream ins = wrk.getInputStream();
        OutputStream outs = wrk.getOutputStream();
        OutputStreamWriter osw = new OutputStreamWriter( outs );
        PrintWriter pw = new PrintWriter( osw );
        for( i = 0 ; i < cStr.length ; i++ ){
            pw.print( cStr[i] ); pw.print('\n');
        }
        pw.write( 0x1A );
        pw.flush(); // essential!
        BufferedInputStream bis = new BufferedInputStream( ins );
        Vector v = new Vector() ; // to save strings in
        StringBuffer sb = new StringBuffer(100);
        int ch = bis.read();
        while( ch != 0x1A ){
            if( ch == '\n' ){ // recognize newline character
                v.addElement( sb.toString());
                sb = new StringBuffer( 100 );
            }
            if( ch >= ' ' ){ // ignore any other control code
                sb.append( (char)ch );
            }
            ch = bis.read();
        }
        wrk.close();
        String[] ret = new String[ v.size() ];
        for( i = 0 ;i < v.size() ; i++ ){
            ret[i] = (String)v.elementAt( i );
```

```
        }
        return ret ;
    }catch(IOException e){
        System.out.println("ChatThread " + e );
        e.printStackTrace( System.out );
    }
    return null ;
}
```

Naturally, when sending data with this technique, you would have to ensure that the special end-of-file character never occurs in the data.

Writing an Object

As shown in Listing 9.3, the code to read and write an object with Java serialization is very simple. Note that the readObject method may throw a ClassNotFoundException if it can't find the class file needed to build an object.

Listing 9.3: Sending and receiving using object serialization

```
private String[] doChat0( Socket s )throws IOException{
    OutputStream os = s.getOutputStream();
    InputStream is = s.getInputStream();
    ObjectOutputStream oos = new ObjectOutputStream( os );
    oos.writeObject( cStr );
    oos.flush();
    ObjectInputStream ois = new ObjectInputStream(is);
    try {
        String[] rec = (String[])ois.readObject();
        return rec ;
    }catch(ClassNotFoundException ce){
        System.out.println("doChat " + ce );
    }
    return null ;
}
```

Writing a Block of Bytes

An alternate approach is to send the array of String objects as a block of bytes. The central problem with this approach is that you must first send the length of the block so the receiving end will know how much space to allocate. Therefore, convert the String array first to determine the size of the block. To convert the array, write the String contents to a ByteArray-OutputStream; this approach automatically expands as needed. As shown in Listing 9.4, after writing the cStr array, you can obtain a byte array from the closed ByteArrayOutput-Stream.

A DataOutputStream is constructed on the OutputStream obtained from the Socket. After writing the size of the array, the byte array itself is written. Note that I flushed the output stream, but didn't close it to avoid closing the Socket.

Listing 9.4: Sending and receiving String arrays as byte blocks in doChatB

```java
private String[] doChatB( Socket s )throws IOException{
    ByteArrayOutputStream baos = new ByteArrayOutputStream();
    PrintWriter pw = new PrintWriter( baos );
    for( int i = 0 ; i < cStr.length ; i++ ){
        pw.write(cStr[i]);
    }
    pw.close();
    byte[] outb = baos.toByteArray();
    //
    OutputStream os = s.getOutputStream();
    InputStream is = s.getInputStream();
    DataOutputStream dos = new DataOutputStream( os );
    dos.writeInt( outb.length );
    dos.write( outb, 0, outb.length );
    dos.flush();
```

Receiving a block of bytes back from the server is shown in Listing 9.5. A DataInputStream is used to read the block count, and a byte array of the correct size is created. The byte array is used as a source for a ByteArrayInputStream, which in turn is used to build a DataInputStream. I am using the readLine method in spite of the fact that it is deprecated because it works fine for plain text. Because we don't know how many String objects will be created, a Vector is used to hold them as they are read. Finally, the correct size String array is created and filled. In this example, the Socket is closed in the method that calls doChatB.

Listing 9.5: The doChatB method continues

```java
    // Now we read the returned block of bytes
    DataInputStream dis = new DataInputStream(is);
    int ct = dis.readInt();
    byte[] inb = new byte[ ct ];
    dis.read( inb,0,ct );
    // Because we don't know how many strings are in the block use a Vector
    Vector v = new Vector() ;
    ByteArrayInputStream bais = new ByteArrayInputStream( inb );
    dis = new DataInputStream( bais );
    // readLine is deprecated but works fine for this use
    // as long as the characters are ASCII
    String tmp = dis.readLine();
    while( tmp != null ){
        v.addElement( tmp );
        tmp = dis.readLine();
    }
```

```
      String[] ret = new String[ v.size() ];
      for( int i = 0 ; i < v.size(); i++ ){
          ret[i] = (String) v.elementAt(i);
      }
      return ret ;
  }
```

Performance Comparison

I compared the performance of these three approaches on my Windows NT Workstation 4.0 dual Pentium III 233MHz processor system by allowing various numbers of chat simulation threads to run for 100 seconds and watching the CPU utilization on the Performance Monitor. The chat simulator also recorded the average round-trip time for sending a small array of String objects and receiving a somewhat larger array from the simulated chat server.

The lowest CPU utilization and shortest roundtrip was produced by the direct String writing techniques with recognition of the end of transmission using the special end-of-file character. The techniques sending binary blocks and the version using object serialization were about the same and much slower. However, all the methods started creating Connect-Exception exceptions when they tried to reach a rate of 200 data exchanges per second even though CPU utilization had not approached 100%.

I conclude that the special end-of-file character is preferable if you can be sure that the data can never contain that character. Otherwise, object serialization has the advantage of being easy to program.

The Revised Chat Servlet

The chat servlet example using cookies from Chapter 3 was easily modified to communicate by socket to a chat database server instead of with a local ChatRoom object. In view of the fact that I could easily prevent a spurious end of file character from appearing in the chat messages, and noting the efficiency of directly writing strings as found in the test cases, a transmission method similar to Listing 9.2 was chosen. The code for the modified servlet starts in Listing 9.6. The variables, initialization, and doGet method are very similar to those used in Chapter 3.

Listing 9.6: The start of the ChatSokServ servlet source code

```
package com.JSPbook.Chap09;

import java.io.*;
import java.util.* ;
import java.net.* ;
import javax.servlet.*;
import javax.servlet.http.*;
```

```java
public class ChatSokServ extends HttpServlet
{
  static String alias = "http://localhost/servlet/chatsocserv" ;
  static public String host = "localhost";
  static public int port = 5995 ;
  static String version = "1.01";
  static String[] listCmd = { "LIST" };

  static String chatRows = "12" ;
  static String chatCols = "72" ;
  static String inputRows = "6" ;
  static String inputCols = "72" ;

  Throwable lastErr ;
  int errCt ;

  public void init(ServletConfig config) throws ServletException
  { // host and port could be read in here
    super.init(config);
    System.out.println("ChatSocServ init");
  }

// the only GET is the initial entry
  public void doGet(HttpServletRequest req, HttpServletResponse resp)
      throws ServletException, IOException
  {
    resp.setContentType("text/html");
    PrintWriter out = new PrintWriter(resp.getOutputStream());
    out.println("<HTML>");
    out.println("<HEAD><TITLE>ChatSocServ Output</TITLE></HEAD>");
    out.println("<BODY>");
    out.println("<h2 ALIGN=CENTER>Welcome to Chat</h2><br>");
    //
    try {
      out.print( getRoomsAsForm() );
    }catch( Exception e ){
      e.printStackTrace( out );
      out.println("<br><hr>");
    }
    out.println("<hr><center>version: " + version + "</center><br>\r\n" );
    out.println("</body>");
    out.println("</html>");
    out.close();
  }
```

The first method with major changes is **doPost**, as shown in Listing 9.7. The same possible user interaction cases (initial entry, sending a message, refreshing the user's view without sending a message, and quitting) must be detected and handled. The difference is that instead of getting a local **ChatRoom** object, the parameters are collected into a **String** array and sent to the chat server.

Listing 9.7: The doPost method of ChatSokServ

```java
public void doPost(HttpServletRequest req, HttpServletResponse resp)
    throws ServletException, IOException
{
  resp.setContentType("text/html");
  PrintWriter out = new PrintWriter(resp.getOutputStream());
  String action = req.getParameter( "chatgo" ); // initial entry
  String handle = null ;
  String room = null ;
  String error = "" ;
  int phase = 0 ;
  if( action != null ){ // because chatgo was found
      // here is where a password check would go
      handle = req.getParameter( "handle" );
      room = req.getParameter("room"); // the code
      if( handle == null || handle.length() < 4 || room == null ){
        phase = 8 ;
      }
      else {
        Cookie hC = new Cookie( "handle", handle );
        hC.setMaxAge( 600 ); hC.setVersion( 1 );
        Cookie rC = new Cookie( "room", room );
        rC.setMaxAge( 600 ); rC.setVersion( 1 );
        resp.addCookie( hC );
        resp.addCookie( rC );
      }
  }
  else { // not initial entry
    // action should be either "Send" "Refresh" or "Quit"
      action = req.getParameter("action");
      Cookie[] cks = req.getCookies();
      for( int i = 0 ; i < cks.length ; i++){
        if( cks[i].getName().equals("handle")) {
           handle = cks[i].getValue() ;
        }
        if( cks[i].getName().equals("room")){
           room = cks[i].getValue();
        } // reset the time limit
        cks[i].setMaxAge( 600 ); cks[i].setVersion( 1 );
        resp.addCookie( cks[i] );
      }
      if( handle == null || room == null || action == null ){
        error = "handle, room or action missing "; phase = 9 ;
      }
      else {
        if( action.equals("Send"))phase = 1 ;
        if( action.equals("Refresh")) phase = 2 ;
        if( action.equals("Quit")) phase = 3 ;
      }
  }
```

```
      if( room == null ){ error = "null value for room"; phase = 9 ;
      }
      String[] singleCmd = new String[ 1 ] ;
      String[] doubleCmd = new String[ 2 ] ;
      String cmdStr = "" ;
      out.println("<HTML>");
      out.println("<HEAD><TITLE>ChatSokServ Output</TITLE></HEAD>");
      out.println("<BODY>");
      out.println("<h2>IN doPost method of ChatSokServ</h2>");
      try {
      switch( phase ){
        case 0 : // new entry
          singleCmd[0] = "ENTER:" + room + "," + handle ;
          doCommand( out, singleCmd,"", 0 );
          break ;
        case 1 : // "Send" - entry with text to be added
          doubleCmd[0] = "SEND:" + room + "," + handle ;
          doubleCmd[1] = getMsg( req );
          doCommand( out, doubleCmd, "", 1 );
          break ;
        case 2 : // "Refresh" - don't add text
          singleCmd[0] = "REFRESH:" + room + "," + handle ;
          doCommand( out, singleCmd, getMsg( req ), 2 );
          break ;
        case 3 : // "Quit"
          singleCmd[0] = "QUIT:" + room + "," + handle ;
          doCommand( out, singleCmd, "", 3 );
          break ;
        case 8 : // user failed to enter usable handle
          badHandleMsg( out, handle ); break ;
        case 9 : // parameters not found, serious problem
          out.println("<h2>Serious problem - " + error +
              " notify operator.</h2>" );
          break ;
        default :
          out.println("Unknown phase " + phase );
      }
      }catch(Throwable et){
        out.print("Serious Problem<br>\r\n");
        et.printStackTrace( out );
      }
      out.println("</BODY>");
      out.println("</HTML>");
      out.close();
    }
```

The doCommand method shown in Listing 9.8 sends a command to the chat server using the chatCmd method and decides what to do with the result based on the response and the command type. For a user that is leaving, it writes the current contents of the chat room but leaves off the message text area and buttons.

Listing 9.8: The doCommand method gets a response from the chat server

```
public void doCommand( PrintWriter out, String[] cmd, String msg, int phase ){
    String[] rslt = chatCmd( cmd );
    if( rslt == null ){
        out.println( "Bad return from chatCmd<br>\r\n");
        return ;
    }
    if( phase == 3 ){ // exiting
        sendChatTA( out, rslt );
        out.println("Goodbye<br>" );
    }
    else {
        sendChatTA( out, rslt );
        sendMsgTA( out, msg );
    }
}
```

The chatCmd method shown in Listing 9.9 creates a socket connection, sends the command array, and receives the result. Note the use of the finally clause to ensure that the socket is closed in all cases. Also shown in this listing, the doChatCom method uses a PrintWriter object to send the String contents from the array followed by an end-of-file character. After sending the last character, it waits for a response and builds an array of String objects.

Because a PrintWriter does not automatically send characters to the OutputStream-Writer it is created with, it is necessary to call the flush method. Many programmers have wasted many hours trying to debug socket communication programs due to failing to flush an output stream.

Listing 9.9: The chatCmd method makes the socket connection

```
// creates socket connection and calls doChatCmd, traps exceptions
public String[] chatCmd(String[] cmd ){
    String[] rslt = null ;
    Socket sok = null ;
    try {
        sok = new Socket( host, port );
        rslt = doChatCom( cmd, sok );
        sok.close();
        sok = null ;
        return rslt ;
    }catch(IOException xe ){
        lastErr = xe ; errCt++ ;
        return null ;
    }finally{
```

```
          try {
            if( sok != null ) sok.close();
          }catch(Exception ef){
          }
      }
   } // end chatCmd

   // sends the contents of cStr using <ctrl>Z to signal end,
   // reads reply a byte at a time, looking for <ctrl>Z
   public String[] doChatCom(String[] cStr, Socket wrk){
     int i ;
     try {
       InputStream ins = wrk.getInputStream();
       OutputStream outs = wrk.getOutputStream();
       OutputStreamWriter osw = new OutputStreamWriter( outs );
       PrintWriter pw = new PrintWriter( osw );
       for( i = 0 ; i < cStr.length ; i++ ){
         pw.print( cStr[i] ); pw.print('\n');
       }
       pw.write( 0x1A );
       pw.flush(); // essential!
       BufferedInputStream bis = new BufferedInputStream( ins );
       Vector v = new Vector() ; // to save strings in
       StringBuffer sb = new StringBuffer(100);
       int ch = bis.read();
       while( ch != 0x1A ){
         if( ch == '\n' ){ // recognize newline character
           v.addElement( sb.toString());
           sb = new StringBuffer( 100 );
         }
         if( ch >= ' ' ){ // ignore any other control code
           sb.append( (char)ch );
         }
         ch = bis.read();
       }
       wrk.close();
       String[] ret = new String[ v.size() ];
       for( i = 0 ;i < v.size() ; i++ ){
         ret[i] = (String)v.elementAt( i );
       }
       return ret ;
     }catch(IOException e){
         System.out.println("ChatThread " + e );
         e.printStackTrace( System.out );
     }
     return null ;
   }
```

The chat user sees a page that has two text area forms, one for the current chat room contents and one for typing a message. These are created by the methods shown in Listing 9.10 that are called after a command has been sent to the chat server and a response has been obtained.

Listing 9.10: Methods to create the form parts of the user page

```java
// creates the textarea form for current chat contents
private void sendChatTA( PrintWriter out, String[] rslt ){
    out.println("<form><textarea rows=\"" + chatRows +
            "\" cols=\"" + chatCols + "\" >");
    for( int i = 0 ; i < rslt.length ; i++ ){
        out.println( rslt[i] );
    }
    out.println("</textarea></form>");
}

private void sendMsgTA(PrintWriter out, String wrk ){
    out.println("<form METHOD=\"post\" action=\"" + alias + "\" >" );
    out.println("--- Use the box below to enter your text ---<br>");
    out.println("<textarea rows=\"" + inputRows    +
            "\" cols=\"" + inputCols + "\" name=\"msg\" >" );
    out.print(wrk);
    out.println("</textarea><br>");
    doButton( out,"action","Send");
    doButton( out,"action","Refresh");
    doButton( out,"action","Quit");
    out.println("</form><br>");
}
```

In the getRoomsAsForm method, shown in Listing 9.11, a LIST command is sent to the chat server, which returns an array of String objects that creates a selection list on the resulting HTML form.

Listing 9.11: The getRoomsAsForm method

```java
public String getRoomsAsForm(){
    StringBuffer sb = new StringBuffer(1000);
    String[] list = chatCmd( listCmd );
    sb.append("<center>Please select a chat room,<br>");
    sb.append("enter a Handle, and click the Enter button<br>");
    sb.append("<form method=\"post\" action=\"" + alias + "\" > ");
    for( int i = 0 ; i < list.length ;i++ ){
        sb.append( list[i] ); sb.append("\r\n");
    }
    sb.append("<br>");
    sb.append("Handle: <input TYPE=\"TEXT\" VALUE=\"\"" );
    sb.append(" name=\"handle\"><br>\r\n");
    sb.append("<input TYPE=\"submit\" VALUE=\"Enter Chat\"" );
    sb.append(" name=\"chatgo\">\r\n");
    sb.append("</form></center><hr>\r\n");
    return sb.toString();
}
```

Any text typed by the user into the message entry text area is recovered from the request and turned into a single `String` in the `getMsg` method, as shown in Listing 9.12. A call to the `replace` method in the `String` class is used to ensure that there is no extraneous end-of-file character in the message. This listing also includes some utility methods unchanged from the chat servlet in Chapter 3.

Listing 9.12: The getMsg method replaces any eof with space

```
public String getMsg(HttpServletRequest req){
   String[] s = req.getParameterValues("msg");
   if( s == null ) return "" ;
   StringBuffer sb = new StringBuffer( 100 );
   for( int i = 0 ; i < s.length ; i++ ){
     sb.append( s[i].replace( (char)0x1A, ' ' ) );
     if( i + 1 < s.length ) sb.append( "\r\n" );
   }
   return sb.toString();
}

// convenient utility
public void doButton( PrintWriter out, String name, String value){
   out.println("<INPUT TYPE=\"SUBMIT\" value=\"" +
     value + "\" name=\"" + name + "\" >" );
}

public void badHandleMsg( PrintWriter out, String handle ){
   out.println("<center><h2>The handle you entered is not usable</h2>");
   // switch here for various reasons
   out.println("<h2>" + handle + " is too short </h2></center>" );
   out.print( getRoomsAsForm());
}
}
```

The Chat Server Program

The ChatRoom and related classes from Chapter 3 have been modified to fit the database server model. The following are the main components of the resulting system:

ChatSokServer   This class provides the initial main method and creates a `ServerSocket` to listen for commands from the chat servlet. It also reads a properties file to establish the titles and codes for the chat rooms.

ChatThread   When a `Socket` connection has been established, it is handed off to an instance of this extension of `Thread`. After receiving a message, it performs the required operation, possibly including creation of a `ChatItem`, and returns a result. A `ChatThread` handles only a single transaction and dies after the `Socket` is closed.

ChatRoom   This class is essentially unmodified from Chapter 3. The static methods keep track of a ChatRoom instance for each room. Each ChatRoom instance keeps a Vector of recent ChatItem objects and can supply the text on demand. ChatRoom is Runnable and has a low priority Thread that wakes up from time to time to trim older ChatItems.

ChatItem   This class is modified from Chapter 3 to provide a constructor compatible with the String array that ChatThread receives.

The ChatSokServer Class

I'll begin this discussion with the main ChatSokServer class. The program expects to find a file name on the command line. This file contains the port number to be used and information on the chat rooms to be created, as shown in Listing 9.13. The number after the comma gives the target number of ChatItem objects to keep in memory.

Listing 9.13: Example properties file

```
# properties for ChatSokServer - everything not port is a room code
# code=room title,#  where # is chat item limit
port=5995
jsrv=Java Servlets Fans,20
jsp=JavaServer Pages,20
frth=Forth Fanatics,20
small=Smalltalk Chatter,20
```

Listing 9.14 shows the import statements, static variables, and main method. Note that, after creating a ChatSokServer object and starting its Thread, the main method enters a loop that blocks, waiting for console input. Typing any character except <Ctrl>Z and pressing <Return> causes output of status information to the console. The <Ctrl>Z input stops the server.

Listing 9.14: The main chat server program

```
package com.JSPbook.Chap09;

import java.net.* ;
import java.io.* ;
import java.util.* ;

public class ChatSokServer implements Runnable
{
  static String version = "1.03 July 9, 2000";
  static String[] instruc = {
    "ChatSokServer requires the name of a properties",
    "file on the command line."
  };
```

```
// start with the name of the properties file
public static void main(String[] args ){
  System.out.println( version );
  if( args.length == 0 ){
    for( int i = 0 ; i < instruc.length ; i++ ){
      System.out.println( instruc[i]);
    }
    System.exit(1);
  }
  File f = new File( args[0] );
  Properties p = new Properties();
  ChatSokServer css = null ;
  Thread t = null ;
  try{
    p.load( new FileInputStream( f ) );
    css = new ChatSokServer( p );
    t = new Thread( css );
    t.start();
  }catch(Exception e){
    e.printStackTrace( System.err );
    System.exit(2);
  }
  System.out.println("enter <ctrl>z<return> to stop");
  while( true ){
    int ch = 0 ;
    try {  ch = System.in.read();
    }catch(IOException ex){}
    if( ch == -1 ){ // special eof value
      System.out.println("Stop signalled");
      css.stop();
      try { t.join();
      }catch(InterruptedException ie){}
      System.exit(0);
    }
    System.out.println( css.toString() );
  }
}
```

Listing 9.15 shows the constructor and instance variables for the ChatSokServer class. The constructor uses a Properties object created in the main method by reading a file.

Listing 9.15: Instance variables and constructor for ChatSokServer

```
// instance variables
Properties sokprop ;
int port = 5995 ;
String[] rooms ; // code,full room name
//
```

```
boolean running ;
int recCt = 0 ;
int ticCt = 0 ;
ServerSocket srvSok ;

public ChatSokServer( Properties p ){
  sokprop = p ;
  sokprop.list( System.out );
  Enumeration e = sokprop.propertyNames();
  Vector v = new Vector();
  while( e.hasMoreElements()){
    String name = (String)e.nextElement();
    if( name.equals("port") ){
      port = Integer.parseInt(sokprop.getProperty(name));
    }
    else { // room codes are other property values
      String tmp = name + "," + sokprop.getProperty( name );
      v.addElement( tmp );
    }
  }
  rooms = new String[ v.size() ] ;
  for( int i = 0 ; i < v.size() ; i++ ){
    rooms[i] = (String)v.elementAt(i);
  }
  ChatRoom.initChatRooms( rooms );
  running = true ;
}
```

Now we come to the central part of the chat server. In the run method shown in Listing 9.16, the ServerSocket that listens for client connections is created. In the while loop, it waits until either a new connection is accepted or the internal timer causes an InterruptedException. The accept method creates a new Socket using a port assigned by the operating system. This Socket is used to create a ChatThread object, which has its priority set lower than the main Thread to ensure that the main Thread goes back to looking at the ServerSocket as quickly as possible.

Listing 9.16: The run method handles the ServerSocket

```
public void run(){
  System.out.println("ChatSokServer.run starts");
  try {
    srvSok = new ServerSocket( port );
    srvSok.setSoTimeout( 1000 ); // effective interrupt every sec
  }catch(SocketException se){
    System.out.println("Unable to set socket timeout " + se );
    return ;
  }catch(IOException x2){
    System.out.println("Unable to create socket " + x2 );
  }
```

```
    while( running ){
      try {
        Socket wrk = null ;
        wrk = srvSok.accept();
        ChatThread ct = new ChatThread( wrk );
        ct.setPriority( Thread.NORM_PRIORITY - 1 );
        ct.start();
        recCt++ ;
         // wrk.close(); is executed by ChatThread
      }catch(InterruptedIOException ie){
        ticCt++ ;
        //System.out.println("tick");
      }catch(IOException ioe ){
        System.out.println("Unplanned " + ioe);
        ioe.printStackTrace(System.err );
        running = false ;
      }
    } // end while
  }
```

Finally, Listing 9.17 shows some utility methods. The stop method simply sets the running flag to false so that the next time the ServerSocket times out or accepts a connection will be the last cycle of the main loop.

Listing 9.17: Utility methods in ChatSokServer

```
    public String toString()
    { StringBuffer sb = new StringBuffer("ChatSokServer transactions: ");
      sb.append( Integer.toString( recCt ));
      sb.append( " tick count: " );
      sb.append( Integer.toString( ticCt ));
      sb.append("\r\n");
      return sb.toString() ;
    }

    public void stop(){ running = false ;}

    public void finalize() throws Throwable
    {
      if( srvSok != null ) srvSok.close();
    }
  }
```

The ChatThread Class

The pattern I have used here, in which a client connection is handed off to a separate Thread for processing is typical of distributed computing. In this version, I create a new ChatThread for every connection, which has the added overhead of creating the Thread and adding it to the Thread scheduling mechanism in the JVM, then destroying it a few milliseconds later. A more efficient approach would be to redesign the class so we could maintain a pool of available ChatThread objects and simply hand the new Socket to the next available one for processing.

The existing class has the virtue of simplicity, as shown starting in Listing 9.18. The comment at the start of the listing shows the five commands that ChatThread needs to recognize. Four static String arrays that correspond to the various error messages might be required.

Listing 9.18: Start of the ChatThread code

```java
package com.JSPbook.Chap09;
import java.net.* ;
import java.io.* ;
import java.util.* ;

public class ChatThread extends java.lang.Thread
{
  /* possible commands that ChatRoom needs to respond to
     LIST - return <li> formated strings for room selection
     ENTER:roomcode,handle -
     QUIT:roomcode,handle
     REFRESH:roomcode,handle
     SEND:roomcode,handle  (followed by multiple lines)
  */

  static String[] badData = { "Transmission error" } ;
  static String[] badCommand = { "Command can't be interpreted","") ;
  static String[] badRoom = { "Roomcode not found","" };
  static String[] unknownCmd = { "Unknown command","" };
  Socket wrk ;
  InputStream ins ;
  OutputStream outs ;
  String command, roomcode,handle ;

  // constructor just attaches socket
  ChatThread( Socket s ){ wrk = s ;
  }
```

As shown in Listing 9.19, the run method gets a String array from the Socket by calling the getStr method, and then it processes the array according to the contents of the first String. The LIST command gets separate processing because it does not involve a particular chat room name. If a valid ChatRoom is found for a given roomcode, the doCommand method is called. Note that all the action is enclosed in a try block so that the Socket will be closed in the finally block, no matter what errors are encountered.

Listing 9.19: The run method in ChatThread

```java
public void run(){
    try {
        String[] outs = null ;
        String[] rslt = getStr();
        if( rslt == null || rslt.length == 0 ){
            outs = badData ;
        }
        else {
          String tmp = rslt[0];
          if( tmp.startsWith("LIST")){
            outs = new String[1];
            outs[0] = ChatRoom.getRoomsAsSelect();
          }
          else {
            if( parseCmd( tmp ) ){
                ChatRoom cr = ChatRoom.getChatRoom( roomcode );
                if( cr == null ){
                    outs = badRoom ;
                    outs[1] = roomcode ;
                }
                else {
                    outs = doCommand( cr, rslt );
                }
            }
            else { outs = badCommand ; outs[1] = tmp ;
            }
          }
        }
        sendStr( outs );
    }catch(IOException e){
        System.out.println("ChatThread " + e );
        e.printStackTrace( System.out );
    }finally{
        try {
          wrk.close();
        }catch(IOException e2){}
    }
}
```

The parseCmd method shown in Listing 9.20 takes apart the first String in the array received from the servlet and sets the command, roomcode, and handle variables. The doCommand method is called with a ChatRoom reference for a particular roomcode variable and uses the command variable to select the correct function.

Listing 9.20: This method parses all commands except LIST

```
// command string known to not be LIST return true if ok
private boolean parseCmd(String s){
  int p1 = s.indexOf(':');
  int p2 = s.indexOf(',');
  if( p1 > 0 && p2 > p1 ){
    command = s.substring(0,p1);
    roomcode = s.substring(p1 + 1, p2 );
    handle = s.substring( p2 + 1 );
    return true ;
  }
  return false ;
}

// command has been parsed from line
public String[] doCommand( ChatRoom cr, String[] msg ){
  String[] rslt = unknownCmd ;
  if( command.equals("ENTER")){
    cr.addUser( handle );
    rslt[0] = cr.getCurrent();
  }
  if( command.equals("QUIT")){
    cr.removeUser( handle );
    rslt[0] = cr.getCurrent();
  }
  if( command.equals("REFRESH")){
    rslt[0] = cr.getCurrent();
  }
  if( command.equals("SEND")){
    ChatItem item = new ChatItem(handle, msg);
    cr.addMsg( item );
    rslt[0] = cr.getCurrent();
  }
  return rslt ;
}
```

The getStr and sendStr methods shown in Listings 9.21 and 9.22 contain the only code specific to the method chosen for communication with the client.

Listing 9.21: The method that receives a String array

```
// this reads a byte at a time, looking for ctrlZ
public String[] getStr(){
  try {
    ins = wrk.getInputStream();
    outs = wrk.getOutputStream();
    BufferedInputStream bis = new BufferedInputStream( ins );
    Vector v = new Vector() ; // to save strings in
    StringBuffer sb = new StringBuffer(100);
    int ch = bis.read();
```

```
    while( ch != 0x1A ){
      if( ch == '\n' ){ // recognize newline character
        v.addElement( sb.toString());
        sb = new StringBuffer( 100 );
      }
      if( ch >= ' ' ){ // ignore any other control code
        sb.append( (char)ch );
      }
      ch = bis.read();
    } // while until eof
    String[] rec = new String[ v.size() ];
    for( int i =0 ; i < v.size() ; i++ ){
      rec[i] = (String)v.elementAt(i);
    }
    return rec ;
  }catch(IOException e){
      return null ;
  }
}
```

> **Listing 9.22: The method that sends a String array**

```
    void sendStr( String[] snd ) throws IOException {
      OutputStreamWriter osw = new OutputStreamWriter( outs );
      PrintWriter pw = new PrintWriter( osw );
      for( int i = 0 ; i < snd.length ; i++ ){
        pw.print( snd[i] ); pw.print('\n');
      }
      pw.write( 0x1A );
      pw.flush();
    }

    public void finalize(){
      if( wrk != null ){
        try{ wrk.close();
        }catch(IOException e){}
      }
    }
  }
}
```

The ChatItem Class

In the original ChatItem class used in Chapter 3, the constructor took two String objects, one for the author handle and one for the message content. In order to work with the String arrays transmitted to ChatSokServer, I added another constructor, as shown in Listing 9.23, that takes the message content from a String array.

Listing 9.23: The ChatItem class

```java
package com.JSPbook.Chap09;

import java.io.*;

public class ChatItem implements Serializable
{
  String author ;
  String content ;
  long timestamp ;

  public ChatItem( String handle, String msg ){
    author = handle ; content = msg ;
    timestamp = System.currentTimeMillis();
  }
  // msg[0] is the command:room,handle line which we skip
  public ChatItem( String handle, String[] msg ){
    if( msg == null || msg.length <= 1 ){
      content = "";
    }
    else {
      StringBuffer sb = new StringBuffer( 200 );
      for( int i = 1 ; i < msg.length ; i++ ){
        sb.append( msg[i] ); sb.append('\n');
      }
      content = sb.toString();
    }
    author = handle ;
    timestamp = System.currentTimeMillis();
  }

  public String toString()
  {
    return author + ": " + content + "\r\n------\r\n" ;
  }
}
```

Using Remote Method Invocation

Remote Method Invocation (RMI) is the standard Java approach to communication between distributed objects. The RMI library and utilities provide for socket communication of objects, just like we did with the object serialization example earlier in the chapter but without exposing the programmer to the details. To the programmer, it looks like you are executing a method on a local object. But in the background, RMI is carrying out the method on a separate system and returning the results to you transparently. These are the essential components of RMI:

The rmiregistry utility.   This utility program registers network objects that are available for RMI invocation so that they can be located by client programs.

The RMI package of classes and interfaces.   Your client and server must use the appropriate classes from the java.rmi and java.rmi.server packages.

Client interfaces or stubs.   These automatically generated classes provide the interface between your program and the RMI system.

The easiest way to see how all this works is to convert the chat server and servlet to using RMI. This is about the simplest possible use of RMI, but I don't have space to go into all of the possible improvements and embellishments.

The Chat Server with RMI

The first step in converting the server is to define the interface it will make available to remote objects. This has to be done by extending the Remote interface in the java.rmi package, as shown in Listing 9.24. Note that every method throws RemoteException. In the event that any Error or Exception is thrown in the server program, it will be enclosed in a RemoteException for transmission to the client. I created a method in the interface for every function the chat server is expected to provide.

Listing 9.24: The ChatInterface as used with RMI

```
package com.JSPbook.Chap09;
import java.rmi.*;

public interface ChatInterface extends java.rmi.Remote
{
    public String getRoomsAsSelect()throws RemoteException ;
    public String usrEnter( String room, String handle )
        throws RemoteException;
    public String usrSend( String room, String handle, String msg)
        throws RemoteException;
    public String usrRefresh( String room )throws RemoteException;
    public String usrQuit( String room, String handle )
        throws RemoteException;
}
```

The next step is to create the server class that implements the ChatInterface. This class must extend UnicastRemoteObject in the java.rmi.server package, as shown in Listing 9.25. The main method is practically identical to that in ChatSokServer (Listing 9.14) with the addition of these lines near the end:

```
ChatInterface ci = new ChatRMIServer();
Naming.rebind( host, ci );
```

Note that we use `ChatInterface` as the type of the reference to the `ChatRMIServer` object. This interface is registered with the `rmiregistry` program with the call to the `rebind` method of the `Naming` class. When this call occurs, the registry verifies that it can find the class files needed to implement the remote interface and is then ready to respond to client operations on that interface.

Listing 9.25: The ChatRMIServer class

```java
package com.JSPbook.Chap09;

import java.net.* ;
import java.io.* ;
import java.util.* ;
import java.rmi.* ;
import java.rmi.server.*;
import com.JSPbook.Chap09.*;

public class ChatRMIServer extends java.rmi.server.UnicastRemoteObject
      implements com.JSPbook.Chap09.ChatInterface
{
  static String version = "1.02 July 11, 2000";
  static String[] instruc = {
    "ChatRMIServer requires the name of a properties",
    "file on the command line. "
  };
  static String host = "//localhost/ChatRMIServer" ;
  static String[] rooms ; // code,full room name
  static Properties chatProp ;

  // start with the name of the properties file
  public static void main(String[] args ){
    System.out.println( version );
    if( args.length == 0 ){
      for( int i = 0 ; i < instruc.length ; i++ ){
        System.out.println( instruc[i]);
      }
      System.exit(1);
    }
    File f = new File( args[0] );
    chatProp = new Properties();
    try{
      chatProp.load( new FileInputStream( f ) );
      Enumeration e = chatProp.propertyNames();
      Vector v = new Vector();
      while( e.hasMoreElements()){
        String name = (String)e.nextElement();
        if( name.equals("host") ){
            host = chatProp.getProperty(name);
        }
```

```
        else { // room codes are other property values
           String tmp = name + "," + chatProp.getProperty( name );
           v.addElement( tmp );
        }
      }
      rooms = new String[ v.size() ] ;
      for( int i = 0 ; i < v.size() ; i++ ){
         rooms[i] = (String)v.elementAt(i);
      }
      ChatRoom.initChatRooms( rooms );
      ChatInterface ci = new ChatRMIServer();
      Naming.rebind( host, ci );
      System.out.println("Registered:" + host );
   }catch(Exception e){
      e.printStackTrace( System.err );
      System.exit(2);
   }
}
```

The instance methods of ChatRMIServer simply provide implementations for the methods the ChatInterface requires, as shown in Listing 9.26. Note that we must have a no-arguments constructor for the class.

Listing 9.26: The instance methods of ChatRMIServer

```
// instance methods
// no args constructor throwing RemoteException is required
public ChatRMIServer(  ) throws RemoteException {
   super();
}

public String crErr( String room ){
   return "Chat Server Error - " + room + " not found." ;
}
    // required by ChatInterface
public String getRoomsAsSelect()throws RemoteException{
   return ChatRoom.getRoomsAsSelect() ;
}
public String usrEnter( String room, String handle )
    throws RemoteException{
   ChatRoom cr = ChatRoom.getChatRoom( room );
   if( cr == null ) return crErr( room ) ;
   cr.addUser( handle );
   return cr.getCurrent() ;
}
public String usrSend( String room, String handle, String msg )
    throws RemoteException {
   ChatRoom cr = ChatRoom.getChatRoom( room );
   if( cr == null ) return crErr( room ) ;
   cr.addMsg( new ChatItem( handle,msg ) );
   return cr.getCurrent() ;
```

```
    }
    public String usrRefresh( String room )throws RemoteException {
      ChatRoom cr = ChatRoom.getChatRoom( room );
      if( cr == null ) return crErr( room ) ;
      return cr.getCurrent() ;
    }
    public String usrQuit( String room, String handle )throws RemoteException
    {
      ChatRoom cr = ChatRoom.getChatRoom( room );
      if( cr == null ) return crErr( room ) ;
      cr.removeUser( handle );
      return cr.getCurrent() ;
    }
  }
```

The other classes used in the chat server, `ChatRoom` and `ChatItem`, are unchanged from the `ChatSokServer` version. Isn't that convenient?!

Creating the Stubs

When the server classes have been compiled, it is time for a magic pass by the `rmic` utility. This standard part of the JDK uses introspection to examine the interface class and create *stub* and *skeleton* classes that will accomplish the RMI communication. Here is an example of the command line to run `rmic`, where the `-keepgenerated` option requests that the generated source code files not be erased and the `-d` option gives the base directory for the class.

```
>rmic -keepgenerated -d d:\JSPservletBook\Chap09\RMI
      com.JSPbook.Chap09.ChatRMIServer
```

The classes created by `rmic` are named `ChatRMIServer_Skel` and `ChatRMIServer_Stub`. The stub carries out the client side, and the skeleton handles the server side of the RMI communication. You must ensure that your servlet code can find the stub, and the server code can find the skeleton classes.

It is extremely instructive to examine the code that `rmic` generates for these classes. Complete documentation for the options that can be used with `rmic` are provided in the tooldocs section of a normal JDK documentation installation. Note that some IDEs such as Visual Cafe may carry out execution of `rmic` automatically.

RMI on the Servlet Side

Only a few changes are needed to convert the socket-based chat servlet to using RMI. The first change is in the `init` method, as shown in Listing 9.27. We obtain a reference to an object implementing `ChatInterface` by calling the `lookup` method of the `Naming` class. Note that we have this reference as an instance variable, so we have to guard against more than one request trying to use it at the same time.

Listing 9.27: Start of the ChatRmiServ servlet source code

```
package com.JSPbook.Chap09;

import java.io.*;
import javax.servlet.*;
import javax.servlet.http.*;
import java.rmi.* ;

public class ChatRmiServ extends HttpServlet
{
  static String alias = "http://localhost/servlet/chatrmiserv" ;
  static String host = "rmi://localhost/ChatRMIServer" ;
  static String version = "1.01";
  static String chatRows = "12" ;
  static String chatCols = "72" ;
  static String inputRows = "6" ;
  static String inputCols = "72" ;

  ChatInterface chi = null ;
  Exception initException = null ;
  public void init(ServletConfig config) throws ServletException
  {
    super.init(config);
    try {
      chi = (ChatInterface) Naming.lookup( host );
      System.out.println("Connected");
    }catch(Exception e){
      initException = e ;
      System.out.println("Failed to connect to " + host );
      e.printStackTrace( System.out );
    }
  }
```

The doGet method and most of the doPost method are unchanged, so I am resuming the listing with the part of doPost that is changed. Naturally, the complete code is on the CD. As shown in Listing 9.28, everywhere the socket-based chat servlet created String commands and called the doCommand method, we now call a method in the ChatInterface object. Behind the scenes, the stub class serializes the parameters, sends them to the server, and then gets back the String results.

Listing 9.28: The portion of doPost that is changed from ChatSokServ

```
out.println("<HTML>");
out.println("<HEAD><TITLE>ChatRmiServ Output</TITLE></HEAD>");
out.println("<BODY>");
out.println("<h2>In doPost method of ChatRmiServ</h2>");
```

```
     try {
     synchronized( chi ){
     switch( phase ){
       case 0 : // new entry
         sendChatTA( out, chi.usrEnter( room, handle ));
         sendMsgTA( out, "" );
         break ;
       case 1 : // "Send" - entry with text to be added
         sendChatTA(out, chi.usrSend( room, handle, getMsg(req)));
         sendMsgTA( out, "" );
         break ;
       case 2 : // "Refresh" - don't add text
         sendChatTA(out, chi.usrRefresh( room ));
         sendMsgTA( out, getMsg(req) );
         break ;
       case 3 : // "Quit"
         sendChatTA(out, chi.usrQuit( room, handle ));
         break ;
       case 8 : // user failed to enter usable handle
         badHandleMsg( out, handle ); break ;
       case 9 : // parameters not found, serious problem
         out.println("<h2>Serious problem - " + error +
             " notify operator.</h2>" );
         break ;
       default :
         out.println("Unknown phase " + phase );
     }
     } // end synchronized on chi
     }catch(Throwable et){
       out.print("Serious Problem<br>\r\n");
       et.printStackTrace( out );
     }
     out.println("</BODY>");
     out.println("</HTML>");
     out.close();
   }
```

When a new user enters the chat servlet, it is the doGet method that creates a page with a form that permits selection of the chat room and entry of a handle. The form is generated with the getRoomsAsForm method shown in Listing 9.29. This method is changed from the socket-based servlet because it now calls a method in the ChatInterface.

Listing 9.29: The getRoomsAsForm method

```
     public String getRoomsAsForm() throws RemoteException {
       StringBuffer sb = new StringBuffer(1000);
       if( chi == null ){
         sb.append("Servlet failed to initialize due to " );
         sb.append( initException.toString() );
         sb.append( "<br>\r\n");
       }
```

```
    else {
       sb.append("<center>Please select a chat room,<br>");
       sb.append("enter a Handle, and click the Enter button<br>");
       sb.append("<form method=\"post\" action=\"" + alias + "\" > ");
       synchronized( chi ){
          sb.append( chi.getRoomsAsSelect() );
       }
       sb.append("<br>");
       sb.append("Handle: <input TYPE=\"TEXT\" VALUE=\"\"" );
       sb.append(" name=\"handle\"><br>\r\n");
       sb.append("<input TYPE=\"submit\" VALUE=\"Enter Chat\"" );
       sb.append(" name=\"chatgo\">\r\n");
       sb.append("</form></center><hr>\r\n");
    }
    return sb.toString();
}
```

The sendChatTA method is changed slightly, as shown in Listing 9.30, because it no longer has to deal with a String array but a simple String.

___

Listing 9.30: The sendChatTA creates the textarea form for current chat contents

```
private void sendChatTA( PrintWriter out, String rslt ){
   out.println("<form><textarea rows=\"" + chatRows +
               "\" cols=\"" + chatCols + "\" >");
   out.println( rslt );
   out.println("</textarea></form>");
}
```

The sendMsgTA, getMsg, doButton, and badHandleMsg methods are unchanged from the socket-based servlet, so we are done with changes to the servlet.

Putting It All Together

Assuming that you have created the interface for your remote server and written the server side program that will implement the interface, here are the steps required to get your RMI-based servlet running.

1. Compile the server side program. Note that even the slightest change to the server side program requires that step 2 be repeated.

2. Run the rmic utility to create the stub and skeleton classes if your IDE doesn't do it automatically.

3. On the server (which can be localhost), start the rmiregistry utility if it is not running already. The server side classes must be on the classpath that rmiregistry sees.

4. Start the server program and confirm that the registration step worked. You did put a System.out.println in after the Naming.rebind call didn't you?

5. Compile the servlet code. Be sure you are using the same version of the interface class as the server-side code and that the call to `Naming.lookup` uses the correct address and name for the server. Put the stub class resulting from step 2 in the proper directory for the servlet engine to see it.

6. It's time to test. Remember that any change to the interface requires you to start over at step 1.

Java supports a number of different approaches to socket-based communication between a servlet and custom database servers. Examples in this chapter have demonstrated communication at three levels of abstraction. With basic streams, the programmer has to work at the individual byte level. Object serialization offers a fast and convenient level of abstraction, while Remote Method Invocation removes all the socket handling details from the programmer's concerns.

CHAPTER 10

Connecting to Legacy Programs

- The Runtime API

- The Process API

- Executing Legacy Common Gateway Interface (CGI) Programs

- Executing System Commands

If your Web site has been online for a while, you probably have a collection of programs such as Perl scripts that carry out useful functions you don't want to give up. Many programs of great utility are simply not set up to be easily interfaced to servlets and JSP with the techniques we have examined so far. In this chapter, we will examine and experiment with the API that Java provides for executing programs that use CGI, command line, and console interfaces.

The Java Runtime and Process APIs

The standard Java library provides a way to execute a program that will run independently of the Java Virtual Machine (JVM) and yet still communicate with it. This facility is accessed through a `java.lang.Runtime` object. When the JVM executes a Java program, such as a servlet engine, a single instance of the `Runtime` class is created to carry out various functions that depend on the underlying operating system. Using the `Runtime` methods, you can execute a command with the various permutations of the `exec` method. The `exec` method returns a `java.lang.Process` object that serves as your connection to the otherwise independent process started by `exec`.

Using the Runtime API

You access the current `Runtime` object with the static method `getRuntime`, as in this example:

```
Runtime rt = Runtime.getRuntime();
```

There are four versions of the `exec` method in `Runtime`; they differ only in the way parameters are supplied:

exec(String[] cmdarray, String[] envp) This is the most general form of `exec`. The other three versions are provided for convenience, but their input is converted to use this form. The first element in *cmdarray* is the name of the command to be executed, and the remaining elements are the command line parameters. The *envp* array is used to set environment variables that will be seen by the new process.

exec(String cmd) In this simplest version, the `String` contains a complete command line just as you might enter it at the console. A `StringTokenizer` is used to take the `String` apart into the *cmdarray*, and `null` is provided for *envp*.

exec(String **cmd**, String[] **envp**) Similar to the previous version but with an environment String array provided by the programmer.

exec(String[] **cmdarray**) In this version, the *cmdarray* is provided by the programmer, and null is assumed for *envp*.

The exec method always calls the SecurityManager checkExec method with the first String in the command array. If the Thread calling exec does not have the proper permission required to execute that command, a SecurityException is thrown. The default Java SecurityManager class checks the file system to verify whether your program is authorized to execute the file. Your servlet engine may provide a more restrictive SecurityManager, or you may want to create one because the open-ended ability to exec programs is very powerful.

Using the Process API

If an exec method executes without causing an exception, it returns a Process object that is now your sole link with the newly started program. Process is an abstract class. The actual class of the object returned depends on the JVM implementation. Your ability to communicate with the new program is extremely limited. You can get input and output streams to communicate with the standard input and output streams, as described here:

getOutputStream() This method returns an OutputStream object that you can use to send data to the new program's standard input. Typically, you won't work directly with this stream but will create a buffered stream instead.

getInputStream() The InputStream returned lets you read the standard output stream from the new program. Typically, you'll use a buffered stream here also.

getErrorStream() The InputStream returned lets you read the standard error stream from the new program. This is also typically buffered.

The JDK documentation warns that because of limitations in the buffering mechanisms of the underlying operating system, your program should try to catch the output from the standard streams as quickly as possible. You should definitely not rely on the following streams to act like files with an infinite capacity.

waitFor() The Thread calling this will wait for the process to terminate if it has not already done so. It returns immediately if the process has already terminated. The exit value from the process will be returned as an int. The waiting Thread can be interrupted by another Thread, in which case, an InterruptedException will be thrown.

exitValue() If the process has terminated, this method returns the exit value as an int. Do not call exitValue unless you're sure the process has terminated, or you will get an IllegalThreadStateException.

destroy() This method forces the operating system to terminate the process represented by the Process object.

Note the following important points about exec:

- The program you start will not have a console window.
- There's no guarantee that the process will be executed concurrently with your Java program.
- If you discard the Process object, the created process may continue independently.

Testing a Process Interface

After spending many hours debugging online servlets and JSPs—and seeing way too many "page not found" and other cryptic browser messages—I'm convinced that any testing you can do in a more controlled environment is good. This testing is even more important when you're trying to use Java's Process objects to work with legacy programs. Therefore, I've created a Java application that you can use to experiment with executing programs with the Runtime exec method and communicating with them using Process objects. The application presents two user interfaces: one for setting up the call to exec and one for manipulating the Process object.

Setting Up a Call to exec

As you learned in the previous section, the most generalized call to the exec method of the Runtime class takes the following form:

```
exec( String[] cmds, String[] env )
```

The first String in the cmds array designates the program to be run, and the remaining are command line options.

Figure 10.1 shows the user interface for setting up the call to exec. The upper field has the name of the program to be executed, in this case, the **java** interpreter. Because java.exe is on my PATH, I did not have to type in the complete path. This field can also be filled by using a file dialog box activated by an option on the File menu.

The text area in the middle of the interface accepts lines that will become command line options. Therefore, the inputs shown in the figure are the equivalent of executing the following:

```
java TestKeyin "Parameter one is a Phrase" Parameter_two
```

The text area at the bottom of the interface accepts lines setting environment variables. When you have all the parameters set up, click the Execute! button to perform a call to exec. If an exception is generated by the call to exec, it will appear in the text field below the Execute! button. If exec works, the interface switches to the Process view, as shown in Figure 10.2.

FIGURE 10.2

The interface for Process
input and output

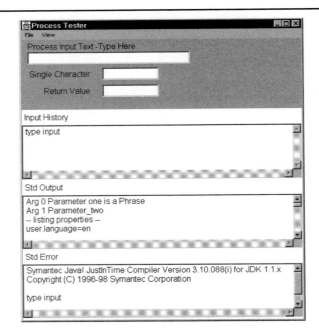

The process view provides for typing in text to be sent to the standard input stream and for displaying the output by the process to the standard output and standard error streams. The group of fields at the top of the window provides for input of characters and display of the value returned when the waitFor method of Process returns.

Accepting character input to be sent to the process is complicated by the fact that a Java TextField does not accept some non-printing characters. To get around this problem, the interface also provides for sending a single character that may be input as a decimal value. The remainder of the process view consists of text areas that record the input characters and the output received from the Process object.

There are three classes in the Process Tester application:

> **ProcessTestFrame** This class provides the main window, which is the interface for the exec method and menus.
>
> **ProcessPanel** This class provides the process view.
>
> **LabeledPanel** A utility display used in ProcessPanel.

The ProcessTestFrame Class

This listing is rather long because of all the interface components that must be created, but it's basically a simple program. The program was created using the Visual Cafe environment, which inserts certain special comments for use in the interface constructor. However, it contains nothing specific to the Visual Cafe environment and will compile with JDK 1.2. Listing 10.1 shows the start of the class, the instance variables, and the constructor. The first few listings are just for the sake of completeness; the interesting stuff starts with Listing 10.6.

Listing 10.1: Start of the ProcessTestFrame class source

```java
package com.JSPbook.Chap10;

import java.awt.*;
import java.io.*;
import java.util.* ;

public class ProcessTestFrame extends java.awt.Frame
{
  Process proc ;
  int procRet ;
  String[] cmds ;
  String[] envs ;
  boolean fComponentsAdjusted = false;

  public ProcessTestFrame()
  {
    //{{INIT_CONTROLS
    setLayout(new CardLayout(0,0));
    setFont(new Font("Dialog", Font.PLAIN, 16));
    setSize(465,481);
    setVisible(false);
    findFileDlg.setMode(FileDialog.LOAD);
    findFileDlg.setTitle("Locate Executable File");
    //$$ findFileDlg.move(48,492);
    processPanel.setLayout(new GridLayout(4,1,0,0));
    add("card1", processPanel);
    processPanel.setBackground(java.awt.Color.white);
    processPanel.setBounds(0,0,465,481);
    processPanel.setVisible(false);
    execPanel.setLayout(new GridLayout(3,1,0,0));
    add("card2", execPanel);
    execPanel.setBounds(0,0,465,481);
    execPanel.setVisible(false);
    execTop.setLayout(null);
    execPanel.add(execTop);
    execTop.setBounds(0,0,465,160);
    label1.setText("Exec Parameters - Program");
    execTop.add(label1);
    label1.setBounds(0,0,288,36);
```

```
        execTop.add(execFileTF);
        execFileTF.setBounds(12,48,432,24);
        goButton.setLabel("Execute!");
        execTop.add(goButton);
        goButton.setBackground(java.awt.Color.lightGray);
        goButton.setBounds(12,84,216,24);
        execTop.add(exceptionTF);
        exceptionTF.setBounds(12,120,432,24);
        execPanel.add(commandsTA);
        commandsTA.setBounds(0,160,465,160);
        execPanel.add(environmentTA);
        environmentTA.setBounds(0,320,465,160);
        setTitle("Process Tester");
        //}}

        //{{INIT_MENUS
        menu1.setLabel("File");
        menu1.add(findFileMI);
        findFileMI.setLabel("Find Executable File");
        menu1.add(saveMI);
        saveMI.setLabel("Save All Text");
        menu1.add(separatorMenuItem);
        separatorMenuItem.setLabel("-");
        menu1.add(exitMenuItem);
        exitMenuItem.setLabel("Exit");
        mainMenuBar.add(menu1);
        menu2.setLabel("View");
        menu2.add(viewExecMI);
        viewExecMI.setLabel("View Exec Parameters");
        menu2.add(viewProcessMI);
        viewProcessMI.setLabel("View Process");
        mainMenuBar.add(menu2);
        //$$ mainMenuBar.move(0,492);
        setMenuBar(mainMenuBar);
        //}}

        //{{REGISTER_LISTENERS
        SymWindow aSymWindow = new SymWindow();
        this.addWindowListener(aSymWindow);
        SymAction lSymAction = new SymAction();
        exitMenuItem.addActionListener(lSymAction);
        viewExecMI.addActionListener(lSymAction);
        viewProcessMI.addActionListener(lSymAction);
        findFileMI.addActionListener(lSymAction);
        goButton.addActionListener(lSymAction);
        saveMI.addActionListener(lSymAction);
        //}}
        processPanel.setVisible(true);
    }
```

The code continues in Listing 10.2 with another constructor, the main method, and typical Visual Cafe initialization routines.

Listing 10.2: ProcessTestFrame code continued

```java
public ProcessTestFrame(String title)  {
  this();
  setTitle(title);
}

public void setVisible(boolean b)  {
  if(b){
    setLocation(50, 50);
  }
  super.setVisible(b);
}

static public void main(String args[])  {
  try  {
      (new ProcessTestFrame()).setVisible(true);
  }
  catch (Throwable t)  {
    System.err.println(t);
    t.printStackTrace();
    System.exit(1);
  }
}

public void addNotify()
{
  Dimension d = getSize();
  super.addNotify();
  if (fComponentsAdjusted)
    return;
  setSize(getInsets().left + getInsets().right + d.width, getInsets().top + ➡
  getInsets().bottom + d.height);
  Component components[] = getComponents();
  for (int i = 0; i < components.length; i++)
  {
    Point p = components[i].getLocation();
    p.translate(getInsets().left, getInsets().top);
    components[i].setLocation(p);
  }
  fComponentsAdjusted = true;
}
```

Listing 10.3 shows the interface components declared and initialized in the Visual Cafe style, plus a couple of utility methods.

Listing 10.3: Declaration of the various interface components

```
//{{DECLARE_CONTROLS
java.awt.FileDialog findFileDlg = new java.awt.FileDialog(this);
com.JSPbook.Chap10.ProcessPanel processPanel = new ➡
com.JSPbook.Chap10.ProcessPanel();
java.awt.Panel execPanel = new java.awt.Panel();
java.awt.Panel execTop = new java.awt.Panel();
java.awt.Label label1 = new java.awt.Label();
java.awt.TextField execFileTF = new java.awt.TextField();
java.awt.Button goButton = new java.awt.Button();
java.awt.TextField exceptionTF = new java.awt.TextField();
java.awt.TextArea commandsTA = new java.awt.TextArea();
java.awt.TextArea environmentTA = new java.awt.TextArea();
//}}

//{{DECLARE_MENUS
java.awt.MenuBar mainMenuBar = new java.awt.MenuBar();
java.awt.Menu menu1 = new java.awt.Menu();
java.awt.MenuItem findFileMI = new java.awt.MenuItem();
java.awt.MenuItem saveMI = new java.awt.MenuItem();
java.awt.MenuItem separatorMenuItem = new java.awt.MenuItem();
java.awt.MenuItem exitMenuItem = new java.awt.MenuItem();
java.awt.Menu menu2 = new java.awt.Menu();
java.awt.MenuItem viewExecMI = new java.awt.MenuItem();
java.awt.MenuItem viewProcessMI = new java.awt.MenuItem();
//}}

class SymWindow extends java.awt.event.WindowAdapter
{
  public void windowClosing(java.awt.event.WindowEvent event)
  {
    Object object = event.getSource();
    if (object == ProcessTestFrame.this)exitNow() ;
  }
}

private void exitNow(){
  if( proc != null ) proc.destroy();
  processPanel.stop();
  System.exit( 0 );
}
```

Listing 10.4 shows the inner class that is used to respond to action events from the menus and the Execute! button on the exec preparation panel.

Listing 10.4: The SymAction inner class catches action events

```java
class SymAction implements java.awt.event.ActionListener
{
  public void actionPerformed(java.awt.event.ActionEvent event)
  {
    Object object = event.getSource();
    if (object == exitMenuItem)
      exitMenuItem_ActionPerformed(event);
    else if (object == viewExecMI)
      viewExecMI_ActionPerformed(event);
    else if (object == viewProcessMI)
      viewProcessMI_ActionPerformed(event);
    else if (object == findFileMI)
      findFileMI_ActionPerformed(event);
    else if (object == goButton)
      goButton_ActionPerformed(event);
    else if (object == saveMI)
      saveMI_ActionPerformed(event);
  }
}

void exitMenuItem_ActionPerformed(java.awt.event.ActionEvent event)
{
  exitNow();
}

void viewExecMI_ActionPerformed(java.awt.event.ActionEvent event)
{
  CardLayout cards = (CardLayout)getLayout();
  cards.show(this,"card2");
}

void viewProcessMI_ActionPerformed(java.awt.event.ActionEvent event)
{
  CardLayout cards = (CardLayout)getLayout();
  cards.show(this,"card1");
}
```

There are two ways to create the String that names the program to be executed: You can type it in directly, or you can browse for it using the FileDialog that is activated by the "Find Executable File" menu item. The method that handles this dialog is shown in Listing 10.5.

Listing 10.5: The method that is used to browse for a program

```java
void findFileMI_ActionPerformed(java.awt.event.ActionEvent event)
{
  findFileDlg.show();
  String path = findFileDlg.getDirectory();
  String name = findFileDlg.getFile();
  if( path == null || name == null ) return ;
  File f = new File( path, name );
  if( !f.exists() ) return;
  execFileTF.setText( f.getAbsolutePath() );
}
```

Now we're getting to the interesting part. Listing 10.6 shows the method that is executed when the Execute! button is clicked. It creates two `String` arrays from the contents of the `TextField` and `TextArea` components of the interface by calling the `prepare` method. The actual execution is carried out by a new `ExecMonitor` object.

Listing 10.6: The method that starts the execution process

```java
void goButton_ActionPerformed(java.awt.event.ActionEvent event)
{
  String exs  = execFileTF.getText();
  if( exs.length() < 2 ) {
     return ;
  }
  cmds = prepare( exs, commandsTA.getText());
  envs = prepare( null, environmentTA.getText());
  for( int i = 0 ; i < cmds.length ;i++ ){
     System.out.println( cmds[i] );
  }
  new ExecMonitor().start();
  CardLayout cards = (CardLayout)getLayout();
  cards.show(this,"card1");
}

 // cmd is null for environment
private String[] prepare( String cmd, String text ){
  StringTokenizer st = new StringTokenizer( text, "\n");
  int ct = st.countTokens();
  if( cmd != null ) ct++;
  String[] ret = new String[ ct ];
  int i = 0 ;
  if( cmd != null ) ret[i++] = cmd ;
  while( st.hasMoreTokens() ){
    ret[i++] = st.nextToken() ;
  }
  return ret ;
}
```

This is the most important part of the `ProcessTestFrame` class. We have to use a `Thread` that is separate from the `Thread` that handles interface events to execute the `Runtime exec` method. Otherwise, the user interface would be frozen, and we would not be able to continue. We accomplish this with the inner class named `ExecMonitor`, which is shown in Listing 10.7. The `Process` object returned by the call to exec is passed to the `ProcessPanel`.

Listing 10.7: The ExecMonitor inner class

```
class ExecMonitor extends Thread {
  public void run(){
    Runtime rt = Runtime.getRuntime();
    try {
      proc = rt.exec( cmds, envs );
      processPanel.attachProcess( proc );
      procRet = proc.waitFor();
      processPanel.procReturn( procRet );
      exceptionTF.setText("None - returned " + procRet );
      proc = null ;
    }catch(Exception ex){
      exceptionTF.setText( ex.toString() );
      processPanel.procReturn(ex);
      proc = null ;
    }
  }
}
```

The Save All Text menu item is provided to let you save the contents of all the various text components in both the `exec` preparation and process panels. This is a handy way to save all the relevant test conditions and results. As shown in Listing 10.8, it simply gets a file path and name, creates a `PrintWriter`, and outputs the contents of the various text components to the file.

Listing 10.8: The method that handles the Save All Text menu item selection

```
void saveMI_ActionPerformed(java.awt.event.ActionEvent event)
{
  FileDialog dlg = new FileDialog(this, "Saving Text in" ,
   FileDialog.SAVE );
  dlg.show();
  String path = dlg.getDirectory();
  String fname = dlg.getFile();
  if( path == null || fname == null ) return ;
  try {
    File f = new File(path, fname );
    PrintWriter pw = new PrintWriter( new FileWriter( f ) );
    dumpExec( pw );
    processPanel.dumpProcess( pw );
    pw.close();
```

```
      }catch(IOException ex){}
    }

  private void dumpExec( PrintWriter pw ){
    pw.println( new Date().toString());
    pw.println( "Process Tester - exec parameters");
    String exs  = execFileTF.getText();
    // create arrays as used by exec
    cmds = prepare( exs, commandsTA.getText());
    envs = prepare( null, environmentTA.getText());
    int i ;
    for( i = 0 ; i < cmds.length; i++ ){
      pw.print( "cmd " + i + " :" );
      pw.println( cmds[i]);
    }
    pw.println("env entries = " + envs.length );
    for( i = 0 ; i < envs.length ; i++ ){
      pw.print("env " + i + " :" );
      pw.println( envs[i] );
    }
  }
}
```

The LabeledPanel Utility Class

I created the LabeledPanel class to make it simpler to add three labeled text areas to the
ProcessPanel class. As Listing 10.9 shows, it simply incorporates a label and a
java.awt.TextArea component. Methods are provided for adding a String or a single
character to the TextArea display. The odd-looking comments were added by Visual Cafe.

Listing 10.9: The LabeledPanel class

```
package com.JSPbook.Chap10;

import java.awt.*;
import java.beans.*;

public class LabeledPanel extends java.awt.Panel
{
  public LabeledPanel( String title )
  {

    //{{INIT_CONTROLS
    setLayout(new BorderLayout(0,0));
    Insets ins = getInsets();
    setSize(430,270);
    msgTA.setEditable(false);
    add("Center",msgTA);
    msgTA.setBounds(0,0,100,40);
    topP.setLayout(new FlowLayout(FlowLayout.LEFT,5,2));
```

```
    add("North",topP);
    topP.setBackground(java.awt.Color.white);
    topP.setBounds(0,0,20,40);
    //}}
    topP.add( new Label( title ));
    //{{REGISTER_LISTENERS
    //}}
  }

  //{{DECLARE_CONTROLS
  java.awt.TextArea msgTA = new java.awt.TextArea();
  java.awt.Panel topP = new java.awt.Panel();
  //}}

  public void clear(){ msgTA.setText(""); }
  public String getText(){return msgTA.getText();}
  public void addText(String s){ msgTA.append( s ); }
  public void addChar( int ch ){
    StringBuffer sb = new StringBuffer( msgTA.getText() );
    sb.append( (char)ch );
    msgTA.setText(sb.toString());
  }
}
```

The ProcessPanel Class

After a Process has been created, you can interact with it through the interface provided by this class derived from java.awt.Panel. Listing 10.10 shows the instance variables and the attachProcess method. The attachProcess method creates the two input streams and single output stream that communicate with the Process; it then creates a Thread to execute the run method.

Listing 10.10: The start of the ProcessPanel class

```
package com.JSPbook.Chap10;

import java.io.* ;
import java.util.* ;
import java.awt.* ;

public class ProcessPanel extends java.awt.Panel implements Runnable
{
  Process proc ;
  BufferedInputStream inStd, inErr ; // read from stdout and stderr
  BufferedOutputStream outStr ; // writes to process stdin
  boolean running = false;
```

```
public void attachProcess(Process p ){
  proc = p ;
  inStd = new BufferedInputStream( p.getInputStream());
  inErr = new BufferedInputStream( p.getErrorStream());
  outStr = new BufferedOutputStream( p.getOutputStream());
  Thread t = new Thread(this);
  t.setPriority(Thread.MIN_PRIORITY);
  running = true ;
  t.start();
}
```

The Thread attached to the run method shown in Listing 10.11 executes with a low priority so as to not interfere with the user interface thread. It continuously looks for available bytes from the input streams and directs them to the appropriate LabeledPanel for display.

Listing 10.11: The run method in ProcessPanel

```
public void run(){
  try {
    while( running ){
      while( inStd.available() > 0 ){
        stdOutP.addChar( inStd.read() );
      }
      while( inErr.available() > 0 ){
        stdErrP.addChar( inErr.read() );
      }
    }
  }catch(IOException ex){
      System.out.println("ProcessPanel.run " + ex );
  }
}
public void stop(){ running = false ; }
```

The constructor for ProcessPanel, shown in Listing 10.12, is pretty straightforward.

Listing 10.12: The ProcessPanel constructor

```
public ProcessPanel()
{
  //{{INIT_CONTROLS
  setLayout(new GridLayout(4,1,0,0));
  setSize(398,492);
  ppTopP.setLayout(null);
  add(ppTopP);
  ppTopP.setBackground(java.awt.Color.cyan);
  ppTopP.setBounds(0,0,398,123);
  label1.setText("Process Input Text -Type Here");
  ppTopP.add(label1);
  label1.setBounds(12,4,240,18);
  ppTopP.add(inputToProcTF);
```

```
inputToProcTF.setBackground(java.awt.Color.white);
inputToProcTF.setBounds(12,24,312,24);
label3.setText("Single Character");
label3.setAlignment(java.awt.Label.RIGHT);
ppTopP.add(label3);
label3.setBounds(12,56,120,24);
ppTopP.add(singleCharTF);
singleCharTF.setBackground(java.awt.Color.white);
singleCharTF.setBounds(156,56,108,24);
label2.setText("Return Value");
label2.setAlignment(java.awt.Label.RIGHT);
ppTopP.add(label2);
label2.setBounds(24,90,108,24);
processReturnTF.setEditable(false);
ppTopP.add(processReturnTF);
processReturnTF.setBackground(java.awt.Color.white);
processReturnTF.setBounds(156,90,108,24);
//}}

setSize(430,270);
add(historyP);
add(stdOutP);
add(stdErrP);

//{{REGISTER_LISTENERS
SymAction lSymAction = new SymAction();
inputToProcTF.addActionListener(lSymAction);
singleCharTF.addActionListener(lSymAction);
//}}
}

//{{DECLARE_CONTROLS
java.awt.Panel ppTopP = new java.awt.Panel();
java.awt.Label label1 = new java.awt.Label();
java.awt.TextField inputToProcTF = new java.awt.TextField();
java.awt.Label label3 = new java.awt.Label();
java.awt.TextField singleCharTF = new java.awt.TextField();
java.awt.Label label2 = new java.awt.Label();
java.awt.TextField processReturnTF = new java.awt.TextField();
//}}
LabeledPanel historyP = new LabeledPanel("Input History");
LabeledPanel stdOutP = new LabeledPanel("Std Output");
LabeledPanel stdErrP = new LabeledPanel("Std Error");
```

As shown earlier in Figure 10.2, there are two TextField components for input of a String of characters or a single character. When a field has the focus and the user hits the Enter key, an ActionEvent is generated and passed to the ActionListener created by the inner class shown in Listing 10.13.

A String input in the inputToProcTF text field will be written character by character to the outStr output stream, followed by a carriage return character. This simulates typing a line of characters to the standard input of the process. Unfortunately, the java.awt.Text-Field won't accept certain control characters, such as Ctrl-Z, so we also have to have the singleCharTF input field. A single character typed here followed by a return will be sent to the standard input; more than one character will be interpreted as a decimal number and sent to the standard input.

Characters sent by either method will also be added to the historyP LabeledPanel. Note that we always have to call the flush method of the output stream to ensure that the characters will actually be sent.

Listing 10.13: This inner class catches events

```
class SymAction implements java.awt.event.ActionListener
{
  public void actionPerformed(java.awt.event.ActionEvent event)
  {
    Object object = event.getSource();
    if (object == inputToProcTF)
      inputToProcTF_ActionPerformed(event);
    else if (object == singleCharTF)
      singleCharTF_ActionPerformed(event);
  }
}

void inputToProcTF_ActionPerformed(java.awt.event.ActionEvent event)
{
  try {
    byte[] tmp = inputToProcTF.getText().getBytes();
    for(int i = 0 ; i < tmp.length ; i++){
      outStr.write( tmp[i] );
      historyP.addChar((char)tmp[i]);
    }
    outStr.write( '\r' );
    outStr.flush();
    historyP.addText( "\n" );
    inputToProcTF.setText("");
  } catch (Exception e) {
  }
}
// send a single character - may do conversion from decimal
void singleCharTF_ActionPerformed(java.awt.event.ActionEvent event)  {
  String tmp = singleCharTF.getText();
  if( tmp.length() == 0 ) return ;
  singleCharTF.setText( "" );
  try{
    if( tmp.length() == 1 ){ // single character in box
      outStr.write( tmp.charAt(0) );
```

```
            outStr.flush();
            historyP.addText( tmp );
            return ;
        }
         // assume a decimal number
        int ch = Integer.parseInt( tmp );
        outStr.write( ch ); outStr.flush();
        historyP.addChar( ch );
    }catch( Exception e){ // including NumberFormatException
        System.out.println( e );
    }
}
```

Listing 10.14 finishes up the `ProcessPanel` listing with some utility methods.

Listing 10.14: Some utility methods in ProcessPanel

```
        public void procReturn( int x ){
          processReturnTF.setText("Returned " + x );
        }
        public void procReturn( Exception e ){
          processReturnTF.setText( e.toString() );
        }

        public void dumpProcess( PrintWriter pw ){
          pw.println("Process Panel contents");
          pw.println("Return value : " + processReturnTF.getText() );
          pw.println("Input History : " + historyP.getText() );
          pw.println("Std Output: " );
          pw.println( stdOutP.getText());
          pw.println("Std Error: " );
          pw.println( stdErrP.getText());
        }
    }
```

For initial tests of the `ProcessTestFrame` program (as shown earlier in Figure 10.2), I used the simple Java program shown in Listing 10.15. This exercises the various functions by echoing input characters to the `System.err PrintStream` and printing various other items to `System.out`.

Listing 10.15: The TestKeyin program

```
    import java.io.* ;
    import java.util.* ;

    public class TestKeyin{

      public static void main(String[] args ){
        for( int i = 0 ; i < args.length ; i++ ){
          System.out.println( "Arg " + i + " " + args[i] );
        }
```

```
Properties sysP = System.getProperties();
sysP.list( System.out );
int ch = 0 ;
StringBuffer sb = new StringBuffer();
try {
  while( ch != 0x1A ){ // 26 decimal
    ch = System.in.read();
    sb.append((char) ch );
    if( ch < ' ' ){
      System.err.println( sb.toString() );
      sb = new StringBuffer();
    }
  }
}catch(IOException e){
  System.err.println( e.toString() );
}
}
}
```

Using a Process in a Servlet

To demonstrate various aspects of using **exec** and **Process** in a servlet, I'm going to use the very simplified servlet shown in Listing 10.16. This servlet uses the **ProcMonitor** class (Listing 10.17) to start an external process and catch the outputs of that process.

As in the **doGet** method, inputs to **ProcMonitor** are hard-coded in this example. This is just to keep the listing short. In a practical servlet, these values could come from an HTML form or properties file. The listing shows the inputs used to execute a Perl script. Outputs are simply written to the HTML page.

Listing 10.16: The ProcServlet code

```
package com.JSPbook.Chap10;

import java.io.*;
import javax.servlet.*;
import javax.servlet.http.*;

public class ProcServlet extends HttpServlet
{
  static String execstr = "Perl" ;
  static String cmdstr = "e:\\scripts\\Hello.pl" ;
  static String envstr = "ProcVersion=1.0\nProcDate=July 26, 2000" ;
  static String instr = null ;
  static String prestr = "" ;
  static String poststr = "" ;
```

```
   public void doGet(HttpServletRequest req, HttpServletResponse resp)
   throws ServletException, IOException
   {
     resp.setContentType("text/html");
     PrintWriter out = new PrintWriter(resp.getOutputStream());
     out.println("<HTML>");
     out.println("<HEAD><TITLE>ProcServlet Output</TITLE></HEAD>");
     out.println("<BODY>");
     out.println("<h2>Start ProcServlet get</h2>");
     ProcMonitor procM = new ProcMonitor( );
     try {
     int ret = procM.doExec(execstr,cmdstr,envstr,instr,prestr,poststr );
     out.println("ProcMonitor returns " + ret + "<br>\n");
     out.println("stdOut result: " + procM.getStdOut() + "<br>");
     out.println("stdErr result: " + procM.getErrOut() + "<br>");
     }catch(Exception e){
         e.printStackTrace( out );
     }
     out.println("</BODY>");
     out.println("</HTML>");
     out.close();
   }
 }
```

The class I'm using with this servlet to execute the Perl script is `ProcMonitor`, shown in Listing 10.17. In contrast with the classes used in the `ProcessTestFrame` application, this class makes some simplifying assumptions so that it can be run by the servlet `Thread`. It assumes that the output will be text and the volume written to the standard error stream will be small. It also assumes that the process that is started will not get hung up in a loop.

The output streams are written to `StringBuffer` objects for later retrieval by the servlet. Simple formatting for each line can be provided by the `prestr` variable, which is written at the start, and the `poststr` variable, which is written at the end of the line.

As with the earlier example, the command and environment variables are handed to the `ProcMonitor` as simple `String` objects that are taken apart into `String` arrays by the `prepare` method. The reason for this approach is that it allows you to accept user commands typed into a text area from a form.

Listing 10.17: The ProcMonitor class

```
   package com.JSPbook.Chap10;

   import java.io.* ;
   import java.util.* ;

   public class ProcMonitor {
```

```
Process proc ;
// the assumption is that stdout will be text .
BufferedReader inStd, inErr ; // read from stdout and stderr
BufferedOutputStream outStr ; // writes to process stdin
StringBuffer stdOutSB, stdErrSB ;
String prestr, poststr ;
boolean running = false;

public int doExec( String exs, String cmd, String env, String input,
          String pr, String po){
  prestr = pr ; poststr = po ;
  String[] cmds = prepare( exs, cmd );
  String[] envs = prepare( null, env );
  Runtime rt = Runtime.getRuntime();
  try {
     proc = rt.exec( cmds, envs );
    watchProcess( proc, input );
    return proc.waitFor();
  }catch( Exception ex){
      System.out.println("ProcMonitor.doExec " + ex );
      return -1 ;
  }
}

   // cmd is null for setup of environment
private String[] prepare( String cmd, String text ){
  StringTokenizer st = new StringTokenizer( text, "\n");
  int ct = st.countTokens();
  if( cmd != null ) ct++;
  String[] ret = new String[ ct ];
  int i = 0 ;
  if( cmd != null ) ret[i++] = cmd ;
  while( st.hasMoreTokens() ){
    ret[i++] = st.nextToken() ;
  }
  return ret ;
}

   // if not null, input goes to the process standard input
public void watchProcess(Process p, String input )throws IOException {
  proc = p ;
  inStd = new BufferedReader( new InputStreamReader(
              p.getInputStream()));
  inErr = new BufferedReader( new InputStreamReader(
              p.getErrorStream()));
  stdOutSB = new StringBuffer();
  stdErrSB = new StringBuffer();
```

```
    if( input != null ){
      outStr = new BufferedOutputStream( p.getOutputStream());
      outStr.write( input.getBytes() );
      outStr.flush();
    }
    String tmp ;
    while( (tmp = inStd.readLine()) != null ){
        stdOutSB.append( prestr );
        stdOutSB.append( tmp );
        stdOutSB.append(poststr);
    }
    while( (tmp = inErr.readLine()) != null ){
        stdErrSB.append( tmp ); stdErrSB.append("\r\n");
    }
  }

  public String getStdOut(){return stdOutSB.toString(); }
  public String getErrOut(){return stdErrSB.toString(); }
}
```

ProcServlet with a Perl Script

Because many Web sites have been running Perl scripts to handle CGI processes, there is a significant investment in these scripts that we would like to take advantage of. Fortunately, Perl is oriented to using environment variables for input and standard streams for output, so it fits the capabilities of the **exec** method well. Listing 10.18 shows a simple script that echoes the environment variables as list items.

Listing 10.18: The Perl script used in the example

```
print "<h2>Hello World</h2>\n";
print "<ul>\n";
@key_names = keys(%ENV) ;
foreach $key (@key_names ){
  print "<li>$key =  $ENV{ $key }</li>\n";
}
print "</ul>";
print "<h2>How about that!</h2>\n";
```

Figure 10.3 shows the result of accessing the Perl script with the **ProcServ** servlet. Notice that the only environment variables found are the two that were input through the call to **exec**. In contrast, when the same script is accessed directly as a CGI process, it finds all the system's environment variables, as shown in Figure 10.4. This is a very important point to consider when you are trying to use existing Perl scripts through a servlet.

FIGURE 10.3

Output by the Perl script through the servlet

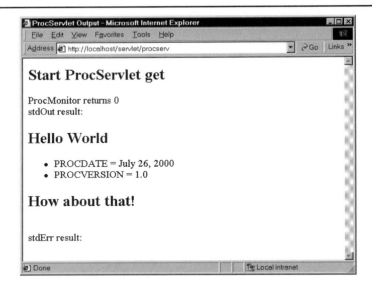

FIGURE 10.4

Output by the Perl script with normal CGI

NOTE A Perl script executed using **exec** will see only the environment variables provided by **exec**; it will not see the normal system environment variables that your existing scripts may depend on.

ProcServlet with System Commands

Many Windows commands that you typically type at the command line do not execute programs but instead execute routines inside the command *shell*. The consequence of this is that we can't **exec** a **dir** command and get a directory listing. However, there's a simple solution. We can **exec** a Windows batch file! This means that a servlet can write a batch file and execute it to accomplish potentially very complex tasks. As a simple example, I used the following batch file (named getdir.bat)

```
REM batch file test of commands
dir /od %1
```

with the following settings for the variables in **ProcServlet**:

```
static String execstr = "e:\\scripts\\getdir.bat" ;
static String cmdstr = "e:\\scripts\\*.pl" ;
static String envstr = "" ;
static String instr = null ;
static String prestr = "<br>\n" ;
static String poststr = "" ;
```

The resulting display is shown in Figure 10.5. Note that the batch file processing is the equivalent of typing the individual lines at the command prompt for the home directory of the JRun servlet engine because that is the "current" directory for the servlet engine.

FIGURE 10.5

The page produced by executing a batch command

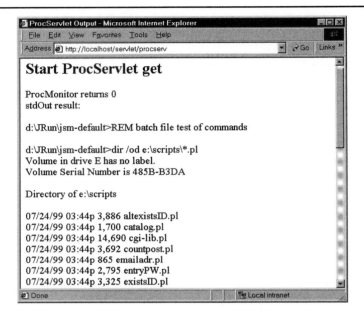

A carefully planned batch file can enable a Java servlet or JSP to accomplish complex processing by legacy programs. However, by using a batch process, you give up all the security features of Java. The open-ended nature of executing a batch file presents a security problem that you need to consider.

CHAPTER 11

Custom Tag Libraries

- The Basics of Custom Tag Libraries

- How Custom Libraries Are Added to a Server

- Tags with Custom Attributes Set at Runtime

- Tags That Process Body Text

- A Tag to Process XML Data

- Nesting and Cooperating Tags

One of the most exciting capabilities now coming to fruition with the JavaServer Pages 1.1 API is the custom tag library. This extremely flexible mechanism allows Java developers to create an entire library of tags that may be intermixed with the standard JSP tags and HTML markup. This innovation is being rapidly adopted by the industry because it holds out the promise of Web site development systems that let programmers concentrate on the data while Web page designers concentrate on presentation.

Using Tag Libraries with JSP

The JavaServer Pages API provides a very elegant facility for creating your own specialized toolkit of tags. The JSP engine treats these tags just like the standard JSP tags to create Java code that is compiled into servlets.

These tag libraries make it easier for Java programmers to provide Web page designers with the specialized information retrieval capability required to support a particular application while staying clear of the presentation details. The latest crop of Web design tools is expected to provide extensive support for tag libraries.

The following steps are involved in creating and applying a custom tag library:

1. Create a Java class (or classes) that implements the required interfaces.
2. Create a tag library description of the attributes and methods in XML.
3. Create a jar file containing the classes and the library description.
4. Place the jar file where the JSP engine can find it.
5. Create JSP pages that refer to the custom tags.

Tags create objects that are similar to Java Beans in the following ways:

*   Variables can be set with attributes.
*   Objects created by tags can access the various standard JSP objects.
*   Objects created by tags can write output to the `response` object.
*   Tag-created objects can share variables.
*   Tags can be nested, allowing for complex behavior.

The JSP API calls for six standard tags (which Sun calls *actions*) that use the same syntax as custom tags. These tags, which were introduced in Chapter 2, are `jsp:forward`, `jsp:get-Property`, `jsp:include`, `jsp:plugin`, `jsp:setProperty`, and `jsp:useBean`.

The uses of custom tags range from very simple to quite complex. We will look at some simple uses first.

Using Simple Custom Tags

The following examples use the Tomcat server, which follows the directory structure called for by the servlet 2.2 API very closely. Not all servlet engines have completely adopted these standards, so your working directory may have a different structure. The following diagram shows some of the most important file locations:

```
C:/tomcat
    +- conf <-- server.xml file defining the JSPbook application
    +- work <-- JSP engine created java and class files for JSP pages
    +- webapps
        +- JSPbook
            +- Chap11    <-- html and jsp pages
            +- Web-inf   <-- web.xml file for this application
                +- jsp   <-- taglib.tld Tag Library Descriptor file
                +- classes
                    +- com
                        +- JSPbook
                            +- Chap11   <- tag handler classes
```

An entry in the `server.xml` file defines the JSPbook application, and this definition keeps all the servlet and other Java class files separate from those in other applications by using a separate class loader. This organization is all part of Sun's plan to make Web applications portable between servers and more secure.

The taglib Directive and the JSP Engine

All custom tag uses require that you declare the library to be used in a taglib directive statement that gives a unique identifier for the tag library and the short name that you will be using for it in the page. The format is similar to the page and includes directives in that it starts with `<%@`. Two attributes are required—`uri` and `prefix`—as shown here:

```
<%@ taglib uri="pathtoLib" prefix="tagprefix" %>
```

The `uri` (Universal Resource Identifier) attribute gives a unique identifier for the library, such as `/jspbooktaglib`, and the `prefix` attribute is the short name you will use in subsequent tags. For example, here is the directive used in the simple taglib example provided with the Tomcat 3.1 server.

```
<%@ taglib uri="http://java.apache.org/tomcat/examples-taglib" prefix="eg" %>
```

It is important to note that although the `uri` attribute gives a URL-like Web location, it is really being used as a unique identifier. The JSP engine does not go looking at that URL because the `web.xml` file that defines parameters for the application contains the following

```
<taglib>
    <taglib-uri>
    http://java.apache.org/tomcat/examples-taglib
```

```
    </taglib-uri>
    <taglib-location>
        /WEB-INF/jsp/example-taglib.tld
    </taglib-location>
  </taglib>
```

which links the `uri` attribute with the actual location on the server. Details of this usage are laid out in the JSP 1.1 and servlet 2.2 APIs.

A Simple Tag Example

This example uses the simplest kind of tag, one without a body. Listing 11.1 shows the complete JSP page with which we will test the tag. Note that the `taglib` directive line uses the `uri` attribute with a value of `JSPbook/taglib` and uses the `prefix` attribute with the value `ch11`. The resulting tag is `<ch11:mem />`, combining the prefix for the library with the name of the tag handler class. You must supply a non-empty prefix that is not on the list reserved by Sun, namely `jsp`, `jspx`, `java`, `javax`, `servlet`, `sun`, and `sunw`.

Listing 11.1: The sosimple.jsp file

```jsp
<html><!-- sosimple example of simple taglib use -->
<title>Example Tag Use</title>
<body>
<%@ taglib uri="JSPbook/taglib" prefix="ch11" %>

<h2>JVM working memory</h2>

<ul>
<ch11:mem />
</ul>
Using simple custom tag <b>mem</b><br>
<hr>
</body>
</html>
```

Locating the Tag Library Definition

To make the JSP engine aware of the relation of the `uri` specified in the `taglib` directive to the tag library defining file, make the following entry in the `web.xml` file for the JSPbook application:

```
  <taglib>
    <taglib-uri>JSPbook/taglib</taglib-uri>
    <taglib-location>
```

```
        /WEB-INF/jsp/JSPbook-taglib.tld
    </taglib-location>
</taglib>
```

The `web.xml` entry says that tags in the tag library with the `uri` attribute of "JSPbook/taglib" are defined in a file named "JSPbook-taglib.tld" found in the `"WEB-INF/jsp` directory relative to the base directory of this application.

The Structure of a TLD File

Relating the name used in tags to the Java class files that implement tag handler functions is accomplished in the Tag Library Descriptor (TLD) file, which should have a ".tld" file type. As you can see from Listing 11.2, the DTD for this file is defined by Sun.

Listing 11.2: The JSPbook-taglib.tld file

```xml
<?xml version="1.0" encoding="ISO-8859-1" ?>
<!DOCTYPE taglib
    PUBLIC "-//Sun Microsystems, Inc.//DTD JSP Tag Library 1.1//EN"
    "http://java.sun.com/j2ee/dtds/web-jsptaglibrary_1_1.dtd">

<!-- a tag library descriptor for JSPbook Chapter 11 examples -->

<taglib>
  <!-- after this the default space is
      "http://java.sun.com/j2ee/dtds/jsptaglibrary_1_2.dtd"
  -->

  <tlibversion>1.0</tlibversion>
  <jspversion>1.1</jspversion>
  <shortname>JSPbook</shortname>
  <uri>JSPbook/taglib</uri>
  <info> A simple tab library for the JSP and Servlets book examples
  </info>

  <tag>
    <!-- the minimum tag example -->
    <name>mem</name>
    <tagclass>com.JSPbook.Chap11.MemTag</tagclass>
    <info> Display JVM memory stats </info>
  </tag>

</taglib>
```

The following list provides a short description of the purpose of each of these XML elements:

tlibversion   Your version number for the library.

jspversion   The JSP specification version it uses.

shortname A convenient name that could be used with an authoring tool to organize access to the library.

uri The unique URI for this library.

info Descriptive information for the library.

tag Each tag handler class must have a tag entry, which can be any of the following:

    name The name to be used in tags for this class.

    tagclass The full package and class name for the tag handler class.

    info Optional additional descriptive text.

I will discuss other possible entries within a tag as we come to examples.

The MemTag Tag Handler Class

The basic interface `Tag` in the `javax.servlet.jsp.tagext` package defines the methods required for communication between the custom tag and the Java code that creates a page. For convenience, this package includes the `TagSupport` basic class implementing the `Tag` interface. This can be used as the starting point for simple custom tags.

The Java code created by the JSP engine calls methods defined in the `Tag` interface according to a strict set of rules.

1. `setPageContext( PageContext pc )` The `PageContext` carries references to all the stock objects used in a JSP.

2. `setParent( Tag t )` If the tag handler is enclosed in another custom tag, this is the reference to it. In a simple tag, the reference is null.

3. If the tag defines attributes, calls will be made to the `set` methods for each attribute, using values from the tag. The naming convention for `set` methods is the same as that used for Java Beans, so if you have defined an attribute named `myData`, the JSP engine will call `setMyData( value )`, where `value` is the `String` associated with the `myData` attribute in the tag. Note that naming attributes with an initial uppercase letter may not work right!

4. `doStartTag()` This is where your custom tag starts to work. The `doStartTag` method must return either `EVAL_BODY` or `SKIP_BODY` of the `int` constants defined in the `Tag` interface. This constant is used by the JSP code to control what happens next. Simple tags without a body must return `SKIP_BODY`.

5. `doEndTag()` This is always called, even if the tag is an empty one. It returns either `EVAL_PAGE` or `SKIP_PAGE`.

6. `release()` This method is guaranteed to be called after the last use of the tag but before the page is completed.

The four int constant return values defined in the Tag interface are:

SKIP_PAGE   Skip the remaining page code.

EVAL_PAGE   Continue executing the page code.

EVAL_BODY_INCLUDE   Evaluate the tag body into the page output stream.

SKIP_BODY   Skip evaluation of the tag body.

Now let's look at the code for the MemTag class. As you can see in Listing 11.3, this class extends the TagSupport class. As you may recall from Listing 11.1, the tag usage is

```
<ch11:mem />
```

without a body, so all the work is done in the startTag method.

Listing 11.3: The MemTag class

```
package com.JSPbook.Chap11;

import javax.servlet.jsp.* ;
import javax.servlet.jsp.tagext.* ;
import java.io.* ;

public class MemTag extends TagSupport
{
  // start tag does everything
  public int doStartTag() throws JspException {
    JspWriter out = pageContext.getOut();
    Runtime rt = Runtime.getRuntime();
    long total, free, used ;
    total = rt.totalMemory();
    free  = rt.freeMemory();
    used  = total - free ;
    try {
      out.println("<li>Total Memory " + total + "</li>");
      out.println("<li>Used by Tomcat " + used + "</li>");
      out.println("<li>Free Memory " + free + "</li>");
      return SKIP_BODY ; // no body of course
    }catch(IOException ex){
      throw new JspException( ex.toString() );
    }
  }
  public int doEndTag() throws JspException {
    return EVAL_PAGE ; // to continue the page
  }
}
```

When the class is compiled, the resulting class file goes into this directory

```
/WEB-INF/classes/com/JSPbook/Chap11
```

along with other servlets in the same package and belonging to the same Web application. When viewing the sosimple.jsp page shown in Listing 11.1, you get a display similar to the one shown in Figure 11.1.

FIGURE 11.1
Viewing the
sosimple.jsp page

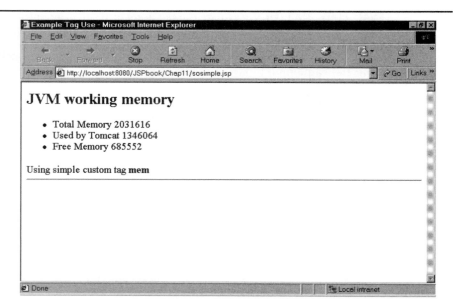

More About PageContext

As discussed in Chapter 2 (Table 2.2), a JSP has a set of objects that are always present on a page, including a `pageContext`. The `PageContext` class in the `javax.servlet.jsp` package holds various references and communicates them to servlets, Java Beans, and tag handler objects.

The `PageContext` class is actually an abstract class that is extended by each JSP engine, but a tag handler always refers to `PageContext`. Here is the code generated by the JSP engine to create the `pageContext` variable passed to a tag handler:

```
_jspxFactory = JspFactory.getDefaultFactory();
response.setContentType("text/html;charset=8859_1");
pageContext = _jspxFactory.getPageContext(this, request, response,
                    "", true, 8192, true);
```

Inside a tag handler, you can use the `pageContext` to get the implicit variables, which are always available in a JSP page, by using these methods:

getOut()   Returns the out object, a `javax.servlet.jsp.JspWriter`.

getRequest()   Returns the request object, a javax.servlet.ServletRequest.

getResponse()   Returns the response object, a javax.servlet.ServletResponse.

getSession()   Returns the session object, a javax.servlet.http.HttpSession.

getServletConfig()   Returns the config object, a javax.servlet.ServletConfig.

getServletContext()   Returns the application object, a javax.servlet.Servlet-Context.

getException()   Returns the exception object, a java.lang.Exception, but only if the page directive includes isErrorPage="true".

getPage()   Returns a reference to the enclosing JSP page object.

You can also store and retrieve object references by name and scope with this code:

```
setAttribute( String name, Object obj, int scope )
setAttribute( String name, Object obj )
getAttribute( String name, int scope )
getAttribute( String name )
findAttribute( String name, int scope )
```

The scope constants reflect the different degrees of permanence of storage of an attribute reference.

PAGE_SCOPE   The reference remains available until the service (with servlets) or _jspService (with JSP classes) method returns.

REQUEST_SCOPE   The reference remains available until the current request is completed.

SESSION_SCOPE   The reference remains available as long as the session is valid.

APPLICATION_SCOPE   The reference remains available as long as the servlet engine is running.

Using Tag Attributes

Custom tags have an extremely convenient arrangement for passing attribute values to tag handler classes. Methods in the tag handler class can use the JavaBeans style setXxx method naming convention, and the method will be called with the matching attribute value. For example, if your tag handler has a String variable named mystr, you can have the value of that variable set from an attribute value in the JSP tag if you meet the following conditions:

- The tag handler provides a setMystr(String s) method.
- The tag library descriptor for the tag has a matching <attribute> entry.
- An attribute in the custom tag takes the form mystr="somevalue".

If these conditions are met, the JSP engine will create the necessary code to take the `mystr` attribute value and call the `setMystr` method with it. This capability goes far beyond setting `String` values because the value `String` can be automatically converted into any of the primitives—`boolean`, `byte`, `char`, `int`, `long`, `float`, or `double`—or their matching wrapper class objects.

Defining Attributes in a Tag Library

Each attribute in a tag must have a matching section in the XML file describing the tag library. This section defines whether or not the attribute is required and whether or not the value might be set at runtime by an expression:

name   This is the name that will be used in the tag.

required   Possible values are `true`, `false`, `yes`, and `no`. If the attribute is not present, the default is `false`. If this is set `true` and the attribute is not supplied in a tag, the JSP engine will generate an error when it attempts to generate the Java source code.

rtexprvalue   Think of this as an abbreviation for "runtime expression value." Possible values are `true`, `false`, `yes`, and `no`, and the default is `false`. If `true`, the code generated must allow for the attribute value to be generated by an expression at runtime.

Example Tags with Attributes

As an experimental test of Tomcat's ability to correctly initialize a variety of attributes, I created the class shown in Listing 11.4. This class has member variables and setter methods for the primitives `boolean`, `byte`, `char`, `int`, `long`, `float`, and `double` and their matching wrapper class objects.

Listing 11.4: A tag handler class with a variety of attributes

```
package com.JSPbook.Chap11;

import javax.servlet.jsp.* ;
import javax.servlet.jsp.tagext.* ;
import java.io.* ;

public class AttribTag extends TagSupport
{
    private boolean flagA ;
    private Boolean flagB ;
    private byte byteA ;
    private Byte byteB ;
    private char charA ;
    private Character charB ;
    private double dubA ;
```

```
    private Double dubB ;
    private float floatA ;
    private Float floatB ;
    private long longA ;
    private Long longB ;
    private int intA ;
    private Integer intB ;

    public void setFlagA( boolean b ){flagA = b ; }
    public void setFlagB( Boolean b ){flagB = b ; }
    public void setByteA( byte b ){ byteA = b ; }
    public void setByteB( Byte b ){ byteB = b ; }
    public void setCharA( char c ){ charA = c ; }
    public void setCharB( Character c ){charB = c ; }
    public void setDubA( double d ){ dubA = d ; }
    public void setDubB( Double d ){ dubB = d ; }
    public void setFloatA( float a ){ floatA = a ; }
    public void setFloatB( Float b ){ floatB = b ; }
    public void setLongA( long x ){ longA = x ; }
    public void setLongB( Long x ){ longB = x ; }
    public void setIntA( int a ){ intA = a ; }
    public void setIntB( Integer b ){ intB = b ; }

      // start tag does everything
    public int doStartTag() throws JspException {
      JspWriter out = pageContext.getOut();
      try {
        out.println("boolean and Boolean " + flagA + " " + flagB + "<br>");
        out.println("byte and Byte " + byteA + " " + byteB + "<br>");
        out.println("char and Character " + charA + " " + charB + "<br>");
        out.println("double and Double " + dubA + " " + dubB + "<br>");
        out.println("float and Float " + floatA + " " + floatB + "<br>");
        out.println("long and Long " + longA + " " + longB + "<br>");
        out.println("int and Integer " + intA + " " + intB + "<br>");
      return SKIP_BODY ; // no body of course
      }catch(IOException ex){
        throw new JspException( ex.toString() );
      }
    }
    public int doEndTag() throws JspException {
      return EVAL_PAGE ; // to continue the page
    }
  }
```

An example JSP page to exercise the AttribTag class is shown in Listing 11.5, and the resulting browser display is shown in Figure 11.2. Note that instead of converting the charA attribute value as an integer into a char, the conversion simply took the first character of the string.

Listing 11.5 A JSP page using the example class

```
<html>
<title>Example Tag Use</title>
<body>
<%@ taglib uri="JSPbook/taglib" prefix="ch11" %>

<h2>Attribute Conversion Test</h2>

<ch11:attr flagA="true" flagB="false" byteA="27" byteB="37"
    charA="31" charB="41" dubA="8765.432" dubB="76.432"
    floatA="0.1234" floatB="1.035" longA="123000456" longB="234000567"
    intA="32000" intB="64000" />

Using simple custom tag <b>attr</b><br>
<hr>
</body>
</html>
```

FIGURE 11.2

The browser display from the AttribTag tag manager

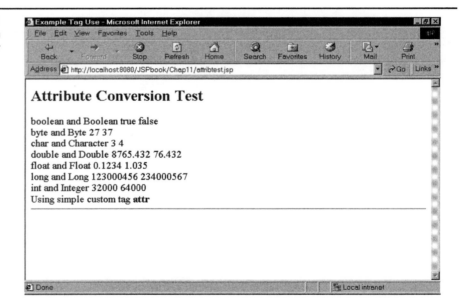

WARNING Not all JSP engines handle this automatic conversion process the same way. When I used this taglib and JSP with the Orion server, it objected to the input of a String with more than one character to the **char** and **Character** input conversions.

The tag library descriptor shown in Listing 11.6 names the tag and all the attributes the tag will require. When generating the Java code for the JSP page, the JSP engine reads this description first and creates a `TagAttributeInfo` object for each attribute.

Listing 11.6: The tag library descriptor for AttribTag

```
<tag><!-- setting attributes example -->
  <name>attr</name>
  <tagclass>com.JSPbook.Chap11.AttribTag</tagclass>
  <info> Test conversion of attributes </info>
  <attribute> <name>flagA</name><required>true</required>
  </attribute>
  <attribute> <name>flagB</name><required>true</required>
  </attribute>
  <attribute> <name>byteA</name><required>true</required>
  </attribute>
  <attribute> <name>byteB</name><required>true</required>
  </attribute>
  <attribute> <name>charA</name><required>true</required>
  </attribute>
  <attribute> <name>charB</name><required>true</required>
  </attribute>
  <attribute> <name>dubA</name><required>true</required>
  </attribute>
  <attribute> <name>dubB</name><required>true</required>
  </attribute>
  <attribute> <name>floatA</name><required>true</required>
  </attribute>
  <attribute> <name>floatB</name><required>true</required>
  </attribute>
  <attribute> <name>longA</name><required>true</required>
  </attribute>
  <attribute> <name>longB</name><required>true</required>
  </attribute>
  <attribute> <name>intA</name><required>true</required>
  </attribute>
  <attribute> <name>intB</name><required>true</required>
  </attribute>
</tag>
```

Attributes with Runtime Values

You can also provide for setting an attribute with a value determined at runtime. Of course, your tag library could also obtain these values by using the request object that is available through the `PageContext`, but setting the attribute has two advantages:

- You can test the page with hard-wired values.
- Web designers using your tag library can see what is going on more easily.

In this example, let's suppose that we are teaching an online course in JavaServer Page creation. The HTML page for student login is shown in Listing 11.7.

Listing 11.7: The HTML form for student login

```
<html>
<head><title>Introduction to JavaServer Pages</title>
</head>
<body>
<h2 ALIGN=center>Welcome to the Online Training Center
</h2>
<h3 ALIGN=center>Course: Introduction to JavaServer Pages</h3>
<br />
<center>
<table WIDTH=500 BORDER=0>
<tr ALIGN=LEFT VALIGN=MIDDLE>
<td><center>Please enter your Student ID and password to logon:</center>
<br /><br />
<form METHOD="POST" ACTION="http://localhost:8080/JSPbook/Chap11/signin.jsp" >
<input TYPE=HIDDEN NAME="course" VALUE="jsp01" >
<input TYPE=TEXT VALUE="" NAME="stuid" SIZE=10 MAXLENGTH=8 > Student ID ➥
<br /><br />
<input TYPE=PASSWORD VALUE="" NAME="stupw" SIZE=10 MAXLENGTH=8 > Password ➥
<br /><br />
<input TYPE="SUBMIT" VALUE="LOGON" ><br /><br />
</form>
</td></table></center><br /><br />
</body>
</html>
```

Listing 11.8 shows the JSP code for the signin.jsp page. I have left out the details of reporting the current student status to save space. The important thing to note here is the way the values for the **studentId** and **studentPw** attributes are set directly from the request. Also note that the ch11:**signin** tag appears before anything has been written to the body of the page, and that the closing tag appears after the course status information. Text between the opening and closing tags is called the body of the tag. In this case, the value returned by the **doStart-Tag** method controls whether or not the body is displayed.

Listing 11.8: The signin.jsp page

```
<html><head>
<title>Student Signin</title></head>
<body>
<%@ taglib uri="JSPbook/taglib" prefix="ch11" %>
<ch11:signin studentId="<%= request.getParameter("stuid") %>"
             studentPw="<%= request.getParameter("stupw") %>"
             course="<%= request.getParameter("course") %>" >
```

```
<h2>Student Login for <%= request.getParameter("stuid") %></h2>
<h3>Course Status</h3>
(.... course status information would go here... )
</ch11:signin>
<hr>
<center>Version 1.0</center>
</body>
</html>
```

The JSP page shown in Listing 11.8 worked fine with the Orion JSP server but failed with Tomcat 3.1. Following the advice of a message on the Tomcat users mailing list, I substituted single quotation marks so that single and double quotation marks alternated in the tag; this enabled it to work under Tomcat. The resulting tag looked like this:

```
<ch11:signin studentId='<%= request.getParameter("stuid") %>'
             studentPw='<%= request.getParameter("stupw") %>'
             course='<%= request.getParameter("course") %>' >
```

Listing 11.9 shows the code for the SignInTag class that is the tag handler for the ch11:signin tag. To save space, I am using a simple checkValidity method; naturally, a real application would use a database in addition to checking for the correct size of the input attributes. Note that if the checkValidity method returns true, the doStartTag method returns the EVAL_BODY_INCLUDE constant. This instructs the calling JSP to continue evaluating the body of the tag. If checkValidity returns false, the HTML page will contain an error message generated in doStartTag, and none of the body of the tag will be included.

Listing 11.9: The tag handler for student signin

```
package com.JSPbook.Chap11;

import javax.servlet.jsp.* ;
import javax.servlet.jsp.tagext.* ;
import java.io.* ;

public class SignInTag extends TagSupport
{
  static final int ID_LENGTH = 8 ;
  static final int PW_LENGTH = 8 ;
  static final int COURSE_LENGTH = 3 ;

  String studentId, studentPw, course ;
  public void setStudentId( String s ){ studentId = s; }
  public void setStudentPw( String s ){ studentPw = s ; }
  public void setCourse( String s ){ course = s ; }

  // start tag does everything
  public int doStartTag() throws JspException {
    if( checkValidity()) return EVAL_BODY_INCLUDE ;
    JspWriter out = pageContext.getOut();
```

```
    try {
    out.println("<h2>Unable To Enter Course</h2>");
    out.println("<p>There is a problem with one or more of the values " +
      "you entered for Student ID or Password.</p>" );
    out.println("<p>Use your browser <b>Back</b> button to return to the" +
      " signin page.</p>");
    return SKIP_BODY ;
    }catch( Exception e ){
      throw new JspException( e.toString() );
    }
  }

  /* In a real application this would consult a database to
     see if the studentID was valid for the course and the
     password was valid for the ID. We simulate this by just
     checking the value length.
  */
  private boolean checkValidity(){
    if( studentId.length() < ID_LENGTH ||
        studentPw.length() < PW_LENGTH ||
        course.length() < COURSE_LENGTH ){
      return false ;
    }
    return true ;
  }
}
```

For the JSP engine to generate the code required to correctly set attributes at runtime, the tag library descriptor must contain a `rtexprvalue` of `true`. The tag description for the `SignIn-Tag` tag handler is shown in Listing 11.10.

Listing 11.10: Entry in the tld for the signin tag

```
<tag> <!-- tag illustrating runtime attribute setting -->
<name>signin</name>
<tagclass>com.JSPbook.Chap11.SignInTag</tagclass>
<info>A tag to check student id and password</info>
<attribute><name>course</name><required>true</required>
          <rtexprvalue>true</rtexprvalue>
</attribute>
<attribute><name>studentId</name><required>true</required>
          <rtexprvalue>true</rtexprvalue>
</attribute>
<attribute><name>studentPw</name><required>true</required>
          <rtexprvalue>true</rtexprvalue>
</attribute>
</tag>
```

In the preceding example, the JSP page was able to either skip or include the body of the tag according to the value returned by **doStartTag**. Next, we explore tag handlers that can manipulate the tag body directly.

Interacting with a Body Element

Now let's look at tags that are able to process a body element. To do this, a tag handler class must implement the BodyTag interface and be able to work with a BodyContent object. The methods that the BodyTag interface adds to the java.jsp.tagext.Tag interface are described here:

doInitBody   You use this method to perform any setup that's required before looking at body content.

doAfterBody   This method is called after the body has been evaluated. It returns an int constant that controls whether or not body evaluation is repeated.

setBodyContent   This method is called to pass your tag handler a new BodyContent object.

The BodyContent class extends JspWriter, which is the class JSP pages use for output. A BodyContent object acts as a sort of reusable buffer that can hold the text of body content for reuse. To show how the BodyContent class and the Tag and BodyTag methods interact, I have created a simple example tag manager.

A Simple BodyTag Example

The PlainBody tag manager class implements the BodyTag interface. I chose this approach rather than extending the BodyTagSupport class because I wanted to show all the interface methods. The javax.servlet.jsp.tagext package provides the BodyTagSupport class as a convenient base for when you need to override only a few methods.

As shown in Listings 11.11 and 11.12, every method writes a message to System.out when it is called so that we can see the way the JSP engine uses the interface. With the Tomcat server under Windows, the System.out stream is directed to the MDOS console. Listing 11.11 shows the instance variables and the methods required by the Tag interface.

Listing 11.11: The PlainBody tag manager instance variables and Tag interface methods

```
package com.JSPbook.Chap11;

import javax.servlet.jsp.* ;
import javax.servlet.jsp.tagext.* ;
import java.io.* ;

public class PlainBody implements BodyTag
{
  Tag parent ;
  PageContext pageContext ;
  BodyContent bodyContent ;
  int count ;
```

```
// the methods required by Tag interface
public int doStartTag(){
  System.out.println("doStartTag called");
  return EVAL_BODY_TAG ; // requests new BodyContent
} // other legal return is SKIP_BODY
// EVAL_BODY_INCLUDE is not legal because this class implements BodyTag

public int doEndTag(){
  System.out.println("doEndTag called");
  return EVAL_PAGE ;
} // other legal return is SKIP_PAGE

public Tag getParent(){
  System.out.println("getParent called");
  return parent ;
}
public void setParent( Tag t ){
  System.out.println("setParent called");
  parent = t ;
}
public void setPageContext( PageContext ctx ){
  System.out.println("setPageContext called");
  pageContext = ctx ;
}

public void release(){
  System.out.println("release called");
}
```

The methods added by BodyTag are shown in Listing 11.12. Note that in the **doAfterBody** method, we print the contents of the bodyContent variable.

Listing 11.12: The methods required by the BodyTag interface

```
// these are added in BodyTag
public void setBodyContent( BodyContent bdy ){
  bodyContent = bdy ;
  System.out.println("setBodyContent called");
}

public void doInitBody(){
  String tmp = bodyContent.getString();
  System.out.println("doInitBody called - content " + tmp );
  count = 5 ;
}

public int doAfterBody(){
  String tmp = bodyContent.getString();
  System.out.println("doAfterBody called - content " + tmp );
  return SKIP_BODY ;
}  // other legal return is EVAL_BODY_TAG
   // which would start new cycle
}
```

The entry in the tag library descriptor file for PlainBody is simply this:

```
<tag> <!-- the minimum BodyTag implementation -->
    <name>plainbody</name>
    <tagclass>com.JSPbook.Chap11.PlainBody</tagclass>
    <info>Prints msg with every call</info>
</tag>
```

To exercise the tag manager, I created the JSP page shown in Listing 11.13. Note that it has HTML markup before and after the tag and inside the body of the tag.

Listing 11.13: A simple JSP page using PlainBody

```
<html>
<title>Simplest Body Tag Use</title>
<body>
<%@ taglib uri="JSPbook/taglib" prefix="ch11" %>

<h2>Before Tag</h2>
<ch11:plainbody >
Inside the tag body,
2nd line inside the tag body.
</ch11:plainbody>
<h2>After Tag</h2>
<hr>
</body>
</html>
```

Here is the sequence of events that occurs when the JSP is viewed as revealed by the System.out output captured in the DOS console window:

```
setPageContext called
setParent called
doStartTag called
setBodyContent called
doInitBody called
doAfterBody called - content
Inside the tag body,
2nd line inside the tag body.

doEndTag called
release called
```

To see exactly what is going on, let's look at the Java source code that the Tomcat servlet engine writes. Listing 11.14 shows the part of the code starting with the call to doStartTag. I cleaned up some of the weird variable names that the servlet engine makes up, and I removed some extraneous comment lines.

Listing 11.14: Part of the Java code generated from the JSP

```
int startTagRet = _jspx_th_ch11_plainbody_0.doStartTag();
if ( startTagRet == Tag.EVAL_BODY_INCLUDE)
    throw new JspTagException("Because tag handler class ➥
    com.JSPbook.Chap11.PlainBody implements BodyTag, it can't return ➥
    Tag.EVAL_BODY_INCLUDE");
if ( startTagRet != Tag.SKIP_BODY) {
    try {
        if (startTagRet != Tag.EVAL_BODY_INCLUDE) {
            out = pageContext.pushBody();
            _jspx_th_ch11_plainbody_0.setBodyContent((BodyContent) out);
        }
        _jspx_th_ch11_plainbody_0.doInitBody();
        do { // now writing to the BodyContent obtained from pushBody
            out.write("\r\nInside the tag body,\r\n2nd line inside the tag➥
            body.\r\n");
        } while (_jspx_th_ch11_plainbody_0.doAfterBody() ==
                        BodyTag.EVAL_BODY_TAG);
    } finally {
        if (_jspx_eval_ch11_plainbody_0 != Tag.EVAL_BODY_INCLUDE)
            out = pageContext.popBody();
    }
}
```

To provide for special processing of the body text, after the startTag method returns
EVAL_BODY_TAG, the pageContext object method pushBody is called. This temporarily
stores the current out reference, the JspWriter that is used earlier in the page to output
plain HTML. The pushBody method returns a reference to a new BodyContent object that
temporarily is stored in the out variable and passed to the tag manager object with setBody-
Content.

Next, all the page content between the start and end tags is written to this BodyContent
object. This is how the tag manager gains access to the body text. Note that although in our
example this text is written in a single statement, the text captured in the BodyContent object
could include output from beans or other tags.

Let's look at the code immediately following the call to initBody:

```
do { // now writing to the BodyContent obtained from pushBody
    out.write("\r\nInside the tag body,\r\n2nd line inside the tag body.\r\n");
} while (_jspx_th_ch11_plainbody_0.doAfterBody() ==
                BodyTag.EVAL_BODY_TAG);
```

Note that as long as doAfterBody returns the EVAL_BODY_TAG constant, the cycle of writing
the body text to the BodyContent object and calling doAfterBody will continue.

Writing a New Body

In the example code of Listing 11.12, the body text was swallowed by the tag manager, and nothing from the body area appeared in the page output. The tag manager can also generate output that is written to the page output. Recall that the text in the tag body area is written to a BodyContent object obtained by:

```
out = pageContext.pushBody() ;
```

which temporarily hides the JspWriter object that writes the page response. However, you can still access that JspWriter inside the tag manager and write directly to the page response.

I'll illustrate this with a simple modification of the PlainBody class, which is to be called ModifyBody. Because only one method is changed, you will have to look on the CD for the full source code. The modified doAfterBody method is shown in Listing 11.15. The call to the BodyContent method getEnclosingWriter gets a reference to the JspWriter that was in use when pushBody was called.

Listing 11.15: The doAfterBody method of the ModBody class

```
public int doAfterBody() throws JspTagException {
  String tmp = bodyContent.getString();
  bodyContent.clearBody();
  try { // get access to the writer that was "pushed"
    JspWriter tout = bodyContent.getEnclosingWriter() ;
    tout.println("<h" + count + ">" + tmp + "</h" + count + ">" );
  }catch(IOException e ){
      throw new JspTagException("ModifyBody.doAfterBody " + e.toString() );
  }
  if( --count == 0 ) return SKIP_BODY ;
  return EVAL_BODY_TAG ;
}
```

This example also demonstrates repeated evaluation of the body content. The count variable is decremented with each repetition, and the method keeps returning the EVAL_BODY_TAG constant until the count reaches zero.

To conclude this simple example, I created a JSP page with the following tag usage:

```
<%@ taglib uri="JSPbook/taglib" prefix="ch11" %>
<h2>Famous Quote</h2>
<ch11:modbody >What, me worry?
</ch11:modbody>
```

When accessed, this page produced the output shown in Figure 11.3.

FIGURE 11.3
The ModifyBody tag repeats
the tag body content

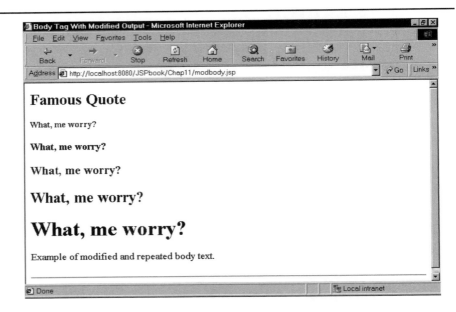

Working with Body Content

Okay, you are probably saying, "so a custom tag can get the content of the tag body, but what can we do with it?" Here are some of the possible uses that occur to me right off hand.

XML "Data Island" in a JSP Page

The text in the BodyContent object that is passed to the tag manager can be accessed as a String (as in the example in Listing 11.12) or as a character stream with a java.io.Reader interface. This means that it could provide input for any Java process that works with an input stream of characters. An obvious candidate is an XML parser or an XSLT (Extensible Stylesheet Language for Transformations) engine.

XSLT is an especially attractive use because it can easily control the appearance of the resulting HTML page. I used the Apache organization's XSLT processor named **xalan** for the following demonstration. This toolkit is available at no charge at the Apache Web site.

The basic idea of XSLT is to transform an XML-formatted data file by applying rules that are supplied in the XSL language, also expressed in XML format. This application is an excellent example of separating presentation of data (controlled by Web designers) from data storage (controlled by programmers). You may see the term "Data Island" applied to this use of XML-encoded data embedded in a page.

As an input data source, I am using the pubs.xml file from Chapter 6, which contains entries for books and articles. The JSP page is shown in Listing 11.16. Note that all the body of the tag is XML formatted XSLT rules.

WARNING When XML is used in the tag body, the first line of XML should immediately follow the start tag on the same line. Otherwise, the XML processor sees a starting empty line and chokes.

Listing 11.16: The JSP page demonstrating XSLT processing

```
<html>
<title>Using XSLT Tag</title>
<body>
<%@ taglib uri="JSPbook/taglib" prefix="ch11" %>
<h1>Publication Data from XML file</h1>

<ch11:xslttag source="f:/ApacheXML/books.xml" ><?xml version="1.0"?>
<xsl:stylesheet xmlns:xsl="http://www.w3.org/1999/XSL/Transform" version="1.0">
<xsl:template match="/">
<xsl:comment>Bill plays with XSLT!</xsl:comment>
  <xsl:apply-templates/>
  </xsl:template>
  <h2>Books</h2>
  <xsl:template match="Book">
   <i>Title:</i><b><xsl:value-of select="Title" /></b><br />
   <i>Author:</i><b><xsl:value-of select="Author" /></b><br /><br />
  </xsl:template>
  <h2>Articles</h2>
  <xsl:template match="Article">
    <i>Article:</i><b><xsl:value-of select="Title" /></b><br />
    <i>Publication:</i><b><xsl:value-of select="Publisher" /></b><br />
    <i>Author:</i><b><xsl:value-of select="Author" /></b><br /><br />
  </xsl:template>
</xsl:stylesheet>
</ch11:xslttag>
<hr>
</body>
</html>
```

The tag manager is surprisingly simple because the XSLProcessor does all the work. As shown in Listing 11.17, the XsltTag class extends the BodyTagSupport convenience class in the javax.servlet.jsp.tagext package. In the doAfterBody method, the source file and the tag body are turned into input streams for the XSLTProcessor, while the output Jsp-Writer is recovered from the bodyContent object.

Listing 11.17: The XsltTag source code

```java
package com.JSPbook.Chap11;

import javax.servlet.jsp.* ;
import javax.servlet.jsp.tagext.* ;
import java.io.* ;

import org.xml.sax.SAXException;
import org.apache.xalan.xslt.* ;

public class XsltTag extends BodyTagSupport
{
  String source ;
  public void setSource(String s ){ source = s ; }

  public int doAfterBody() throws JspTagException {
    String err = "";
    StringReader sreader = new StringReader( bodyContent.getString());
    bodyContent.clearBody();
    try {
     FileReader fsource = new FileReader( source );
     System.out.println("Source file opened");
     JspWriter tout = bodyContent.getEnclosingWriter() ;
        // the XSLTProcessorFactory obtains a new XSLTProcessor object.
     XSLTProcessor processor = XSLTProcessorFactory.getProcessor();
     processor.process(new XSLTInputSource( fsource),
                   new XSLTInputSource( sreader ),
                   new XSLTResultTarget( tout ));
    }catch( SAXException se ){
        err = se.toString();
        if( se.getException() != null ){
           err += " caused by: " + se.getException().toString() ;
        }
    }catch( Exception e ){
        throw new JspTagException("ModifyBody.doAfterBody " + e.toString() );
    }finally{
        System.out.println("Err:" + err );
    }
    return SKIP_BODY ;
  }

}
```

As we discussed in Chapter 3, debugging servlets and JSP is trickier than debugging Java applications because there are so many different processes. Using an XML parser adds even more complexity, which is why I put such detailed exception reporting in this method. Note that both the XML data file source and the XSL text from the tag body have to be parsed, so there are two possible sources of an SAXException. You should certainly verify that any XML data file is valid and well formed before trying to work with it in a Web server. Figure 11.4 shows the output of the JSP page in Listing 11.16.

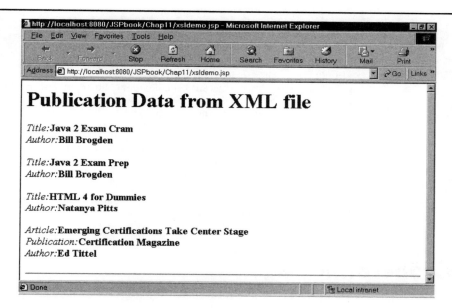

FIGURE 11.4
The browser view of the
xsldemo.jsp page

SQL Query

Another popular use of body tag processing is database query formulation. You may recall from Chapter 8 that we formulated a query String as shown here:

```
SELECT Text FROM errsql WHERE isbn = '1576102912' AND Significance <= 1 AND ➡
printing = 1
```

This type of statement could easily be formulated in the body of a tag as in the following mock-up:

```
<ch11:sqltag source="BooksDB">
SELECT Text FROM errsql
    WHERE isbn = '<%= request.getParameter("ISBN")%>'
    AND Significance <= 1
    AND printing = 1
</ch11:sqltag>
```

However, there is a possible hidden problem in this example. The body text actually consists of several text lines with leading and trailing spaces. If this were submitted directly to a database engine, it might not be parsed correctly. Listing 11.18 shows a simple routine that collects all the body text lines into a single String, removing extra spaces yet ensuring that at least one space separates the text from each line.

Listing 11.18: A utility routine to clean up body text

```
// this removes all line feeds and extra spaces
// from the body text to make a single line
private String getBodyAsString(){
  StringBuffer sb = new StringBuffer( 200 );
  BufferedReader br = new BufferedReader( bodyContent.getReader() );
  try {
    String tmp = br.readLine().trim();
    while( tmp != null ){
      sb.append( tmp );
      sb.append( ' ' );  // replace line end with space
      tmp = br.readLine();
      if( tmp != null )tmp = tmp.trim();
    }
  }catch(IOException e){} // impossible under the circumstances
  return sb.toString().trim();
}
```

Cooperating Tags

There is no obstacle to using multiple custom tags on a single JSP page, but they must all belong to the same tag library and have entries in the tag library descriptor file. Recall that the first call from a JSP page to a tag handler class is **setPageContext**. A tag handler can create one or more objects that are shared with following tags by saving the object(s) in the Page-Context using one of these methods:

```
setAttribute( String name, Object obj, int scope )
setAttribute( String name, Object obj )
```

and later retrieving the object(s) with one of these methods:

```
getAttribute( String name, int scope )
getAttribute( String name )
findAttribute( String name, int scope )
```

Enclosing tags have special methods available to provide shared objects. The methods described here are in the TagSupport utility class of the javax.servlet.jsp.tagext package.

getParent() Returns a Tag reference for the directly enclosing tag.

findAncestorWithClass(Tag child, Class class) Returns a Tag reference found by looking at the hierarchy of tags that enclose the child tag for a tag of type class. After the enclosing tag reference is found, it can be used to address the Tag object directly to share data.

The Tag Extension API

The tag extension API is so large and full of neat features that I have been able to demonstrate only a few of them. At this point, I would like to quickly review the classes and interfaces in the `javax.servlet.jsp.tagext` package. You are most likely to use the following classes and interfaces:

Tag   The basic interface defines the methods required for communication between the custom tag and the Java code that creates a page.

TagSupport   The basic class implementing the `Tag` interface and providing many utility methods. This is typically the starting point for simple custom tags.

BodyTag   An interface extending `Tag` that provides methods to be used in classes that modify a body of text.

BodyTagSupport   The basic class implementing the `TagSupport` interface. More complex tag functionality can be obtained by extending this class.

TagExtraInfo   If you want to provide custom validation of attribute values when a JSP is translated into Java source code or provide for your tag to generate scripting variables, you can use an extension of `TagExtraInfo`.

VariableInfo   Custom tags that create scripting variables are described by `VariableInfo` objects in cooperation with a `TagExtraInfo` object.

Tag Library Resources

Many people are jumping on the custom tag bandwagon. Somebody may have already released exactly the tag you need, so look around. The following are some resources I recently found.

- Sun's tag library project:

    `http://java.sun.com/products/jsp/taglibraries.html`

- The Apache organization "Taglibs" collection:

    `http://jakarta.apache.org/taglibs/index.html`

- The JRun tag library at Allaire's site, which includes many Enterprise JavaBean-related tags:

    `http://www.allaire.com/`

- Independent sites devoted to JSP tags:

    `http://jsptags.com/`

    `http://sourceforge.net/projects/jsptags/`

CHAPTER 12

Applet-to-Servlet Communication

- Using the URLconnection Class

- Using URL Streams

- Writing and Reading Objects between Applet and Servlet

- Application of Applet-Servlet Communication

For a while, it looked like applet usage was on its way out. Almost any business applet could be replaced with a collection of JavaScript pages that were almost as good and were smaller and less likely to have browser compatibility problems.

Today, most browsers comply with the Java Runtime 1.1, so there are fewer browser compatibility problems to worry about. Furthermore, Sun's browser plug-in can provide JDK 1.2 compatibility if necessary. Most importantly, as Java-based application servers grow in complexity and users expect more capability from an interface, we find that there is a place for Java applets. With the convenient communication classes developed in this chapter, your applets and servlets can talk back and forth with ease.

A Little Background

NOTE   I (Bill) have asked Paul Wheaton to provide most of the material for this chapter in view of his extensive work with applet - servlet communication. Here is the background information on how he got involved with this subject and evolved the utility classes we will be presenting.

I once worked on a project that involved taking satellite pictures of Earth. Users were presented with a map they could zoom in and out, then they could draw a polygon on the map representing an area they want photographed. Try to get JavaScript to do that!

This applet needed a variety of services from the server. Because all the server-side software was to be developed in Java, RMI seemed to be a natural solution. Unfortunately, Internet Explorer does not support RMI.

The data also needed to pass through corporate firewalls. Many firewalls block all ports except port 80, the standard port for Web pages. Sometimes port 80 is served only through a proxy, so the one thing that definitely works is sending an HTTP GET or POST command and getting back an HTML document.

The GET command has some size limitations, so POST is preferred. However, to do a true POST, you have to convert all your data to text and then URL-encode it. What a hassle!

Through some evolutionary trial and error, I've created what I call the applet-to-servlet object pipeline. Using Java's object serialization capability, the applet sends an object to the servlet. The servlet does some processing and sends an object back to the applet. What could be simpler?

The Bare Necessities

I spent a great deal of time finding a simple solution to the problem I am about to relate, but I didn't mind because the effort yielded excellent results (or maybe it was because I was being paid by the hour).

First I'll show you the applet side—without an applet. Applications are a little easier to work with, so I'll get everything working as an application first and mash it into an applet later. To make this work, I need to create a connection, send an object, and receive an object. I encapsulated each of these needs into appropriately named methods. First up is establishing a connection with the servlet with the `getConnection` method, as shown in Listing 12.1.

Listing 12.1: The getConnection method

```
private URLConnection getConnection( String servlet ) throws
IOException
{
  URL u = new URL( servlet );
  URLConnection con = u.openConnection();
  con.setDoInput( true );
  con.setDoOutput( true );
  con.setUseCaches( false );
  con.setRequestProperty("Content-type","application/octet-stream");
  con.setAllowUserInteraction( false );
  return con ;
}
```

The wacky thing is that while I nowhere mention POST, POST is what it does. During my experiment, this method was once more than a hundred lines long. Fortunately, further experimenting made it nice and simple.

Next, I need to send the object to the servlet:

```
private void sendObject( URLConnection con , Object obj ) throws
IOException
{
  ObjectOutputStream out = new ObjectOutputStream(
con.getOutputStream() );
  if ( obj != null )
  {
    out.writeObject( obj );
  }
  out.close();
}
```

The connection object already has an output stream. I just connect an object stream to it. As long as an object stream is used on the other side of the connection, this works smoothly. (I'll talk about the servlet side later.) Now I need a way to receive an object from the servlet; that's shown in Listing 12.2.

Listing 12.2: The receiveObject method

```
private Object receiveObject( URLConnection con ) throws Exception
{
  ObjectInputStream in = new ObjectInputStream(
con.getInputStream() );
  Object obj = in.readObject();
  in.close();
  return obj ;
}
```

The nice thing here is that `in.readObject()` will wait quite a long while until data is ready for the servlet. This works out really well when the Net is congested.

For almost all my distributed computing experiments, I have the client send a string to the server, make the server reverse the string, send the reversed string back to the client, and have the client display the reversed string. This way, I have proof that the data is being transferred correctly both ways. My test program looks like Listing 12.3.

Listing 12.3: The PipelineApp class

```
import java.io.* ;
import java.net.* ;

public class PipelineApp
{
  private static final String servlet = "http://localhost/servlet/➥
  PipelineServlet";

  private static URLConnection getConnection() throws IOException
  {
    URL u = new URL( servlet );
    URLConnection con = u.openConnection();
    con.setDoInput( true );
    con.setDoOutput( true );
    con.setUseCaches( false );
    con.setRequestProperty("Content-type","application/octet-stream");
    con.setAllowUserInteraction( false );
    return con ;
  }
```

```java
 private static void sendObject( URLConnection con , Object obj )
throws IOException
  {
    ObjectOutputStream out = new ObjectOutputStream( con.getOutputStream() );
    if ( obj != null )
    {
      out.writeObject( obj );
    }
    out.close();
  }

 private static Object receiveObject( URLConnection con ) throws
Exception
  {
    ObjectInputStream in = new ObjectInputStream(
con.getInputStream() );
    Object obj = in.readObject();
    in.close();
    return obj ;
  }

 public static void main( String[] args ) throws Exception
  {
    URLConnection con = getConnection();
    sendObject( con , "The Tick sez Spoooooon!" );
    String s = (String)receiveObject( con );
    System.out.println( s );
  }
}
```

I made a tiny change in getConnection by using "servlet" directly instead of getting it via a parameter. I also made the methods static so they can be used by main. A quality program would catch the exceptions, but I'm just going to let them dump all over the screen—after all, this is just a prototype!

On to the Servlet!

Those brilliant and charming engineers at Sun designed servlets, so I don't have to worry about the connection. Every servlet comes with a first-class connection to the client. So all we need are methods for receiving an object and sending an object:

```java
private Object receiveObject( HttpServletRequest req ) throws
Exception
{
  ObjectInputStream in = new ObjectInputStream( req.getInputStream() );
  Object obj = in.readObject();
  in.close();
  return obj ;
}
```

Note that here I am using the servlet standard object `HttpServletRequest`, which comes complete with an input stream. I just wrap it with an object stream. To send an object, I use this code:

```
private void sendObject( HttpServletResponse resp , Object obj )
   throws Exception
{
  ObjectOutputStream out = new ObjectOutputStream( resp.getOutputStream() );
  out.writeObject( obj );
  out.close();
}
```

The standard servlet object `HttpServletResponse` conveniently comes with an output stream. In this object pipeline (Listing 12.4), all objects are sent via an HTTP POST command, so I need to inherit from `HttpServlet` and override `doPost()`.

Listing 12.4: First try at PipelineServlet

```
import java.io.* ;
import javax.servlet.* ;
import javax.servlet.http.* ;

public class PipelineServlet extends HttpServlet {

  private Object receiveObject( HttpServletRequest req ) throws Exception
  {
    ObjectInputStream in = new ObjectInputStream( req.getInputStream() );
    Object obj = in.readObject();
    in.close();
    return obj ;
  }

  private void sendObject( HttpServletResponse resp , Object obj )
  throws Exception
  {
    ObjectOutputStream out = new ObjectOutputStream(  resp.getOutputStream() );
    out.writeObject( obj );
    out.close();
  }

  public void doPost( HttpServletRequest req , HttpServletResponse
  resp )
  {
    try {
      Object obj = receiveObject( req ) ;
      // reverse the String.
      String old = (String)obj ;
      String s = "";
```

```
        for( int i = old.length() - 1 ; i >= 0 ; i-- )
        {
            s += old.charAt( i );
        }
        sendObject( resp , s );
    } catch ( Exception e ){
        System.out.println( "Clang! Thunk: " + e );
    }
  }

}
```

I fire up my servlet server and run PipelineApp, and I see "!noooooopS zes kciT ehT" It works! Now I need to convert my application into an applet, as shown in Listing 12.5.

Listing 12.5: The Pipeline application turned into an applet

```java
import java.applet.* ;
import java.awt.* ;
import java.awt.event.* ;
import java.io.* ;
import java.net.* ;

public class PipelineApplet extends Applet implements ActionListener
    {

    private static final String servlet =
"http://localhost/servlet/PipelineServlet";
    private Label text ;   // shows my results

    private URLConnection getConnection() throws IOException
    {
     URL u = new URL( servlet );
     URLConnection con = u.openConnection();
     con.setDoInput( true );
     con.setDoOutput( true );
     con.setUseCaches( false );
     con.setRequestProperty("Content-type","application/octet-stream");
     con.setAllowUserInteraction( false );
     return con ;
    }

    private void sendObject( URLConnection con , Object obj ) throws
IOException
    {
        ObjectOutputStream out = new ObjectOutputStream(
con.getOutputStream() );
        if ( obj != null )
        {
            out.writeObject( obj );
        }
```

```
  out.close();
}

private Object receiveObject( URLConnection con ) throws Exception
{
  ObjectInputStream in = new ObjectInputStream( con.getInputStream() };
  Object obj = in.readObject();
  in.close();
  return obj ;
}

public void actionPerformed( ActionEvent e )
{
  try
  {
    URLConnection con = getConnection();
    sendObject( con , text.getText() );
    String s = (String)receiveObject( con );
    text.setText( s );
  }catch( Exception ex ) {
    System.out.println( "Curses!  Foiled again: " + ex );
  }
}

public void init()
{
  Button b = new Button("reverse!");
  b.addActionListener( this );
  add( b );
  text = new Label("The Tick sez Spoooooon!");
  add( text );
}
}
```

Note that my three methods are the same except they aren't static anymore. I could have left them static, but I don't like to do that unless it is necessary.

For the applet, I introduced a button and a label. The label holds the text that is being reversed. The button activates the pipeline and, therefore, reverses the string. I'm properly catching all my exceptions now.

Here are the contents of pipeline.html I used to view the applet:

```
<HTML>
<BODY>
  <applet CODE=PipelineApplet.class WIDTH=300 HEIGHT=300 >
  </applet>
</BODY>
</HTML>
```

With your servlet engine running, fire up your Web browser and head for `http://local-host/pipeline.html`. You should see something like Figure 12.1.

FIGURE 12.1
Before and after reversing the String

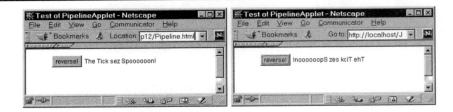

Each time you click on the button, the text is sent to the `PipelineServlet`. The `PipelineServlet` reverses the text and sends it back to the applet. The applet then shows the new text.

TIP   Only serializable objects can be passed through the object pipeline. This means that your object's class must implement `java.io.Serializable`. If there are any objects within your object, they must also be serializable. Most core Java classes implement `Serializable`.

WARNING   Watch out for some classes in some versions of Microsoft Internet Explorer that don't serialize correctly. `Hashtable` and `Vector` are two known problems; there may be others. Just to be safe, I stick to passing only my own classes that are passing just primitive types (`int`, `long`, `char`, `double`), strings, and arrays.

Introducing Reusability

For every type of transaction that the applet needs to do with the server, I make a servlet. Some people like to have one do-it-all servlet, but in that case, the servlet has to spend time figuring out which task it has been given. I could send a variety of polymorphic objects that have a common `doYourThing()` method, but I think having a lot of servlets is far simpler—and keeping things simple is the most important thing to me.

So I have a lot of servlets. Instead of copying my send and receive methods to every servlet, I want just one copy of the methods. In addition, I think this is a good place to implement the Facade Pattern (GoF 95). If I need to make the pipeline work differently, I can do it in one place instead of a lot of places. I decided to make a class that holds general-purpose stuff for servlets. These two methods will be my first addition, as shown in Listing 12.6.

Listing 12.6: The Servlets utility class

```java
package com.javaranch.common ;

import java.io.* ;
import javax.servlet.http.* ;

public class Servlets
{

   // since this class just holds static methods, I don't want anybody to➥
   instantiate it
   private Servlets(){}

   public static Object getObjectFromClient( HttpServletRequest req ) throws➥
   Exception
   {
     ObjectInputStream in = new ObjectInputStream( req.getInputStream() );
     Object obj = in.readObject();
     in.close();
     return obj ;
   }

   public static void sendObjectToClient( HttpServletResponse resp , Object obj )
     throws Exception
   {
     ObjectOutputStream out = new ObjectOutputStream( resp.getOutputStream() );
     out.writeObject( obj );
     out.close();
   }

}
```

I put this class in a package into which I put all my stuff that can be reused among projects. My naming convention for the package is nothing more than my domain name backward, followed by a directory-tree-like structure. Things that are common to other packages are put in a package called "common." I own the domain javaranch.com, so I use com.javaranch.common for things common to various projects. On my site I have the rules roundup game, which is in the package com.javaranch.roundup.

I made the methods static because I could see no need to instantiate an object to use these methods. They are very much standalone methods. I changed the names of the methods a bit. After all, because this class will serve all sorts of functions for servlets, "sendObject()" just isn't very clear. Now my test servlet looks like Listing 12.7.

Listing 12.7: PipelineServlet modified to use the Servlets utility

```java
import javax.servlet.* ;
import javax.servlet.http.* ;
import com.javaranch.common.* ;

public class PipelineServlet extends HttpServlet {

  public void doPost( HttpServletRequest req , HttpServletResponse resp )
  {
    try {
      Object obj = Servlets.getObjectFromClient( req ) ;
    // reverse the String.
      String old = (String)obj ;
      String s = "";
      for( int i = old.length() - 1 ; i >= 0 ; i-- )
      {
    s += old.charAt( i );
      }
      Servlets.sendObjectToClient( resp , s );
    }
    catch ( Exception e )
    {
  System.out.println( "Clang! Thunk: " + e );
    }
  }
}
```

It's still a bit clunky. Listing 12.8 shows an improved base class for all my servlets that communicate with applets to extend instead of extending HttpServlet.

Listing 12.8: The ObjectServlet class, an improved base for servlets

```java
package com.javaranch.common ;

import javax.servlet.* ;
import javax.servlet.http.* ;
import java.io.* ;

public abstract class ObjectServlet extends HttpServlet
{
    // override this method
  public Object doObject( Object obj ) throws Exception
  {
      return null ;
  }
```

```
    public final void doPost( HttpServletRequest req ,
HttpServletResponse resp )
    {
      try
      {
        Object obj = Servlets.getObjectFromClient( req ) ;
        obj = doObject( obj , req );
        Servlets.sendObjectToClient( resp , obj );
      }
      catch ( Exception e )
      {
System.out.println( "Clang! Thunk: " + e );
      }
    }
  }
```

The idea is that rather than extend `HttpServlet` and override `doPost()`, you extend `ObjectServlet` and override `doObject` as shown in Listing 12.9.

Listing 12.9: PipelineServlet as an extension of ObjectServlet

```
import com.javaranch.common.* ;

public class PipelineServlet extends ObjectServlet
{
    public Object doObject( Object obj )
    {
// reverse the String.
      String old = (String)obj ;
      String s = "";
      for( int i = old.length() - 1 ; i >= 0 ; i-- )
      {
  s += old.charAt( i );
      }
      return s ;
    }
}
```

Now we'll give the applet a bit of a makeover. Three methods can be moved to a common class: `getConnection()`, `sendObject()`, and `receiveObject()`. However, if you think about it, these three methods always occur right in a row. Why not consolidate them into one method, as I have done with the **send()** method in the class shown in Listing 12.10.

Listing 12.10: A utility class for the applet side

```
package com.javaranch.common ;

import java.io.* ;
import java.net.* ;
```

```java
public class HTTP
{

  private static URLConnection getConnection( String servlet )
      throws IOException
  {
    URL u = new URL( servlet );
    URLConnection con = u.openConnection();
    con.setDoInput( true );
    con.setDoOutput( true );
    con.setUseCaches( false );
    con.setRequestProperty("Content-type","application/octet-stream");
    con.setAllowUserInteraction( false );
    return con ;
  }

  private static void sendObject( URLConnection con , Object obj )
      throws IOException
  {
    ObjectOutputStream out = new ObjectOutputStream( con.getOutputStream() );
    if ( obj != null )
    {
       out.writeObject( obj );
    }
    out.close();
  }

  private static Object receiveObject( URLConnection con ) throws Exception
  {
    ObjectInputStream in = new ObjectInputStream( con.getInputStream() );
    Object obj = in.readObject();
    in.close();
    return obj ;
  }

  // returns null if there are any problems
  public static Object send( String servlet , Object obj )
  {
    Object returnVal = null ;
    try
    {
       URLConnection con = getConnection( servlet );
       sendObject( con , obj );
       returnVal = receiveObject( con );
    }
    catch( Exception e )
    {
       System.out.println( "HTTP: " + e );
    }
    return returnVal ;
  }
}
```

Now take a look at my sexy lean applet in Listing 12.11!

Listing 12.11: The PipelineApplet using the HTTP utility class

```java
import java.applet.* ;
import java.awt.* ;
import java.awt.event.* ;
import com.javaranch.common.* ;

public class PipelineApplet extends Applet implements ActionListener
{

  private static final String servlet = "http://localhost/servlet/➡
  PipelineServlet";
  private Label text ;   // shows my results

  public void actionPerformed( ActionEvent e )
  {
    text.setText( (String)HTTP.send( servlet , text.getText() ) );
  }

  public void init()
  {
    Button b = new Button("reverse!");
    b.addActionListener( this );
    add( b );
    text = new Label("The Tick sez Spoooooon!");
    add( text );
  }
}
```

Status, Logs, and Debugging

When something isn't working, I'm always quick to move the blame away from my flawless code. However, this is really hard to do when the guy you normally blame has been out sick for a week. So there must be something wrong with the server—or maybe the network. After all, if my applet dies the moment it tries to get the first thing over the pipeline, the only possible causes are the network, the server, and me. My ego tells me that I need to develop something that proves there is some kind of problem with the server or the network. My first attempt is pretty straightforward. I add the Listing 12.12 code to my `ObjectServlet` class.

Listing 12.12: A first step at debugging the ObjectServlet class

```java
public void doGet( HttpServletRequest req , HttpServletResponse resp )
{
  try
  {
    PrintWriter out = resp.getWriter();
```

```
      out.println( "working!" );
    }
    catch( Exception e )
    {
      System.out.println( "GET fail: " + e );
    }
  }
}
```

Now when I direct my browser to `http://localhost/servlet/PipelineServlet`, I see the message "working!"

Okay, so the network is working and the server is working, but how do I know that doPost is being activated? Counters! Every time doPost() is activated, we'll have it increment a counter that can be seen through doGet(). And while we're at it, why not have a counter for doGet, too. The result is Listing 12.13.

Listing 12.13: Adding debugging aids to ObjectServlet

```
package com.javaranch.common ;

import javax.servlet.* ;
import javax.servlet.http.* ;
import java.io.* ;

public abstract class ObjectServlet extends HttpServlet
{
  private int getCount = 0 ;
  private int postCount = 0 ;

    // override this method
  public Object doObject( Object obj ) throws Exception
  {
      return null ;
  }

  public final void doPost( HttpServletRequest req , HttpServletResponse resp )
  {
    postCount++ ;
    try
    {
      Object obj = Servlets.getObjectFromClient( req ) ;
      obj = doObject( obj );
      Servlets.sendObjectToClient( resp , obj );
    }
    catch ( Exception e )
    {
        System.out.println( "Clang! Thunk: " + e );
    }
  }
}
```

```
    public void doGet( HttpServletRequest req , HttpServletResponse resp )
    {
       getCount++ ;
       try
       {
         PrintWriter out = resp.getWriter();
         out.println( "working!" );
         out.println( "GET count = " + getCount );
         out.println( "POST count = " + postCount );
       }
       catch( Exception e )
       {
 System.out.println( "GET fail: " + e );
       }
    }
  }
```

Now I direct my browser to `http://localhost/servlet/PipelineServlet` and hit Reload (or Refresh for IE) several times, and I see the GET counter increment. If I have my applet running in another window, I can click the button a couple of times and then hit Refresh on the status browser, and the POST counter increments.

Now I know that POST is being called. But then what? Something must be going wrong . . . gulp . . . in my code! So I sprinkle some `System.out.println()` statements throughout the code. I wade through the servlet server logs to find the problem. I figure out the problem, but leave the `println()` statements there so that if anything else goes wrong, I can still have the information. After doing something like this in several servlets, the servlet logs get pretty huge and klunky. There has to be a better way.

I have an `ErrorLog` class that I created a couple of years ago that should come in handy. There's not much to it. Create an `ErrorLog` object, tell it where to send the error messages it gets, and then send it error messages. At any time, you can tell it to send its messages somewhere else—including nowhere.

To pull this off, I need to be able to add to the log and redirect the log while the servlet is running , and I need to see the log. Because the rest of this book has brought you up to speed on servlets, you'll find the resulting code (Listing 12.14) to be bulky, but not complicated.

Listing 12.14: Adding logging capability

```
package com.javaranch.common ;

import javax.servlet.* ;
import javax.servlet.http.* ;
import java.io.* ;
```

```java
public abstract class ObjectServlet extends HttpServlet
{
  private int getCount = 0 ;
  private int postCount = 0 ;

  private ErrorLog log = new ErrorLog();

    // turn logging to memory on and off
  protected void setLogMemory( boolean on )
  {
      log.setInternalLog( on );
  }

    // turn logging to console on and off
  protected void setLogConsole( boolean on )
  {
        log.setConsole( on );
  }

    // add messages to the log
  public void logMessage( String s )
  {
      log.add( s );
  }

    // override this method
  public Object doObject( Object obj ) throws Exception
  {
        return null ;
  }

  public final void doPost( HttpServletRequest req , HttpServletResponse resp )
  {
    postCount++ ;
    logMessage( "start POST" );
    try
    {
     Object obj = Servlets.getObjectFromClient( req ) ;
     obj = doObject( obj );
     Servlets.sendObjectToClient( resp , obj );
    }
    catch ( Exception e ) {
       logMessage( "Clang! Thunk: " + e );
    }
    logMessage( "stop POST" );
  }
```

```java
public void doGet( HttpServletRequest req , HttpServletResponse resp )
{
  getCount++ ;
  try
  {
    String url = req.getRequestURI(); // we'll need this for interaction
    PrintWriter out = resp.getWriter();
    resp.setContentType("text/html");
    out.println("<html>");
    String parm = req.getParameter("log");
    if ( parm == null )
    {
      out.println( "POST count = " + postCount + "<p>" );
      out.println( "GET count = " + getCount + "<p>" );
      out.print("logging to stdout.log is currently " );
      if ( log.isConsoleLogOn() )
      {
        out.println( "on . . . . <a href=" + url +
        "?log=conoff>turn off</a><p>" );
      }
      else
      {
        out.println( "off . . . . <a href=" + url +
              "?log=conon>turn on</a><p>" );
      }
      out.print("logging to memory buffer is currently ");
      if ( log.isInternalLogOn() )
      {
        out.println( "on . . . . <a href=" + url +
              "?log=memoff>turn off</a><p>" );
        String[] s = log.getList();
        if ( s == null )
        {
          out.println("no log messages.<p>");
        }
        else
        {
          out.println("log messages:<p><ul>");
          int i ;
          for( i = 0 ; i < s.length ; i++ )
          {
            out.println( "    <li>" + s[ i ] + "<p>" );
          }
          out.println("</ul>");
        }
      }
    }
```

```
          else
          {
            out.println( "off . . . . <a href=" + url + "?log=memon>turn on➡
            </a><p>" );
          }
        }
        else
        {
          if ( parm.equals("conon") )
          {
            log.setConsole( true );
            out.println("future log entries will now be routed to stdout.log<p>");
          }
          else if ( parm.equals("conoff") )
          {
            log.setConsole( false );
            out.println("further log entries will not be routed to ➡
            stdout.log<p>");
          }
          else if ( parm.equals("memon") )
          {
            log.setInternalLog( true );
            out.println("future log entries will now be kept in memory<p>");
          }
          else if ( parm.equals("memoff") )
          {
            log.setInternalLog( false );
            out.println("The memory log has been erased and further log➡
            entries will not be kept in memory<p>");
          }
        }
        out.println( "\n\n<p><a href=" + url + ">get new servlet data</a><p>" );
        out.println("</html>");
        out.close();
      }
      catch( Exception e )
      {
        System.out.println( "GET fail: " + e );
      }
    }
  }
```

Note that I am now specifying the content type as HTML. This is because I'm allowing the status/log screen user to be able to change the status of the servlet by clicking on hyperlinks. Console logging is the old, moldy, boring stuff that went out to the servlet server log files.

Memory logging is the good stuff. You can turn this on, monkey with the applet (which monkeys with the servlet), and hit Reload to see what happened. It defaults to off so it doesn't hog memory.

Problems with Complicated Objects

Something in the network was haunting me. As the project progressed, the pipeline became less stable. At first I thought it was a fluke, but as time passed, there were more pipeline failures.

I modified PipelineApp and PipelineServlet so I could try passing different objects and different quantities of objects. If I sent a half megabyte byte array, it would work fine. If I sent an object array with a couple hundred simple objects, it would fail. One hundred would be fine. If I sent an object array with a couple dozen sophisticated objects, it would barf. But five sophisticated objects would be okay.

The problem seemed to have something to do with the total number of objects. The solution was to write all the objects to a byte array and send the byte array. On the receiving end, I had to get the byte array and convert that to objects. Because the problem was happening only in the direction from the servlet to the applet, I only implemented it there.

In the HTTP class, I added a method called `convertByteArrayToObject()` and made the appropriate changes to `receiveObject()`, as shown in Listing 12.15.

Listing 12.15: Serializing to a byte array in the utility class

```
private static Object convertByteArrayToObject( byte[] b ) throws Exception
{
   ObjectInputStream in = new ObjectInputStream( new ByteArrayInputStream
   ( b ) );
   return in.readObject();
}

private static Object receiveObject( URLConnection con ) throws Exception
{
   ObjectInputStream in = new ObjectInputStream( con.getInputStream() );
   byte[] b = (byte[])in.readObject();
   in.close();
   return convertByteArrayToObject( b );
}
```

In the Servlets class, I added a method called `convertObjectToByteArray()` and made the appropriate modifications to `sendObjectToClient()`, as shown in Listing 12.16.

Listing 12.16: Methods to convert objects to byte arrays

```
private static byte[] convertObjectToByteArray( Object obj ) throws IOException
{
   ByteArrayOutputStream b = new ByteArrayOutputStream();
   ObjectOutputStream out = new ObjectOutputStream( b );
   out.writeObject( obj );
   return b.toByteArray();
}
```

```
public static void sendObjectToClient( HttpServletResponse resp ,
        Object obj ) throws Exception
{
   byte[] b = convertObjectToByteArray( obj );
   ObjectOutputStream out = new ObjectOutputStream( resp.getOutputStream() );
   out.writeObject( b );
   out.close();
}
```

Compression

As my first applet-to-servlet pipeline project drew to a close, we started focusing on optimization. Because the applet was going to be made available via the Internet, we had to test the speed of the applet over a 28.8kb connection. Some of the data transfers were quite slow, so I offered to compress the data on-the-fly. Sounds impressive, doesn't it?

It took less than half an hour to figure out how to do it and implement it. In HTTP.sendObject(), I changed this line

```
ObjectOutputStream out = new ObjectOutputStream( con.getOutputStream() );
```

to

```
ObjectOutputStream out = new ObjectOutputStream( new
                      GZIPOutputStream( con.getOutputStream() ) );
```

and in HTTP.receiveObject(), I changed this line

```
ObjectInputStream in = new ObjectInputStream( con.getInputStream());
```

to

```
ObjectInputStream in = new ObjectInputStream(
                      new GZIPInputStream( con.getInputStream()));
```

In Servlets.getObjectFromClient(), I changed this line

```
ObjectInputStream in = new ObjectInputStream( req.getInputStream() );
```

to

```
ObjectInputStream in = new ObjectInputStream(
                      new GZIPInputStream( req.getInputStream()));
```

and in Servlets.sendObjectToClient(), I changed the following line

```
ObjectOutputStream out = new ObjectOutputStream( resp.getOutputStream() );
```

to

```
ObjectOutputStream out = new ObjectOutputStream(
                      new GZIPOutputStream( resp.getOutputStream() ) );
```

That's all it took to insert zip stream functionality into my object streams. The complete code for the final version of the utilities is on the CD-ROM that came with this book, and any improvements will be posted at my Web site at www.javaranch.com.

The ease with which the compression function was added to the applet to servlet communication utilities is a testament to the elegance possible with object-oriented programming and the Java standard library.

Expanding Object Communication Concepts

Communicating a single object back and forth between applet and servlet may, at first glance, seem inadequate for heavy-duty applications. However, this impression is false due to the fact that Java interface building and collection classes are serializable. Any user interface that you would care to build from AWT or Swing components can be built on the server dynamically or retrieved as a serialized object from a database and sent to a skeleton applet in the user's browser. Even complex user data can be placed in a Java collection such as Vector or Hashtable for return to the servlet.

Transmitting a User Interface

For an example, I am going to create a Panel with labels and text fields, send it to an applet, and process the user's input. The Panel creation is handled by the class shown in Listing 12.17.

Listing 12.17: Class to create a Panel on the server

```
package com.JSPbook.Chap12;

import java.awt.* ;

public class PanelPrep
{
  static String[] labelTxt = {
    "First Name", "Last Name", "eMail Address", "Preferred handle"
  } ;
  static String[] fieldName = {
    "fname", "lname", "email", "handle"
  } ;

  // creates a Panel with various fields
  public Object testOne(String name, String label ){
    Panel p = new Panel( new GridLayout( 1 + (labelTxt.length * 2), 1, 2, 2) );
    p.setBackground( Color.cyan );
```

```
        p.setName( name );
        p.add( new Label( label ) );
        for( int i = 0 ; i < labelTxt.length ; i++ ){
          p.add( new Label( labelTxt[i] ));
          TextField tf = new TextField();
          tf.setName( fieldName[i] );
          p.add( tf );
        }
        return p ;
      }
    }
```

The `java.awt.Panel` class is one of the most used containers for organizing AWT (Abstract Windowing Toolkit) user interfaces. It inherits all functionality from the `Container` class, so you should look at the `Container` class documentation for details of the methods. Containers maintain an ordered list of graphic components they hold, and they use a `Layout Manager` to arrange these containers. In the example, the `GridLayout` spaces the components vertically and lets them occupy the full width of the `Panel`.

Another important point is that all AWT components can be assigned a name, just like the input fields of an HTML form. In the `PanelPrep` code, a name was assigned to each of the `TextField` objects. We will later use this name when user input data is returned to the servlet.

An alternative to creating a user interface with AWT components is the so-called Swing toolkit. Swing components, which are considered a "standard extension" to the Java libraries, are much more flexible than AWT components but are also somewhat more complex to work with. Swing components are also serializable, but they can't be mixed with the regular AWT components.

Transmitting the Panel

For the purposes of this chapter, the example servlet will just transmit a single `Panel` and receive the user's input from that interface. Obviously, a real application would involve many more interface elements, but this serves to illustrate the principle. Listing 12.18 shows the `AwtObjectServlet` source code.

Listing 12.18: The AwtObjectServlet class

```
package com.JSPbook.Chap12;

import java.io.*;
import java.util.* ;
import javax.servlet.*;
import javax.servlet.http.* ;
import com.javaranch.common.* ;
```

```
public class AwtObjectServlet extends com.javaranch.common.ObjectServlet
{
  String version = "1.00 8/01";
  public void init(ServletConfig config) throws ServletException
  {
    super.init(config);
    System.out.println("AwtObjectServlet initialized " + version );
  }

   // overrides the method in ObjectServlet
  public Object doObject( Object obj )throws Exception {
    //System.out.println("AwtObjectServlet got " + obj );
    if( obj instanceof String ){
      return new PanelPrep().testOne("Name Panel",
  "Please Enter The Following") ;
    }
    if( obj instanceof Hashtable ){
      Enumeration en = ((Hashtable)obj).keys();
      while( en.hasMoreElements()){
String key = (String)en.nextElement();
System.out.println( key + " = " + ((Hashtable)obj).get(key) );
      }
      return "OK" ;
    }
    return "Unknown" ;
  }

  public void service( HttpServletRequest req, HttpServletResponse rsp )
     throws IOException, ServletException {
    try {
      super.service( req, rsp );
    }catch(IOException e){
e.printStackTrace( System.err );
    }
  }
}
```

The initial request goes to the service method in `ObjectServlet`, which calls the `doPost` method in `ObjectServlet`.

WARNING   That method calls `getObjectFromClient` in the Servlets utility class and passes the resulting `Object` to the `doObject` method we have overridden. The `Object` returned from `doObject` is serialized and returned to the client.

On the Applet Side

The fact that I am using JRun and the 1.2 JDK as a servlet engine introduced an important complication that I had not foreseen. Because the `Panel` was being created by a 1.2 version library, I ran into a problem with the JVM and library in normal Microsoft and Netscape browsers, which are only compatible with the 1.1 JDK.

In order for object serialization to work, the class files available to the JVM on the receiving side must be compatible with the class files used in the creation of the objects being serialized. Java has two ways of checking for version compatibility. If the class has a `final static long` variable named `serialVersionUID`, that value must be identical or an exception is thrown. If the class does not have that variable, the `ObjectOutputStream` computes a version number based on all the fields and method signatures.

Many of the AWT components used the same `serialVersionUID` values in the 1.2 JDK as they did in the 1.1 JDK. Unfortunately, `GridLayout` was not one of them, so my JDK 1.1 compatible browsers could not deserialize the object. To get around this problem, I installed the 1.2 compatible Java browser plug-in.

Special HTML Tag for the Plug-In

In order for the browser to call the plug-in instead of using the built-in JVM, a special version of the `<applet>` tag had to be used. Fortunately, Sun provides a conversion utility that turns a simple applet tag like this

```
<applet code="ObjTestApplet.class" width="500" height="400" >
<param name=contact value="/servlet/objectsupply">
</applet>
```

into the `<OBJECT>` tag you see in Listing 12.19. I have left in all the HTML comments that the conversion utility creates. Normally, however, you would remove those after verifying that the converted code works.

Listing 12.19: The HTML page as modified to use the Java plug-in

```
<html>
<head>
<title>Testing Object Transmission</title>
</head>
<body BGCOLOR="#FFFFFF" TEXT="#000000">
<font FACE=VERDANA>
<h2 ALIGN=CENTER>Click Next To Continue
</h2><br>
<center>
<!--"CONVERTED_APPLET"-->
<!-- CONVERTER VERSION 1.0 -->
<OBJECT classid="clsid:8AD9C840-044E-11D1-B3E9-00805F499D93"
WIDTH = "500" HEIGHT = "400"  codebase="http://java.sun.com/products/plugin➥
/1.2/jinstall-12-win32.cab#Version=1,2,0,0">
<PARAM NAME = CODE VALUE = "ObjTestApplet.class" >

<PARAM NAME="type" VALUE="application/x-java-applet;version=1.2">
<PARAM NAME="contact" VALUE ="/servlet/objectsupply">
<COMMENT>
```

```
<EMBED type="application/x-java-applet;version=1.2" java_CODE = ➥
"ObjTestApplet.class" WIDTH = "500" HEIGHT = "400"  contact = "servlet➥
/objectsupply"  pluginspage="http://java.sun.com/products/plugin/1.2➥
/plugin-install.html"><NOEMBED></COMMENT>

</NOEMBED></EMBED>
</OBJECT>

<!--
<APPLET  CODE = "ObjTestApplet.class" WIDTH = "500" HEIGHT = "400" >
<PARAM NAME = contact VALUE ="servlet/objectsupply">

</APPLET>
-->
<!--"END_CONVERTED_APPLET"-->

</center>
<hr>

</body>
</html>
```

The ObjTestApplet

The applet I created to receive and display the serialized panel is also simple. It is created with a BorderLayout in which the serialized panel will be displayed as the "Center" component, and it has a Button to start the transfer process. The applet was created with the Visual Cafe IDE so it has the Visual Cafe special comments, as you can see in Listing 12.20.

Listing 12.20: The start of the ObjTestApplet source code

```
import java.net.* ;
import java.io.* ;
import java.util.* ;
import java.awt.*;
import java.applet.*;
import com.javaranch.common.* ;

public class ObjTestApplet extends Applet
{
  Panel currentP = null ;
  String servlet = "/servlet/objectsupply" ;
  String server ;

  public void init()
  {
    //{{INIT_CONTROLS
    setLayout(new BorderLayout(0,0));
    setFont(new Font("SansSerif", Font.PLAIN, 16));
    bottomP.setLayout(new FlowLayout(FlowLayout.CENTER,5,5));
```

```
      add("South",bottomP);
      bottomP.setBackground(java.awt.Color.cyan);
      bottomP.setBounds(0,233,426,33);
      nextB.setLabel("Next");
      bottomP.add(nextB);
      nextB.setBackground(java.awt.Color.lightGray);
      nextB.setBounds(194,5,38,23);
      //}}

      //{{REGISTER_LISTENERS
      SymAction lSymAction = new SymAction();
      nextB.addActionListener(lSymAction);
      //}}
      String tmp = getParameter("contact");
      if( tmp != null ) {
  servlet = tmp ;
      }
   }

   //{{DECLARE_CONTROLS
   java.awt.Panel bottomP = new java.awt.Panel();
   java.awt.Button nextB = new java.awt.Button();
   //}}

   class SymAction implements java.awt.event.ActionListener
   {
     public void actionPerformed(java.awt.event.ActionEvent event)
     {
       Object object = event.getSource();
       if (object == nextB)
  nextB_ActionPerformed(event);
     }
   }
```

Now we come to the interesting part—what happens when the button is clicked, as shown in Listing 12.21. To send an Object using the HTTP utility class, we need a String representation of the servlet address. Note that if the server variable has not set, we create it by using the getDocumentBase method of the Applet class. The first time the button is clicked, the currentP variable will be null, and the Object transmitted is the "Next" String. The Panel object that is returned is added to the applet in the "Center" position. Then a call to validate forces the applet to re-evaluate the layout and display of all contents, and the new panel is displayed.

Listing 12.21: The code that receives an object

```
     void nextB_ActionPerformed(java.awt.event.ActionEvent event)
     { Object obj = null ;
       try {
         if( server == null ){
```

```
URL url = getDocumentBase();
URL srvUrl = new URL(url.getProtocol(), url.getHost(),
  url.getPort(), servlet );
server = srvUrl.toExternalForm();
 System.out.println("server:" + server );
    }
    if( currentP == null ){
obj = com.javaranch.common.HTTP.sendE( server, "Next");
    }
    else {
Hashtable params = harvestText();
obj = com.javaranch.common.HTTP.sendE( server, params );
    }
    if( obj instanceof Panel ){
currentP = (Panel) obj ;
add("Center", currentP );
validate();
    }
    System.out.println("Returned " + obj );
  }catch(Exception e){
    e.printStackTrace( System.out );
  }
 }
```

On the other hand, if the currentP variable contains a Panel, the harvestText method is called to grab the current contents of the TextField components, and the resulting Object is sent to the servlet. As you can see in Listing 12.22, harvestText creates a Hashtable using the name assigned to each TextField as a key for the contents.

Listing 12.22: The method that creates a Hashtable from the user input

```
private Hashtable harvestText(){
  Hashtable ret = new Hashtable();
  Component[] cmp = currentP.getComponents();
  ret.put("Form name", currentP.getName());
  for( int i = 0 ; i < cmp.length ; i++ ){
    if( cmp[i] instanceof TextField ){
TextField tf = (TextField) cmp[i] ;
//System.out.println( tf.getName() + " = " + tf.getText() );
ret.put( tf.getName(), tf.getText() );
    }
  }
  return ret ;
 }
}
```

Figure 12.2 shows an example of the applet in action, with partially filled in text fields. Any field that is not filled in will be transmitted to the servlet as an empty String instead of a null value.

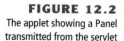

FIGURE 12.2
The applet showing a Panel
transmitted from the servlet

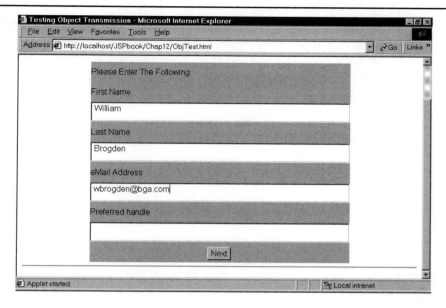

Using a Hashtable Instead of getParameter

In a conventional servlet design, you typically retrieve data from an HTML form by using the getParameter method of the HttpServletRequest object in the doPost method. The equivalent information can be obtained from an applet in a Hashtable object.

Potential Applications

The example I just discussed doesn't do anything that an HTML form could not accomplish. The real advantage of applet-to-servlet communication by object serialization becomes apparent only when you consider more complex interfaces. Here are some examples drawn from the requests for help that I have seen on Java-related newsgroups:

User Drawn Images   Many applets let a user draw and color an image with various tools. An image is easily converted to an array of byte or int primitives, which in turn is easily serialized. Because the HTTP utility object transmission scheme applies compression to the serialized Object, image transmission can be quite fast.

Encrypted Content   If your application involves sensitive information, you certainly don't want to communicate it in the clear. Following the examples discussed here and using Java's encryption and signing classes, you can encrypt any object transmission.

Analog Controls   Complex settings such as those on an audio mixer can be represented by `Scrollbar` objects or, using Swing components, by `JSlider` objects.

Complex Logic   Applet-based games are always of interest but have generally used pretty simple interfaces. Using object serialization, strategic maps and user decisions of any desired degree of complexity can be transmitted.

The Servlet and JSP APIs

While working with the servlet and JSP APIs, I have found the JDK documentation to be very thorough from a class documentation standpoint, but not very useful from a functional standpoint. The formal Servlet 2.2 and JSP 1.1 APIs also seem to be hard to integrate into real practices. The purpose of this appendix is to present the most frequently used APIs from a functional point of view, along with hints on usage.

Just to review, we are concerned with the following packages:

javax.servlet   The basic generalized servlet package.

javax.servlet.http   Specialized extensions for Web pages.

javax.servlet.jsp   Classes for creating JavaServer Pages.

javax.servlet.jsp.tagext   Specialized extensions to JSP classes that permit creation of custom tag libraries.

Setting Parameters for Applications

The servlet and JSP APIs treat parameters as having a scope that reflects the parts of the system in which the parameter has validity. The different scopes in order of decreasing extent are Server, Application, Session, Request, and Page. Each is described here:

Server Scope   Parameters visible to all applications.

Application Scope   Sun uses the "Web application" term to refer to the collection of servlets, JSP, and other resources installed in a particular server address space. The **Servlet-Context** class is intended to let all these resources share information by means of mutually accessible stored objects in "application scope." The application scope affects the interpretation of relative URL specifications.

Session Scope   As you learned in Chapter 3, servlets and JSP pages can save information specific to a user in an **HttpSession** object managed by the servlet engine. Objects stored this way are said to have "session" scope.

Request Scope   A request can actually be processed by several pages because of the forwarding mechanism. The request object can carry additional objects with it.

Page Scope   In JSP engine-created servlets, this is the scope of a single page.

Servlet Creation

Because servlet methods are defined in an interface and interfaces cannot define constructors, all initialization of a servlet is carried out in the `init` method. The servlet engine is guaranteed to call `init` after the servlet object is constructed and before any request is handled. The `init` method is handed a `ServletConfig` object that can be used to obtain initialization parameters. Remember this distinction:

- `ServletConfig`—Objects using this interface hold information used during servlet initialization. A frequent source of mysterious runtime errors in servlets occurs when the programmer forgets to include a call to `super.init()` in an `init()` method.

- `ServletContext`—Objects using this interface let a servlet locate information about the servlet engine it is running in and its environment. You can get a `ServletContext` from the `ServletConfig` object.

All servlet engines provide for defining initialization parameters to be passed to a given servlet. The conventions by which the server administrator can set these parameters vary between servlet engines, but the basic idea remains the same. Hopefully, more vendors will be moving to Sun's standard approach using XML.

A parameter name is associated with a text value. Programmers familiar with Java applets will note the parallel with the way in which an applet container (the browser) provides named parameters to an applet. The three methods that `ServletConfig` provides are shown in Table A.1.

TABLE A.1: The ServletConfig methods

Returns	Method	Usage
String	getInitParameter(String name)	This method returns a `String` corresponding to the name or returns null if no such parameter exists.
Enumeration	getInitParameterNames()	This method returns an `Enumeration` over all the names in the set of parameters.
ServletContext	getServletContext()	This method gets the `ServletContext` the servlet is operating in.

Table A.2 lists the methods your custom servlet must provide for.

TABLE A.2: The Servlet interface methods

Returns	Method	Usage
void	init(ServletConfig config)	Called by the servlet container before any user requests are submitted. Remember to call `super.init( config )`.
void	destroy()	Called by the servlet container to indicate to a servlet that the servlet is being taken out of service.
ServletConfig	getServletConfig()	Returns a `ServletConfig` object, which contains initialization and startup parameters for this servlet. Note: This reference will be null if you forget to have your `init` method call `super.init( config )`.
String	getServletInfo()	Optional method to return information about the servlet, such as author, version, and copyright.
void	service(ServletRequest req, ServletResponse res)	Called by the servlet container to allow the servlet to respond to a request.

HttpServlet Methods

The `HttpServlet` class adds methods to support HTTP protocol requests. Your custom servlet class should override at least one of these methods, as shown in Table A.3.

TABLE A.3: The HttpServlet methods that are commonly overridden

Override this method	To support this request
doGet(HttpServletRequest req, HttpServletResponse resp)	HTTP GET
doPost(HttpServletRequest req, HttpServletResponse resp)	HTTP POST
doPut(HttpServletRequest req, HttpServletResponse resp)	HTTP PUT
doDelete(HttpServletRequest req, HttpServletResponse resp)	HTTP DELETE

The ServletContext Interface

The servlet engine creates an object implementing this interface and makes it available to servlets. This is the primary path for communication between a servlet and the enclosing servlet container. Each Web application, which may contain many servlets and JSP, shares a `ServletContext`. Table A.4 summarizes the methods by which objects and parameter settings are shared through `ServletContext`. The remaining methods are summarized in Table A.5.

TABLE A.4: ServletContext methods related to parameters and attributes

Returns	Method	Usage
Object	getAttribute(String name)	Returns the servlet container attribute with the given name, or null if there is no attribute by that name.
Enumeration	getAttributeNames()	An **Enumeration** containing the attribute names (Strings) in this servlet context.
void	removeAttribute(String name)	Removes the attribute with the given name from the servlet context.
void	setAttribute(String name, Object object)	Binds an object to a given attribute name in this servlet context.
String	getInitParameter(String name)	Returns a **String** containing the value of the named context-wide initialization parameter, or **null** if the parameter does not exist.
Enumeration	getInitParameterNames()	Returns the names of the context's initialization parameters as an **Enumeration** of **String** objects, or an empty **Enumeration** if the context has no initialization parameters.

TABLE A.5: More ServletContext methods

Returns	Method	Usage
ServletContext	getContext(String uripath)	Returns a **ServletContext** object that corresponds to a specified URL on the server.
String	getMimeType(String file)	Returns the MIME type of the specified file, or null if the MIME type is not known.
RequestDispatcher	getNamedDispatcher(String name)	Returns a **RequestDispatcher** object that acts as a wrapper for the named servlet.
RequestDispatcher	getRequestDispatcher(String path)	Returns a **RequestDispatcher** object that acts as a wrapper for the resource located at the given path.
String	getRealPath(String path)	Returns a **String** containing the real path for a given virtual path.
java.net.URL	getResource(String path)	Returns a **URL** to the resource that is mapped to a specified path.
InputStream	getResourceAsStream(String path)	Returns the resource located at the named path as an **InputStream** object.
String	getServerInfo()	Returns the name and version of the servlet container on which the servlet is running.
int	getMajorVersion()	Returns the major version of the Java Servlet API that this servlet container supports (i.e., 2 for version 2.2).
int	getMinorVersion()	Returns the minor version of the Servlet API that this servlet container supports.

Getting Request Information

User request information comes to your servlet as an object implementing the
javax.servlet.ServletRequest or the javax.servlet.http.HttpServletRequest
interface created by the servlet engine. Servlets that extend
javax.servlet.GenericServlet or implement the javax.servlet.Servlet interface
get a ServletRequest object named req. JSP pages always get an HttpServletRequest
object named request because JSP pages are used only in an HTTP context.

The basic methods for getting request information are all in the ServletRequest interface
(see Table A.6), whereas HttpServletRequest adds some methods for getting protocol
information.

TABLE A.6: Getting user request parameters from ServletRequest

Returns	Method	Usage
Enumeration	getParameterNames()	The names of parameters parsed out of the request are made available as an Enumeration rather than a String array because the name – value pairs are stored in a Hashtable, and Hashtable objects return the list of all keys as an Enumeration.
String	getParameter(String name)	This method returns the String value corresponding to a parameter name or returns null if the name does not appear in the request. It is a wise precaution to always check the returned value versus null. If there may be more than one parameter with the same name, this method returns only the first one in the request.
String[]	getParameterValues(String name)	If there may be more than one value associated with a particular name, this method should be used. The String array that is returned preserves the original order of the parameters. If no parameter with this name exists, null is returned.

Methods Added by HttpServletRequest

This interface extends ServletRequest and adds a number of useful methods as shown in
Table A.7. Most of these methods are related to getting at information in the HTTP header
or characterizing the way the request has come to the servlet. None of the get methods that
access the header information by the header name is sensitive to case.

TABLE A.7: HttpServletRequest methods characterizing the request

Returns	Method	Return value
String	getContextPath()	The portion of the request URI that indicates the context of the request.
long	getDateHeader(String name)	The value of the specified request header as a long value that represents a **Date** object.
String	getHeader(String name)	The value of the specified request header. The name is not case sensitive.
Enumeration	getHeaderNames()	An enumeration of all the header names this request contains.
Enumeration	getHeaders(String name)	All the values of the specified request header as an **Enumeration** of **String** objects.
int	getIntHeader(String name)	A convenience method that tries to convert the specified request header into an **int** value. Returns minus 1 if the header does not exist. Throws **NumberFormatException** if the header value can't be converted, so use cautiously.
String	getMethod()	The name of the HTTP method with which this request was made (for example, GET, POST, or PUT).
String	getPathInfo()	Any extra path information associated with the URL the client sent when it made this request.
String	getPathTranslated()	Translates any extra path information after the servlet name but before the query string into a real path.
String	getQueryString()	The query string that is contained in the request URL after the path.
String	getRequestURI()	The part of this request's URL from the protocol name up to the query string in the first line of the HTTP request.
String	getServletPath()	The part of this request's URL that calls the servlet.

HttpServletRequest Methods Related to Security

As near as I can tell, the security methods listed in Table A.8 are not yet widely supported in servlet engines.

TABLE A.8: Security related methods in HttpServletRequest

Returns	Method	Return value
String	getAuthType()	Returns the name of the authentication scheme used to protect the servlet, for example, "BASIC" or "SSL," or null if the servlet was not protected.
String	getRemoteUser()	In sessions using authentication, returns the login of the user or null if the user has not been authenticated.
Principal	getUserPrincipal( )	Returns a java.security.Principal object containing the name of the current authenticated user.
boolean	isUserInRole(String role)	Returns true if the authenticated user is included in the specified logical "role."

Methods Related to Sessions and Cookies

Because a cookie is a concept tied to the HTTP protocol, all cookie and session methods related to requests are in the **HttpServletRequest** class as shown in Table A.9. Methods such as **getRequestedSessionId** refer to the session ID that was attached to the request, as either a cookie or a rewritten URL. They all return null if there was no session attached to the request.

TABLE A.9: HttpServletRequest methods related to sessions and cookies

Returns	Method	Return value/use
Cookie[]	getCookies()	Returns an array containing all the Cookie objects the client sent with this request.
String	getRequestedSessionId()	Returns the session ID specified by the client.
HttpSession	getSession()	Returns the current session associated with this request, or if the request does not have a session, creates one.
HttpSession	getSession(boolean create)	Returns the current HttpSession associated with this request or, if there is no current session and create is true, returns a new session.
boolean	isRequestedSessionIdFromCookie( )	Returns true if the requested session ID came in as a cookie (as opposed to a rewritten URL).
boolean	isRequestedSessionIdFromURL( )	Checks whether the requested session ID came in as part of the request URL.
boolean	isRequestedSessionIdValid()	Checks whether the requested session ID is still valid.

Other Methods in ServletRequest

I have tried to group the methods shown in Table A.10 by functional area instead of alphabetic order. If you want alphabetic order, use the standard JDK documentation files provided with Tomcat or the JSDK.

TABLE A.10: Some more ServletRequest methods

Returns	Method	Return value/use
void	setAttribute(String name, Object obj)	This method is used when you want to store an object in a ServletRequest object that will be handed to another servlet for processing.
Object	getAttribute(String name)	This method retrieves a stored object or returns null if no such object exists.
Enumeration	getAttributeNames()	Returns an Enumeration over all the names of available attributes.
void	removeAttribute(String name)	Removes an attribute by name.
ServletInputStream	getInputStream()	An object for reading a stream of binary data from the request using the InputStream methods.
BufferedReader	getReader()	A BufferedReader would be used to read and parse the request body text line by line instead of using the parsed parameters.

HttpSession and Cookie-Related Classes

I guess this is the best place to list HttpSession and Cookie-related classes and methods. An HttpSession object is used to maintain state information between transactions with a particular user.

HttpSession Objects implementing this interface allow the programmer to store information about a user between individual page visits or transactions. Servlet engines provide methods for keeping track of HttpSession objects using unique IDs. See Chapter 3 for examples.

HttpSessionBindingListener This interface is analogous to the many listener inter-faces in Java GUI design. A programmer would implement this interface in an object that needed to be notified when it was attached to or detached from an HttpSession object.

Cookie These objects are used to manipulate cookie information that is sent by the server to a browser and returned on subsequent requests. Cookie information in a request is turned into Cookie objects by the HttpServletRequest.

HttpUtils Static methods in this class are useful occasionally.

HttpSessionBindingEvent Objects of this type are used to communicate information to HttpSessionBindingListener objects when it is attached to or detached from an HttpSession object.

HttpSession Methods

Notice the similarity between the *attribute*-related method names listed in Table A.11 and those used in ServletRequest. An earlier API included HttpSession methods using *value* rather than *attribute* (for example, getValue), but these are deprecated in the interest of more consistent method naming.

TABLE A.11: Methods in HttpSession

Returns	Method	Return value/use
Object	getAttribute(String name)	Returns the object attached with the specified name or returns null if no object has the name.
void	setAttribute(String name, Object obj)	Attaches the object to this session with this name. Any previous reference with this name is lost.
Enumeration	getAttributeNames()	An **Enumeration** of **String** objects containing the names of all the objects attached to this session.
void	removeAttribute(String name)	Removes the object with this name from the session.
long	getCreationTime()	The system time when this session was created, as in `System.currentTimeMillis()`.
long	getLastAccessedTime()	The last time the client sent a request associated with this session; same scale as `getCreationTime`.
int	getMaxInactiveInterval()	The maximum time interval, in seconds, that the servlet container will keep this session open between client accesses.

TABLE A.11: Methods in HttpSession *(continued)*

Returns	Method	Return value/use
void	setMaxInactiveInterval(int interval)	Sets the time, in seconds, between client requests before the servlet container will invalidate this session.
void	invalidate()	Invalidates this session and unbinds any objects bound to it.
boolean	isNew()	Returns true if the client does not yet know about the session or if the client chooses not to join the session. This is usually called right after calling the getSession method of an HttpServletRequest object.
String	getId()	Returns the unique identifier assigned to this session.

HttpSessionListener Interface Methods

If an object is being stored in a session and needs to "know" when it has been attached to a session or when it is being dropped from a session, you can have that class implement the HttpSessionListener interface. It will have to implement these two methods:

valueBound(HttpSessionBindingEvent event) The object that it is being bound to a session. The event carries the session ID and the name the object is bound with.

valueUnbound(HttpSessionBindingEvent event) The object that is being unbound from a session, possibly because the session expiring.

Cookie Methods

The Cookie constructor uses a String name and a String value. Note that the name cannot use arbitrary characters, but must conform to RFC 2109. Names are not case sensitive. Table A.12 shows useful methods in the Cookie class.

TABLE A.12: Methods in the Cookie class

Returns	Method	Return value/use
Object	clone()	Overrides the standard Object.clone method to return a copy of this cookie. Note, however, that you still have to cast the reference to Cookie.
String	getValue()	Returns the value of the cookie.
void	setValue(String newValue)	Assigns a new value to a cookie after the cookie is created.
String	getComment()	The comment describing the purpose of this cookie, or null if no comment was attached.
void	setComment(String purpose)	Attach a comment that describes a cookie's purpose.

TABLE A.12: Methods in the Cookie class *(continued)*

Returns	Method	Return value/use
String	getDomain()	Returns the domain name set for this cookie.
void	setDomain(String pattern)	Set the domain within which this cookie should be presented.
void	setPath(String uri)	Set the path to which the client should return the cookie.
int	getMaxAge()	Returns the maximum age of the cookie, specified in seconds. The default, minus 1, indicates the cookie should persist until the browser shuts down.
void	setMaxAge(int expiry)	Sets the maximum age of the cookie in seconds. A value of zero means discard immediately.
String	getName()	The name of the cookie.
String	getPath()	The path on the server to which the browser returns this cookie.
boolean	getSecure()	Returns true if the browser is sending cookies only over a secure protocol; returns false if the browser can send cookies using any protocol.
void	setSecure(boolean flag)	Indicates to the browser whether the cookie should only be sent using a secure protocol, such as HTTPS or SSL.
int	getVersion()	Returns the version of the protocol this cookie complies with.
void	setVersion(int v)	Sets the version of the cookie protocol this cookie complies with.

Specialty Objects Associated with Request

The RequestDispatcher interface defines two methods that enable one servlet or JSP to forward to or include the output of another servlet or file resource on the server. You obtain a RequestDispatcher object from the ServletRequest object with a constructor that specifies the resource to be attached. The object is created by the servlet engine as in this example:

```
RequestDispatcher rd = req.getRequestDispatcher(String path);
```

Using this object, you call either of these methods:

```
forward( ServletRequest req, ServletResponse resp )
include( ServletRequest req, ServletResponse resp )
```

Setting Response Information

In this section we consider the classes and methods involved in sending response data to a user.

ServletResponse   An object implementing this interface must be created by the servlet engine and passed to the servlet's `service` method to be used for output of the MIME body to the client.

HttpServletResponse   An extension of the `ServletResponse` interface, which adds methods specific to HTTP transactions.

ServletOutputStream   A class for writing a stream of binary data as part of a response.

Methods in ServletResponse

The servlet engine creates an object implementing the `ServletResponse` interface before your servlet or JSP is called. The methods in this class are shown in Table A.13.

TABLE A.13:   Methods in the ServletResponse interface

Returns	Method	Return value/use
void	setBufferSize(int size)	Sets the preferred buffer size for the body of the response.
void	flushBuffer()	Forces any content in the buffer to be written to the client.
void	reset()	Clears any data that exists in the buffer as well as the status code and headers.
int	getBufferSize()	The actual buffer size used for the response.
boolean	isCommitted()	Returns true if the response has been committed.
String	getCharacterEncoding()	Returns the name of the charset used for the MIME body sent in this response.
Locale	getLocale()	Returns the Locale assigned to the response.
ServletOutputStream	getOutputStream()	This is the output stream to use for writing binary data in the response. Note that you cannot change output stream types after one is selected. It is an extension of `java.io.OutputStream` and can be used to create specialized output streams such as `ObjectOutput-Stream` or `ZipOutputStream`.

TABLE A.13: Methods in the ServletResponse interface *(continued)*

Returns	Method	Return value/use
PrintWriter	getWriter()	This is the output stream to use for writing character text. Because it does a character conversion according to the content type and locale, you should set those parameters before writing any data. You can call the **flush()** method to force the data out. The **close()** method must be called when your servlet has finished writing output, or the client may never receive anything.
void	setContentLength(int len)	Sets the length of the content body in the response. In HTTP servlets, this method sets the HTTP Content-Length header. This must be called before any content is actually sent. Although a content length is not required for all content types, in general it is required for binary types.
void	setContentType(String type)	Sets the content type of the response. The response type will be one of the MIME types and may optionally include character encoding information. An example of the type for html in the "Latin-4" character set for Northern European languages would be "text/html; charset=ISO-8859-4". If the character set is not specified, the default of ISO-8859-1 (ASCII) will be used.
void	setLocale(java.util.Locale loc)	Sets the locale of the response, setting the headers (including the Content-Type's charset) as appropriate.

Methods Added by HttpServletResponse

The HttpServletResponse interface extends ServletResponse and adds some useful methods specific to HTTP output as shown in Table A.14. It also defines a bunch of constants corresponding to the response status codes, such as the infamous "404 – page not found" message.

Note that the header methods using **add** can add values to an existing header creating a comma-separated list, whereas the methods using **set** replace any existing header.

TABLE A.14: Methods in the HttpServletResponse interface

Returns	Method	Return value/use
void	addCookie(Cookie cookie)	Adds the cookie to the response. This method can be called multiple times, but note that browsers might only accept 20 cookies from a given source or might be set to refuse all cookies.
void	addDateHeader(String name, long date)	Adds a response header with the given name and date-value. The date parameter is of course in the System.currentTimeMillis() style, but the header value will be text in the specific HTTP format as in Tue, 15 Nov 1994 08:12:31 GMT.
void	setDateHeader(String name, long date)	Sets a response header with this name and date-value. Any previously set header with this name is lost, so watch it.
void	addHeader(String name, String value)	Adds a response header with the given name and value. If the header already exists, adds the value to the existing value with comma separation between values.
void	setHeader(String name, String value)	Sets a response header with the given name and value. If the header already exists, replaces it.
void	addIntHeader(String name, int value)	Adds a response header with the given name and integer value. Naturally, the value is converted to a String when attached to the header.
void	setIntHeader(String name, int value)	Sets a response header with the given name and integer value.
boolean	containsHeader(String name)	Returns true if the named response header has already been set.
void	sendRedirect(String location)	Sends a temporary redirect response to the client using the specified redirect location URL.
String	encodeRedirectURL(String url)	Encodes the specified URL for use in the sendRedirect method or, if encoding is not needed, returns the URL unchanged.
String	encodeURL(String url)	Encodes the specified URL by including the session ID in it, or if encoding is not needed, returns the URL unchanged.
void	sendError(int sc)	Sends an HTTP error code to the client.
void	sendError(int sc, String msg)	Sends an error code with a descriptive message.
void	setStatus(int sc)	Sets the status code for this response.

JSP Output to Response

An instance of the JspWriter class, called out, is created automatically in the _jspService method from a PageContext. A JspWriter object is similar to a java.io.PrintWriter object in that it writes a character stream with a specific encoding. However, a significant difference is that JspWriter output methods can throw an IOException. In the PrintWriter class, an IOException is handled internally, and the programmer has to call checkError() to determine if an exception was thrown.

The capability of throwing an IOException is essential for managing the buffering behavior of the JspWriter.

Errors and Exceptions

The servlet API provides the specialized exception classes ServletException and UnavailableException, which are described here:

ServletException   A general purpose exception used throughout the servlet API. The various constructors shown in Table A.15 provide various ways to incorporate another Exception or Error with or without an explanation. Use the method getRootCause() to extract the incorporated Exception or Error from a ServletException.

UnavailableException   This exception is to be thrown when a servlet needs to indicate that it is temporarily or permanently unavailable. The cause might be lack of availability of a database server or system maintenance. Table A.16 explains the usefulness of this exception.

TABLE A.15: ServletException constructors

Constructor	Usage
ServletException()	Constructs a new servlet exception.
ServletException(java.lang.String message)	Constructs a new servlet exception with the specified message.
ServletException(java.lang.Throwable rootCause)	Constructs a new servlet exception when the servlet needs to throw an exception and includes a message about the "root cause" exception that interfered with its normal operation.
ServletException(java.lang.String message, java.lang.Throwable rootCause)	Constructs a new servlet exception when the servlet needs to throw an exception and includes a message about the "root cause" exception that interfered with its normal operation, including a description message.

TABLE A.16: UnavailableException constructors

Constructor	Usage
UnavailableException(java.lang.String msg)	Constructs a new exception with a descriptive message indicating that the servlet is permanently unavailable.
UnavailableException(java.lang.String msg, int seconds)	Constructs a new exception with a descriptive message indicating that the servlet is temporarily unavailable and giving an estimate of how long it will be unavailable.

The capability of throwing an IOException is essential for managing the buffering behavior of the JspWriter.

JSP Errors and Exceptions

Remember that the JSP API provides for special designation of a JSP error handling page as discussed in Chapter 5. This is accomplished with a page directive such as the following:

```
<%@ page language="java" errorPage="/JSPbook/Chapt02/whoops.jsp" %>
```

Any JSP page that is designated as the error page must include a tag similar to the following

```
<%@ page language="java" isErrorPage="true" %>
```

that sets the isErrorPage parameter. This ensures that the page will have a default variable named exception that will refer to the actual error or exception. This variable will refer to one of the two error-related classes, JspException and JspError. These classes have no particular extra methods beyond those in the parent class, java.lang.Exception. Table A.17 shows the constructors for JspException and JspError.

TABLE A.17: Constructors for JspException and JspError

Constructor	Usage
JspException()	Construct a JspException.
JspException(String msg)	An exception with a message.
JspError()	Note that JspError descends from JspException.
JspError(String msg)	Adds a message to the error.

HTTP Status and Error Codes

The HttpServletResponse interface includes constants for all the HTTP status and error codes, shown in Table A.18. This is essentially the same information as in the HTTP 1.1 standard, RFC 2616. The general classification of codes can be summarized as follows:

- 100 series - Informational, process continues.
- 200 series - Success.
- 300 series - Redirection, further action required to complete the request.
- 400 series - Client error, the request contains bad syntax or cannot be fulfilled.
- 500 series - Server error, the server failed to fulfill an apparently valid request.

TABLE A.18: HTTP constants for status codes

Constant name	Value	Meaning
SC_CONTINUE	100	The client can continue.
SC_SWITCHING_PROTOCOLS	101	The server is switching protocols according to Upgrade header.
SC_OK	200	The request succeeded normally.
SC_CREATED	201	The request succeeded and created a new resource on the server.
SC_ACCEPTED	202	A request was accepted for processing but was not completed.
SC_NON_AUTHORITATIVE_INFORMATION	203	The meta information presented by the client did not originate from the server.
SC_NO_CONTENT	204	The request succeeded, but there was no new information to return.
SC_RESET_CONTENT	205	The agent *should* reset the document view that caused the request to be sent.
SC_PARTIAL_CONTENT	206	The server has fulfilled the partial GET request for the resource.
SC_MULTIPLE_CHOICES	300	The requested resource corresponds to any one of a set of representations, each with its own specific location.
SC_MOVED_PERMANENTLY	301	The resource has permanently moved to a new location, and future references should use a new URI with their requests.
SC_MOVED_TEMPORARILY	302	The resource has temporarily moved to another location, but future references should still use the original URI to access the resource.

TABLE A.18: HTTP constants for status codes *(continued)*

Constant name	Value	Meaning
SC_SEE_OTHER	303	The response to the request can be found under a different URI.
SC_NOT_MODIFIED	304	A conditional **GET** operation found that the resource was available and not modified.
SC_USE_PROXY	305	The requested resource *must* be accessed through the proxy given by the Location field.

Now for the error codes! Table A.19 lists those.

TABLE A.19: HTTP error code constants

Constant name	Value	Meaning
SC_BAD_REQUEST	400	The request sent by the client was syntactically incorrect.
SC_UNAUTHORIZED	401	The request requires HTTP authentication.
SC_PAYMENT_REQUIRED	402	Reserved for future use.
SC_FORBIDDEN	403	The server understood the request but refused to fulfill it.
SC_NOT_FOUND	404	The requested resource is not available.
SC_METHOD_NOT_ALLOWED	405	The method specified in the Request-Line is not allowed for the resource identified by the Request-URI.
SC_NOT_ACCEPTABLE	406	The resource identified by the request is capable of generating only response entities that have content characteristics not acceptable according to the accept headers sent in the request.
SC_PROXY_AUTHENTICATION_REQUIRED	407	The client *must* first authenticate itself with the proxy.
SC_REQUEST_TIMEOUT	408	The client did not produce a request within the time the server was prepared to wait.
SC_CONFLICT	409	The request could not be completed due to a conflict with the current state of the resource.
SC_GONE	410	The resource is no longer available at the server and no forwarding address is known.
SC_LENGTH_REQUIRED	411	The request cannot be handled without a defined Content-Length.
SC_PRECONDITION_FAILED	412	The precondition given in one or more of the request-header fields evaluated to false when it was tested on the server.
SC_REQUEST_ENTITY_TOO_LARGE	413	The server refuses to process the request because the request entity is larger than the server is willing or able to process.

TABLE A.19: HTTP error code constants *(continued)*

Constant name	Value	Meaning
SC_REQUEST_URI_TOO_LONG	414	The server refuses to service the request because the Request-URI is too long for the server to interpret.
SC_UNSUPPORTED_MEDIA_TYPE	415	The server refuses to service the request because the entity of the request is in a format not supported by the requested resource for the requested method.
SC_REQUESTED_RANGE_NOT_SATISFIABLE	416	The server cannot serve the requested byte range.
SC_EXPECTATION_FAILED	417	The server could not meet the expectation given in the Expect request header.
SC_INTERNAL_SERVER_ERROR	500	An error inside the HTTP server prevented it from fulfilling the request.
SC_NOT_IMPLEMENTED	501	The HTTP server does not support the functionality needed to fulfill the request.
SC_BAD_GATEWAY	502	The HTTP server received an invalid response from a server it consulted when acting as a proxy or gateway.
SC_SERVICE_UNAVAILABLE	503	The HTTP server is temporarily overloaded and unable to handle the request.
SC_GATEWAY_TIMEOUT	504	The server did not receive a timely response from the upstream server while acting as a gateway or proxy.
SC_HTTP_VERSION_NOT_SUPPORTED	505	The server does not support or refuses to support the HTTP protocol version that was used in the request message.

NOTE   Note on diagnosing error codes: Microsoft's Internet Explorer has a "friendly" mode that will prevent you from seeing actual error messages from a servlet or JSP. To turn it off, start at the Tools menu and follow this command sequence:

Tools -> Internet Options -> Advanced -> Show Friendly Http Error Messages

The JavaServer Pages API

The variables shown in Table A.20 are always created in a JSP page with the exception of `exception`, which is available only when the page directive includes the `isErrorPage` attribute with a value of true as in this example:

```
<%@ page language="java" isErrorPage="true" %>
```

TABLE A.20: The implicit JSP page variables

Variable name	Type	Usage
Request	A descendent of `javax. servlet.ServletRequest`	Represents the user's request.
Response	A descendent of `javax. servlet.ServletResponse`	Creates the output response.
pageContext	A `javax.servlet.jsp. PageContext` object	Contains attributes of this page.
session	A `javax.servlet.http. HttpSession`	Contains arbitrary variables attached to this user's session.
application	A `javax.servlet.ServletContext` object	Contains attributes for the entire application, affects the interpretation of several other tags.
out	A `javax.servlet.jsp.JspWriter` object	The output stream for the response
config	A `javax.servlet.ServletConfig` object	Contains servlet initialization parameter name – value pairs, and the **ServletContext** object.
page	An object reference pointing to *this*	The current servlet object.
exception	A throwable object	Only pages designated as error pages in the page directive have this object.

The `JspPage` and `HttpJspPage` interfaces are very simple, as shown in Table A.21. Because the JSP engine is responsible for creating the `_jspService` method, you only need to worry about defining the `jspInit` and `jspDestroy` methods.

TABLE A.21: Methods in the JspPage and HttpJspPage interfaces

Method	Interface	Usage
`void jspDestroy()`	JspPage	The method called when the **JspPage** is about to be destroyed. Use this to clean up any resources.
`void jspInit()`	JspPage	The method invoked when the **JspPage** is initialized. Use this to set up parameters.
`void _jspService( HttpServletRequest request, HttpServletResponse response)`	HttpJspPage	The method created by the JSP engine to write the body of the JSP page.

The PageContext Class

PageContext is an abstract class. The JSP engine will provide a class extending PageContext for a particular server. A PageContext object manages all the resources used by the servlet that the JSP engine writes. It is important to note that resource management recognizes several different scopes.

Access to the Standard Variables

The PageContext class provides methods to get references to the standard (implicit) JSP variables listed in Table A.20. Because these variables are automatically defined in your JSP page, the PageContext methods shown in Table A.22 are mainly of use in other classes.

TABLE A.22: PageContext methods for getting implicit variables

Implicit variable	Type	PageContext method
Exception	Exception	getException()
Out	JspWriter	getOut()
Page	Object	getPage()
Request	ServletRequest	getRequest()
response	ServletResponse	getResponse()
config	ServletConfig	getServletConfig()
application	ServletContext	getServletContext()
session	HttpSession	getSession()

Table A.23 shows the PageContext methods used for recovery of various objects. Note that the scope variables refer to constants in the PageContext class (see Table A.25).

TABLE A.23: PageContext methods related to attribute storage and recovery

Returns	Method	Usage
Object	getAttribute(String name)	The object associated with the name in the page scope. Returns null if the object does not exist.
void	removeAttribute(String name)	The named object, in any scope, is removed.
void	setAttribute(String name, Object attribute)	Attach this object to the PageContext in page scope.

TABLE A.23: PageContext methods related to attribute storage and recovery *(continued)*

Returns	Method	Usage
Object	getAttribute(String name, int scope)	The object associated with the name in the specified scope. Returns null if there is no such object.
void	removeAttribute(String name, int scope)	Removes the object reference associated with this name.
void	setAttribute(String name, Object obj, int scope)	Attach the object with this name and the specified scope.
Enumeration	getAttributeNamesInScope(int scope)	Returns an **Enumeration** of **String** objects over all named attributes in this scope.
int	getAttributesScope(String name)	Returns the scope of the named attribute.
Object	findAttribute(String name)	Searches for this name in page, request, session (if valid), and application scope(s) in order and returns the value associated or null.

Table A.24 summarizes the **PageContext** methods that didn't fall into any of the previous categories.

TABLE A.24: The remaining PageContext methods

Returns	Method	Usage
void	forward(String relativeUrlPath)	Redirects, or "forwards," the current **ServletRequest** and **ServletResponse** to another active component in the application.
void	handlePageException(Exception e)	This method is called from the **try-catch** clause that includes your JSP page code. As such, it redirects the exception to the specified error page for this JSP, or if none was specified, it performs custom action.
void	include(String relativeUrlPath)	The resource specified is processed as part of the current **ServletRequest** and **ServletResponse**.

TABLE A.24: The remaining PageContext methods *(continued)*

Returns	Method	Usage
void	`initialize( Servlet servlet, ServletRequest request, ServletResponse response, String errorPageURL, boolean needsSession, int bufferSize, boolean autoFlush )`	The initialize method is called to initialize an uninitialized **PageContext** so that it can be used by a JSP implementation class to service an incoming request and response in a `_jspService()` method. Creating this call is handled by the JSP engine.
JspWriter	`popBody()`	Return the previous JspWriter "out" saved by the matching **pushBody()** and then update the value of the "out" attribute in the page scope attribute namespace of the **PageContext**. See Chapter 11 for examples.
BodyContent	`pushBody()`	Return a new **BodyContent** object, save the current "out" **JspWriter**, and update the value of the "out" attribute in the page scope attribute namespace of the **PageContext**.
void	`release()`	Reset the internal state of a **PageContext** object so it can be reused. Calling this method is handled by the JSP engine.

The **PageContext** class defines a number of static constants mostly related to scope definition. Table A.25 summarizes these constants.

TABLE A.25: Constants in the PageContext class

Type	Name	Usage
String	APPLICATION	Name used to store **ServletContext** in **PageContext** name table.
int	APPLICATION_SCOPE	Application scope: Named reference remains available in the **ServletContext** until it is reclaimed.
String	CONFIG	Name used to store **ServletConfig** in **PageContext** name table
String	EXCEPTION	Name used to store uncaught exception in **ServletRequest** attribute list and **PageContext** name table.
String	OUT	Name used to store current **JspWriter** in **PageContext** name table.
String	PAGE	Name used to store the **Servlet** in this **PageContext**'s name tables.
int	PAGE_SCOPE	Page scope (default): The named reference remains available in this **PageContext** until the return from the current servlet `service()` invocation.
String	PAGECONTEXT	Name used to store this **PageContext** in its own name tables.
String	REQUEST	Name used to store **ServletRequest** in **PageContext** name table.

TABLE A.25: Constants in the PageContext class *(continued)*

Type	Name	Usage
int	REQUEST_SCOPE	Request scope: The named reference remains available from the **ServletRequest** associated with the servlet until the current request is completed.
String	RESPONSE	Name used to store **ServletResponse** in **PageContext** name table.
String	SESSION	Name used to store **HttpSession** in **PageContext** name table.
int	SESSION_SCOPE	Session scope (valid only if this page participates in a session): The named reference remains available from the **HttpSession** (if any) associated with the servlet until the **HttpSession** is invalidated.

The JspWriter Class

The JspWriter class extends the java.io.Writer abstract class. The purpose of this class is to provide output functionality similar to the BufferedWriter and PrintWriter classes in JSP context, as shown in Table A.26. An important difference is that JspWriter methods can throw an IOException whereas PrintWriter does not.

TABLE A.26: JspWriter buffer management method summary

Returns	Method	Usage
void	clear()	Clear the contents of the buffer. Throws an IOException if any contents have been flushed to the output stream to warn your application that some output has already been sent.
void	clearBuffer()	Clear the current contents of the buffer but does not throw an exception if some data has already been sent.
void	close()	Close the stream, flushing it first.
void	flush()	Flush the stream.
int	getBufferSize()	The current buffer size.
int	getRemaining()	The unused space in the buffer.
boolean	isAutoFlush()	The state of the auto-flush flag.

The output methods in Table A.27 parallel those of the java.io.PrintWriter class, but they can throw an IOException if there is a problem with the output stream.

TABLE A.27: The JspWriter output methods

Returns	Method	Usage
void	newLine()	Write a line separator.
void	print(boolean b)	Print a boolean value.
void	print(char c)	Print a character.
void	print(char[] s)	Print an array of characters.
void	print(double d)	Print a double-precision floating-point number.
void	print(float f)	Print a floating-point number.
void	print(int i)	Print an integer.
void	print(long l)	Print a **long** integer.
void	print(java.lang.Object obj)	Print an object.
void	print(java.lang.String s)	Print a **String**.
void	println()	Terminate the current line by writing the line separator string.
void	println(boolean x)	Print a boolean value and then terminate the line.
void	println(char x)	Print a character and then terminate the line.
void	println(char[] x)	Print an array of characters and then terminate the line.
void	println(double x)	Print a double-precision floating-point number and then terminate the line.
void	println(float x)	Print a floating-point number and then terminate the line.
void	println(int x)	Print an integer and then terminate the line.
void	println(long x)	Print a **long** integer and then terminate the line.
void	println(java.lang.Object x)	Print an **Object** and then terminate the line.
void	println(java.lang.String x)	Print a **String** and then terminate the line.

The javax.servlet.jsp.tagext Package

When writing custom JSP tags, you will be concerned with only a few of the classes in this package. Your custom tag must extend either the Tag or BodyTag interface. The **Tag** methods are shown in Table A.28.

TABLE A.28: The Tag interface methods

Returns	Method	Usage
int	doEndTag()	Process the end tag.
int	doStartTag()	Process the start tag for this instance.
Tag	getParent()	For nested tags, returns the parent.
void	release()	Called on a Tag handler to release state.
void	setPageContext(PageContext pc)	Set the current page context.
void	setParent(Tag t)	Set the current nesting Tag of this Tag.

The Tag interface is for custom tags that do not process a body. You have to add the methods shown in Table A.29 to be able to handle body content.

TABLE A.29: The BodyTag interface adds these methods

Returns	Method	Usage
int	doAfterBody()	Perform actions after some body has been evaluated.
void	doInitBody()	Prepare for evaluation of the body.
void	setBodyContent(BodyContent b)	Setter method for the bodyContent property.

The BodyContent Class

This class inherits from JspWriter (Tables A.26 and A.27), adding methods that provide for buffering character information and manipulating it, as shown in Table A.30. Also note that the flush method has to be redefined because a BodyContent object is not attached to an output stream but only to an internal buffer.

TABLE A.30: Methods in the BodyContent class

Returns	Method	Usage
void	clearBody()	Clear the body buffer, typically in preparation for re-reading the body into it.
void	flush()	Redefine the flush() method of JspWriter because you can't flush a BodyContent. Throws an IOException if called.
JspWriter	getEnclosingWriter()	Get the enclosing JspWriter.
Reader	getReader()	Return the value of this BodyContent as a Reader.
String	getString()	Return the value of the BodyContent as a String.
void	writeOut(java.io.Writer out)	Write the contents of this BodyContent into a Writer output stream.

GLOSSARY

100% Pure Java   The designation for classes and applications that comply with Sun's criteria for total independence from the underlying operating system.

absolute positioning   Placing and sizing Component objects with reference to pixel coordinates; useable only when a Container has a null layout manager.

abstract   A Java keyword describing classes or methods that define a runtime behavior but that don't provide a complete implementation. You can't create an object from an abstract class, but an object created from a class extending the abstract class can be referred to with the abstract class name.

abstract path name   The internal path designation inside a File object that is independent of the underlying operating system.

Abstract Window Toolkit (AWT)   The package of Java interfaces, classes, exceptions, and errors that create a Java GUI using the GUI components of the underlying platform. The AWT is simpler than the "swing" GUI package.

accessibility   The javax.accessibility package stipulates interfaces that provide ease-of-use Java application features for users with disabilities.

Active Server Pages (ASP)   Microsoft's technology for embedding code inside HTML pages to create dynamic Web pages.

adapter   Design pattern for converting or adapting one class interface to another. For example, there are classes in the java.awt.event package that support the creation of event listeners.

Adjustable (interface)   Java interface (java.awt.Adjustable) that stipulates methods for handling changeable control, such as a scroll bar.

algorithm   A problem-solving operation that proceeds one step at a time to accomplish a specific program task.

alpha   The typical designation given a program or application that is undergoing initial (internal) testing before being released for testing outside the company that developed it. *See also* beta.

alpha value   A computer graphics term indicating degree of opacity. Together with the more familiar RGB (red, green, and blue) intensity values, alpha is part of Java color representation. When Java represents a graphics pixel as an int value, the alpha value is in the high byte.

American Standard Code for Information Interchange (ASCII)   The ubiquitous computer industry standard for encoding text and control characters; internally, Java uses Unicode, a superset of ASCII printing characters.

anonymous   Unnamed Java local class declared and instantiated in a single statement.

API   *See* application programming interface.

applet A Java program that operates within a Java Virtual Machine (JVM), supplied by the user's Web browser. You can think of the browser as providing an applet container that lets it run on the client machine more or less independently of the underlying operating system.

application A Java program that runs on a client machine and that can access all the client system's resources. *See also* applet.

application programming interface (API) Calling conventions or instruction set used by an application to access operating system and library services.

Application Service Provider (ASP) An Internet server that provides more than simple Web pages.

Application Services Sun's classification of a collection of interface improvements that is included in the Java Foundation Classes (JFC).

argument Java method call data item that can designate a Java primitive or object.

ArithmeticException Java runtime exception that indicates integer nonfloating-point division by zero.

array Group of data items that share the same type, in which a 32-bit integer index addresses each data item uniquely.

Arrays (class) Java class (java.util.Arrays) that includes static methods for operations on primitives, arrays, and object references.

ASCII *See* American Standard Code for Information Interchange.

ASP *See* Active Server Pages; *see* Application Service Provider.

assignable Relationship between an object reference and a reference variable when both are the same type or the variable is an ancestor of the object reference in the class hierarchy.

assignment Java operators that assign a value to a variable; for example, = and +=.

atomic A program step that cannot be interrupted by another Thread is said to be atomic. All Java assignment operations with 32-bit variables are atomic, but 64-bit variable (long and double) operations are not.

automatic (local) variable Variable declared inside a method, to which memory is automatically allocated when the method is called.

AWT *See* Abstract Windowing Toolkit (sometimes called the Annoying Windowing Toolkit by frustrated programmers).

bean *See* Java bean.

beta The typical designation given a program or application that is under development and is released for testing outside the company that developed it; usually the step just prior to commercial release. *See also* alpha.

bitwise An operator that works on individual bits; an operator that manipulates Java integer primitive types on an individual-bit basis.

block A section of Java code that is contained within matching { and } characters.

break A Java keyword governing two programmatic actions. Used alone, it prompts continuation of program execution after the present code block; used with a statement label, it prompts continuation of program execution after the code block tagged by that label. *See also* `continue`.

byte An eight-bit Java integer-type primitive that is treated as a signed integer.

Byte (class) The Java wrapper class for values of eight-bit byte primitives.

bytecode Java Virtual Machine (JVM) instruction in platform-independent format, such as that used with Java applets.

CAB (cabinet) Microsoft's format for compressed class and other resource files and for distributing installation files.

case-insensitive Programming language naming convention that does not distinguish between upper- and lowercase letters.

case-sensitive Programming language naming convention that distinguishes between upper- and lowercase letters; in other words, "Text" and "text" are read differently. Java is case-sensitive.

cast Reserved word (not presently used); syntax for changing Java expression type, for example, casting an int value to a long value.

catch Java keyword that declares specific exception type and that creates a block of code or clause that executes when that exception contained in code with a `try` statement is thrown.

CGI *See* Common Gateway Interface.

char Java integer primitive variable that represents Unicode characters as 16-bit unsigned integers.

Character (class) The Java wrapper class for char values.

checked exceptions Java programmatic exceptions that require explicit handling code.

child In context of object oriented programming, any object that inherits from and obtains information from another object; a Java class that inherits from another class (parent of superclass).

class In general context of object oriented programming, a method for grouping objects that share some characteristic or characteristics; all Java classes descend from the `Object` class.

Class (class) The Java class (`java.lang.Class`) that indicates the runtime type of any object.

class file The outcome of compiling a Java class.

class method Java method declared `static` and attached to an entire class, rather than to objects in the class.

class modifiers   Java keywords (`public`, `abstract`, and `final`) that establish class properties or characteristics.

class variable   A variable (`static`) that belongs to a Java class rather than to a class instance of the class.

ClassCastException   An exception that is thrown whenever the JVM identifies an attempt to cast an object reference to an incompatible type.

clone method   Java method in the `Object` class that can generate a copy of an object.

Collection (interface)   Java interface (`java.util.Collection`) that defines basic behavior for Collections API objects.

Collections API   Java 2 set of classes and interfaces that provide a number of methods for handling collections of objects.

Collections (class)   Java class (`java.util.Collections`) containing `static` methods applicable to collections.

Color (class)   Java class (`java.awt.Color`) that encompasses red, green, and blue intensities of screen color. *See also* alpha.

Common Gateway Interface (CGI)   The conventions governing communication between Web servers and auxiliary programs, such as search engines. Scripts or executables that support interaction between users (via browsers) and Web servers.

Comparator (interface)   Java interface (`java.util.Comparator`) that provides the means of access between custom classes and `Arrays` class sorting and searching methods.

completeness   Java term denoting whether a class behavior is fully developed or requires further development by subclasses.

Component (class)   Java abstract class (`java.awt.Component`) that is the parent of all screen components in the AWT graphics package except those related to menus.

constraints   Java object that is passed to a layout manager that implements the `LayoutManager2` interface and that defines the way in which a component is handled.

constructor   Special kind of member function called on the creation of a class instance using `new`; initializes the object. Java classes can declare none, one, or many constructor methods.

constructor chaining   A Java constructor that calls another constructor, according to a specific set of Java-enforced rules.

container   In Sun's terminology, the environment a Java applet, servlet, or EJB operates in is a specialized container that is required to provide specific services.

Container (class)   The Java class (`java.awt.Container`) that is the ancestor for all AWT GUI objects that contain and manage interface components.

contentPane   In Swing primary container classes, such as JFrame, the container to which all interface components are added.

continue   Java keyword used in two contexts: Inside a looping construct, it causes continuation of execution with the next innermost loop activity; when used with a statement label, it moves control to the next labeled loop. *See also* break.

controller   In the Model-View-Controller design pattern, the controller provides functions or services for communicating user input to the model and view(s).

conversion   Used in a Java expression, conversion changes the expression type.

cookie   A small chunk of text data stored by a Web browser as a consequence of visiting a Web site. This data is returned to the Web server on subsequent visits to the site and may be used to identify a user.

daemon Thread   Daemon is a UNIX term for programs that operate in the background and handle requests for network services. Java Threads can be tagged daemon by the setDaemon method as a way of distinguishing them from user threads, and they are generally JVM utilities, such as the garbage collection Thread. A Java application stops when the only Threads left running are daemon Threads.

deadlock   Situation in which two or more Java Threads need the same resource and consequently come to a stop.

decorator   Java design pattern in which an attached object adds functions to a core class.

decrement   Operator (--) attached to a primitive numeric variable that subtracts one from the variable.

deep copy   Programming term for a method of cloning objects that copies both the object and all objects to which that object refers. The clone method in the Object class is not a deep copy.

delegate   Object that handles a component's look and feel (Swing convention) or that combines view and controller functions (Model-View-Controller design pattern).

delegation (model)   Java 1.1 event model in which event-generating components transfer event handling to specific event listeners.

deprecated   JDK (Java Developers' Kit) term that indicates a method whose use is no longer recommended.

deserialize   To reconstruct a Java object stored by serialization, usually by use of ObjectInputStream.

destructor   C++ method that cleans up for a user-defined object type, reclaiming designated memory and other resources. Java uses automatic garbage collection rather than destructors. *See also* finalize.

Dimension (class)   Java class (java.awt.Dimension) objects typically used for reading and setting a component's width and height.

directives   In JavaServer Pages, directives are tags that define general policies or conditions for a page or part of a page.

Distributed Computing   In general, an architecture in which programs running on different physical computers cooperate to solve a problem by communicating over a network.

DLL   *See* dynamic link library.

doclet   Java program developed with classes in `sun.tools.javadoc` for customizing javadoc output.

Document Object Model (DOM)   An approach to processing an XML document in which the entire document is stored in memory as a parsed hierarchy of elements. Also, in Web browsers, the hierarchical structure of the HTML document.

DOM   *See* Document Object Model.

double (double precision)   Java 64-bit floating-point primitive type.

Double (class)   Java wrapper class for `double` primitive values.

Drag & Drop   JFC (Java Foundation Classes; in the `java.awt.dnd` package) that supports moving data between Java applications and between Java and native applications.

dynamic link library (DLL)   Executable packages or modules that a programmer can bring into memory and link to as needed by an application.

dynamic method lookup   The manner in which the JVM (Java Virtual Machine) locates and calls the appropriate method at runtime based on an object's actual (rather than reference) type.

editable   A property of `TextArea` and `TextField` components that is true if the contents can be changed by a user.

enabling events   Java method (`enableEvents`) in `java.awt.Component` called to enable creation of user interface events. The exact events enabled are determined by an event mask.

encapsulation   Term used in object oriented programming for enclosing information and behavior within an object, hiding its structure and implementation from other objects. Encapsulation allows programmers to modify the way the object's internal functions, without affecting any other code using the object.

Enumeration (interface)   Java 1.0 interface (`java.util.Enumeration`) that stipulates the manner in which a collection generates a series of the collection's elements, using `nextElement` and `hasMoreElements` methods. Sun intends that `Enumeration` be replaced by the Java 2 `Iterator` interface but it is still widely used.

equals   Java method that compares two object references and returns `true` when the objects' content is identical. The `Object` class default `equals` method returns `true` when both references the same object.

Error (class) Java class (java.lang.Error) that is the parent class of all Java error classes and a subclass of Throwable. Errors are typically conditions that a program cannot recover from, such as running out of memory.

escape sequence A character string for encoding a character that is not a normal keyboard character or would cause trouble for the Java compiler.

event listener Java object that is registered with a particular control associated with user activity and that is notified when a specific event takes place.

event mask A java.awt.Component class feature that dictates the types of GUI events the object generates.

Exception (class) Java class (java.lang.Exception) that is the parent class of all Java exceptions and a subclass of Throwable. Exceptions generally signal conditions that the program may be able to recover from.

extends Java keyword used to define a new class that indicates the base class from which the new class will inherit.

Extensible Markup Language (XML) A simplified form of SGML proposed as a standard for creating custom markup languages. The purpose of this is to permit the tags in a document to exactly describe the contents.

Extensible Stylesheet Language (XSL) A proposed specification for transforming and presenting documents created with XML.

field Java variable that defines a particular class characteristic.

File (class) Java class (java.io.File) that manages file and directory path names instead of actual data files.

file separator Character that indicates the division of path and file name components.

filter (file I/O sense) Package of interfaces (java.io) that specifies filtering methods for input and output streams and file names.

filter (image sense) The Java java.awt.image package provides so-called filter classes for transforming image information.

final Java keyword that stipulates that a class cannot have subclasses. Applied to a member method, this stipulates that the method cannot be overridden by subclasses. Applied to a member variable, it stipulates the variable is a constant whose value cannot be changed once it is set.

finalize Object method executed by the Java garbage collection process when the memory that object occupies is to be reclaimed. Typically used to ensure that system resources are recovered when an object is discarded.

finally Java keyword for attaching a code block that always has to be executed to a try block.

float Java 32-bit floating-point primitive type.

Float (class) Java wrapper class for float primitive values.

Font (class) Java class (java.awt.Font) that holds specific font information.

font family Class or group of fonts with common design or font family characteristics.

FontMetrics (class) Java class (java.awt.FontMetrics) whose objects are required for all positioning calculations for a particular font.

form A structure used in HTML pages to create elements that can accept user input and transmit it to a Web server using CGI conventions.

garbage collection JVM (Java Virtual Machine) process of locating and recovering memory that is allocated to objects the program can no longer use.

GIF *See* Graphics Interchange Format.

graphical user interface (GUI) A computer user interface that uses graphical elements, windows, and a pointing device; Mac OS, Windows, and X11 are examples of GUIs; supported by JVM.

Graphics Java class (java.awt.Graphics) that supplies the context for drawing components and screen images.

graphics context Hardware-specific information used by an operating system in allowing applications to draw on a graphics device, such as the computer screen.

Graphics Interchange Format (GIF) Ubiquitous HTML-compressed graphics file format (.gif file extension) for inline graphic elements. Unisys owns the format's patent. *See also* Joint Photographic Experts Group (JPEG).

Graphics2D (class) Java 2 class (java.awt.Graphics2D) that extends Graphics.

GUI *See* graphical user interface.

hashcode In computing context, a characteristic number derived from a data item's contents that allows a program or application to locate the item quickly by operating on the number.

hashCode The method in every Java object that generates an int primitive hashcode value characteristic of the object.

Hashtable (class) Java class (java.util.Hashtable) object that stores Object references denoted by "key" objects using the key's hashcode.

heavyweight components Java GUI interface components that use a corresponding operating system peer. In contrast to "lightweight" components in the "Swing" GUI toolkit.

hex (hexadecimal) Mathematical base 16 system used in computer programming that uses alphanumeric characters 0 through 9 and A through F or a through f.

hidden variable In an HTML form, a hidden variable holds information that cannot be seen or modified by the user but which will be transmitted to the Web server.

hierarchical   Logical arrangement of elements, also called a tree structure, in which every element with the exception of the root object has parents and might or might not have child objects (children). Examples of this structure can be found in the Java class library, XML documents, and computer file systems.

HTML   *See* HyperText Markup Language.

HttpServlet (class)   The base class in the `javax.servlet.http` package extended by servlets that need to respond to GET and POST operations.

HyperText Markup Language (HTML)
The document markup language used to create Web pages and standardized by the W3C.

Hypertext Transfer Protocol (HTTP)
The set of rules (protocols) based on TCP/IP that provides the foundation for communication between Web clients and servers.

IDE   *See* Integrated Development Environment.

identifier   Name given an item in a Java program or application.

IEEE   *See* Institute of Electrical and Electronics Engineers.

Image (class)   Java abstract class (`java.awt.Image`) that defines how graphics representation information is held.

implements   Java keyword in class declarations that precedes a list of one or more interfaces for which the class supplies methods.

implicit variables   In a JavaServer Page, these variables are always created.

import   Java source code file statement that informs the Java compiler as to which package holds classes used in the code.

increment   Operator (++) attached to a primitive numeric variable that adds one to that variable to which it is attached.

IndexOutOfBoundsException   Java exception thrown when an attempt is made to address a nonexistent array element; `ArrayIndexOutOfBoundsException` and `StringIndexOutOfBoundsException` are subclasses of `IndexOutOfBoundsException`.

inheritance   In object oriented programming, relationship among hierarchically arranged objects by which some objects (children) are granted attributes of another object (parent).

init (applet method)   By convention, a method that belongs to a Java applet's initial class and that is called by a Web browser's JVM after the applet object is created, but before it is displayed.

init (servlet method)   A method that belongs to a Java servlet class and that is called by the servlet engine after the servlet object is created, but before it services any user requests.

initialize; initialization   Setting a variable's starting value.

inner class Nested class or interface with access to all member fields and methods of the class in which it is nested, including any declared `private`.

InputStream (class) Java `abstract` base class (`java.io.InputStream`) for various Java classes that read data as a byte stream.

Insets (class) Java class (`java.awt.Insets`) used in graphic interfaces containing an object that delineates border widths on all sides of a container.

instance An object created from a specific class is said to be an instance of that class.

instance fields The set of distinct member variables for each class instance.

instance methods Member methods that are executable only through a reference to a class instance.

instance variable Java variable that is part of a class instance instead of the class itself (class or `static` variable).

instanceof Logical operator used to determine the type of a reference in an expression.

Institute of Electrical and Electronics Engineers (IEEE) Professional organization that develops computer hardware and software standards, as well as standards for the electronics industry.

int Java 32-bit integer primitive type that is always treated as a signed integer.

Integer (class) Java wrapper class for `int` values.

Integrated Development Environment (IDE) Application development system that incorporates in one package programming tools, such as a source code editor, compiler, debugger, and project tracking functions.

interface Similar to a Java class definition, but this provides only method declarations, not implementations. A Java class is free to implement as many interfaces as needed.

International Organization for Standardization (ISO) Group comprised of national standards organizations from 89 countries that establishes international standards for telecommunications and technology.

interrupt Java `Thread` class instance method; if `Thread` is in `sleep` or `wait` state, calling `interrupt` wakes the `Thread` and generates `InterruptedException`; otherwise, the interrupted flag is set.

interrupted (Thread private variable) Java flag set to `true` when a `Thread` is interrupted.

interrupted (Thread static method) Java `static` method that a running `Thread` uses to determine whether it has been interrupted.

InterruptedException Exception that can be generated when a `Thread` that is sleeping or waiting is interrupted. The `Thread` cannot continue with what it was doing, but must instead handle the exception.

IOException (class) Java class (`java.io.Exception`) that is the parent class of all exceptions related to I/O processes; e.g., opening and reading a file.

isInterrupted Java `Thread` class instance method by which a `Thread` can be queried to determine whether or not it has been interrupted.

ISO *See* International Organization for Standardization.

Iterator (interface) Java interface (`java.util.Iterator`) intended to replace `Enumeration` as the preferred method of examining elements in a collection.

J2EE *See* Java 2 Enterprise Edition.

J2ME *See* Java 2 Micro Edition.

J2SE *See* Java 2 Standard Edition.

JAR (Java ARchive) File format similar to Zip for collecting multiple resources (such as class files and Java class libraries) in a single file.

Java 2 Enterprise Edition (J2EE) The largest of Sun's collection of Java utilities and libraries, designed for creation of Internet applications.

Java 2 Micro Edition (J2ME) Sun's collection of Java utilities and libraries that have been reduced in size and complexity to fit small computing environments such as Palm Pilot.

Java 2 Standard Edition (J2SE) Sun's collection of Java utilities and libraries designed to fit most developer's needs.

Java 2D Group of Java classes that provides a number of advanced graphics methods.

Java bean Reusable software component written for a specific function or use and that meets the JavaBeans standard for getting and setting instance variable values.

Java Communications API Group of Java classes and operating-system-specific code that supports direct interaction with serial and parallel I/O ports.

Java Database Connectivity (JDBC) The collection of Java classes in the `java.sql` package that enables Java programs to connect to SQL-style databases.

Java Development Kit (JDK) Java package of development tools, utilities, a class library, and documentation that is downloadable from the `java.sun.com` Web site.

Java Foundation Classes (JFC) Sun's name for the collection of five Java toolkits (Swing, Java 2D, Accessibility, Drag & Drop, and Application Services) for creating advanced GUIs in Java 2.

Java Native Interface (JNI) Java interface (API) that gives programmers access to a host system's language and determines Java's interaction with native code modules.

Java Runtime Environment (JRE) A collection of programs and libraries for a particular operating system that enables execution of Java programs, but doesn't include the compiler or classes used in the compiler.

Java Virtual Machine (JVM)   Nonphysical (virtual) computer that is part of the Java run-time environment and interprets Java bytecodes, providing the foundation for the cross-platform features of Java programs.

JavaBeans   Java programming standard for components that complies with a standard interface.

javac   Java application that starts the compiler.

javadoc   Java utility that allows automatic documentation by processing source code and producing reference pages in HTML format.

JavaScript   Web page scripting language developed by Netscape (originally called Live-Script) that controls the way in which Web pages appear in browsers. Provides limited support for embedded Java applets.

JavaServer Pages (JSP)   The Java API that allows a programmer to combine HTML and Java code in a single document to create a dynamic Web page.

JComponent (class)   Java class (`javax.swing.Jcomponent`) that is base class for the Swing visual components.

JDBC   *See* Java Database Connectivity.

JDK   *See* Java Development Kit.

JFC   *See* Java Foundation Classes.

JIT   *See* Just In Time.

join   **Thread** class instance method for coordinating **Threads**.

Joint Photographic Experts Group (JPEG)   Compressed graphics file format (.jpg file extension) supported by JVM and often found in Web pages. *See also* Graphics Interchange Format (GIF).

JNI   *See* Java Native Interface.

JPEG   *See* Joint Photographic Experts Group.

JRE   *See* Java Runtime Environment.

JSP   See JavaServer Pages.

jspDestroy (JSP method)   A method that is always called just before a Web server removes JSP code from memory.

jspInit (JSP method)   A method that is always created in a JSP page and is always called before a user request is processed.

jspService (JSP method)   A method that is always created in a JSP page to process a user's HTTP request.

Just In Time (JIT)   Technology that speeds up the execution of Java programs by dynamically replacing the Java bytecode with machine language on-the-fly as methods are called.

JVM   *See* Java Virtual Machine.

label   An identifier followed by a colon appended to a Java statement; used only with **break** and **continue** statements.

layout manager An object for controlling screen component position and size within a `java.awt.Container` object.

lightweight components Java interface components that lack an operating system peer and for which the JVM carries out all screen drawing and event processing.

List (interface) Java interface (`java.util.List`) that supplies an ordered collection of object references.

listener Java 1.1 event model object registered with a generating component that is informed about a particular class of events.

local class Java inner class defined within a member method that can access all class members and all local `final` variables.

local variable *See* `automatic` variable.

lock The equivalent of a variable associated with every object that controls access to the object by threads. Locks can be manipulated only by the JVM in the process of synchronizing access to the object.

long Java 64-bit integer primitive type; always treated as signed integer. *See also* `double` (double precision).

Long (class) Java wrapper class for `long` values.

low-level event Java events that are close to operating system raw events, for example, mouse movements.

main (application method) Java `static` method required by a Java application's initial class and that is executed by the JVM after loading the class, to start the application.

manifest File in all JAR files that provides supplementary information about other files in the JAR (such as digital signatures and encryption information). Manifest information is accessed via the `java.util.jar.Manifest` class.

Map (interface) Java interface (`java.util.Map`) that requires the class implementing it to associate unique key objects with value objects. Classes implementing `Map` include `Hashtable` and `SortedMap`.

marshalling In distributed computing techniques, the process of assembling objects and variables for transmission to a remote process.

maximumSize Parameter that applies to graphic interface objects descended from `JComponent`; set with `setMaximumSize` method.

MAX_PRIORITY Java `Thread` class constant.

member Java variables, methods, and inner classes declared as part of a class are called members of the class.

member class Java inner class not declared as `static`, nor within a member method.

MenuComponent (class) Java class (`java.awt.MenuComponent`) that is the parent class of all `java.awt` classes that is used in displaying screen menus.

method Java class function that is named and for which specific input parameters and return types are declared.

method signature Combination of name and parameters that distinguishes one method from another.

minimumSize A parameter applicable to Java components that descends from JComponent (set with the setMinimumSize method) which stipulates the smallest amount of space a layout manager will give the component.

MIME *See* Multipurpose Internet Mail Extensions.

MIN_PRIORITY Java Thread class constant.

model In the Model-View-Controller design pattern, the Java object that contains data.

Model 1 Refers to a JSP application architecture in which the JSP code does both the primary decision-making and formatting. In Model-View-Controller terminology, the JSP page is both controller and view, while JavaBean objects handle the model function.

Model 2 Refers to a JSP application architecture in which the primary decision-making is handled by a servlet which delegates display to JSP pages using a RequestDispatcher. In Model-View-Controller terminology, the controller is a servlet, while JSP handles only the view.

Model-View-Controller Design pattern in which data is held by the model object and displayed by the *view* object, and a controller object informs both model and view objects of user input.

modulus (modulo) Java operator (%) used with either integer and floating-point types that divides the left operand by the right operand and returns the result.

monitor JVM mechanism that uses object locks in controlling Thread access to objects.

multiple inheritance In object oriented programming, inheriting variables and methods from more than one class. Java does not provide for multiple inheritance.

Multipurpose Internet Mail Extensions (MIME) A standard way of denoting content type in a resource; originated for use with e-mail but now widely used in network applications.

multitasking Process by which an operating system runs or appears to be running more than one program simultaneously.

multithreading Characteristic of a runtime environment that executes multiple independent paths (threads) within a program, allowing each thread access to the entire program's main memory and resources.

namespace Complete set of class and method names and other program items that the Java compiler tracks to identify an item uniquely.

NaN *See* Not a Number.

narrowing conversion (primitives) Java process of converting one primitive type to another primitive type that might lose information; for example, the conversion of int to byte eliminates extra bits.

narrowing conversion (reference type)   Java process of converting a reference type to a subclass; for example, a conversion from `Object` to `String`.

NEGATIVE_INFINITY   Java constant defined in the `Float` and `Double` classes that results from the floating-point division of a negative floating-point primitive by zero.

nested top-level inner class or interface   Java inner class that's declared `static` and handled in the same way as any other Java outer class.

new   Java keyword indicating the creation of a new object or array.

NORM_PRIORITY   Java `Thread` class constant.

Not a Number (NaN)   Java special floating-point constant that denotes results of arithmetical operations, such as taking the square root of a negative number, that don't have a correct numerical representation; defined in the `Float` and `Double` classes.

notify   Java `Object` class method that causes a `Thread` on the object's wait list to become runnable; `Thread` does not run until allowed to do so by the JVM scheduling mechanism.

notifyAll   Similar to `notify`, but causes all `Threads` on the object's wait list to become runnable.

null   Java special literal value that is used for the value of an uninitialized reference variable.

object   A class instance.

Observable (class)   Java class (`java.util.Observable`) that supplies basic methods or procedures for adding and notifying objects that implement the `Observer` interface; in `Observer-Observable` design pattern, object whose change in state is of interest to an `Observer`.

Observer (interface)   Java interface (`java.util.Observer`) that designates the `update` method used by `Observable` objects in notifying `Observer` objects.

OutputStream (class)   Java `abstract` base class (`java.io.OutputStream`) for classes that writes data as a stream of bytes.

overloading   Refers to a Java class containing multiple methods with the same name, but different parameter lists; called *overloading the method name*.

overriding   A subclass method supercedes (overrides) a superclass method with the same return type and signature as a method.

package   Collection of associated Java classes and interfaces organized into distinct namespaces.

parent   In a hierarchical system, any class that is the ancestor of another class.

path separator   Character that separates paths in a list; as in the Windows environment variable PATH. The `File` class supplies the `pathSeparator String` appropriate to a given environment.

peer   An operating system GUI object that corresponds to some Java AWT object.

pixel (picture element)   Smallest visible, addressable unit on a monitor or other output device and used in Java to define size and location of screen and image operations.

pointer   A C programming language mechanism that provides indirect access to objects and variables; not available in Java.

polymorphic   An object's capacity to have multiple identities, based on the object's interfaces, inheritance, and overloaded methods.

port address   On computer networks based on TCP/IP, the socket identifier at a given network address for which a program or a service looks.

POSITIVE_INFINITY   Java constant defined in the Float and Double classes that results from floating-point division of a positive floating-point primitive by zero.

preferredSize   Parameter assigned to components descended from Jcomponent; set with the setPreferredSize method.

primary container   A Swing object that has an operating system peer and that can support an independent window.

primitive   Java types (boolean, char, byte, short, int, long, float, and double) that are stored and accessed directly in binary form.

priority   Value from 1 to 10 that is assigned to Threads and that the JVM uses in determining which Thread is to run next.

private   Java keyword used to tag variables and methods that can be accessed only by methods declared within the same class.

promotion   Compiler process that uses widening conversion of a number to a type a particular operation requires.

protected   Keyword used to tag variables and methods that can be accessed only by methods of classes in the same package or by methods of classes for which that class is the superclass.

protocol   Rules that govern a transaction or data transmission between devices.

public   Java keyword for modifying visibility of classes and members, making them accessible by all objects, regardless of package boundaries.

random access   The ability of a programmer to move a file pointer to any point in a file and begin reading or writing at that point.

Reader (class)   Java abstract base class (java.io.Reader) for classes that read data as a stream of 16-bit Unicode characters.

reference   In Java, the process handled by the JVM by which a programmer works a "pointer" to an object (object reference) rather than directly with an object's physical memory address.

reference variable   All Java variables with the exception of primitives.

Reflection API Java API comprised of classes that enable a program to ascertain the constructors, methods, and variables available in any class, as well as the interface the class implements.

Remote Method Invocation (RMI) Java communications standard for distributed computing that allows a Java program to execute a method on an object that resides on another system or JVM as if it were a local object.

resume Java Thread instance method (deprecated) that allows continuation of a suspended Thread.

RMI *See* Remote Method Invocation.

root The one item or object from which all others descend in a hierarchical system.

Runnable Java interface (java.lang.Runnable) that defines the Threads run method.

RuntimeException Java class (java.lang.RuntimeException) that is the parent class of every exception that doesn't require declaration in a method throws clause.

SAX *See* Simplified API for XML.

scope The identifier attribute that controls the identifier's accessibility to other parts of a program.

semantic event An event that includes additional logic; contrasted with low-level event.

serialize To convert a Java object into a byte stream that is formatted in a way that allows reconstruction of the object.

server Network computer that supplies resources and services to client computers.

servlet Java program that runs in a servlet container on a Web server and processes network requests (typically these are http requests.)

servlet container The environment in which a servlet runs. The servlet API defines a number of services that a servlet container must provide.

session In servlet and JSP applications, a session maintains information about a user during the course of interaction with an application.

Set (interface) Java interface (java.util.Set) that is an extension of the Collection interface that holds object references and that is restricted so as to prevent duplication of references; hence, every reference is unique.

SGML *See* Standard Generalized Markup Language.

shallow copy Copy produced by the clone method in the Object class that copies only the values of reference variables.

short Java 16-bit integer primitive variable type; always treated as signed integer.

Short (class) Java wrapper class for short values.

sign bit   Most significant bit in the Java `byte`, `short`, `int`, and `long` primitives, which, when turned on, causes a number to be interpreted as negative.

signature   Java method's name along with the type and order of parameters in its argument list.

Simple Object Access Protocol (SOAP)
A recent proposal for a standard way to transmit requests to objects over the Internet using XML documents.

Simplified API for XML (SAX)   An approach to processing XML documents in which the parser identifies and parses elements as it encounters them in a single pass through the document. The user of SAX must provide methods to process the parsed elements.

singleton   Design pattern that allows the creation of only one instance of a class; a `static` class method controls access to the instance.

sleep   Java `static` method of the `Thread` class, which when called, causes the calling `Thread` to sleep for a specified number of milliseconds.

SOAP   *See* Simple Object Access Protocol.

socket   On computer networks, the combination of a computer address and a port number that provides a unique channel of communications.

Socket (class)   Java class object (`java.net.Socket`) representing a single network socket connection; can supply an `InputStream` and `OutputStream` for communication.

SortedSet (interface)   Java interface, an extension of `Set`, that maintains references in a sorting order determined by the `compareTo` method.

SQL   *See* Structured Query Language.

stack trace   Formatted text output that can provide the history of a `Thread`'s execution of a method that throws an exception or results in an error.

Standard Generalized Markup Language (SGML)   A standard for annotating text documents with tags that expresses the structure of the document and how the content should be treated. SGML served as the basis for HTML and XML.

start (applet method)   The Java method that a Web browser's JVM calls after the initial display of the applet and whenever the Web page that contains the applet is redisplayed.

static   Java method or variable tag that indicates the variable or method belongs to a class, rather than to a class instance.

static fields   Member fields of a Java class attached to the class itself, as opposed to fields attached to class instances.

static methods   Member methods of a Java class that execute in the environment of the class rather than a particular class instance.

stop   Java `Thread` instance method (deprecated) that causes a `ThreadDeath` exception and brings a `Thread` to an abrupt halt, often with unpredictable and unwanted results.

stream   A sequence (stream) of bytes that can be read only in sequence from start to finish.

Structured Query Language (SQL)   A standard for creating and accessing the contents of relational databases via text statements.

subclass   Class that extends (indirectly or directly) another class; all Java classes (except `Object`) are subclasses of the `Object` class.

super   Java keyword that refers to parent class variables, methods, or constructors.

superclass   In Java class hierarchy, ancestor of a class; the immediate ancestor is the direct superclass. *See also* `extends`, parent.

suspend   Java `Thread` instance method (deprecated) that stops a `Thread` until the `resume` method is called.

Swing   Set of advanced Java interface components that is an improvement on original AWT components; standard extensions for Java 2.

synchronized   Java keyword that activates a method's or code block's monitor mechanism.

syntax   Explicit rules for constructing code statements, including particular values and the order or placement of symbols.

System (class)   Java class (`java.lang.System`) composed of `static` methods and variables that the JVM initializes when a program starts.

tag   In markup languages such as HTML, XML, and JSP pages, a tag is a special character sequence that is not part of the document text but defines additional information.

taglib   In JSP technology, a programmer can define his own library of special purpose Java functions identified by tags. A special `taglib` directive tells JSP to use a particular library.

TCP/IP   *See* Transmission Control Protocol/Internet Protocol.

Thread (class)   Java class (`java.lang.Thread`) that encloses a single thread of control in the JVM and defines its behavior.

ThreadDeath   Special type of error that brings a `Thread` to a stop.

ThreadGroup (class)   Java class (`java.lang.ThreadGroup`) the objects of which are used by the JVM to define a set of `Thread` objects and to govern operations on the set.

throw   A Java statement that causes normal statement processing to halt and starts processing of an exception; must be associated with a `Throwable` object.

Throwable (class)   Java class (`java.lang.Throwable`) that is the parent class of every Java exception and error class.

throws   Java keyword that is employed in method declarations to introduce a list of the exceptions that method can throw.

timestamp   Java `long` primitive variable that holds the system time for an event's occurrence.

toString   Method possessed by all Java reference types that the compiler uses to evaluate statements that include `String` objects and the + operator.

Transmission Control Protocol/Internet Protocol (TCP/IP)   Suite of communications protocols developed to support mixed network environments, such as the Internet.

try   Java statement that constructs a code block in which an exception can occur; must be followed by at least one associated `catch` clause and/or a `finally` clause.

type   A Java object's class or interface. In object oriented programming in general, an object's interface is sometimes considered separately from its implementation, resulting in a further division into class and type.

UDP   *See* User Datagram Protocol.

unary   Java operators, such as ++, that affect one operand.

unchecked exceptions   Exceptions descending from `RuntimeException` for which the compiler doesn't require a programmer to provide explicit handling code.

Unicode   International ANSI 16-bit standard for the representation of alphabets (includes over 65,000 characters, including graphics). Java uses the 2.0 version of Unicode (`http://www.unicode.org`).

URL (class)   Java class (`java.net.URL`) that represents a Uniform Resource Locator for a Web server.

User Datagram Protocol (UDP)   A connectionless packet communication protocol (alternative to TCP/IP) for simple communication among programs; considered unreliable because a packet can be lost completely.

user Thread   Any Java `Thread` that has not been tagged as a daemon.

variable shadowing   Java variables in the same scope that can prevent direct access to other variables that have the same identifier.

Vector (class)   Java class (`java.util.Vector`) object that comprises extensible array of `Object` references.

view   Java command that creates a specific model data display in the Model-View-Controller design pattern.

viewport   Logical window in which part of the Java `JViewPort` view object is viewable.

visibility   Level of access a Java class grants to other Java classes.

W3C   *See* World Wide Web Consortium.

wait   Java `Object` class method that when called by a `Thread` releases the `Thread`'s lock on the object, causes the `Thread` to become inactive, and places the `Thread` on the object's wait list.

wait list   List of Java Threads that is attached to a particular object and waiting for notification.

wait set   *See* wait list.

Web application   A collection of servlets, JSP pages, HTML files, image files, and other resources that exists in a structured hierarchy of directories on a server.

Web Application Resource (WAR)   A collection of all files needed to create a Web application in a single file using the zip compression algorithm. Specified in the servlet 2.2 API.

widening conversions   Primitive types conversions that do not lose magnitude information or reference types conversions from a subclass to a class located higher in the class hierarchy.

widget   Programmer jargon for a component of a user interface, such as a checkbox or button.

World Wide Web Consortium (W3C)   The organization that creates standards for the Web (www.w3.org).

wrapper classes   Java classes that correspond to each of the primitive types, providing related utility functions.

Writer (class)   Java abstract base class (java.io.Writer) of classes that write data as a stream of 16-bit characters.

XML   *See* Extensible Markup Language.

XSL   *See* Extensible Stylesheet Language.

INDEX

Note to the Reader: Page numbers in **bold** indicate the principal discussion of a topic or the definition of a term. Page numbers in *italic* indicate illustrations.

B

I

J

Q

R

S

X

Z